The Age of Water

Number Nine: Environmental History Series

M A R T I N V. M E L O S I ,

General Editor

ANDRÉ E.
GUILLERME

The Age of Water

The Urban Environment
in the North of France,
A.D. 300–1800

TEXAS A&M UNIVERSITY PRESS
COLLEGE STATION

Library of Congress Cataloging-in-Publication Data

Guillerme, André, 1945–
 [Temps de l'eau. English]
 The age of water : the urban environment in the North of France,
A.D. 300–1800 / André E. Guillerme.
  p.   cm. — (Environmental history series ; no. 9)
 Bibliography: p.
 Includes index.
 ISBN 0-89096-270-7 (alk. paper) : $29.50
  1. Municipal water supply—France—History.   2. Cities and towns—
France—History.   3. Hydraulic structures—France—History.
I. Title. II. Series.
HD4465.F8G85   1988
363.6'1'0944—dc19   88-3209
                                                                CIP

FOR MARÈME

CONTENTS

Introduction

Even today, the old European city, circled with boulevards, clings to the banks of a river or stream that engineering has not covered over. But the city's hydrographic system, reduced to scatterings of surface water isolated by the major engineering and sanitation works undertaken in the nineteenth century, no longer functions except marginally—for esthetic or recreational purposes. The views of cities from earlier times—the *vedute*—provide an entirely different urban waterscape: the city and its outskirts were surrounded by large moats and penetrated by numerous canals around which the activities of the port and local crafts were concentrated.

Contrary to a widely held view, this hydrographic system did not originate naturally. Its gradient, profile, and dimensions were planned and worked out over many centuries—from as early as the decline of the Roman Empire—for military purposes. Defense, like attack, was from the earliest times the great strength of West Europeans;[1] for protection they surrounded their cities with well-built moats. Later, the hydrographic system assumed other functions, such as driving watermills, draining swamps, and, in the twelfth century, providing for the needs of urban artisans.

It is the history of these bodies of water—the history of contact, then rupture, between city and water—that I should like to trace here, by looking for the origins of the hydraulic networks and analyzing their development, in selected cities in northern France.

Assigning a date to the building of canals will allow us to locate urban expansion both temporally and spatially, and to understand better the diverse planning policies of feudalism and the royal state. When Rollo, duke of Normandy, extended the city of Rouen at the beginning of the tenth century on *terra nova* reclaimed from the Seine, he put coopers and smiths there who would be useful to the expansion of trade with northern Europe. Toward the middle of the twelfth century, Henry the Liberal decided to make the region of Champagne one of the richest in Europe; with alacrity he endowed the cities in the region with hydraulic equipment and recruited experienced technicians. At the end of the fifteenth century, Louis XI reorganized textile production by encouraging a new kind of craftsmanship that was better adapted, as we shall see, to the urban ecosystem of the age. The medieval or post-medieval city, whose urban planning measures shaped the economy for generations, knew how to master the hydric environment, and it is precisely on this point that these cities differed fundamentally from the earlier Gallo-Roman or the later industrialized city, both of which dreaded surface water.

During the sixteen centuries covered in this study, urban technology underwent considerable change. From the beginning and up to the tenth century, the predominant artisanal industries—mainly those working with wood (coopering), clay (pottery), metals (armoring and minting), and hides (parchment making)—required only a minimum of water consumption. During the Middle Ages, on the other hand, new techniques evolved requiring large quantities of water that transformed the city into a replica of Venice—or even, during the Renaissance, into an archipelago. Finally, discoveries made at the end of the eighteenth century in the field of inorganic chemistry introduced techniques that used less water.

The present study deals with the history of urban planning, but it also deals with the specifics of urban techniques and their effect on the environment. The history of technical innovation has all too frequently focused on the single aspect of invention, neglecting sociological and ecological frameworks and allied technologies; taking the production of means for the means of production; and separating, for example, printing from the production of paper, and ballistics from the manufacture of gunpowder.[2] In the same way, the history of science, which pays more attention to genius than to its commonplace origins, has usually recognized the social dimension only in biographies of the illustrious.[3] I try to show here that the evolution of science, and even more so of technology, depends as well upon the collective imagination of artisans and craftsmen.

For example, if we look at developments in chemical technology from the fourteenth to the eighteenth centuries, we see that urban chemical activities throughout that period were founded on one and the same principle—namely, the slow techniques of maceration, which result, sooner or later, in the putrefaction of bodies. Until Lavoisier, work

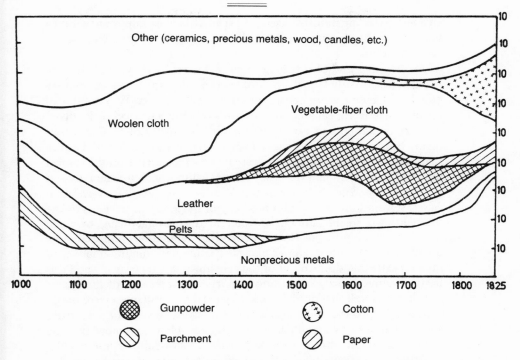

Figure 1. Distribution of Exports by the Cities in This Study between the Eleventh and Nineteenth Centuries, in Percentage of Total Exports.

in experimental chemistry also used these same techniques. This long period, called by Philippe Ariès the time of the macabre, was one of fascination with dead bodies and their decomposition.[4] It began at the end of the thirteenth century and closed with the eighteenth, when a new era was born, one that would repudiate death, chasing putrefaction out of the city and ushering in a new chemical technology based not on decomposition, but on the use of minerals. Lavoisier's revolution in chemistry, considered by Kuhn to be simply a matter of epistemics,[5] gave rise to something of vaster dimensions affecting the entire social body as mentioned in Alain Corbin's *The Foul and the Fragrant: Odor and the French Social Imagination*.[6] This transition from the "stinking city" of the Ancien Régime to the polluted city of the Industrial Age was brought about slowly but ineluctably by a series of shifts in awareness—political and cultural, symbolic and everyday, scientific and technical, economic and ecological.[7] The eighteenth century was both the ending of the era of "macerating" craftsmanship and the beginning of an energy-wasting industrialized age. It was the most important century for water management[8] and bore within it the protoplasm of a new science: hydraulics.

At the other end of this long reign of the macabre we find that the Middle Ages, with feudalism, had worked out an urban technology based on dynamic water consumption and water purity. We continue to assume that Europeans of the twelfth and thirteenth centuries lived without sanitation and cared little about the quality of their environment. But we need to look at the hard facts. Although it may be true that in Europe at that time there were no general treatises on the subject of urban pollution—not the case in the Muslim world, incidentally—it is nonetheless true that during the Middle Ages hospitals were relocated, sewers were dug, and a new way of hygiene was developed: the frequenting of steam baths. In addition, textile manufacturing, to which the cities in the north of France owed their reputation, required large quantities of running water. This water contained minute amounts of mineral salts that drained out of the calcium-rich substrate of the Paris basin. Chemical analysis not only confirms the presence of these salts but shows as well that products used by northern craftsmen were fungicidal and helped the rivers to cleanse themselves. Its care for pure water and air demonstrate that the medieval city knew how to remove from its midst what might threaten the well-being of its wealthier inhabitants.

All these elements played their part in demographic evolution. According to historians, a demographic maximum was attained in Europe at the end of the thirteenth century, not to be surpassed until the beginning of the nineteenth. As I shall try to show, this notion may need to be corrected. In fact, beginning early in the twelfth century, city dwellers set up sanitation systems that served to increase longevity. Because of this, demographic saturation was attained in Europe, especially in northern France, as early as the twelfth century. On the other hand, under the Ancien Régime, the low level of sanitation, combined with practices that encouraged fungous proliferation, severely limited the average life span, and the city, by disproportionately enlarging its ditch networks for military protection, slowly created a microclimate, or "greenhouse effect," that made the city a less healthy and more dangerous place in which to live. Historical analysis reveals the severe deteriorations sustained by the urban ecological milieu after the High Middle Ages.

The Paris basin is one of the best-defined regions in France in terms of environmental or ecological unity[9] and urbanization continued there, somehow, from Roman times onward. Unlike the cities of the south or the center of France, the cities of the north established congenial relationships with their rivers, all of which flowed slowly and regularly. The Paris basin—which I shall call, for purposes of convenience, northern France—today contains several hundred cities. By the end of the thirteenth century it already counted almost sixty, according to the survey done by Jacques Le Goff.[10] I have selected eighteen of these sixty, using as my criterion the standard by which medieval urbanization is usually measured—namely, the number of houses of mendicant orders within the city at the end of the thirteenth century—and I have excluded those urban areas that were located too far away from Paris, the center of the region and already paramount even at this early date.[11] Fourteen of these cities were regional centers of *civitas* during Roman times. As such, they became episcopal sees and played a predominant political and economic role during the first feudal age. Twelve of them were destined to become the capitals of *départements* at the time of the French Revolution, which shows how steady their importance has remained throughout history.

The formation of the surface hydraulic network can be approached by studying two elements: the moats that encircled the city, and the canals cut inside and outside city walls. The former will guide us especially toward structures of urbanization; the latter will allow us to probe into the technological systems that set the pace for two millennia.

From the end of the third century to the beginning of the fifth, the Roman world was in a period of crisis. In order to protect itself, the open city retreated back onto one part of itself, surrounded itself with a thick rampart edged with a wide moat—the first hydrographic inscription carved onto the surface of the earth. These changes were certainly intended for military use, but they were primarily intended to afford supernatural protection: upon closer examination we see that the rivers that were diverted to fill the moats had names derived etymologically from the Gallic order of the sacred. Urban space, at least in the north of the Roman Empire, thus became sacralized, reviving Celtic culture that had been smothered by three centuries of colonization. Etymological analysis of the names of waterways reveals the fundamental sacred role played by Jupiter Taranis in the protection of the cities of the late Roman Empire, a role substituted in the Christian calendar by the Rogation Days and the feast of the Ascension.

From the end of the Carolingian era to the end of the twelfth century, while the Normans were taking advantage of internal quarrels among the last of the Carolingians and another ideology—feudalism—

was taking shape, a new, much thicker wall was built to enclose the colonial city buried now under six centuries of ruins and landfill, and feudal authorities gave the old urban system new foundations. These activities occurred in two phases—in the tenth and eleventh centuries to control the population, and in the twelfth century for economic reasons.

The construction of intramural water networks was carried out as each particular case necessitated: by shoring up the banks of existing waterways, draining swamps, or using the grid left by the network of Roman roads, excavated and then fed by water diverted from nearby rivers. Entrenched behind their moats, the cities with the most waterways would come to resemble little Venices with quick-flowing streams.

The network was put to use for the watermills that produced meal. From the twelfth century on, it was used to maintain the "river trades," the crafts that then began to take precedence over milling. Inasmuch as the increase in the number of watermills reflects demographic evolution, I will try to calculate this evolution using the mills as the standard of evaluation. Industrial crafts that have been studied elsewhere with respect to organization and production will here be examined for their effect on the environment. The same holds for the analysis of certain collective facilities such as hospitals, public steam baths, and sewers.

In the middle of the fourteenth century, the Hundred Years' War began, provoking an economic and political crisis, resulting in the decline of feudalism and the reinforcement of the royal state. From then until the beginning of the seventeenth century, urban fortifications evolved with the progress made in armaments. The moat widened disproportionately, in direct proportion to the number of defeats suffered by defenders. As a result, the balance in the urban ecosystem was forfeited. War had imposed a no-man's-land around the city.

The activities that had made extensive use of the intramural waterways since the middle of the thirteenth century were adapted to new economic and military conditions. The streams of flowing water became stagnant pools. The accumulation of detritus and rubble in the streets lowered houses, which artisans now used for their crafts into the pervading underground dampness. Moreover, dampness was considered salubrious for the population as a whole. At the same time, a new filiform hydraulic system had developed in the no-man's-land left by the wars. The city was thus entirely bathed in vapors.

Beginning in the last quarter of the seventeenth century, the moats began to be filled in, and by about a hundred years later reduction of the intramural water system had been undertaken almost everywhere.

A detailed study of the "burial" of the system would take as long as this study of its origins. Without going into the precise details of its disappearance, I shall nonetheless try to delineate, in the final part of my study, its essential determinants—namely, scientific thinking and innovations in fungicidal technology.

The Age of Water

I

Sacred Cities

The years A.D. 270–430, the period of the late Roman Empire, are noted for the political, social, and economic turmoil that profoundly altered the urban land- and waterscape. In Europe this period began with the revolt of the *bagaudes*, bands of starving peasants and slaves particularly known for burning and pillaging cities, and continued with the damage done in the north of Gaul by the Germanic invaders who eventually succeeded in breaking through the Rhine frontier. The efforts of the badly shaken empire to deal with these problems only accentuated the constraints it faced. In 272, Aurelian forced the *curies*, the middle levels of society, to pay a tax on abandoned estates. Diocletian, his successor, began a sweeping reform that was simultaneously administrative (the creation of dioceses), military (the creation of an army of reserves, the *comitatenses*, stationed in the outermost cities of the empire), and financial (the reorganization of and increase in direct taxation, and the devaluation of money). However, these measures only increased the progressive impoverishment of the *curies*, which in turn accelerated the breakdown of the control apparatus itself, the city, which was by now a fortress or castle (*castrum*), huddled over one part of the vast urban area it had once occupied. This period was also marked by the growing predominance of Christianity and its recognition as the official religion in the middle of the fourth century. The urban environment owed much to this historic turn of events.

To be sure, sociopolitical upheavals were only one facet of the disturbances that had already brought about a change in mentality in the preceding period. We see this quite clearly in religious testimony: the spread of gnosis in reaction to the pretentiousness of the Pax Romana; the mortification and self-punishment of the Christian martyrs; the development of demonology in the works of Plotinus, Marcus Aurelius, and Palladius; the sexual abstinence and self-loathing reported by Galen and Origen; the visionary exaltation repeatedly emphasized in the writ-

3

ings of Apuleius; and finally, the return to certain Celtic cults in Gaul and Brittany. Such examples as these would seem to indicate that strong feelings of moral insecurity and collective anxiety existed throughout the Roman Empire, feelings that were more exacerbated the farther one moved toward the northern borders of the empire, where the effects of urban and Roman culture remained the most fragile.[1]

During this troubled period, municipal authorities—in spite of financial difficulties—put ramparts and ditches around parts of their cities, abandoning the earlier theories of the aediles, who had advocated an open and airy city: "Everywhere we see walls surging up over the remains of foundations that have just been rediscovered."[2]

The function of these walls and ditches has always been interpreted as military. And these enclosures did, in fact, use certain strategic extremities of the urban relief—for example, the summit of a hill in Senlis and Noyon; a spur at Le Mans, Chartres, and Auxerre; an island in Paris, Châlons-sur-Marne, and Meaux; the bottomland of a valley in Evreux, Rouen, Beauvais, Soissons, and Amiens. In Reims and Sens, two provincial capitals, the wall enclosed the greater part of the city of the second century. In every case, these fortifications were surrounded by a line of U-shaped ditches, the width of which—some fifteen meters at Noyon, Beauvais, and Senlis; nearly thirty at Sens and Reims— meant that any offensives would have to be sieges. These walls were used throughout the Middle Ages, and especially in the Carolingian era, for defense: sacred relics dispersed in outlying abbeys could be brought there in moments of panic.

Until now, historians have generally considered the sudden transformation of these urban areas from two points of view. According to one, the phenomenon was the sign either of ruralization—urban exodus—or of the ultimate withdrawal of Roman culture confronted with barbarianism. The other point of view insisted on the idea of the strategic citadel as a material refuge for a population scattered over the remains of the city of the second century. These two currents of thought need not be rejected: both are founded upon solid arguments.[3] However, microtopographic analysis of these cities raises a number of doubts concerning the "obvious" options worked out by the Gallo-Roman strategists. The question can indeed be asked why one site should be selected rather than another, all potentials for defense being equal. Why did Lutèce prefer the Ile de la Cité to the Château-Hautefeuille, location of the ancient forum? Why did Beauvais prefer to surround itself with water diverted from the Thérain—certainly far more costly and less strategic—rather than from the Liovette? Why did Le Mans choose a promontory, rather than the area around its forum, which was much

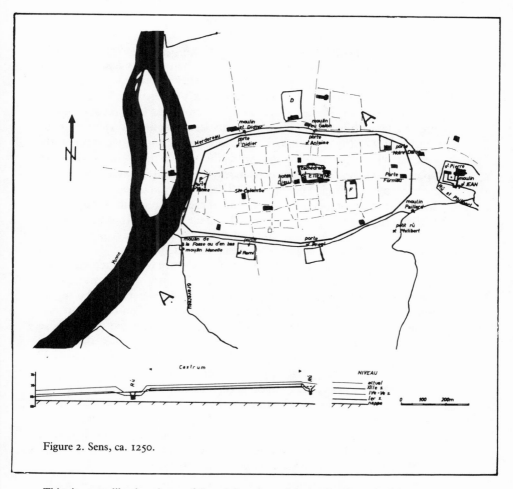

Figure 2. Sens, ca. 1250.

This city map, like the others to follow, is based on originals taken from the Schéma Directeur d'Aménagement et d'Urbanisme of each city. To it has been added a cross-section of the city (lower lefthand corner) corresponding to the A-A vector of the city in the map above it. This cross-section shows the ever-higher ground levels of the city over the course of time: *nappe* = water table; *Ier s.* = 1st century (A.D.); *IVe–Ve s.* = 4th to 5th century; *actuel* = present-day; *niveau* = level.

Other abbreviations:

A = Augustinians
C = cathedral
D = Dominicans
F = Franciscans
H.D. (Hôtel-Dieu) = hospital (public)
P = palace
baines = baths
bourg = district, neighborhood, borough
clos = enclosed field
enceinte = enclosure (wall, rampart)

fosse = ditch
limite de la ville romaine (médiévale) = limits of the Roman (or medieval) city
merdançon, merdereau = toilet ditch
moulin (or *m.* or *M.*) = mill
ND = Notre Dame
porte (or *pte.*) = gate
pré = meadow
rú or *ruisseau (ruiss.)* = small stream, brook
tour = tower

better supplied with water from the spring of Saint-Julien? Why did Auxerre retreat into a corner of its plateau when the city had other sites that were easier to defend? These, and other questions, are left unanswered by the study of poliorcetics, the art of seige warfare.

Another series of questions arises concerning the long period following the late Roman Empire when Christian sanctuaries were built in the vicinity of the ramparts. These churches or abbeys were generally erected within Roman cemeteries on the site of the tomb of the first apostle of the diocese, whose existence was then antedated to the second century by Carolingian panegyrists. That is, they claimed that the saint had lived at a time before the building of the urban fortifications, when Christianity had not yet penetrated northern Gaul. It can easily be imagined how oral tradition moved the tomb of the first martyr, and this is generally what scholars have maintained.

But from the point of view of probability, there is every reason for us to search for other, less uncertain, preferably more structural, motivations for the founding of these first Christian monuments. The fact is that the Gallo-Roman city developed at the intersection of at least two roads and had at its disposal four necropolises, situated along these roads on the periphery of the city.[4] In the majority of cases, the Christian sanctuary was set up in the immediate proximity and upstream of the diversion channel that brought water to the city moats or ditches. There would thus seem to have been a relationship between the first abbeys and the diversion channels, as between the channels and the location of the site of the *castrum*. The role of the hydraulic system, put into place at the end of the third century and, more generally, that of the geographical contours of the city in the development of the new city of the late Roman Empire have been underestimated.

Le Mans and Auxerre chose to retreat back onto the highest points of their sites, where Celtic religious remains were the most abundant. Fitted into the chevet of the cathedral at Le Mans is a menhir that women to this day touch as an aid to fertility. Within the walls of Auxerre stood a temple dedicated to Icauni, the divinity of the river Yonne, as well as a sacred tree and another monument perhaps consecrated to Materna, the Mother. Senlis and Noyon—Augustomagus and Noviomagus—new cities of the first century created after the Bellovaques had surrendered, chose to build on sites that were the most religious from the Roman point of view—namely, the forum and its temples, located at the highest point of the city, as mentioned in later vitae of the first martyr of Senlis, Saint Rieul.

For cities built on heights, holiness dwelt in the hill that supported the new *castrum*, as it had the Roman forum, or, in Le Mans and Chartres, the pre-Roman oppidum. This holiness beneath the soil added to that of the soil itself, which was protected by the religious monuments transported there. And the ramparts were covered over with building material extracted from the temples constructed in accordance with sacred Roman legislation, the *res sanctae;* they too were part of the city's religious patrimony. Each city celebrated feast days for the dedication of its towers, walls, and moats, as one of Saint Eloi's admonishing sermons shows. This accumulation of sacred memorabilia appears even more clearly in and around valley cities. *Castra* were surrounded by ditches filled with water diverted from a neighboring river. This was certainly for additional military protection; especially in the north of Gaul, where clashes could be sudden and violent. These ditches defined the shape of the urban landscape for centuries to come, and for certain cities—for example, Reims and Sens—they would serve later as the outlines for the boulevard loops of urban peripheries in the twentieth century.

The construction of these canals and ramparts took decades, sometimes centuries. Roman coins discovered from time to time in walls give at best an approximate indication of age; they cannot be used to date the beginning or the end of construction work. A part of the walls of Sens was erected as early as the years 276–282, but the recent discovery of a mosaic on the site of the old prison shows that the rampart did not yet exist in that section of the city at the end of the fourth century. Completion of the city's enclosure took more than a century. The enclosures of Amiens and Reims took some forty years, it seems. Generally speaking, this is probably the length of time that should be estimated for the construction of ramparts in the late Roman Empire, a point that strengthens my belief that strictly military aspects were not the all-determining factors. Other considerations must be taken into account—namely, esthetic, economic (insofar as supervising the work was in the domain of the *curies*), and especially religious.

The Power of Taranis

Beauvais

Caesaromagus was well drained by the Liovette (or Calais) Brook, the basin of which extends over more than five thousand hectares. The aediles chose, however, to divert the Thérain, or Thara, as recorded in a document dated 879,[5] by means of the two-kilometer-long Gonard ca-

The Age of Water

Table 1.
Lucien-Taranis Parallels

	Lucien	Taranis
Origination	born of Lucius: light	god of light
Relationship to time	an old man	represents time
Type of immolation	flagellation, then decapitation	flagellation, then decapitation
Symbolization of eternity	a body radiating light	light

nal, in order to surround the city with water. The name "Thara" un-doubtedly derives from Taranis, the Gallic god who epitomized the Indo-European sacerdotal function, that of the Druids.[6] It is easy to understand why Beauvais would want to envelop itself with this peaceful divinity, who seems not to have lost all his influence at the dawning of the fourth century. Much later, one of the sources of this stream, christianized under the name of Saint-Arnoult, would be the site of the last procession of a pagan nature (in 1258).

To offset the all-powerful god that bathed Beauvais,[7] Christianity imposed its own holy personage: Saint Lucien, the city's first martyr, whose Latin name, Lucianus, is related to *lux*, "light," one of Taranis's attributes. The three vitae of Lucien,[8] the oldest of which dates from the end of the ninth century, detail parallels between the saint and the god, as shown in Table 1.

Chilpéric I founded the Abbey of Saint-Lucien on the site where the relics of the first martyr of Beauvais had been found, near the road to Rouen, on the Thérain—in a rival position, so to speak. The protection of the city was thus incumbent upon a Christian hero who retained the attributes of the Gallo-Roman divinity. The metamorphosis of the sacred was accomplished through the inauguration of a new space (the abbey), as if a competing *topos* ("place," "space"), equally sacred and significant, had to be substituted for the urban area surrounded by its sanctified walls and ditches.

The same thing will be seen for Evreux, capital of the Aulerques Eburovices, whose old *oppidum* ("town"), Mediodunum—"Old Evreux"—seems to have been abandoned not long after the Roman conquest.[9]

8

Evreux

At the end of the third century, the city of Evreux took refuge behind a twofold diversion of the Iton, abandoning the rest of its urban area on the hillsides. The Iton, designated Itona on one of the maps of Charles the Bald, also carries a second name: Hesilina *fluvius,* or Eseline. The parallel here with Esus (Hesus) is significant. Esus was a well-known Gallic divinity. Scholars are unanimous in attributing to him the protection of Nautes (ships), thus of all river commerce, and hence of rivers in general. For Lucan, this god was related to Taranis.[10] The first legendary apostle of Evreux was named Taurin (Taurino). His vita, written in the ninth century, refers to the attributes and functions of Taranis: Taurin was named bishop by Saint Denis and came to Evreux, where he was warmly received by Lucius, whose name evokes Lucien and "light."[11] Before Taurin arrived at the city gates, the devil transformed himself three times to try to force the saint to turn back; he successively took on the form of a bear, a lion, and a bull—which could be the three animals of Taranis. But Taurin overcame them all by his virtue. On the third day, the devil carried off Euphrasie, the daughter of Lucius, and threw her into a fire, another mode of sacrifice offered to the Gallo-Roman divinity. Taurin brought her back to life. Then, after other miracles, he decided to chase the demon once and for all from the temple of Diana, where an idol was located. Under threats, the devil emerged from the idol in the form of an "Ethiopian as black as soot," wearing a long beard and shooting gleaming sparks of fire from his mouth. We know that Taranis, usually represented with a long beard, a symbol of wisdom and time, was in command of the night, thus was credited with the coming of the day, the "gleaming" day. This devil in the temple of Diana was carried off by the Angel of the Sky, "brilliant as the sun." The correlation between these two entities, Taurin and Taranis, is thus conclusive.

It was the Bishop Laudulfe, probably a contemporary of Clothaire I, who discovered the tomb of Saint Taurin. While praying, preoccupied by the search for the saint's remains, he saw a column "brilliant as the sun," a completely "Taranien" light, descending from the sky down to the spot where the saint was buried. Laudulfe founded a chapel dedicated to Saint Martin there, between the two arms of the Iton, upstream from Evreux. Why did he choose the apostle of the Gauls? Perhaps because Martin was the protector of the Merovingians; more certainly because he stood as the guarantor of Christianity threatened by a paganism that was still very much alive; and especially because Taurin had not yet been invested with all the Christian virtues of his legend. In the life of

9

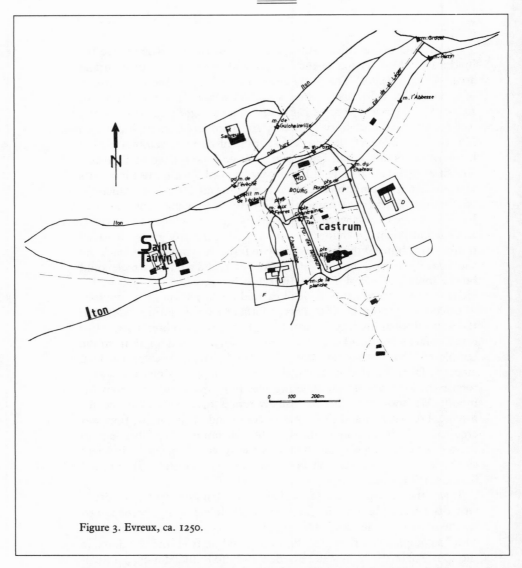

Figure 3. Evreux, ca. 1250.

Taurin we probably must recognize that of Taranis reformulated; Taranis was still present, so to speak, at the time of the writing of Taurin's earliest vita, during the ninth century. Whatever the reason, Laudulfe's intention was clearly to substitute the Taurin-Iton, or Martin-Iton, pairing for the Taranis-Esus pairing, in order to protect the city. It was a question of sanctifying a clearly delimited extraurban space, which would thus hold a kind of religious counterpower over a city still too markedly pagan from the presence of the river Eseline and the god Taranis. The Christianization of the outskirts of the city took place in the middle of the sixth century, at a time when Christianity was flourishing: Gregory of Tours is the best witness.

Local Divinities

Soissons

The Aisne River runs along the eastern side of Augusta Suessionum. The ground configuration would have lent itself to the diverting of this river (sanctified under the name Aciona) along three sides of the city walls dating from the late Roman Empire. In spite of this, it was one of the branches of the Crise, a modest tributary of the Aisne, that was diverted to bathe the ramparts of Soissons, which was to become the capital of Clovis and Clothaire, founders of the French royal line.[12] The name "Crize" (thirteenth century), Crisia or Crizia (twelfth century), seems to derive from the Gallic *crispus*, "curly," "frizzy." The discovery at nearby Pommiers (the former *oppidum* of the Suessiones) at the end of the nineteenth century of more than a thousand medals dedicated to Criciru, who is represented with curly, waving hair, would seem to confirm this etymology.[13] This divinity is not well known, but I would readily see him as the principal god of the Suessiones in the era before Roman colonization and associated with the mythic king of this people, Divitiac. The coins show him as well with curly hair. On the reverse side, a horse accompanies the legend *Deiovigeagos*, whose root,

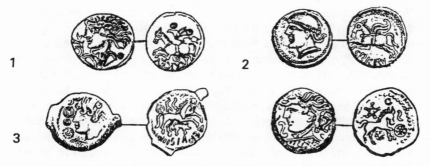

Figure 4. Coins of the Suessiones, Gallo-Roman Inhabitants of Soissons:
1) Silver Coin Depicting Cricuru;
2) Bronze Coin Inscribed Cricironio;
3) Coins Dedicated to Divitiac.

div- or *deio-*, indicates quite well the sacred character of this probably legendary personage.

The parallel between the river Crise and the gods Criciru-Divitiac was continued with the appearance of two other no less important personages from the High Middle Ages, Saints Crépin and Crépinien (Crispin and Crispinian), the first legendary martyrs of Soissons, whose Latin names, Crepinus and Crepinianus, mean "curly" as well. Their biographies shed little new light on the analysis, except for their drowning in the Aisne[14] and the fact that they were twins, which points to the third Indo-European divinity function (see note 6). On the other hand, the founding of the Abbey of Saint-Crépin on the site of two sarcophagi supposedly theirs, in the immediate proximity of the Crise, leaves no doubt about the royal and episcopal wishes of the Merovingians to Christianize the river and the territory of Soissons.[15] Once again, the decisions on the diversion of the Crise around the city at the end of the third century, and on the site of the first monastery at the end of the sixth, were prompted by considerations of sacred hydrography. The Abbey of Saint-Crépin was located between the Crise, the more important divinity, and the Aisne (Aciona), the lesser divinity. The Crépin-Crépinien pairing replaced the Crise-Criciru pairing seen in the two heads that figure on the reverse side of Divitiac coins. Finally, it should be noted in passing that the Crise wells up at Launoy, Alnetium in the medieval texts, a Gallic place name meaning, most likely, "the White" (fem.).

Rouen

Ratomagus was endowed with a number of streams flowing down from hills to the north. Any one of them could have been quite easily diverted. But the *aediles* chose to divert the Robec, or Rodobeccus (924), for more than three kilometers. The root *rod-* is related to the color "red," or to the eponym *Rato-*, for Roth, the local divinity of Rouen.[16] This stream was diverted by means of a paved canal that led right up to the walls of Rouen, supplying water for two of its moats. The Seine, Sequana, fed a third, and the fourth, the Renelle, was used as an outlet for the two springs that welled up inside the temple dedicated to Venus, which was partially destroyed about 630 by the bishop, Saint Romain, and transformed at that time into the church of Notre-Dame.[17] In the eleventh century, three chapels were built, one after the other, on the Renelle, each distant from the other by a hundred meters: Notre-Dame, Saint-Martin, and Saint-Jean—as if their number were in proportion to the holy power of the waters they were supposed to neutralize. The *castrum* of Rouen was thus utterly bathed in a pagan sacredness that christianization would obliterate.

The first mythic apostle of the province, Saint Mellon, was used with this purpose in mind. His subsequent vita recounts that he sacrificed to Mars, the god of war, before his conversion to Christianity. When he arrived at Rouen, Mellon destroyed the idol Roth, god of the Rothomagenses. His name can be related to the Indo-European root *mel-*, which probably designated a dark color, in Latin *mulleus*, "red," "purple," the color attached to the second Indo-European divinity function, that precisely of Mars and of Roth (see note 6).

Christianity made similar use of Saint Romain at the beginning of the seventh century to sanctify the sources of the Renelle, which were thereafter called the wells of Notre-Dame. This bishop, a contemporary of King Dagobert, was also credited with the extermination of a dragon that roamed in the marshes of the Robec at the foot of Mount Gargan. Gargan was the pagan counterpart of the Archangel Michael, the leader of the divine army, who reduced the power of Lucifer (light) by forcing him into the darkness. Gargan, the ruler of thunder and lightning, was another, more warlike, manifestation of Taranis, and folklore frequently endowed him with control over suddenly rising, tumultuous waters, symbolized by a dragon. By having the dragon submit to God, Bishop Romain christianized the Robec. Rouen itself could then be invested with Christian buildings, which until then had been located at a distance from the *castrum*, first in the necropolis on the western side, at Saint-Gervais, a place of silence and meditation.

Mediolanum: Sacred Space

From these examples, which could be multiplied,[18] we must conclude that the choice of the walled part of urban territory at the end of the third century, and the site of the first extraurban abbey in the fifth or sixth, did not simply come about by chance. Quite the contrary, these options were informed by highly religious considerations, all of which revived the Celtic mentality.

Thus the fundamental characteristics of Roman urbanism (the slopes considered important by Vitruvius and Pliny for good aeration and proper run-off, for example) were completely ignored during this era. These characteristics had generally been applied during the laying of foundations in the first century. The late-empire enclosure, built on a rocky spur or dug into the middle of a marsh, was a characteristic of the Celtic *oppidum* as defined by Vegetius.[19]

Unlike cities in the south, most of the cities in the north of Gaul changed their name as they put up enclosures. They chose the name of the tribe or its prinicpal god, as if everything linking individuals converged on one point of land, the Gallo-Roman regional capital, which had retreated into one part of the city. These modifications took place when the greatest weight of religiousness was concentrated on the *castra*. This accumulation of the sacred, this religious "fullness," can perhaps be compared to the Celtic *mediolanum*, that "center of perfection where a kind of religious plenitude can be realized."[20] In addition, the refuge would appear to have been sanctified by a triple consecration: the earth, fitted out with Celtic or Roman temples; the sanctified walls crowning the site; and the ditches bathed by the protective waters of the principal divinity of the tribe, or Taranis, or at least by one of his attributions—the color white, for example. We meet up here again with the Indo-European divinity trifunctionality. The first function, that of the priest, could perhaps be assigned to the diversion channel, or to the hill in the case of cities on heights; the second, the warrior, to the walls and palace of the ruler; and the third, that of producers and makers, to the intramural earth, linked to the chthonian divinities.[21] Thus, the functional concentration of the sacred was added to that of the place itself, the *mediolanum*.[22]

The new Christian religion, which was beginning to take over in the West, rejected this trifunctionality, but constructed churches or abbeys in the Gallo-Roman necropolises on the tomb of the first apostle of the diocese. The edifice was generally built upstream of the city, in the immediate proximity of the diversion channel, as if the Christian authorities wanted to dominate it. This church, which would become the center of an abbey, was also a place of silence and meditation, highlighted in the daily prayers of the monks.[23] The monastery was but the Christian form of the Gallic *mediolanum*, of which Saint Augustine's *City of God,* in 420, is one reflection.

On a mythological level, there were links between the two founders, the holy Christian martyr and the Gallic god. According to the vita of the first bishop of each city, there was always a conflict with the forces of evil—that is, with the local god, frequently a river spirit, as mentioned above. Through the intervention of the apostle, the god was chased out; this relates to one of the first two Indo-European divinity functions. Table 2 summarizes the points at which myth and reality meet.

Above and beyond these mythic conflicts, created by the new religion when confronted with the old, the same vision of the world, the same *Weltanschauung,* in fact united them. Faced with this form of sacred Gallic urbanization, the *mediolanum,* Christianity would urbanize all human space—*urbi et orbi*[24]—several centuries later according to the

Table 2.
Gallo-Roman and Early Christian Confrontation/Assimilation

	Reality	Myth	
Late Empire	river	river-god	confrontation
High Middle Ages	church	apostle	

same model, aided by those centers of perfection, the monasteries. In sum, the deurbanization of the late empire and the high Middle Ages was essentially material, which is what impressed nineteenth- and twentieth-century historians. But in the period from the fourth to the seventh centuries, with its ideology based on the sacred, on the theological, any motion of ruralization is purely illusory. Quite the contrary, what occurred was a form of theological urbanization, or "theography," which we see in the implantation of the Merovingian monasteries, and in the earlier constitution of urban enclosures saturated in religiosity.

During the late empire, diversion channels were cut upstream of the city to provide a sacred flow of water for the entire urban area. This water was governed by the first Indo-European divinity function, Taranis, Criciru, the color white, which at the time of the Celts or under Roman dominion had absorbed some of the attributes of the second function (the red of Rouen, military protection) and of the third, notably in the ditch encircling the *castrum*. These attributes are all to be found in a Christian institution, the Rogation Days, the origins of which are less well known.

The Origin of the Minor Rogation Days

The Rogation Days played an important role in Christian ritual. The major Rogation Days fell near April 25, the feast of Saint Mark. It was probably during the sixth century that they were substituted for the Robigalia, Roman feast days for the protection of cereal grains against rust. The minor Rogation Days were instituted about 470 by Saint Mamert, bishop of Vienne in the south of France (464–77), in order to invoke divine protection against the earthquakes and lightning that threatened the region at that time. At the Council of Orléans in 511, this custom was extended to all of Gaul and was generalized for the Christian world under the pontificate of Leo III at the beginning of the ninth century. The pagan origin of the Rogation Days has not yet been con-

clusively proved: the only attempts so far—limited to the study of
the Roman liturgical calendar—have been fruitless.[25] Only Cerquand's
analysis has established a correlation between the Rogation Days and
Taranis.[26] This analysis, however, has found little support among contemporary liturgists. Nevertheless, his hypothesis should not be completely rejected. It would seem, in effect, that the Rogation Days and
the Ascension are the legacy of one and the same festival dedicated to
the Gallic Taranis or to the Gallo-Roman Jupiter-Taranis. The feasts
of the Gabales, recounted by Gregory of Tours, bear witness to the per-
sistence of this ceremony as late as the fifth century.

The remarkable feature in the origin of the Rogation Days is how
quickly they were adopted by all the Gauls—in less than forty years—
and, in contrast, how long it took for them to be recognized in the Italian world—more than four hundred years. If the origins of the Rogation Days are pagan, they must be sought in France rather than in Italy.
We happen to know the circumstances of their inauguration by Saint
Mamert, thanks to a homily by Saint Avit, the second successor of
Mamert in the diocese of Vienne:

> When ineffable necessity bent the stubborn hearts of the people
> of Vienne toward humility and prayer, then our church found
> succor in the practice of the litanies, which was stronger than
> the magistrates' power. I know that many of you remember the
> terrors of these times, when repeated fires, frequent earth-
> quakes, nocturnal noises, and the apparition of wild beasts
> foretold the ruin of the city. Indeed the forms of animals could
> be seen wandering among the throngs. . . . In the midst of
> these public terrors and anxieties, we came to the solemnities
> of the vigil of Easter. All expected that the feast would bring
> relief, as at the end of a scourge. Then came that venerable
> night whose ceremonies had given birth to the hope of a uni-
> versal pardon. All at once, the thunder began to rumble, with
> an ever-increasing groan up to a final crash, the noise of which,
> like a whiplash, was of such intensity that everyone said after-
> ward that the only thing left now was for chaos to come. The
> public buildings, whose towering constructions covered the
> summit of the citadel, caught fire about dawn. At the news of
> this disaster, the joy of the feast was interrupted. The terrified
> people left the church, all fearing that a flaming beam would
> fall upon their house. But the holy Bishop Mamert remained
> immovable before the altar that had been prepared for the
> solemnities. The ardor of his faith erupting into a river of tears,

he took the power out of the fire, which little by little began to go out. The terror began to calm, the people came back to the church, and the brightness of the candles put out the last glimmers of the burning fire. The bishop resolved posthaste to apply the remedy of penance. Alone with God, on this vigil of Easter, he thought out the plan of the Rogation Days, and put together psalms and prayers that are now sung by the entire Christian universe.[27]

A homily attributed by Christian scholars to Saint Mamert invokes "the Lord to deliver us from our infirmities, to turn the scourge from us, to keep us from all evil, to protect us from the plague, from hail, from drought, from the fury of our enemies; to give us good weather for the health of our bodies and for the fertility of the earth, to let us enjoy peace and calm, and to pardon us our sins."[28]

In both these instances, identical motives prompted the founding of the Rogation Days: the fear of water, fire, and the earth. It would seem that Gallic and high medieval folklore associated lightning, earthquakes, and floods:

1. Taranis, corresponding to the Roman god Jupiter, the god of the thunderbolt, was the greatest of the Gallic divinities. He was also a water god (see above with respect to Thérain of Beauvais), shown by the etymology of "Tarasque," to designate the dragon in the waters of the Rhone at Tarascon. Taranis was also the master of earthquakes: several statuettes from Nîmes show him with a trident. In the region of Narbonne—Vaison, Orange, Nîmes, and Vienne—his cult, under these last two forms, was particularly developed during the Gallo-Roman era.[29] Elsewhere, especially in the regions of Orléans and Mayenne, where crossing rivers was particularly risky, the protection of Taranis was likewise invoked. In support of these assertions, numerous little wheels, the solar symbol of this god, and bronze coins from a later period and until the sixth century, have been discovered near fords.[30] In conclusion, Taranis, and what was left of his memory in the High Middle Ages, presided almost everywhere in Gaul as the protector against dangerous waters.

2. In the Middle Ages, the rogation procession began in the town and ended in a marsh close to the walls of the city: Martainville in Rouen, the Moline in Troyes, the future Saint-Marcel quarter in Paris, the lower town of Poitiers, the environs of Saint-Ayoul in Provins, the Saint-Pantaleon quarter in Sens. These areas were subject to annual flooding; moreover, according to vitae of the tenth century, each had harbored a dragon with pestilential breath until a saintly bishop came to

deliver the population from its curse. The processions of the Rogation Days ritualized this combat. During the first two days, the dragon was placed at the head of the procession, "the tail built up and swollen. But the last day . . . he followed from behind, his tail empty, flattened, and depressed."[31]

We know, to begin with, that humid places, in Europe, are the preferred habitats of snakes. But what sort of logic transforms snakes into dragons? Surface waters swell up and overflow their banks during a flood, rendering the atmosphere loathesome. The snakes flushed out of their lairs suddenly assumed gigantic proportions, those of a dragon. And in fact, the swelling up of beings had a symbolic value for the Celts, signifying the anger associated with the warrior function, and vengeance.[32] On a religious level, only the prayer and fasting of the three days of procession could vanquish, symbolically, the strength of the monster.

3. Most of the extraurban swamps were located in the immediate vicinity of a Mount Gargan (Rouen, Troyes) or near a hill whose name was related to light (mons Lucotinius in Paris), one of the attributes of Taranis. There would thus seem to be a close relationship between the Gallic god of thunder—or his substitute—and the dragon of the swamp. This is confirmed, incidentally, in Gallo-Roman statuary: Jupiter or Jupiter-Taranis crushes a giant anguipe monster, or with a ram's head crushes a serpent, comparable in form to the medieval dragon.

There thus existed in medieval and Gallo-Roman folklore a cause-and-effect relationship vis-à-vis lightning, earthquakes, and floods. As a homily attributed to Mamert, and later on one by Guillaume Durand, bishop of Mendes about 1260, make clear: "Because it was especially during this time that we used to make war, and the fruits of the earth, still green or in flower, were habitually lost or spoiled in diverse manners, we now say litanies to pray to [God] to turn away from us such scourges, to protect us and to defend us from storms of the air, to deliver us from wars and from the enemies of the Christian religion." The Rogation Days, instituted by Mamert, would thus be a substitute for the feast of Taranis, commemorated to prevent the flooding of rivers. Understood in this way, Mamert's actions during the vigil were not simply metaphoric: "The ardor of his faith erupting into a river of tears, he took the power out of the fire, which little by little began to go out." On the contrary, his actions disguised a substitution, a Christian assimilation of the scourges and thus of the non-Christian divinities. Mamert accomplished two things with one religious practice: he reduced the cause and the effect to one identical origin, which now only prayer could neutralize.

It remains to be seen why Mamert chose the three days before the Ascension. The feast of the Ascension appeared for the first time only in the middle of the fourth century in the Byzantine Church and was associated at the time with Pentecost (the fiftieth day after Easter).[33] The establishment of the Ascension on the fortieth day after Easter dates from the years 380–430 for the Roman Church. Liturgists have not given a cogent explanation for the choice of this forty-day reckoning, and the only fact they have established is that the Council of Elvira (near Granada, Spain) (ca. 300) declared that celebrating the fortieth day after Easter was a heretical practice. The celebration thus appears to have been an essentially Gallo-Roman, or Hispano-Roman, activity of pagan origin. It seems furthermore to have been associated with an agrarian ritual: the *Liber pontificalis* states that a blessing of beans, and sometimes of new fruits, was held in Rome on the same day.

In the haziness of the hypotheses, this rite, very probably linked to an earth-fertility rite, might readily be compared to the feast of a little-known Roman divinity, Dea Dia, who "occupied the central place in the liturgy . . . celebrated in May by the Arvales brothers" and who "was the goddess of atmospheric conditions."[34] Hers was a moveable feast, like the Ascension; it lasted for three days in May, like the Rogation Days. A torch-light procession was held the third day, as on the third Rogation day in certain towns in Gaul, according to Gregory of Tours. But nothing is known of the rites associated with this goddess after the first century A.D. Another hypothesis links the ascension of Christ, at least symbolically, with the apotheosis of the Roman emperors, who were carried up into the heavens on a chariot drawn by the four horses of Jupiter; this scenario was introduced by Diocletian about 280.[35] The day consecrated to Jupiter was Thursday (in French, *Jeudi*, from the late Latin *juesdi*, originally *Jovis dies*, Latin, "the day of Jove," i.e., Jupiter). The fiftieth day after Easter is always a Sunday, Pentecost; the fortieth, Ascension day, is always a Thursday.

Whatever the reason, the Ascension was probably a feast of recent institution when Mamert came up with the idea of the Rogation Days. The least one can say, in the absence of more likely hypotheses, is that the Ascension had begun to establish itself in Roman Christianity as a substitute for a pagan feast, associated probably with the cult of the sun (Jupiter and his Gallis equivalent, Taranis), or with a cult of daylight (Dea Dia). Seen in this context, the Rogation Days appear as a prelude to the feast of the Ascension. They are intended as a sort of exorcism of calamities—war, lightning, earthquake, rain, floods, poor harvests— for three days, so that on the fourth day appears the honor and glory of Christ the Conqueror.

Gregory of Tours tells in his *Gloria confessorum* about a rite practiced by farmers of the Gevaudan region, the Gabales:

> There, on the shore of a mountain lake named Allenc, at a certain time, a multitude of people from the country used to make as it were libations in this lake. . . . They came with chariots, brought things to eat and drink, slaughtered animals, and during three days gave themselves up to good living. The fourth day, at the moment of departure, they were assailed by a storm with thunder and tremendous lightning, and there came from the sky rain so strong and hail so violent that the people were all sure that they were going to perish instantly. This was repeated every year, and superstition held sway over these unthinking people.

The bishop of the place then had a sacred basilica built: "The storm was thus from that time removed from that place and never again was it seen to hold sway on a feast day consecrated to God." [36]

Gregory of Tours does not actually designate Taranis, for he always avoided calling pagan divinities by their names. However, what happened on the fourth day of the feast of the Gabales coincides with all that we know about the Gallic Jupiter-Taranis. The bishop of Tours recalls that this fourth day was consecrated entirely to God, just as Ascension day. The correspondence between the long feast of the Gabales' folk, whose bishopric is not far from Vienne where Mamert preached, and the four days of Rogations-Ascension is very clear.

Mamert's actions on the vigil of Easter, and the rapidity with which the Council of Orléans set up the Rogation Days before the Ascension, [37] can now be more easily understood: they were the substitute for a four-day period of libation that the Gallo-Romans set aside for ritual protection against the scourges of nature. Calamities that had formerly been dissociated as to nature and function fell within the competence of an all-powerful god during the late empire, a god whose attributes very closely resembled the Christian *dis-pater* (Jupiter—that is, Jesus Christ). Not only did he protect the people from the forces of evil, but he also protected cities by means of ramparts and by encircling streams. He sometimes delegated his powers to a local divinity: Roth or Criciru, for example. Lug is probably another name by which he was known in certain localities: in Laon, for example, important feasts were sacred to him as late as the eighth century in spite of the multiplication of Christian places of worship. [38] Lugdunum (for example, the "hill of Lugus") was the Latin name of Lyons and Loudun.

Table 3.
Parallels between the Feast of Gabales and the Rogation Days/Ascension.

	Feast of Gabales	Rogation Days and Ascension
Place	By the shore of a lake, on a mountain named Allenc	In a swamp, at the foot of a hill dedicated to Gargan-Taranis
Date	At a certain time of the year	Variable: 37th to 40th day after Easter
Procedure	A crowd indulging in libations	Procession and blessing of swamp with holy water
Accompanying rites	Pieces of cloth and bread thrown into the lake	Small breads tossed into the mouth of the dragon
	Feasting	Feasting is forbidden*
Duration	Three days	Three days
Fourth day	Storm accompanied by tremendous thunder and lightning; heavy rain; violent hail	Formerly the feast of Jupiter
		Ascension: the apotheosis of Christ (blessing of the beans and new fruits in Rome), who rises toward the light of the sun

*Capitulaire d'Hérald de Tours (858): "We want the Rogations to be celebrated with attention and respect, and we want conversations and lewd games to be banished from them. No one, during the triduum, is to go from one house to another, taking part in feasting and banquets and drinking a toast in each house" (*Gallia Christiana*, XIV, 1856, "Instrumenta," col. 44, par. xcv).

Thus, in the northern section of Gaul, the city of the late empire was first and foremost a religious refuge, a *mediolanum* dedicated to Jupiter-Taranis. The military significance of the citadel and palace, the visible representation of Roman culture, had clearly been relegated to a secondary rank. This multisacredness revived ancient traditions: the *templum* or *temenos*, the divine enclosure of the Greeks. But to the extent that Christianity similarly established itself in the urban periphery,[39] the concentration of numinousness within the city walls weakened, subsisting only in a skeleton of stones or ditches, and in folklore.[40] Throughout this entire period, the waters diverted through channels from the rivers with sacred names played a primordial role: they covered the sacred. This network of canals would also influence the urbanization of the eleventh and twelfth centuries, at least for episcopal cities.

2

Peopling the Environs
of the Roman Castles

The half-millennium from the beginning of the late Roman Empire to
the Carolingian era had left the urban military infrastructure almost intact, but its sacred signification had changed as Christianity spread.
The new religion left its mark on the walls of the *castrum:* crosses were
carved into the largest stones in Sens and Reims. Sometimes the city
gates were designated as Christian and sanctuaries of the all-powerful
Archangel Michael, conqueror of demonic forces, were set up there.
The moats had partaken of the faith of the first local apostle, whose al-
leged martyrdom was the sign of his virtuous power. Paganism, its
structures neutralized, had been relegated to the harmless domain of
folklore. The city of God had replaced the city of the gods. The cathedral, baptistry, episcopal palace, and other Christian fixtures now occupied the *castrum,* and the city outskirts were dotted with monasteries
and *cellae* (cells, hermitages). The God of the Christians was ready to
recuperate the space left vacant by pagan disorganization. The imma-
nence of the Christian God would make itself felt, with all its power, in
the smallest places where persons gathered together.

The city of the High Middle Ages was not simply a reliquary; it was
itself a relic, a thing of the past. The praises of the Carolingian monks
hurriedly writing the lives of the apostles of their diocese amply attest to
this fact. In the introduction to the *Cartulaire de Saint Père,* Chartres is
presented as follows by the monk Paul, about 890:

> This is a very populous city, and the most opulent of the cities
> of Neustrie, famous for the thickness of its walls, the beauty of
> its buildings, and the study of the liberal arts. . . . A city that,
> beseiged in the past by Julius Caesar, resisted for ten years and
> indefatigably pushed back the Roman armies and the pha-
> lanxes of Argos. [In fact, the city was built of enormous square

23

stones and provided with high towers, and for this reason it was called the city of stones.] Now, with God's permission, a people totally devoid of Christian virtue is razing it to the ground and putting it to the torch.

The description of Laon, written at about the same time by the author of the *Life of Saint Salaberge*, contains similar references:

Even though it is easy to lay seige to Laon by using entrenchments, the city is well protected by its location on a stone promontory. Indeed, in former times the Vandals, Alamanni, Huns, and other peoples of Germania and Scythia tried in vain to take the city. They were unable to conquer her. Neither portable battlements, nor javelins hurled by their sieging machines, nor battering rams had any effect. Disappointed by their useless efforts, they retreated powerless. In fact no war machine can injure her, for her walls follow the exact contours of the rocky hill and house terrepleins on the inside.

The important role given to the past in these tributes is significant, and it was the same for all the cities in this study until the middle of the eleventh century—that is, until the flourishing of urbanization. The entire *castrum* was like an island of tenacity, longevity, and resistance confronted with the ephemeral nature of daily life. Sacred and profane history, and especially written history, glorified the *castrum*, and its lower walls were to bear the marks of victorious combats like trophies against the wrath of Satan.

Beginning in the ninth century, a new spatial organization, itself a crucible of new infrastructures, slowly began to concentrate around this urban skeleton inherited from the late empire.

Until that time, the Carolingian dynasty had been little concerned with refurbishing urban fortifications. There were several reasons for this. To begin with, these rulers had managed to maintain their power intact; secondly, they conducted their wars outside the kingdom; and finally, they practiced an internal policy of support for the church and the lay nobles who enriched themselves as the population grew.[1] The second dynasty of French kings ushered in an era of collectivization that would lead to the first period of urban growth. That new era included administrative and scribal concentrations in the major cities (often the former regional capitals of the *civitas* of the late empire, whose territory had been reorganized by Charlemagne); religious concentration following the organization of canonical communities near the cathedral; and, finally, concentration of wealth from the Arab reengagement in international commerce—gold and silver began to accumulate in treasuries and reliquaries. Thus in the ninth century the major urban centers became points of accumulation of power and precious metals that the Normans attempted to seize at the first signs of weakness from sovereigns and of resistance to Christianization. For that reason Charles the Bald attempted to hold the Norman invaders downstream on the Seine (Edict of Pîtres, 864) by constructing fortresses—furnished with a supply of water, arable land, and pastures—to withstand long sieges. The model for this plan, taken probably from Vegetius, was incorporated in the castle of Pîtres, built between 862 and 869. The chapter house of Quierzy-sur-Oise (877) anticipated the reinforcement of the palaces of Compiègne, Paris, and Saint-Denis, and of fortresses along the Seine and the Loire.[2] A little later, in 885, the castle of Pontoise was built. About 890, military marches—protective border areas—were established that were capable of containing the Normans on the east (Vermand and Soissons) and on the west (Chartres).

It was in this defensive context, which was prolonged very late into the eleventh century because of conflicts over territorial hegemony, that the first medieval hydraulic networks appeared: the moats of Senlis, Noyon, and Chartres. Unlike those of other cities, the moats here preceded urbanization; that is, they came before the setting up of religious and political superstructures and economic infrastructures.

870–950, Protourbanization

Topographical considerations were the determining factors in the implantation of citadels built at the end of the ninth century by Charles the Bald; they were spread out along the valleys of the Seine and the Oise, close to Senlis and Noyon. It is thus very probable that these two cities were fortified at that time. But neither historical documents nor archeological records reveal any traces of such fortification. Aside from the scarcity of manuscripts dating from that era, the problem is that stone is the only element that would have been mentioned in such texts. Only stone deserved the attention of the poets; if there were none to describe, they resorted to descriptions of Roman walls. Water, ditches, and earthen ramparts were not documented, and copyists, faithfully following the words of authors, did not put these elements on maps, at least until the beginning of the twelfth century. We shall thus have to be content with deductions and conjectures drawn from documents dating from after the period of protourbanization.

Senlis

At the base of the *castrum* in Senlis flows the Nonette, or Old River, mentioned for the first time in the founding deed of the Abbey of Saint-Vincent in 1068. At that time the river spread out to the south of a vast field, called Victellus or Vietellus, belonging to the king. The qualification "old" necessarily implies its opposite, "new" or "young." And indeed, about twenty meters higher, a canal built of earth embankments and still today called the New River is to be found. It was known as early as 1141, when the Saint-Vincent mill, which was never moved from the spot, was mentioned for the first time. The Nonette seems thus to have been diverted at least as early as 1068. Furthermore, at that time the canons of Notre-Dame and Saint-Rieul of Senlis were protected by the *munitiones hujus civitatis* ("fortifications of this city"). As reported in legal drafts dated later, these were arable lands located to the northeast of the *castrum*. Flodoard, describing the ups and downs of the last of the Carolingians, mentions the *munitiones*—especially the towers—put up around the city. Most likely these were entrenchments flanked by large ditches bordering pastures that were later given to the cathedral chapter house.

The three-kilometer-long earth-and-water fortification, reinforced here and there with towers, was enough to assure Senlis of the role of key fortress.[3] The city controlled the road to Saint-Denis and opened onto the territory newly attached to the functions of the duke of Francia, created by Charles the Bald, and occupied successively by the Robertiens and the Capétiens. The wall, properly speaking, would not have been built until much later, in the second half of the twelfth century.

The usefulness of the New River was twofold. On the one hand it drained the Vallée des Joncs ("valley of the rushes") to the east of the city by releasing there a portion of its standing water. The economic context (witness the levees on the Loire) favored the draining of marshy land. The New River was situated more than three meters above the *thalweg* (the pathway running through the bottom of a valley at which the slopes of the two sides meet and forms a natural watercourse); thus, in times of war the valley could be quickly and easily flooded. In addition, from this height the waters of the new ditch could protect both the eastern and western sides of the city of the late empire by placing them out of the deadly range of the crossbow (150 meters). It is worth noting that this moat was built on the outer limits of the old Roman city, where digging was the easiest, away from the ancient buildings still standing at the end of the ninth century. The enclosure must indeed date from this

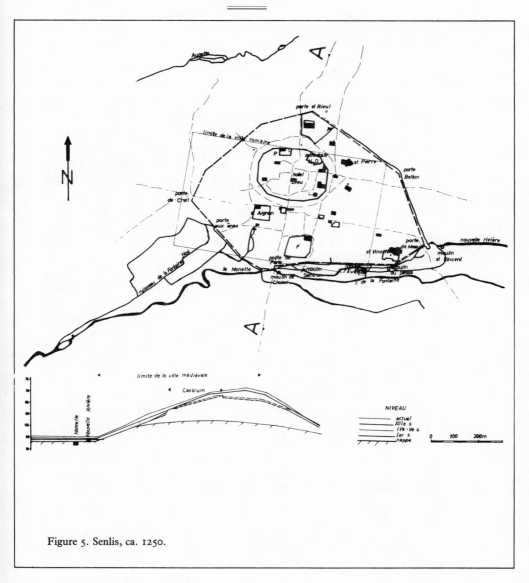

Figure 5. Senlis, ca. 1250.

time: the Normans, and at the height of their power, were defeated outside the city during the winter of 885–86.

Chartres

The defensive network of Chartres can be partially dated from the
same period. On eighteenth-century maps, the Eure is divided into three
branches as it flows into Chartres: the Eure proper, the Fossés Neufs
("new moats"), and the Vieux Fossés ("old moats"). Sometime after 1350, the new moats were cut at the foot of the wall dating from
the twelfth century in order to support it more effectively against
newer forms of war machines. Before that date, the Eure had only two
branches, one of which was natural and had been turning mills since at
least 1029, and the other man-made, which can be identified as early as
1060. At that time, Lanfry, the abbot of Saint-Père, had a ditch cut into
the river, to protect and irrigate the gardens of his abbey.

The diversion of the river was continued to the west by a large ditch
that had been mostly dry. For as long as anyone could remember, it had
always been there, but no one knew when it had been dug out. It is
recalled in a charter of Count Thibaud V that dispensed the bishop's
men, in 1181, from the maintenance of this ditch, next to which stood
wide, newly built, ramparts. One of the boroughs adjoining this ditch
was given the name Muret ("low wall") in 1028. Chartres thus had very
sophisticated fortifications, including a moat, before 1030. One tower,
probably that of the Morard gate, was built about 955 by Count Thibaud the Cheat; his son Eudes I reinforced the northern part with a
stone wall around 987, at the time of the troubles with the dukes of
Normandy—troubles provoked by the king.

The long, wide ditch, abutting the twelfth-century walls, followed a
course that took into careful consideration the outlines of the terrain.
To the north it followed the valley of the Couasnon for two hundred
meters, then joined the ditch hollowed out by the fountain of the Drouaise gate. Water from the fountain flowed into the Eure in front of the
artificial branch cut in the landfill constituted essentially of debris from
fallen Gallo-Roman constructions. On the right bank was a shallow
layer of gravel and dirt, and the water level was clearly lower. A little
more to the east, the canal divided the Gallo-Roman cemetery in two.
This cemetery was used by the Merovingian churches of Saint-André,
Saint-Gilles, and Saint-Leu. To the southwest, the dry ditch was used
to protect the Abbey of Saint-Père, damaged in the Norman raid of 858.

The cutting of the ditches, like the construction of the fortifications,

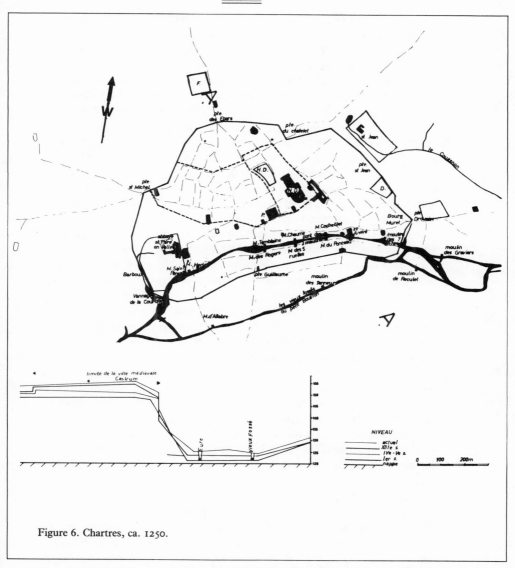

Figure 6. Chartres, ca. 1250.

was demanded by the evolving defensive policy. These works necessitated an abundance of labor, which, it seems, only a powerful local authority still in control and a relatively dense population could bring together. The threat of Norman invasion appears to have been the decisive factor in the creation of the system of protection.

Normans devastated Noyon in 859 and 861, burning the cathedral and the *castrum;* in 890, however, they failed to take the city after six months of siege. In 925 they made their way into the suburbs of the city and managed to set fire to the houses, but the residents of the walled city, allied with those of the suburbs, were able to save the *suburbium*. It appears that Noyon at that time already had in place its twofold defensive system, which would confirm an incident reported by Flodoard in the year 932. The count of Arras, named Alleaume, in conflict with the chapter house of Noyon over the election of the bishop, decided to take over the *castrum* and thus have his claimant named. To accomplish this, he and a handful of his followers scaled the Gallo-Roman ramparts and crawled through one of the windows of the chevet of the cathedral, which had been rebuilt and enlarged after 861.[4] Several days later, outraged inhabitants of the suburbs used the same stratagem and massacred the count and his men. Such ease in entering the inner city was not surprising: all these men lived well within the new fortifications, consisting of towers, one of which, perhaps the future Coquerelle gate, protected the new cathedral and the moat whose point of origin was the Verse.

One last observation: around 880, numerous merchants from Tournai took refuge in Noyon in order to protect themselves from the Normans,[5] but the space limitations of the *castrum*, reduced in size when the cathedral had been expanded, forced them to move outside into a *suburbium*, which they probably helped to isolate in order to resist the Norman siege in 890.

Chartres also experienced Viking (Norman) attacks. The Normans captured and burned the city in 858 but underwent a crushing defeat in 911, after a futile attempt to besiege the city. And they had just destroyed Etampes-les-Vieilles.[6] Here again, the date of the building of the moats must be adjusted to 900, just after the military marches had been set in place.

Senlis, Noyon, and Chartres seem thus to have been fortified at about the same time in order to resist Norman invasions. These defense works were the policy of Charles the Bald, and they were supported by the work of Hugues the Abbot, and even more certainly by Eudes I, who victoriously defended Paris during the winter of 885–86 before being crowned king of France in 888. A long line of demarcation was built up between the lands of the kingdom and those of the under-administered Neustrie, which had in fact already been abandoned to the Normans. This line of fortifications began at Noyon (end of the ninth century); followed the Oise to Compiègne (870), Mézière-sur-Oise (870–80), Creil (880–85), Senlis (end of the ninth century), and Pon-

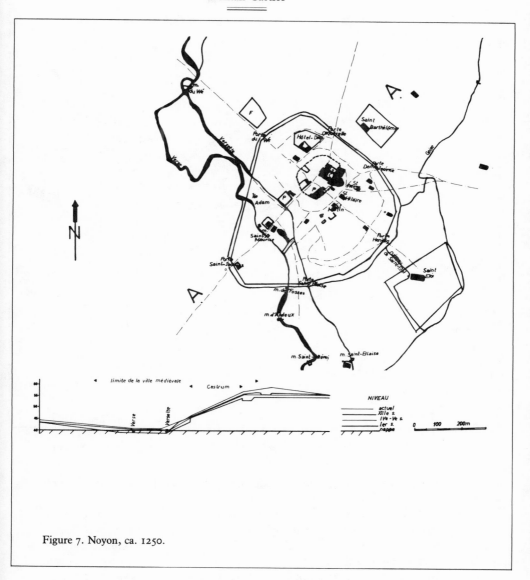

Figure 7. Noyon, ca. 1250.

toise (885); then blocked the Seine at Pîtres (865), Saint-Denis (877–98), and Paris; and was prolonged to the southeast by Chartres (end of the ninth century), Le Mans (869), and Tours (869) on the Loire. Each of these points had a nucleus, solidly fortified and protected by holy relics, and a closed-in space intended for the "self-defense" of the *labo-*

31

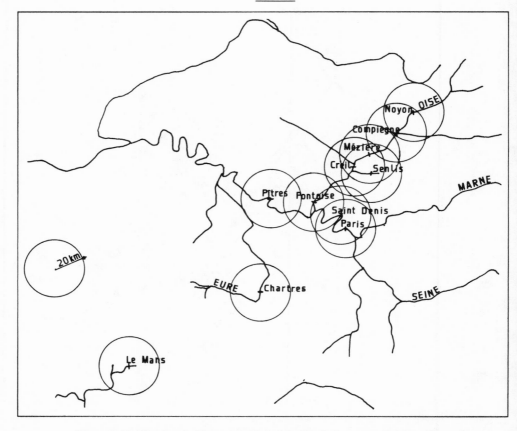

Figure 8. Fortifications in Place at the End of the Ninth Century to Reinforce Natural
Barriers (the Oise and Eure Rivers).

ratores (laborers), dotted here and there with towers manned by *bella-*
tores (warriors).

This type of spatial organization had but one of the distinctive features of urbanization—namely, protection: the moat is an urban characteristic. Political and social structures had not yet established a new
order that would ensure permanent habitation, for the moment still
provisional, and create a distinction among the *laboratores*, between
those who remained tied to the land and those who worked for the convenience of the aristocracy.

This system of urban defense tended to become generalized in the
second half of the tenth century,[7] as a result of lingering tensions between the Carolingian and Robertian dynasties, and especially with the

emergence of feudalism. Under feudalism, the entire civil population was submitted to the will and orders of a warrior aristocracy, which was based on and held together by interpersonal bonds. For the *bellatores*, the defense of a place was associated with concentration of individuals and domination over them. Defensive systems evolved as a consequence. At the end of the ninth century, the newly cut ditches, with their earthen banks and a few towers, had enclosed a space practically devoid of buildings; it was only later that the infrastructures would be set into place. Little by little, starting with the end of the tenth century, would come the construction of fortified palaces, the foundation of new churches and monasteries—abbeys and collegiate churches—and the laying out of intramural canals. This was the first period of urbanization, its feudal character transparent, its portioning out of urban space inept. This was the era summed up for historians by the term *incastellamento*, the beginnings of city life around a *castrum* (in Italian, *castello*). A second phase, better organized spatially and opposed to feudalism, succeeded it at the end of the eleventh century, participating in the emergence of true cities.

950–1050, First Period of Urbanization

Within the framework of the first period of urbanization appeared the fortifications of four cities. Two were former Roman cities, Châlons-sur-Marne and Beauvais, and two were new cities, Etampes and Caen.

Two Old Cities: Châlons-sur-Marne and Beauvais

Two waterways flow into Châlons-sur-Marne: the Mau and the Nau, both man-made canals. They did not exist in Roman times: archeologists have found Roman stone coffins at a depth of more than two meters under the water table and under these rivers. The late-empire enclosure was protected to the west and the south by a loop of the Marne River. The Nau was dug at that time to protect the ramparts and was probably used as a port river, as the name *nautae* ("boatmen"), in the earliest reference to it, would seem to indicate. Nothing is known of the origins of the Mau (Maudum in 1133), which emptied at first into the Moivre, one of the tributaries of the Marne.

In the second half of the tenth century, and in any case before 1028, the church of Saint-Alpin was enclosed in an outgrowth of the enclosure. The new rampart was raised above the right bank of the Nau and continued to the left bank of the Mau. It is possible to antedate the building of a part of the new enclosure by another few decades because

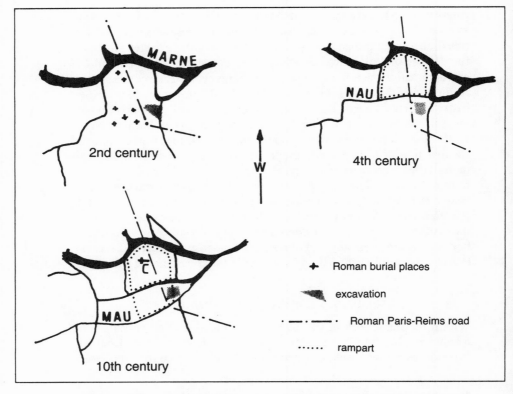

Figure 9. Evolution of the Hydrographic Network in Châlons from the Second to the
Tenth Centuries.

a charter makes clear that about 940 Bishop Bovon wished to rebuild
the walls.

But it seems hardly likely that the northern ramparts were very imposing at that time. A recent excavation between the Mau and the Nau,
to the north of the Roman road, has exposed a reemergent water table
(the ground level during the late empire) of an entirely different nature
from the surface waters. At the time of the Merovingians, that water
table must have fed a bog that was also fed by a stream (which has since
disappeared) originating at the foot of the Saint-Jean hill, flowing along
the church of Notre-Dame-en-Vaux, and merging into the edges of the
bog. Under these conditions, the construction of a solid rampart would
have been impossible, and neither here nor further to the west have any
vestiges from before the medieval epoch been found.

When the Mau was rerouted from the Moivre toward the Marne,

downstream from the city, the entire northern part of Châlons was drained. The waters of the stream running along Notre-Dame-en-Vaux were harnessed, and the bog was dried up by the new drainage channel. This diversion of the Moivre seems not to have been in existence before 931, when King Raoul destroyed the city and put it to the torch.

All things considered, the city was poorly protected along its northern front. Certainly about 940 the ruins had been rebuilt, but in 969 the city was attacked and easily taken by Robert of Vermandois. The Mau must have existed before 1043, for a charter of Henry I with this date mentions a suburb around Notre-Dame-en-Vaux and the presence of the new church of Saint-Germain where the bog had been located. Fifteen years before, a charter of Robert II—and the charter cited above is the confirmation—had made no mention of this *suburbium* but did note the presence of the church of Saint-Alpin inside the walls; a wall must have been constructed to the east of that church.[8]

The hypothesis that the wall was built before the digging of the Mau is untenable, considering the force of the reemergent water table and the claylike nature of the soil directly underneath; any rampart would soon have fallen. Draining the waters and then anchoring the wall directly in clay guaranteed the solidity of the enclosure. We must suppose therefore that the Mau was diverted before 1028 and that the zone around Notre-Dame-en-Vaux and Saint Germain was built up between 1028 and 1043.

The important role played by Châlons-sur-Marne in the dynastic conflicts at the beginning of the eleventh century explain these defensive reinforcements. Robert the Pious used all his power to keep the city out of the hands of his warlike cousin, the count of Champagne. He gave over his royal rights to the bishop, whose interest in fortifications was understandable. It was a question not only of protecting a precarious part of the city, but also of defending a profitable enterprise— namely, the churches and the houses and market clustered around them. Proof of the demographic expansion of the Notre Dame quarter is that it became a parish in 1107.

Begun around 933, the fortifications in Châlons were finished a century later. The Mau was probably created during the half-century that overlapped the millennium, but it was not until the beginning of the fourteenth century that the ramparts were to include Saint-Pierre-aux-Monts and Saint-Jacques.

The ditches of Beauvais can also be dated from the years 1015–30. The Gonard canal, which since the third century had brought the waters of the Thérain to the foot of the *castrum*, now in the years following 1015 fed a long ditch that enclosed the city and its three most out-

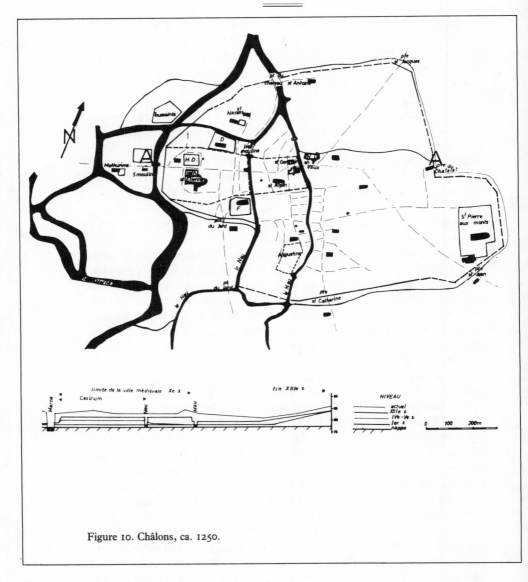

Figure 10. Châlons, ca. 1250.

lying churches: Saint-Laurent to the north, Saint-André to the east, and Saint-Etienne to the south. This ditch was contemporaneous with the canals built within the new urban space by Bishop Roger II.[9]

Two New Cities: Etampes and Caen

A regional capital in the sixth century, with a minting prerogative, Etampes—or Etampes-les-Vieilles, as it was known in the twelfth century—had developed in a bend in the old Roman road leading from Paris to Orléans. Under the Carolingians, it became relatively important; in 770 it received two *missi dominici* ("imperial envoys") from Charlemagne, and in 861 Charles the Bald designated the district around Etampes *a comté* ("county"), whose titular rulers were the dukes of France. But in 911, Rollon, returning from a perilous campaign at Saint-Colombe, Sens, destroyed the town of Etampes and the surrounding area and decimated the population before being defeated before the walls of Chartres. From this devastation there still remained, some time after the year 1000, the ruins of a chapel dedicated to Saint Serin on which Robert the Pious founded the church of Notre-Dame about 1020. The chapel was built at the crossroads of the Roman road and the stone road (*perrey* or *pierre*) leading to the Saint-Pierre borough, whose church had been built about 650 on a large tract of land given to the abbey of Fleury-sur-Loire. Not far from there the powerful abbey of Morigny was built, which held royal prerogatives on the Juine and the Juineteau, of which the rivers of Etampes were tributaries.

Etampes-les-Nouvelles was then built around a castle ordered by Queen Constance about 1015,[10] the church of Notre-Dame, and the collegial church of Saint-Basile founded about 1022 on dependencies of the royal castle. In 1046, Notre-Dame had two mills built on the Chalouette, a diversion of which fed the southern ditch of the new city; these canals had been cut in 1015 at the request of Constance, who wanted to improve the appearance of and enclose the ditches of her new habitation. To the north, at the foot of the Guinette tower, built before 1107 and perhaps at the beginning of the eleventh century, was a pond that has now disappeared. Its outlet followed the natural gradient, parallel to the stone road leading to the borough of Saint-Pierre. All that was necessary was to excavate and enlarge it to make a moat that effectively marked off the northern and western limits of the city. The new city, surrounded by ditches probably under Robert the Pious, could from then on be designated a *castrum*. It took on a trapezoidal shape, covering about forty hectares (the walls would not be built until the end of the twelfth century, or about a century and a half later).

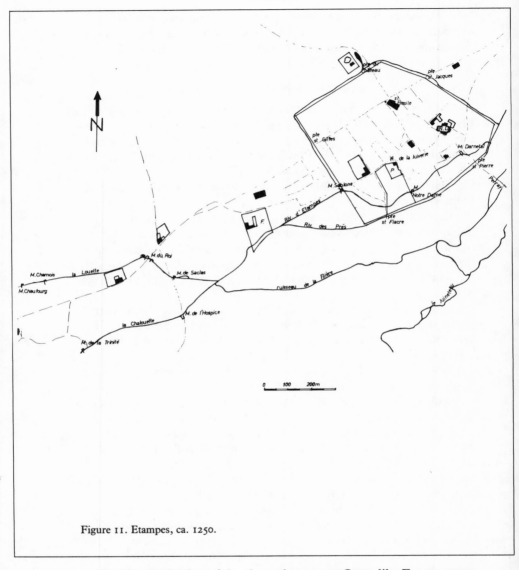

Figure 11. Etampes, ca. 1250.

Until the beginning of the eleventh century, Caen, like Etampes, was confined to the limits of ecclesiastical territories. We have records of two churches there: to the west, Saint-Martin, probably Merovingian, and to the south, Saint-Michel, of Carolingian toponymy.

The island of Saint-Jean, located at the mouth of the Odon and the estuary of the Orne under a layer of mud, was not yet visible during the High Middle Ages except for a central spine formed by the Roman road leading from Bayeux to Lisieux. Caen appeared for the first time between 1021 and 1025 on the left bank facing the island. The city developed under the impetus of William the Conquerer, who founded two abbeys on either side of his ducal residence in the years 1062–64 (that is, two years before the battle of Hastings and the conquest of England). The monks, under the banner of Lanfranc, the future archbishop of Canterbury, carried out improvements on the Orne and diverted the Odon in order to build a port for sea-going vessels once the conquest ended. The limits of Caen were now clearly in evidence: the Orne, the castle from the first half of the eleventh century, and the abbey of Saint-Etienne. A dry ditch, perpendicular to the Odon, joined the river at the castle; another one, parallel to it, linked the castle to the abbey, whose large drainage ditches served as a fourth side.

For Caen, Beauvais, Châlons, and Etampes we should thus note the intimate relationship between the cutting of ditches, the hydraulic improvements carried out, and the implacement of an administrative apparatus in the course of the first half of the eleventh century. Thanks to the diplomacy pursued especially by Robert the Pious and the church, this period put an end to the conflicts among warriors and accorded with the demands made by peace-seeking groups, active since the end of the tenth century.

The efforts made by Robert II to shore up his kingdom were to mark indelibly the urban network of the Paris basin. The Capetian dynasty was still unsteady; the king was just another noble. He was surrounded on the northwest by the wealthy duchy of Normandy, on the northeast by the county (*comté*) of Flanders, on the east and the west by the powerful Eudes II, and on the south by the duchy of Burgundy. Robert the Pious followed by a policy of creating buffer states between his kingdom and the other principalities by supporting as much as possible the archepiscopal church of Reims and by intervening in episcopal elections in places where the power over the city, and thus over the surrounding district, remained divided between the bishop and the count. Thus he supported the election of Roger II in Beauvais (1001), Macaire in Meaux (1008), and Roger II in Châlons (1009), with the support of Fulbert of Reims against Eudes II, who, despite opposition, succeeded in retaining certain prerogatives in episcopal elections, except in Beauvais. In Dreux the king set up a county across from that of Evreux established under Richard I of Normandy, and he managed to maintain a

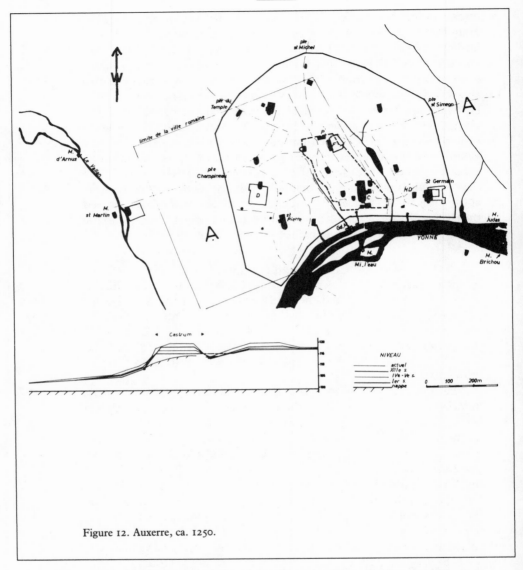

Figure 12. Auxerre, ca. 1250.

viscount in Sens. All in all, territorial possessions, as of 1025, no longer appeared to present a problem, and it was now a question of organizing the centers of strength in those places. The most powerful of the nobles acted along two plans of action, one territorial and the other local.

In order to ensure its regional authority, the nobility developed a policy of urban networks intended to control the new geographical entity, be it kingdom, duchy, or county. Thus, the political "center of gravity" for Paris, Senlis, Meaux, and Orléans was located in the region of Etampes, with good roads, navigable waterways, and proximity to royal lands. Richard III chose Caen for the same reasons: it was located between Bayeux and Lisieux at a day's march from each of them, on a Roman road, and at the extremity of an estuary. But centrality does not explain everything. The kingdom and the duchy, like the county of Flanders, enjoyed territorial integrity, unlike the counties of Eudes II, dispersed on both sides of the Seine. These provinces, with their rich wheat fields and sunny skies (a climactic optimal was enjoyed in the last third of the tenth century), were able to produce farm surpluses marketable in urban centers. This led to a demographic increase that had to be controlled or channeled, in one way or another, toward new centers.

The Champagne region, less densely populated and more extensive, did not develop its urban network, more economic than political, until a century later, under Henry the Liberal. Nor did it undergo the "centralization" that appeared after the year 1000, giving Etampes and Caen the roles of capital cities until the middle of the twelfth century. Given a choice among the king, the duke, and the meddler Eudes, the bishops on the periphery of lay territories were content with maintaining the hegemony of their dioceses. That is, by reinforcing their role as provincial capitals, the episcopal cities could extend urbanization. On the other hand, Auxerre, Laon, and Soissons, where the count and the bishop remained in conflict until the end of the twelfth century, stayed behind their late-empire ramparts. Noyon merely vegetated inside its Carolingian walls.

On the local level, the construction of moats was contemporaneous with the settling of Jewish communities at the foot of the castles. In the eyes of the princes and of the church, these communities were capable of spreading heresy—political as well as religious—but were nonetheless necessary because they held the monopoly on international commerce.

Jewish Enclaves

There is mention of Jewish communities in most of these cities at the end of the twelfth century. In Orléans, Sens, Auxerre, Soissons, Reims, Rouen, Etampes, Troyes, Senlis, and Paris, the Jews lived inside the old city walls from the beginning of the eleventh century, but their settlement within the walls has not yet been analyzed with any precision.

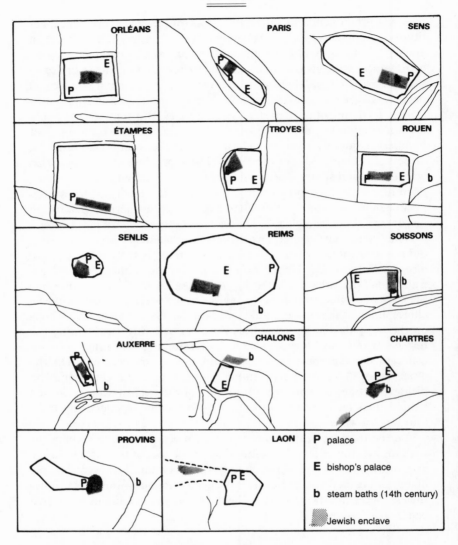

Figure 13. Jewish Enclaves before the Twelfth Century, under the Watchful Eye of Feudal Power.

In Orléans, there was a "Jewry Street" (rue de la Juiverie) in 1238 in the center of the city between the church of Saint-Sauveur ("Holy Savior"), which replaced the synagogue, and the well of the Circumcision. The Jewish community in Sens lived in the western part of the city near the royal palace, where two streets still bear the names Big and Little

Jewry (*la Grande Juiverie, la Petite Juiverie*) on either side of the Roman *decumanus* (tax office). The synagogue became the church of Sainte-Colombe-du-Carrouge about 1240. At the beginning of the thirteenth century the Jewish community in Auxerre occupied the high medieval city center; it was forced out in 1206 and relocated in the Saint-Pierre and Saint-Germain boroughs close to the Yonne River; the synagogue became the church of Saint-Regnobert. In Soissons, the Jewish community established itself inside the former limits of the late-empire city in the immediate proximity of the count's palace; a synagogue was mentioned at the beginning of the thirteenth century in the Street of Coq-Lombard. Rouen still had a Jewish enclosure (*Clos-aux-Juifs*) during the reign of Louis IX; it was situated between the cathedral and the royal palace. Etampes had a large Jewish community at the foot of the royal palace on the Street of the Jews. Provins had two synagogues at the beginning of the thirteenth century; the older was in the heart of the Jewish community, on the western flank of the hill bearing the Carolingian *castrum,* and the other was near the Fish Bridge (*Pont-aux-Poissons*) in the lower city.

Jewish communities at the end of the twelfth century were generally set up closer to the feudal castle than to the cathedral, often at the foot of the fortress and in immediate proximity to the *via publica.* These were precisely the places that were the first to be urbanized and offered the most security during the first stage of medieval urbanization. It can perhaps be conjectured that Jewish communities were set up there as early as the beginning of the eleventh century. Several documents mention these groups toward the middle of the century, but just when they settled into and around the urban space remains difficult to determine.

In Etampes, the Street of the Jews, established about 1020, adjoined the royal palace, located within the walls. According to a judgment of 1210 handed down in a dispute between the canons of Notre-Dame and those of Sainte-Croix (the former synagogue), the synagogue had supposedly been built on property belonging to the collegial church of Notre-Dame, probably given by Robert the Pious in order to firmly establish the patrimony of the new church. Basements on the Street of the Jews are on the same archaeological level as the foundations of the royal palace of Queen Constance. Thus we have two chronological indicators that provide us with good hypotheses about the continuity of the Jewish settlement in Etampes.

In Rouen, where the Jewish community faced massacres between 1008 and 1026 but was later protected by William the Conqueror, recent archeological digs carried out in the *Clos-aux-Juifs* also suggest the regrouping of Jews there about the year 1000.[11] As for Orléans, Reims, and Sens, it would seem that their Jewish communities were settled within the walls at the beginning of the eleventh century. Raoul Glaber spoke of the walls of Orléans; Joseph bar Samuel of Troyes was consulted on the subject of his brothers in Reims; and Robert the Pious in 1015 chased out Count Renard II, who was a protector of the Jews of Sens. We should, however, proceed with caution in assigning dates to the earliest settlements on the basis of these facts alone.

Schwarzfuchs writes: "It is striking that several different Jewish traditions, supported by Christian testimony, date the reappearance of the European Jewish communities right after the battle of Poitiers and at the beginning of the Carolingian era." [12] The institution of the *magister judaeorum*, a functionary who was responsible for Jewish affairs, especially trade and commerce, can also be dated from that time. Until the end of the tenth century, the Jews did not seem to be concerned with the regime in question. They worked both in agriculture and in trade, and lived, like Christians, interspersed with the rest of the population. But the political and religious persecutions led by Robert the Pious against those who contested his fragile power or the society it gave rise to—namely, feudalism—seem to have encouraged the regrouping of Jews.

The heresies that arose about the year 1000 were centered in Orléans, Rouen, Reims, and Sens—the same places where erudite Jews lived who were given to passionate study of the Old Testament. And it was precisely the Old Testament that interested those Christians who rejected baptism, ecclesiastical hierarchy, and transubstantiation; in some cases they followed latter-day self-proclaimed messiahs. Jews were persecuted between 1007 and 1012 for the same reasons that heretics were massacred by the king of France or the duke of Normandy.[13] Papal authority was necessary to put down the repression, which was, it should be noted, more political than religious. Supervision and control of the Jews was then carried out by regrouping them around the base of the local castle and by turning over the concession for the synagogue to authorities of the local church, usually cathedral or collegiate canons. Once the synagogues had been deprived of their faithful, they were transformed into parish churches. This system of social surveillance conformed to the model of *incastellamento*, which by that time had become increasingly prevalent in Western Europe.

The repressions of Robert II and Richard II also forced Jews to go in search of friendlier places to settle, like the county of Flanders, and to avoid, in their diaspora, places that depended on powerful feudal lords: Beauvais, Noyon, Laon. In these three cities Jewish communities would not appear until quite late in the fourteenth century. It is also perhaps from the second quarter of the eleventh century that we can date the settlement of Jews on the urban lands of Eudes II (whose conflicts with Robert the Pious continued)—in Provins, Chartres, and Bar-sur-Aube. At any rate, in the middle of the twelfth century the Jewish communities of these cities no longer resided within the city walls but on the exterior flank of the *castrum*, along the *via publica*, which indicates that they could freely practice their religion and their businesses. An identical settlement pattern appeared in Caen, especially after 1060. The Jews there lived not far from the castle but outside the city; the duke apparently no longer feared the prospect of heresy.

Intramural settlement of Jewish communities, datable from about the year 1000, is a good cut-off point for the first period of urban growth. It suggests that a ditch or a moat was also a means of controlling a population that feudal lords still only barely had under their yoke. Taken in this way, *incastellamento*, like the first period of urbanization, was a form of confinement.

Monasteries were established close to the Jewish communities, perhaps in an effort to reduce heresies but especially because abbeys and collegial institutions administered lay properties. This was because they possessed *scriptoria* for the writing of charters, deeds, and chronicles. This explains the founding of Saint-Frambourg (990) and Saint-Vincent (1068) in Senlis; Saint-Jean in Chartres (1036); Saint-Barthélémy in Noyon (1020); Saint-Hilaire in Orléans (1030); Saint-Amand in Rouen (1030); Notre-Dame in Etampes (1022); and Saint-Etienne in Caen (1063). There was a clear difference, nevertheless, between royal foundations, frequently collegial, and the others, episcopal or county, which were always abbeys. This tendency demonstrates the desire of the Capetians—in particular of Robert the Pious, who had trouble getting the church to recognize his wives—to stay at a distance from the still very powerful papacy upon which the abbeys directly depended.

If the religious orders were centers of writing, they were also to a certain extent transmitters of permanence and political stability. The world of the warriors was essentially mobile but nonetheless depedent on certain fixed points as far as food was concerned. These fixed points were the granaries controlled by feudal lords as far as passing visitors were concerned. These granaries were no longer refilled once a year, as in the past, but on a monthly or even weekly basis, thanks to the commercial activities that were little by little developing within the moats and ditches. The granary was a depository of rural wealth, the pride of local artisans, and a fixture of international commerce.

What can be perceived through this blur of mentalities is the image of Brigitte, the Celtic Minerva, guardian of the hearth and village, the goddess and guarantor of stability and genealogy, virgin and mother, directly opposed to Mercury or Cuchulainn, the perennial itinerants, like the *bellatores*. It is true that during this period women played an important role in the founding of cities. The Duchess Alixe de France, Queen Constance, and the Countess Berthe played a role in the founding of Caen, Etampes, and Provins, respectively. Women also participated in the founding of collegiate churches (Queen Adelaide for Saint-Frambourt in Senlis) and abbeys (Queen Mathilde for the nuns' abbey in Caen). And, at the same time, the church encouraged the creation of chapels dedicated to the Holy Virgin.

The image of city as woman flourished at the beginning of the eleventh century: she was the guardian of heritage and stability, adorned with the wealth brought to her by her artisans and her merchants. The towers and walls kept her safe, just as the palace guarded the women's quarters. And above all she was guaranteed protection by the moats, which permitted the continuation of her productive forces—the merchants and artisans. These urban traits were inherited from the Celtic model, or perhaps even from beyond, from an ancient Indo-European model as well. But they were nonetheless different: they associated the foundational virginity peculiar to antiquity with the matrimonial and rural character of the Carolingian era, and the apparent lewdness denounced by heretical sensitivities.

The Urban Boom

In Senlis, Noyon, Chartres, and Beauvais, the intramural urban space coincided with the confines of the Gallo-Roman city, unlike other episcopal cities whose development came later. They enclosed within their walls most of the abbeys founded in the high Middle Ages on Gallo-Roman cemeteries located on the periphery of the city. Their growth was now obstructed by bogs that the Romans had never tried to drain or by rivers too difficult to divert. The superimposition of two urban surfaces dated a thousand years apart leads to the conclusion that the Gallo-Roman ruins, at least those protected by a moat, must have been above ground, unusable, and irremovable. In the eleventh century, Beauvais and Chartres stood less than a meter above the ground level of the third-century city; Senlis, less than a meter and a half. Given the location of these ruins, and the fact that concrete hardens with age, and given the modest technical capacities available in the ninth and tenth centuries, it is probable that it was easier to leave the ruins alone and extend new water lines up to the limits of the marsh, which was then drained.

The first medieval ditches enclosed the open Roman city, and this was the first symbolic takeover of Roman culture, comparable to the emergence of the vernacular Romance languages and style. In this sense, the moat, both in configuration and in the way it appeared during the course of the tenth and eleventh centuries, remained a key element of the new ideology of feudalism,[14] which also fortified the suburban monasteries and the *castra* by means of rampart and ditch defenses surmounted with wooden palisades. The urban space circumscribed before the middle of the eleventh century would thus condition, by this fact, all urban extension for several centuries to come.

We should avoid generalizations based on these examples, however, first of all because certain cities of the high Middle Ages were naturally protected against certain types of invasion. Auxerre, for example, was surrounded on one side by the Saint-Vigile swamp and on the other by the stagnant waters of the Street Under the Walls (*Rue Sous-Murs*). Paris and Troyes were protected by the Seine; Laon and Provins were inaccessible. Sometimes, when natural defenses were lacking, weak points were reinforced by a palace, as in Rouen. The urbanization of these cities developed without problems at the end of the eleventh century and in the twelfth century between the late-empire enclosure and the suburban boroughs. It was not until the second half of the twelfth century that authorities decided to enclose the city as it thus stood with a double ditch-and-stone line of defense. These were the methods of Henry the Liberal in Troyes and Provins, of Pierre de Courtenay in Auxerre, and of Philip Augustus for all the cities of the kingdom that had not yet been fortified. Châlons, Reims, and Rouen continued to expand.[15]

The diversion channels apparently presented no problems when the base of the rampart was close to the level of running water: this was the case for the valley cities of the late empire. But in the thirteenth century, urban zones were much larger and their periphery rarely flat, and the cutting of ditches turned out to be difficult in places, because there was no running water close at hand, and extensive detours were necessary. These ditches provided the city with a new food supply in the form of fisheries, which the religious communities—who had to abstain from meat some two hundred days of the year—as well as the municipalities eagerly sought to control. Assuming an average production of two hundred kilograms per hectare per year, nearly five tons of fish could be produced annually in the new watercourses in Troyes, Amiens, and Rouen. The building of these ditches required cuttings six meters deep at Amiens, and seven at Beauvais, and nearly four hundred meters long, which meant excavating more than twenty thousand cubic meters of earth for each of these two cities, and just as much perhaps at Soissons and Reims.

The problems were not the same everywhere, and certain cities were fortunate to possess marshy zones on their new borders, or streams that were easily transformable into ditches. Rouen's second enclosure was protected to the north by the Rougemare ("red pond"), and to the east by the Malpalud marsh. Auxerre was protected by the stream of the Valan to the north and by a *thalweg* above the Abbey of Saint-Germain. The lower city in Provins contained numerous watercourses, the branches of which were multiplied, some for the benefit of the ditches. Paris stayed inside the former branch of the Seine, the Marais. The new urban limits in Auxerre, Rouen, Evreux, and Orléans merged with the banks of rivers. In Troyes, Provins, Amiens, and Auxerre, the limits enveloped the former marshes, with drains feeding into external ditches. Excavations preceded wall-building, first of all because they insured a better foundation for the base of the wall in compressible terrain, and secondly because they made it easier for equipment to be moved to the base of the works, by boat rather than by cart.

The most richly endowed abbeys and the cloistered chapter houses, like the walled cities, also entrenched themselves behind walls and dry ditches. This line of demarcation, which was established during the twelfth century, reveals that the practice of *basse justice* (jurisdiction over property matters) was in effect within the enclosure; but even more, it indicates the existence of tensions between the abbeys and the rapidly expanding communities of *cives* ("citizens"), which the religious groups wanted to keep out of their space. The fabric of the medieval city began to take on a "cellular" appearance: boroughs clustered around abbeys or churches to form so many cities-within-cities. Time, urbanization, and the lessening of conflicts with lay persons would dissolve this appearance in the course of the thirteenth century. The medieval city thus developed a continuous network of adjoining houses, with only the fortification wall standing out, for the time being.

These new boundaries no longer surrounded former Roman urban space, as had the ditches cut in the tenth and eleventh centuries; they were at a distance from that space, nullifying it to some extent. This was the beginning of another era, which saw the disappearance of the old late-empire defense works, which were filled in or used as sewers. This was to be an era marked by the recognition of communities, associations, and artisans—that is, of those who worked and lived in the miry places bordering on the rivers. But what now constituted the real or symbolic force of the defenses was no longer the moat or the isolated feudal tower, but the stone wall dotted with gates and prominent towers, built in part with the help of communal finances. Stone was the visible translation of the city's wealth and the strength of its militia: only in this perspective can we comprehend the enthusiasm of municipalities for the construction of the fortifications ordered by Philip Augustus at the moment of his departure for the Crusades, or the extent of the jousting areas or the length of city walls: more than two thousand meters in perimeter on the average; four thousand at Rouen; three thousand at Provins, Amiens, and Chartres. Thereafter the medieval city was no longer limited by the outline of ditches. On the contrary, the city set its own extension limits, as in Paris, Rouen, Reims, Amiens, Orléans, Châlons, and Soissons, which would still be growing at the beginning of the fourteenth century.

Urban defenses must be understood in their intimate relationship with the social category represented by the bourgeoisie. As its members gradually rose in the scale of aristocratic values—lay or religious—from the end of the eleventh century, their defenses, their "self-defense," evolved also, from the ditch mounded with soil behind which they took refuge, a nameless and servile mass, to higher and higher walls, with better and better quarried stones, identical in form, like the individuals of a crowd, and linked together by a cement comparable, on the social level, to a communal charter. The ditch, the quintessential symbol of protourbanization and the first period of urban expansion, yielded to the wall in the course of the twelfth century.

Of course the walls were not complete everywhere. At the beginning of the Hundred Years' War, the western part of Troyes and the southern part of Reims, for example, were separated from the countryside or the river only by earthen banks used for jousting. But the gates, flanked with monumental towers and drawbridges, displayed urban opulence. Their names—the Noyon gate in Amiens, the Rouen gate in Evreux, the Troyes gate in Provins, and the Creil and Meaux gates in Senlis—stressed privileged economic or political relationships with neighboring cities. Paris, by the end of the twelfth century, was already in the lead.[16] The gates also point out the particular role played by pilgrimages in this society: every city had a Saint-Jacques gate. Unlike the gates built in the eleventh century, whose names marked an opening onto the nearby countryside or the suburbs, the gates built in the twelfth century signaled the faraway, the presence of the extraordinary in daily existence. They were the marks of the grafting of the commercial fabric onto earthly roads.

Present-day urban space, the city center or downtown, was thus already laid out by the end of the twelfth century for certain cities and at the latest by the end of the thirteenth for others, with the exception of

Rouen, Paris, Amiens, and Caen, which would continue to expand during the Renaissance. The medieval city had laid its foundations before the beginning of the twelfth century on top of the buried Gallo-Roman city. Later, as we shall see, the city spilled over this former limit to absorb the marshy lands in a "water economy." *Incastellamento* was brought on by dynastic wars and the Norman raids along the valleys of the Oise and the Eure. But at the end of the tenth century or the beginning of the eleventh it took on a more coercive and irreversible nature. The continuous line of the ditch encircling the new city offered spiritual and material security—at the price, however, of surveillance and economic dependence. This ditch-line inscribed something new onto the earth: urban feudalism.

3

Mini-Venices

At the end of the third century the city had retreated into one part of the ancient Gallo-Roman *urbs*. For five hundred years, administrative, political, and religious activities collected here behind the protection of strong ramparts. What was left of the former urban territory had been abandoned to a large extent as ruins and fallow land. Here archeologists frequently encounter a more or less extensive layer of ashes dating from the late Roman Empire or the High Middle Ages, on top of which is a layer of accumulated landfill brought in from elsewhere. Part of this landfill came from the excavation of ditches,[1] and part from the destruction, intentional or otherwise, of buildings outside the walls; the best material was used in wall-building. Everywhere, the ground level rose throughout the Middle Ages: two to three meters in Amiens, Soissons, and Rouen; more than five meters in Orléans; up to one and one-half meters in Chartres, Evreux, Sens, and Reims; and less than a meter in Beauvais and Noyon.[2]

The extraurban landscape thus underwent profound changes in the period between the late empire and the first feudal age. In Orléans or Amiens, residents of the tenth century would no longer have recognized anything of the city of antiquity. In Auxerre or Evreux they would have glimpsed a few ruins covered over by churches of religious orders; at Beauvais and Noyon the network of Roman roads would have been still entirely visible.

A reconstitution of this extraurban landscape, even fragmentary, is neccessary in order to understand the topography of the medieval city. On this site, located between the *castrum* and the limits of the ancient Roman city, the economic power of the West was to be organized. In the course of the eleventh century, a new spatial organization would gradually be transplanted onto the outskirts of the walled city, a territory whose surface had only barely been marked with the external signs of urbanization, or onto other sites located close to the *via publica* that led into the cities of Caen, Etampes, and Provins. The earliest urban expansion had occurred on the banks of waterways and then had established itself in the marshes that Roman urbanization had always avoided; the Romans had preferred airier and less humid sites for their cities. They also sought to distance their cities from the *oppida* of the Gauls, frequently built on marshy land. The rivers located on the outskirts of Roman cities had served only the function of ports; this function would be retained and developed in the Middle Ages.

Water was the economic nerve center of preindustrial urbanization; without water, there would have been neither millers nor weavers, neither dyers nor tanners, nor would communities have existed. Starting with the *castrum* and a few scattered points in the Roman ruins, the men of the tenth century reconquered the abandoned spaces, then headed in the direction of the river and the marsh, both of which had become highly charged with a sense of sacredness during the late empire.

Until the eighth century, the majority of the population was pagan, and it must be supposed that at that time the sacred nature of water retained all its power, in spite of the efforts made by the church to destroy Gallo-Roman sanctuaries. But all those efforts were in vain, for in the Gallic mentality what was important was not the monument, such as a temple, but rather nature, represented by its most visible elements: trees, stones, rivers.

Christian "colonization" followed the guidelines of Roman religion: for example, churches were built over the ruins of pagan temples. Then it went about implacably destroying all elements of Celtic culture. In the case of large areas like sacred forests, the church resorted to massive land-clearing. In the case of marshes, the church tried to exorcise them, to take away the power of Taranis, for in these areas lived the *Vouires* and other reptiles that Christianity associated with the forces of evil. Fortunato recounts that Saint Marcel of Paris successfully drowned a serpent in the Seine. The reptile had entered the tomb of a noblewoman whose life had been very turbulent. At the end of the eighth century, Paul Diacre tells that Saint Clement, sent by Saint Peter to Metz, moved into the area beneath the amphitheater, "and after that no snake could live in the place." In the Carolingian mythology, these snakes became the powerful dragons that the holy bishops—Marcel and Clement, Romain in Rouen, Loup in Troyes, Pavace at Mans, Hilaire at Poitiers—had come to remove, by force if necessary. The more powerful the dragon, the greater the faith of the conqueror and the more Christianity was able to consolidate its position.

Each outlying urban marsh was thus christianized in the very act of writing the lives of the saints and in the processions of the Rogation

Days, which yearly ritualized the putting to death of Gallic beliefs. Thereafter, standing and running water would be nothing more than water. No one would be able to "misuse" them; the Druids who had held the power of Ogmios and Taranis had long since disappeared, and their heirs, still powerful at the time of Saint Eloi or Saint Ouen, were banished from the city and reduced to silence in written texts. The local sacredness of the waters was diluted in the omnipresence of the Christian God. With the blessing of the church, anyone could now drain them, divert them, or change their courses according to the whim of the prince, their secular proprietor.

For three centuries the medieval city was to forge the character of the West, little by little making the economy the basis of its specific nature. The economy in turn could not have developed without a concentration in habitat and industrial infrastructure that drew its resources from the water of the rivers. The development, laying out, and diversion of watercourses had been accomplished during the period of *incastellamento*. Romanesque and Gothic silhouettes were reflected in the mirror of the little Venices that urbanization had conceived.

Nevertheless, economic thought did not at first play a part in the genesis of the hydrographic network. In the very earliest times, the aristocracy treasured the *commoditas* ("pleasantness," "convenience") and charm of water; water was desirable because it was pleasant. So it was when Queen Constance, the wife of Robert the Pious, decided to build her new palace at Etampes in 1015. She chose a site near the river so that the edifice could be surrounded by gardens and she could enjoy all the conveniences offered by a body of water.[3] All in all, this was natural for the daughter of William of Arles; she was probably used to the delights of her native city. The Chalouette was diverted for nearly a kilometer in order to embellish the royal dwelling.

Commoditas was a Carolingian legacy that the Robertians tried to strengthen or reproduce. Orléans, for example, was "in former times, as at the present, the chief residence of the kings of France, because of its beauty, its large population, and also the fertility of its soil and the purity of the water from the river that flows around it," declared Raoul Glaber at the end of the tenth century. Sens, as we are told by the author of the *Second Passion of Saint Savinien*, "then under the control of the Romans, was richer and more glorious than all the other cities of Gaul. The multitude of great nobles living there, the weapons that accumulated there for her defense, the walls and marvelous towers that fortified her, the charm of the stream that waters her, all worked together for her magnificence." Convenience and charm, from the post-Carolingian point of view, were not simply reducible to beauty or landscape; included in the notion was utility: the transportation of wood and grain, the installation of fish ponds, and the use of hydraulic mills for the grinding of royal grain. These three activities can be confirmed very early at Etampes: the mill of Notre-Dame appeared about 1020 with the founding of the chapter house of Notre-Dame. The crafts, however, did not become really well established until about 1130, over a century later.

The development of the hydraulic infrastructures of the cities studied here seems in fact to accord with the same principle of *commoditas*, in two phases. The first phase, when a network of new canals was set in place, which attracted the implantation of mills, harbor fittings, and the crafts to a lesser extent, was contemporaneous with the fortification ditches of the eleventh century. During the second phase, chronologically, the principal concern was with the draining of marshes as an aid to mill construction; this phase often preceded the period of wall-building—the end of the twelfth century. Each city would use inexpensive, creative methods in order to bring water within its walls; some cities would even incorporate the ancient network of streets left by the Romans.

Draining the Marshes: Caen

As early as the second quarter of the eleventh century, Caen had a port and mills on the Orne.[4] But it was only some forty years later that the dukes, notably William the Conqueror, organized the hydrographic network with the help of the Abbey of Saint-Etienne, founded in 1063. About 1065, William, in an inventory of the goods belonging to the abbey, indicated that it possessed the riverbed of the Old Odon between Venoix and the Orne, with its three mills. Between 1066 and 1083, at the instigation of the first three abbots, the New Odon was cut.[5] This canal penetrated the property of the abbey downstream from the city and joined back with the Old Odon at the Saint Peter bridge. In this way, boats coming from the estuary and from newly conquered England were able to unload their cargo within the walls of the powerful abbey itself. The canalization of the Odon was very probably the result of co-operation between William the Conqueror and Abbot Lanfranc. The former had the ramparts built shortly after 1066; the latter bought the lands and directed the work of canalization. About 1080, the New Odon seems to have been completed; the entire project thus took only fourteen years to complete.[6] The rapidity of the construction can be explained by the ready availability of local labor, provided most likely by

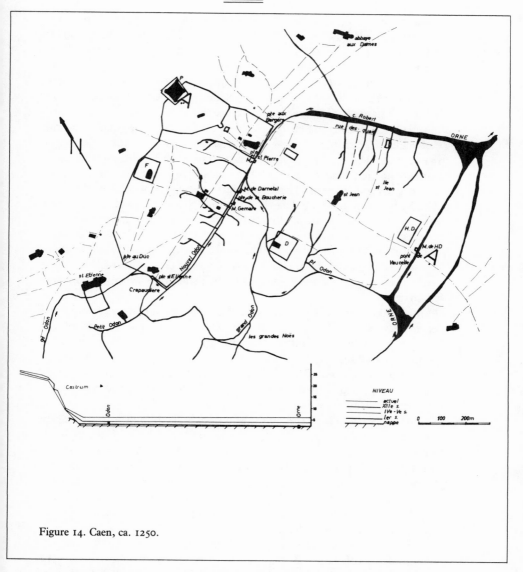

Figure 14. Caen, ca. 1250.

the population of Caen, which then retained the function of keeping the riverbed dredged.

The New Odon, which defined the southern part of the city, also marked the boundary between the calcium-rich plateau and the peat-rich valley, and served as the outlet channel for the waters of the reemergent cross streams on the edge of the plateau, discharging part of the overflow from the headwaters of the Orne above the island of Saint Jean, at the estuary. Once the calcareous zone and its surrounding area had been drained, there remained the task of draining the entire southern part of the island, which was still covered by the waters of the Orne. The construction of two outlet channels began under Robert Courteheuse, the son of William the Conqueror. The Orne was divided into two channels to relieve the congestion at the southern extremity of the island, and the Robert canal, completed in 1104, received the water of the Odon from the north and of the Little Orne, which drained the springs on the western side of the island, along with the excess headwaters of the Orne before the diversion point. The island and its environs were now drained. The Robert canal, which absorbed the high water of the ebb tide of the estuary, was fitted with docks during the first half of the twelfth century. The southern side of the island was fortified with stone bridges that provided more support for the banks of the Orne. In short, everything was ready for the implantation of a new city, but until the fourteenth century this waterscape was embellished only with gardens and pastures.

More than three kilometers of watercourses were laid out around the ducal city during the reigns of William the Conqueror and Robert Courteheuse with the support of the abbots of Saint-Etienne. This grandiose and complex undertaking was facilitated by the presence of numeorus streams of water that had only to be enlarged and interconnected through mere digging in the peat, a substance that offers minimal resistance to shovels.

The construction of this hydraulic network entailed improvements for the abbey and the castle, the provision of millraces for the mills of Saint-Etienne, and improvements of the harbor for the abbey and the ducal city, now the capital of a large kingdom extending from England to Aquitaine. The riverside crafts were the "watermark" of the city. The water of the Odon, unlike that of the Orne valley, was completely upset by these imposing hydraulic works, making use of technical mastery that still astounds engineers.

Caen and Rouen became large maritime ports. They were the achievements of the dukes of Normandy, the heirs of the Vikings, for whom access to the sea was an existential necessity. To the glory of the duchy, these two cities rose up as if to reclaim the ruins of the largest seaport on the English Channel during the Carolingian era, the vanished city of Quentovic, probably near Montreuil-sur-Mer. For two centuries they also weakened the influence of the third-largest Carolingian port of the English Channel, Amiens.

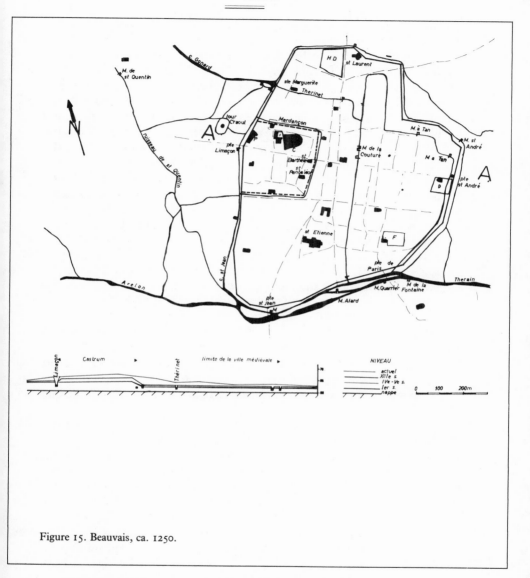

Figure 15. Beauvais, ca. 1250.

Rehabilitation of the Gallo-Roman Patrimony: Beauvais

The canal system worked out in Beauvais was of an entirely different nature. The course of the Thérain through the city, as depicted on old maps, is surprising for many reasons. Its course was formed of rectilinear segments and left well to the west the *thalweg* of the river. The

Gonard canal, cut during the period of the late Roman Empire, was the sole distributor of this network. This same canal also fed the drainage ditches of the city. It is thus likely that the intra- and extramural waterways were dug at the same time.

Artisanal equipage on the peripheral canals is implicitly indicated in the earliest document mentioning the commune, in 1099. A mill belonging to the chapter house of the cathedral at least since 1069 was blocked by the bridges built over the river and by rubbish from the dyers. According to testimony of the townsfolk, the fourth bishop, the predecessor of Ansel (1096–1100), had authorized them to set pilings in the river and to build the bridges. The town won the contest. The bishop mentioned was Guy (1067–93); he was run out of the city by its citizens, reduced to misery by the taxes extorted from them by the prelate. Guy was not able to recover his cathedral until Yves of Chartres intervened, and Guy was then forced to make concessions to the townspeople.[7]

This does not necessarily mean, however, that it was this bishop who was responsible for the diversion of the river into the city. In fact, the mills of Saint-André and Saint-Laurent, which belonged to the cathedral chapter house and were fed by one of the canals of the Thérain, had been built to the north of the city as early as the beginning of the eleventh century.[8] A diversion after this period would have reduced mill production, and the archives of the chapter house would certainly have mentioned it. In the absence of more cogent arguments, it thus seems that the branches of the Thérain diverted into the city were cut at the same time as the ditches—that is, about 1015–30, at the time of Bishop Roger.

This diversion channel ran for three kilometers inside the enclosure, dividing into two arms just after entering the city. One ran toward the north, then bent toward the south, parallel with the other branch. The elaboration of these works required extremely good knowledge of leveling and surveying, unlike the work carried out on the Odon and the Orne. Problems of seepage posed by the chalky substratum in Beauvais were solved by incorporating the ruins of the Gallo-Roman city. Thirteenth-century Beauvais, at least in the places outside the late-empire city, stood but one meter above the ground level of the Roman city. The Roman ruins, especially those of the principal streets, had still been visible in the eleventh century.

Nothing has been published on the canal beds at Beauvais, which were transformed into sewers and covered over between 1946 and 1950. The work was done with the utmost secrecy, behind partitioning that prevented the state archeologist from viewing what was there. Engineers in charge of the work reported that the bottom of the canal was formed of clay and partially paved.

It seems hardly likely that the episcopal authorities of the eleventh century could have afforded the extravagance of lining the new bed of the Thérain with stones, or of making it watertight. But the development of these two diversions coincided perfectly with the Gallo-Roman street grid studied by Leblond.[9] Its north-south gradient encouraged drainage, either by means of an aqueduct, the remains of which, already exposed, had only to be finished off, or else by means of a diversion of the Thérain or the Liovette.

Everything would lead us to suppose that the authorities used the old Roman streets for the improvements on the Thérain—a task that in itself was not very difficult. All that had to be done was to unearth the paving stones that were still in place and to lower by a few decimeters the roadbed, which measured approximately two meters deep in some places. Taking into account that the ground level had risen between the Roman era and the high Middle Ages, the canal would thus have measured one meter deep and two meters wide, with a 2 percent gradient, sufficient to turn the mills on its banks. A relatively modest labor force could have accomplished the task, and in fact the general population of Beauvais, unlike that of Caen, Troyes, or Provins, seems not to have participated in these works. The community retained no rights with respect to this canal; the bishop remained the exclusive owner of the streets, the ground, and the water within the ramparts.[10]

If we refer to the earliest texts that mention the diversion of the Thérain, it seems that canal improvement was first carried out so that mills could be built. Secondarily, and much later—most likely during the third quarter of the eleventh century—dyers set up their trade there; the water had a high calcium content unlike that of the Avelon.

This city's original character was not simply that of technical enterprise. The rectilinear canal system, next to which the streets of Beauvais were laid out, gave the city an urban framework comparable to that of Greco-Roman cities. And it prefigured the urban texture of the *bastides*—the walled cities of the thirteenth century—and on a much larger scale, for Beauvais enclosed some sixty hectares within its new ramparts. In addition, Beauvais seems to have been divided up into lots all at one time; at any rate, urbanization was an accomplished fact there by the end of the twelfth century. Such allotment—land deeds reveal a "checkerboard" patterning of lots—was a remarkable exception for a city at the end of the eleventh century, considering that most cities then were clusters of boroughs in the environs of a *castrum*, or

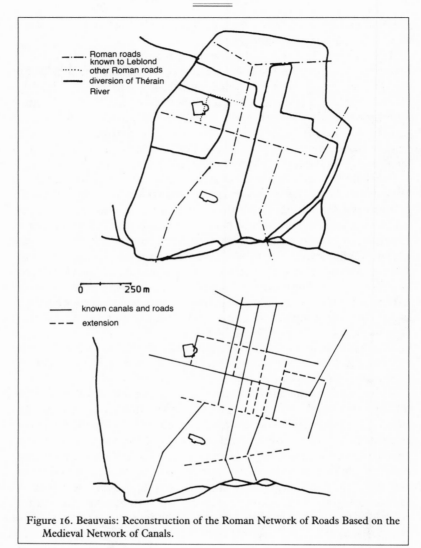

Figure 16. Beauvais: Reconstruction of the Roman Network of Roads Based on the Medieval Network of Canals.

inside the territory of a Merovingian or Carolingian abbey. The divisioning of Beauvais anticipated by a century that of the right bank of Paris—les Halles.

Beauvais was not the only city to rehabilitate the old Gallo-Roman streets for hydrological purposes. At about the same time in Nîmes, the course of the Fontaine, which in former times had flowed along the Régordane road, was diverted onto Domitian's Way, to the north of the

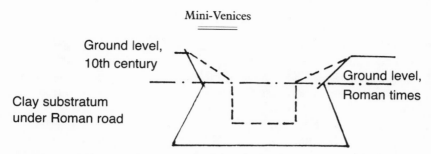

Figure 17. Depiction of Roman Road Turned into a Canal.

cathedral,[11] in order to turn the flour mills. The Versette at Noyon should also be cited; this stream flowed out of the Verse, paralleling it within the city walls. Flowing through a *cardo* ("hinge"), it drained the southern part of the city.[12]

The transformation of Gallo-Roman highways into canals appears as a technique specific to the beginning of the eleventh century. This period was also characterized by the incorporation of ancient building material in architecture. Taking into consideration the ground layout during this same period along the ancient Roman ways, the result was a veritable rehabilitation of the Gallo-Roman urban grid that marked the end of the Carolingian era.

The genealogy of the hydrographic infrastructures set up between the beginning of the tenth century and the middle of the eleventh reveals that the primary concern of this first period of urban growth was milling. This is explained first of all by the soil and the climate. The calcium-rich soil of the Paris basin encouraged cereal cultivation; and during this period the harvests were very certainly abundant, in light of exceptional climactic conditions (it has already been noted that the optimal range of temperatures prevailed during the last third of the tenth century) and improvements in farming methods. But this generalization should not allow us to overlook the fact that certain bishops and abbots and landed nobles were willing to divert or improve their waterways, whereas lay nobles were totally preoccupied with war.[13] The flour mills, which were at the origin of these landscape transformations, were not, in themselves, an "urbanizing" factor: despite their high productivity, they stimulated only a relatively slight increase in employment. Rather, the setting up of mill ponds marked urban territory with the hydrographic network where artisans and craftsmen would later find a place for themselves. In this way milling played a role in what I have called the "first period of urbanization," which saw an influx of labor for heavy work.

Fitting out inland harbors was undertaken primarily by the dukes of

Normandy. Elsewhere, especially in Amiens, this activity did not begin until the middle of the twelfth century, after artisans had already set up their activities. This fact proves quite clearly that the basis of medieval urbanization was not, contrary to what others have asserted, at least for this part of Europe, the setting up of ports.

Milling is concerned only with the energy furnished by a waterfall or a current. Only running water could be utilized by mills, and rarely the water from marshes, for it could not provide the power needed to turn the mill wheels. On the other hand, what would be designated in the thirteenth century as "river trades" did not require a natural flow of water: human ingenuity could furnish it. Water in large quantities, and standing, not running—useless for milling—was an absolute necessity for slaughtering animals and for treating wool, leather, and the primary materials used in their preparation. The marshes that the Romans had avoided, became, once they had been drained, the preferred site for these crafts, and they were the mainspring of medieval urbanization. Crafts were thus linked to the mills and waterways as early as the middle of the eleventh century.

The setting up of this network remains difficult to trace because it was a low-profile activity and could change from day to day. This is at least what would seem to have happened in the twelfth and thirteenth centuries on either side of the *castrum* of Auxerre, surrounded until then by the Saint-Vigile pond to the north and the small peat bogs fed by reemergent springs to the south. This pond or swamp, fed by the hills overlooking Notre-Dame-la-d'Hors, covered more than a hectare during the Middle Ages. As early as the twelfth century it was partially filled with alluvial deposits. Urban development began at the end of the twelfth century and continued during the course of the thirteenth: the Street of the Fields (*rue des Champs*), with a few houses on it, appears in texts as early as 1224, at the same time as the Street of the Large Gardens (*rue des Grands Jardins*), which wound around the left bank of the pond into the upper city through a Gothic gate built into the wall. At the beginning of the fourteenth century, the pond was reduced to a stream, used for irrigating the gardens bordering the houses along the above-mentioned streets. On the other side of the *castrum,* the texts mention the *rue Sous-les-Murs* ("under the walls") at the end of the twelfth century: a stream fed the tanneries and the dye works set up on both sides of this street.

The situation was comparable in Le Mans, where the Isaac rivulet received the waters of the *Vallée de Misère* ("valley of misery") and the Saint Julien spring. At the very end of the eleventh century, the area around the spring was drained and filled in. All around, tanners and textile workers moved in. At Evreux, the tanners diverted a part of the waters of the Iton before 1170, thirty or so meters from the third-century ramparts. At Rouen, the dyers and tanners clustered on the banks of the Petit-Ruissel, the Trou-Patin, and the stream along the Street of the Glassblowers (*rue des Verriers*), diverted from the Robec, whose waters were made to flow through holes two inches in diameter. These workshops had been implanted as early as the beginning of the thirteenth century, long after the mills, but were not enclosed by the new walls until about 1253.

The creation or canalization of waterways for crafts is thus not datable with any certainty, in the absence of written documents. Did it come about spontaneously? This is certainly a possibility, at least for the county of Champagne and the cities of Troyes and Provins, where the ruling princes had pursued a rigid economic policy throughout the twelfth century.

The Fruits of Planning

Troyes

The origins of the different canalizations in Troyes remain hazy, given the absence of documents from before the middle of the twelfth century. The valley of the Seine seems to have been marshy before this period, despite fourth-century improvements on the Moline canal. The Vienne flowed to the south of the late-empire city before emptying into the Seine. The Tréffoir flowed parallel to the Seine before flowing into the Vienne.

About the year 1157, construction work on the count's palace undertaken by the powerful Henry the Liberal was already well underway. For his pleasure, the count decided to have water from the Seine diverted to his palace. To that effect, he had a two-kilometer-long channel dug from the Trévois. The total length was reduced to a few hundred meters thanks to the presence of the Tréffoir, whose course it followed from the Pétal mill to the Paresse mill. There, by means of a wooden passageway, the canal passed over the Vienne and flowed inside the ramparts. Following the northern flank of the former bed of the Vienne, the canal of the Trévois went along the Seine near the Abbey of Notre-Dame-aux-Nonnains, entered the palace of the count, and exited via the Cordé channel, higher than the Seine. This undertaking, requiring very exacting technological methods, seems to have been completed before 1174.[14]

The canal was apparently not for the exclusive use of the palace. In a complaint submitted by the chapter house of Saint-Pierre in 1222, it is

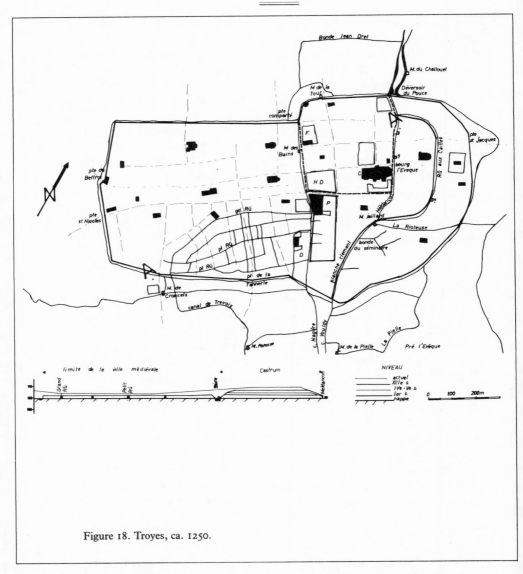

Figure 18. Troyes, ca. 1250.

clear that some forty years earlier Henry the Liberal had had the river diverted in order to clean the city and provide water in case of fires.[15]

Raising the canal level above the former bed of the Vienne River made it possible, in addition, to drain water from the spongy terrain located beneath: it was sufficient to reinforce the right bank with a wall.

Outlets, substituting for former branches of the river, served as drainage channels and released the stagnant waters. Once landfill had been added, the area was suitable for settlement. From approximately 1230 to 1240, tanneries, a rope works, and slaughterhouses were located along this kilometer-long network.[16] In addition, moving the mouth of the Vienne a hundred or so meters upstream from the Seine made available the land that had been swamped in the meanderings of the stream, and the terrain was thus partially stabilized. It was then possible to solidify the base of the ramparts, whose main feature was the Croncels gate, mentioned in 1125.

Provins

As for Provins in the middle of the eleventh century, a large bog extended at the base of the city, fed by the Durtein, the Lambert, the Voulzie, and their tributaries. A layer of peat approximately twelve meters deep covered the site of what would later be the lower city. A single paved road suitable for vehicles led down from the hill where the *castrum* stood. The road crossed the peat marshes in the direction of Troyes. During the twelfth century the lower city was encircled by a long ditch fed by the overflow from the Durtein, the spill-over from the streams of the Auges, and the discharge of the Voulzie through the *Pont-qui-Pleut* ("bridge-that-weeps"). The earth excavated from the cutting of the ditch was then used to raise the base of the ramparts; thereafter, the base was higher than the ground level of the city. Thus banked in and drained of excess water, the marsh was partially dried out.

To absorb more water, the banks were first of all fixed with oak or chestnut pilings driven into the soil. Once the streams had been channeled, the peat all around was scraped off to a depth of one meter; it was then replaced by a one-meter-thick layer of chalk-white soil.[17] This was done during the course of the twelfth century and at the beginning of the thirteenth century, as the city developed.

These rivers were judiciously channeled to prevent flooding. Indeed, the longitudinal profile and cross section of the *rue du Val* ("valley street") show that the bed of the Durtein was located about a hundred meters to the west of where it is today; that of the Voulzie must have extended beyond the *rue Aristide-Briand*. The straight lines of the Marambert stream and the right angles of the Pinte brook were obviously man-made. Shifting the course of the Durtein drained excess water from the entire zone triangulated by the Pont-aux-Poissons, the Pont-Pigy, and the Sainte-Croix church, which then received only the

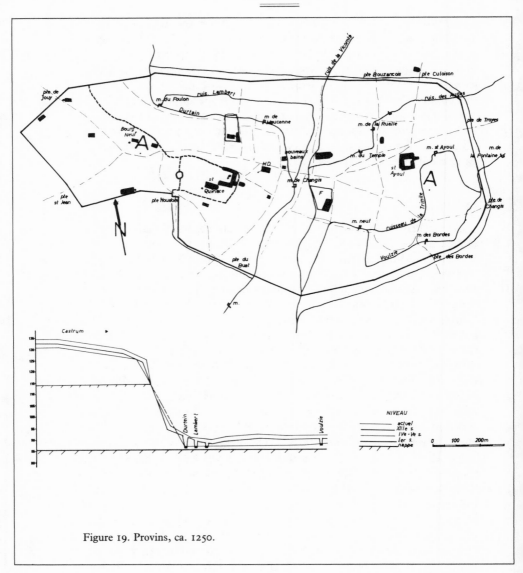

Figure 19. Provins, ca. 1250.

streams of the Auges and the Vicomté, channeled into the "old bed," mentioned for the first time in a deed dating from 1232. It seems, however, that the harnessing of the Durtein goes back to the middle of the twelfth century, before 1166, when the *rue des Teinturiers* ("street of the dyers") is first mentioned.[18] The Marambert stream did not receive its name until 1287. By veering off from the Durtein the Marambert greatly diminished the headwaters of the Durtein, to the advantage of dyers and tanners; this stabilized the entire northern part of the city abutting the ramparts. This canalization seems to have come after the Durtein had been diverted.

The Auges stream was used to supply water for the Buzançais water-mill in 1160. Contained within artificial banks, it could no longer flood the eastern side of the city. As either a cause or a consequence of this canalization, Notre-Dame-du-Val was founded in 1196. Farther to the south, the lands watered by the Voulzie were also cleared in this way during the second half of the twelfth century. In fact, a deed dated 1176 mentions houses built near a canal next to the church of Saint-Ayoul. Later, a text dated 1227 mentions a piece of land bordering on the "old Voulzie." These records must be referring to the Pinte stream, known by that name after 1281, which indeed ran along Saint-Ayoul, parallel-ing the Voulzie. Draining off a part of the waters of the Voulzie as the river entered the city, the Pinte thus freed the neighborhood on the near side of the ditches. Thereafter, buildings began to replace the meadows and pastures, and ramparts could be built with no risk of toppling.

The canalization of the streams in Provins was carried out in the first half of the twelfth century, probably requiring extensive labor and a highly skilled master engineer. This was undoubtedly André le Cémentier,[19] a loyal follower of Henry the Liberal; he had already col-laborated on the construction of the count's palace in Troyes. The ex-tent of similar projects carried out in different places, at the same time as the setting in place of fortifications, sheds light on a form of medieval planning that could also be found at this time in Flanders and Switzer-land. The draining of marshes and the stabilization of land brought added value to drained areas, indeed the basis for an urban economy. The construction of canals for watermills was an element in the kind of feudal economy that Guy Bois has analyzed.[20]

Reims

A similar policy seems to have guided the archbishops of Reims, notably Guillaume aux Blanches Mains and his successor Guy Paré, who held royal title to the Vesle River and its banks. Circa 1190, in order to counteract the uncontrolled urbanization of swampy areas, Guillaume conceded marshy lands to the south of the city to coopers and woodworkers, in return for low taxes. Guy had drained the neigh-borhood known as "Venise" and built a city hall in 1205. About thirty hectares were thus reclaimed from the marsh. At Châlons-sur-Marne,

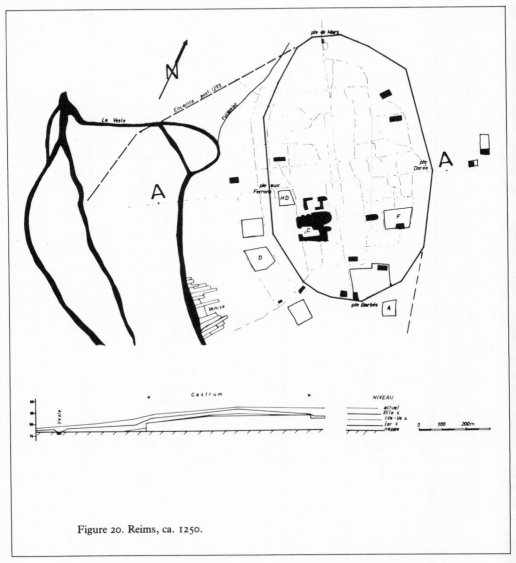

Figure 20. Reims, ca. 1250.

the intentions of the bishops are not so clear, but in the second half of the twelfth century, one of the branches of the Marne was retrenched and its waters rejoined the principal riverbed. The entire northern part of the city, drained and no longer at the mercy of annual floods, was now ready for the installation of crafts. The church of Saint-Nicholas (the patron saint of dyers) was built as early as 1187 in the middle of an island, linked by two bridges to the old city. Several decades later, new ramparts enclosed it inside the city.

The twelfth century thus appears to have been the era of the draining of marshes found at the foot of the *castrum*. It was especially in Champagne that authorities took this initiative. This region, which until then had been neglected and "under-urbanized," was thereafter to recover equal economic footing with Normandy, now worn out by the wars with Philip Augustus. The draining of the marshes, especially in Provins and Troyes, allowed for the installation not only of flour mills, which show how the city depended on rural areas, but also mills for various urban crafts, which would accelerate the industrial development of these cities.

Documentary evidence of harbor improvements on the rivers, on the other hand, remains minimal. Some cities had their own ports during the Carolingian era, replacing the ports built by the Romans at Orléans, Soissons, and perhaps Paris. Fittings appear to have been on the most elementary level: planks and simple pilings driven into the banks. Indeed, it was not until the middle of the twelfth century that cities began to construct docks and warehouses as in Caen and Rouen.

Amiens

Following the example of Provins and Reims, Amiens carried out improvements throughout the twelfth century. Inasmuch as the twelve watermills given by the bishop to his chapter house in 1060 had definitively set the water level of the canals, harbor infrastructures could be built only downstream from those watercourses, on the principal branch of the Somme, in an extension of the Carolingian port.[21] Ever since the end of the eleventh century, the local fleet had been improving and was no longer content simply with inland navigation. Deeper drafts of water were now necessary when coastal traffic penetrated some distance inland, as was the case here.[22]

The city adapted to these new constraints by dredging the Somme in order to facilitate berthing. Responsibility for this work was assumed by the cathedral chapter house, which had the Grand-Pont built on the site of the ford eliminated by the deepening of the principal bed. Then, with the help of the monied faithful, especially the millers, the chapter house invested in the construction of quays built of stone.[23] Grand-Pont (1121), Grand-Quai (1145), Nouveau-Quai (1149)—the very names give some indication of the ambitions of the enterprise. From then on,

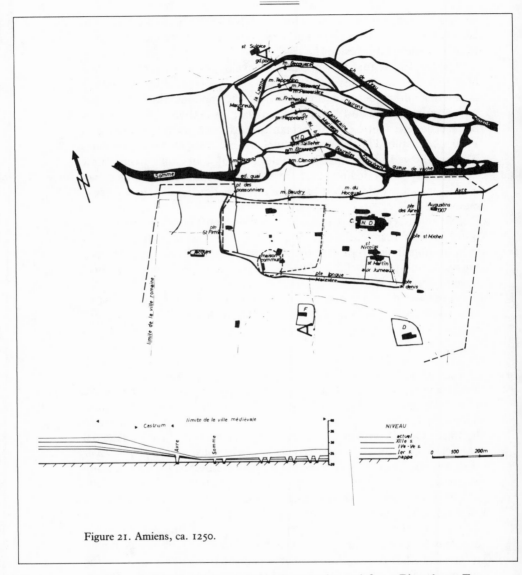

Figure 21. Amiens, ca. 1250.

Amiens would be able to export wheat and woad from Picardy to England.[24] These two products were transported to the docks by road or
river transport: hence the *Chaussée-au-Blé* ("wheat road") commencing
where the highways from Saint-Quentin, Boulogne, and Abbeville
came together at the entrance to the city. Traffic from the upper reaches

of the Somme and the Avre was discharged in the small ports of the Don and the Queue-de-Vache ("cow's tail"), to the east of the city.[25] Skeins of wool arriving from England were then transported to Beauvais, Saint-Quentin, and eventually towns in the Champagne region. The infrastructures, improved again in the thirteenth century, would bring in several thousand pounds yearly, divided among the bishop, the cathedral chapter, and the parishioners.[26]

Apart from these cities oriented toward the English Channel, only Noyon would develop a maritime harbor on one of its streams, the Marquais, by means of a channel fed by the Oise. This modest port, set up in the suburb of Oroir, made it easier for agricultural products of the country to reach the Ile de France.

In short, river ports remained embryonic until the beginning of the thirteenth century;[27] in the Paris basin they were not an important element of urbanization.

Land

The reclamation of marshes and bogs opened up a new land for population expansion. Table 4 shows how much land was reclaimed from swamps. I have added to the table the terrain acquired from ditches filled in during the thirteenth century. This was especially notable as regards the ditches of the *castrum* of Rouen, which were dried out after new walls had been erected, more extensive and farther to the north, by Philip Augustus. In 1224 Louis VIII donated this land for the construction of a hospital for the poor. A similar development took place with the ditches of Soissons when the waters of the Crise were diverted to make room for the new enclosure. Little by little, they were filled in and, at the beginning of the fourteenth century, an agreement made between the count and the municipality opened these new areas for construction.

Although the area gained from the ditches drained in the thirteenth century may appear relatively modest, it is nonetheless true that at Auxerre, Châlons, and Noyon, the land reclaimed from swamps and drainage ditches was 10 percent of the total intramural surface, nearly 15 percent in Troyes and Rouen, and nearly a third in Provins. For Caen and Reims, the new space represented an area as large again as the city of the eleventh century. The conquest of the extraurban marshes remained one of the chief preoccupations of feudal authorities. The soggy lands around the *castrum* were drained of water by raising the ground level, which furnished the stagnant water of the bog with the dynamic force

Table 4.
Land Gained by Draining Extraurban Marshes and Filling in Late-Empire Ditches,
Tenth to Thirteenth Centuries.

City	Surface area reclaimed from swamps (hectares)	Surface area reclaimed from ditches (hectares)	Surface area of medieval city (hectares)	Reclaimed area as percentage of city area
Inside the walls				
Provins	40	0	130	31
Troyes	15	0	105	16
Rouen	14	3	125	14
Auxerre	8 (combined)		70	12
Châlons	8	0	80	10
Noyon	3.5	0.5	40	10
Soissons	0	2	40	5
Senlis	0	1	40	3
Outside the walls				
Caen	40	0	40	100
Reims	30	1	33	90
Evreux	2	0	10	20
Le Mans	1	0	8	12

necessary to make it flow, so useful for the river crafts or the turning of watermills. The utilization of potential energies—whether by watermills or windmills—by whatever means available, seems to have been a leitmotiv of feudalism. Hydrokinetics was a hallmark of this era, a time situated between the period from the late empire to the High Middle Ages, when swamps were endowed with divine powers, and the period from the Renaissance to the Ancien Régime, when urban economics would be based on stagnant water.

The hydrographic policies implemented by these cities of the eleventh and twelfth centuries found their counterpart in the clearing of land in the countryside. The expansion of arable land went hand in hand with the multiplication of watercourses; the increase in cereal yield reflected the "dynamizing" of energies. The diversity of topography underlay the diversity of newly created urban and rural landscapes. Water was to the city what land was to the countryside.

In order to understand more clearly the power of water in medieval cities, we must compare their hydrographic networks with those of Venice, and gauge their development in terms of the length of the waterways inside and outside the city walls.

Table 5.
Water Networks of Cities in Northern France Compared with that of Mid-Thirteenth-Century Venice.

City (century)	Surface area (hectares)	Intramural canals (meters)	Ratio, length/area	Other intramural waterways (meters)	Total intramural waterways (meters)	Ratio, length/area	Cumulative, within 500 m. of city (meters)	Ratio, length/area
Amiens (12th)	75	8,000	107:1	3,000	11,000	147:1	16,000	213:1
Troyes (12th)	105	7,000	67:1	4,500	11,500	110:1	16,000	152:1
Rouen (12th)	125	6,000	48:1	5,500	11,500	92:1	15,000	120:1
Provins (12th)	130	6,500	50:1	3,500	10,000	77:1	15,000	115:1
Beauvais (11th)	90	3,700	41:1	4,000	7,700	86:1	12,000	133:1
Châlons (10th)	80	2,800	35:1	4,000	7,000	88:1	10,000	125:1
Senlis (10th)	40	300	8:1	2,900	3,200	80:1	7,000	175:1
Venice (13th)	**220**	**12,000**	**55:1**	**6,000**	**18,000**	**82:1**	**40,000**	**182:1**
Noyon (13th)	40	1,200	30:1	2,000	3,200	80:1	6,000	150:1
Etampes (10th)	35	1,000	29:1	1,800	2,800	80:1	4,000	114:1
Caen (12th)	40	1,000	25:1	1,100	2,100	53:1	7,000	175:1
Evreux (12th)	15	400	27:1	1,000	1,400	93:1	6,000	400:1
Soissons (12th)	40	—	—	2,200	2,200	55:1	4,000	100:1
Auxerre (13th)	70	700	10:1	2,000	2,700	39:1	5,000	71:1
Chartres (11th)	60	1,200	20:1	1,500	2,700	45:1	5,000	83:1
Paris (12th)	270	4,000	15:1	4,000	8,000	30:1	11,000	41:1
Le Mans (11th)	8	—	—	2,200	2,200	275:1	4,000	500:1
Reims	33	—	—	1,500	1,500	45:1	4,500	136:1
Sens	25	—	—	2,000	2,000	80:1	4,000	160:1
Orléans (12th)	25	—	—	1,000	1,000	40:1	4,000	160:1

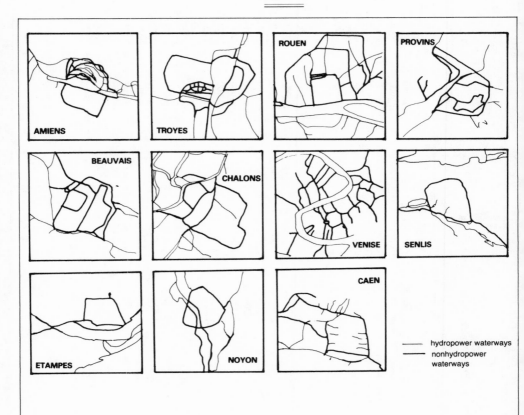

Figure 22. Urban Water Networks in Northern France Compared with That of Venice, Mid-Thirteenth Century.

Venice

The intramural waterscape of a third of these cities in northern France resembled that of Venice at this time; if canals and moats are included, nearly two-thirds. In the entire Paris basin, nearly half of its cities could be compared to the Venice of the thirteenth century.

"Little Venice" was the phrase used by Louis IX to address the city of Amiens. "Venezuela!" cried Amerigo Vespucci, bathed in the dreams of his native Italy, when he discovered the mouth of the Oronoco River. Venice was not just an image, it was a tangible reality in many of the cities of the Middle Ages. Guillaume aux Blanches Mains used this name for one of the sections of Reims that he built up in 1205.

The medieval city was indelibly marked by water, subjected to its power, and scaled to its dimensions. Streets and buildings were made to follow its fluid curves. Herein lies the distinctiveness of the medieval urban landscape.

The setting up of hydrographic networks began in the eleventh century in Caen, Etampes, and Beauvais. It was finished during the third quarter of the twelfth century in Troyes and Provins. A century and a half sufficed for the elaboration of these infrastructures, which were to remain unchanged for seven centuries.

The canals were a topographical fixture; they were also a social fixture in that they were the crucible of medieval communities. They frequently show traces of a unification of townsfolk against the governing aristocracy, especially in Beauvais, Troyes, and Rouen. Finally, they were also an economic fixture: the "river crafts" were located there. The density of the hydraulic network was the visible sign of urban wealth: the most important medieval cities were those with the largest networks, and this prosperity was evident in the areas named *Bourg-Riche* ("rich borough"), set up not far from the canals on well-ventilated sites, behind the "ugly crafts," and isolated in the middle of irrigated verdure. Examples would be the area occupied by the butchers and millers in Soissons (Riquebourg, 1147); lots sold to spinners and merchants in the neighborhood of the Hotoie in Amiens (Bourg-Riche, 1188); and a street used especially for the dwellings of the rich drapers owning mills outside the enclosure in Beauvais (Riquebourg, 1172). Toponyms fix these little pockets of opulence in a twofold societal opposition: with respect to the city center (the residence of the clergy and the lay aristocracy) and with respect to the irrigated lower city (occupied by citizens of ordinary means). The *Bourg-Neuf* ("new borough") was not named in contrast to anything "old," unlike streets named "new," but always signified a settlement on previously unoccupied land: Neubourg-Saint-Croix at Châlons (1248), Bourg-Neuf at Troyes (1128), Villeneuve at Auxerre (1235). These were all named after 1190 and implanted on the periphery of small pockets of older populations, near the city gates, on virgin lands also known as *aires* ("zones," "areas"). The alignment of their basements proves that from the beginning the street layout of these developments was rectilinear, following the example of walled towns and new cities, or the neighborhood of the Halles in Paris, founded by Philip Augustus at the end of the twelfth century. The opulence of these "merchant" boroughs is proof of the wealth that flowed from the "river trades" and the hydrodynamics affecting watermills.

The genealogical record of the mediecal city would be incomplete without a reference to written traditions. The image of the city, irrigated by its canals and ditches, protected by ramparts, delighted chroniclers of the twelfth century, who sang a city's praises. It was no longer a question of a *castrum* or of its resistance to Roman armies. The city was no longer turned toward the past; it now lived in the present.

Oderic Vital wrote (ca. 1148):

> The city of Rouen is very populous, and has been made wealthy by different sorts of commerce. It is an agreeable city due to the number of buildings surrounding the port, the murmur of the running waters, and the charms of the meadows. A large abundance of fruits, fish, and all sorts of products adds to her wealth. The mountains and forests, with which she is surrounded on all sides, the walls, the trenches and other military constructions make the city very pleasant indeed. Much of her luster comes from her churches, as well as the appearance of the houses and buildings.[28]

Caen, "that powerful city, opulent and beautified by rivers, meadows, and fertile fields, receives ships into the port, bringing all sorts of merchandise. This city has such an abundance of churches, houses, and inhabitants that it hardly sees itself as inferior to Paris," according to the glowing praises of Guillaume le Breton. His praise was also intended as flattery to Philip Augustus for his triumphs.[29]

And Reims: "flanked by towers and gates, the city is located on a plain, and enjoys wonderfully salubrious air. Her wide, extremely long walls are of cut stone. The countryside she dominates is very fertile; a small river bathes her, and although the river itself does not bring fertility, it contributes to the charm to be found there."[30]

Finally, a very beautiful text by Radbod painted this practically idyllic portrait of Noyon at the end of the eleventh century:

> The country is fertile and pleasant, with an abundance of wine, fruits and vegetables, and cereals of every type. These nourish a warrior race. . . . The city is surrounded by woods and marshes, and thus well protected against enemy invasions.
>
> The city is located between two streams: to the east flowes

the Goële, and to the west the Marguerite. A third, called the Verse, receives both streams and the waters of all three flow into the Oise, that river of renown, not far from the ramparts. In the vicinity grow many fruit trees, and the radiant soil, enlivened by its meadows and green verdure, is very agreeable to the inhabitants. In addition, to the east as well to the west, the city is so well fortified by rocks, rivers, hills, and valleys all around that it could not be simpler to defend her with just a handful of men against a huge and mighty enemy invasion.[31]

These are just four, from among many other, texts—four eulogies evoking an abundance of sparkling water and the resultant fertility of the extraurban environment. These texts also emphasize the clean air of the city—healthy and pure air—and the life-giving qualities of the rivers that flow all around or penetrate the city. All the city's wealth was the net result.

4

Apparatus and Environment

The economic apparatus of the medieval city, in the form of milling and crafts, grew out of the hydrographic maze whose origins have been sketched above. Both have been treated at considerable length by historians.[1] I will be interested here in pursuing demographic indices, still relatively unknown for this period in spite of numerous attempts to determine the size of urban populations. Focusing on the period when mills were constructed, I shall trace their multiplication. This evolution can be used as a criterion of urbanization, assuming that the quantity of flour produced was proportionate to the number of inhabitants. Any surplus meant for exportation would have been negligible compared with local consumption. We can assume that flour output was in direct proportion to the effective power of mill wheels—that is, to the number of mills in use in the city, keeping in mind that most of the mills had only one wheel, whose effective yield can be considered as constant over a given period of time. The state of milling can thus be used as an index of demography, at least in the twelfth and thirteenth centuries, when hand mills had completely disappeared and all wheat was ground at communal mills. Looking at some of the details of these mills will permit us to better grasp their diversity, and tracing their successive owners will underline the important role played by this type of machinery in social exchange.

As far as the crafts are concerned, I will here consider only their macrodemographic aspects, by analyzing the effect they had on the health of the urban population. Before undertaking this study, I imagined, like most positivist historians, that medieval cities were filthy and heavily polluted. But analysis of pertinent documentation soon revealed that this hypothesis was not based on facts. On the one hand, the disposition of workshops along the rivers influenced the water's capacity to cleanse itself; on the other hand, the building of hospitals in the twelfth century and the creation of steam baths in the thirteenth, show to what extent medieval urban society wished to protect itself from the risks of air and water pollution.

We have perhaps all too often ignored the existence of an "artisanal revolution," which began in the mid-eleventh century and developed in northern France at the end of the same century. The setting up of hydraulic equipment and the implantation of "river crafts," which could be referred to as a "craft industrialization," nevertheless constituted the originality of the second period of urbanization, following the Roman urbanization that had completely changed Gallic society. It has too often been thought that this urban development proceeded helter-skelter. Nothing could be further from the truth: it was planned and implemented with regard to both timing and location in order to take better advantage of the complementarity of different crafts. Aristocratic authorites frequently carried out large-scale plans, increasing the surface area of their cities by as much as tenfold. In the second half of the eleventh century, technological innovations developed on the waterways: flax-retting, rope-making, the spinning and weaving of wool, cloth-dyeing. A part of the labor force was detached from specifically rural activities for the construction of cathedrals, and organized into small interdependent family units. In this way, craft industrialization ensured better development and quality control by artisans themselves, which the former system, based on private, isolated labor, could not guarantee. That the city was also much more independent with respect to its surrounding countryside also contributed to this industrial revolution at the end of the eleventh century: use of the communal flour mill dispensed individuals from the cultivation and theshing of grain, in order for them to perform more specialized tasks. The increase in cash flow, with the city as the principal center of transaction, permitted the economy to go from a barter system to a market system. But, as I have already pointed out, feudal powers were not able to direct urbanization except in cities where their authority was absolute; in these cases, feudal lords, with their ecclesiastical partners, planned the development of urban areas: the organization of fairs, the setting up of new crafts, the control of merchandise—with substantial profits as a result. Where the control of a city was divided between rival powers, industrialization could be carried out only very slowly, even when the city had the necessary hydraulic infrastructures.

Hydraulic Mills

According to Vitruvius (*De architectura*, X, 5) and historians of technology, Greek engineers were the inventors of the watermill. However, Danish archeologists have discovered vestiges of mills dating from the second and third centuries A.D. in the marshes of Jutland, well beyond the Roman *limes*.[2] In Ireland, the first mill is believed to have been built to the northwest of Tara in the second half of the third century by Cormac Long Beard to facilitate the labors of his slave Ciarat.[3] Moreover, milling terminology is largely constituted of Celtic and Germanic elements, such as *bief* ("millrace"), *vanne* ("sluice"), *bond* ("bung"), *gué* ("ford"), *barrage* ("dam"), and *étanche* ("watertight," "staunch"). There are no corresponding terms in Greek or Latin for these words. If, therefore, in spite of these examples, milling has to be maintained as a Greek invention it must be supposed that the peoples of northwestern Europe were capable of greater adaptability to this new technology than were Mediterranean peoples. This fact cannot be neglected in our search for knowledge of hydraulic techniques: milling spread especially in those regions where the dominant Celtic culture was matched with the mentality of the ruling Germanic peoples. Thus it is that England, soon after the Norman Conquest, inventoried 5,624 watermills in the *Domesday Book*, whereas in the Paris basin during the same era there were only a thousand or so mills.

Ausone speaks of the mills near Trèves around 360; Gregory of Tours mentions those on the Suzon, at the gates of Dijon, around 510. The reasons why there was not greater development in northern France remain obscure. Perhaps the slow development must be linked to meager grain harvests, the absence of a clear division of labor, and perhaps more probably to the lack of a strong desire to save time. The first major investment in milling took place in a religious context: the bishop of Trèves or Dijon, the abbots of Saint-Lucien at Auxerre (ca. 665), or of Saint Benoît on the Loire at Orléans (651), or of Saint-Pierre-Le-Vif at Sens—all were concerned about consecrating the maximum amount of time to prayer and the minimum to nonspiritual occupations. Moreover, a mill could very rapidly satisfy the sudden demand for flour occasioned by the transitory presence of an itinerant royal court. Thus it is not surprising to find mention of mills in the Carolingian chapter house records for Noyon and Orléans.

It was thus the goal of physical power (getting work done in less time) that would little by little be implemented by milling during the High Middle Ages. During the later period of urbanization the goal of economic power would be added, and the mill would become a means

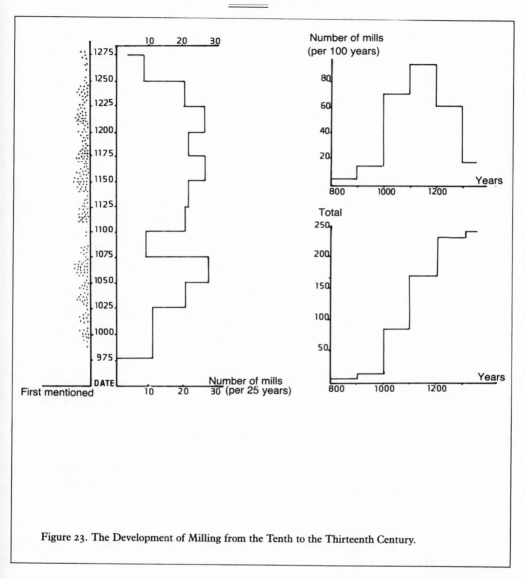

Figure 23. The Development of Milling from the Tenth to the Thirteenth Century.

of earning profits for the nobility: one-tenth (tithe) of the flour milled went to the aristocracy.

From the end of the thirteenth century until the beginning of the nineteenth, before milling had undergone the technical modifications of steel and faced competition with the steam engine, the number of urban

81

and extraurban mills remained relatively constant. More wheels were added to some mills already in place, but the location of mills did not change during this time. The height of the waterfall for overshot mills was fixed as early as 1190 in Chartres, 1222 in Troyes, 1252 in Noyon, and during the fourteenth century for other cities. In this sense, the Middle Ages fixed the energy potentials of these cities for six centuries to come.

Periods of Construction and Demographic Indices

Records of mills generally appear in the context of a donation, litigation, or confirmation of holdings. There is nothing to prove that their actual construction goes back to the same dates: indeed, it would seem logical that they must have been built earlier. The date of construction in some cases can be approximated with a margin of error of about fifty years: this is the case for the mills of the Victoire at Senlis and the Tourelles bridge in Orléans. For most of the mills of Troyes, Caen, and Beauvais, known as the "ditch mills," the margin of error varies from twenty to fifty years. For all the others there is no way to date their construction with any exactitude. In Rouen, the Notre Dame mills were donated by Richard II in 996; eight others built nearby were mentioned for the first time about twenty years later. All these mills belonged to the duke (like most of the mills built in the third quarter of the eleventh century). Before 950, the state of war would account for an absence of building. In Etampes the first mills are documented in a charter from 1046. The building of the city dates from 1015 to 1020; there is a gap of at least twenty-six years between the probable date of construction of the mills and the first written records of them. Thus the dates of the earliest records of mills built prior to the thirteenth century do not exceed their construction by more than a half century. The margin of error tends to decrease in the course of the twelfth century, reaching a maximum of about ten years.

Under these conditions, the chronology of the first records can be formulated. Two periods can now be clearly distinguished: 995–1082, and 1120–1275. Of a total of 230 mills that have been inventoried, 82 were built during the first period and 125 during the second. Between 1083 and 1120, ten mills are mentioned, only two of which are mentioned between 1083 and 1106. The construction of more than a third of the urban flour mills was carried out in the first period, and the remainder during the longer second period.

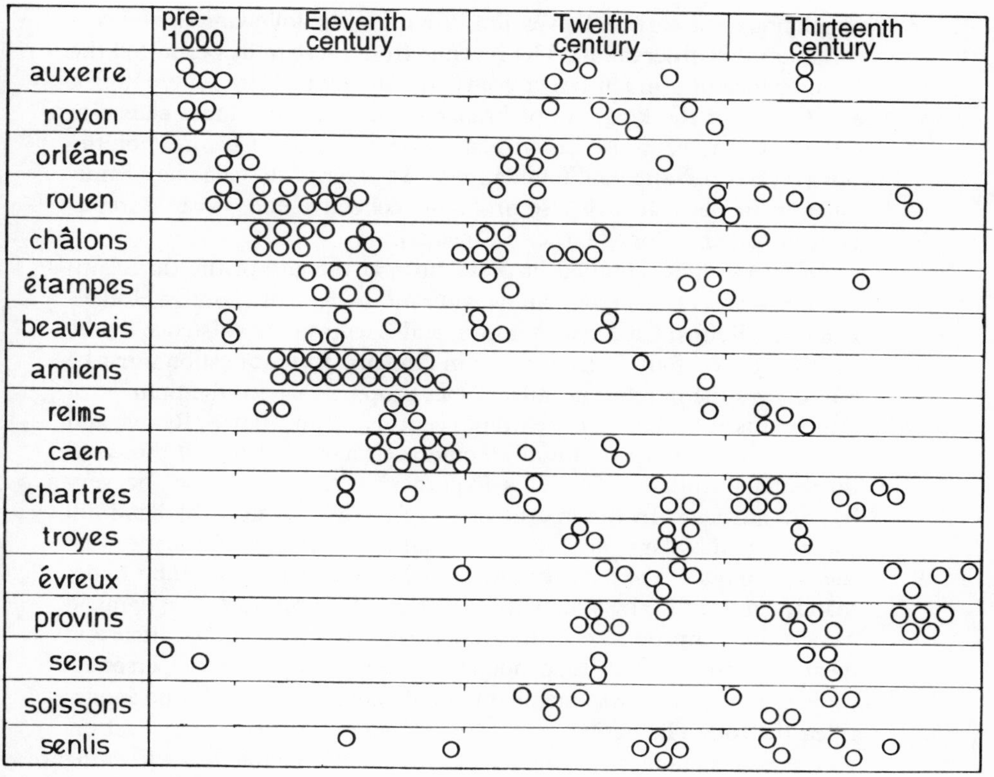

	pre-1000	Eleventh century	Twelfth century	Thirteenth century
auxerre				
noyon				
orléans				
rouen				
châlons				
étampes				
beauvais				
amiens				
reims				
caen				
chartres				
troyes				
évreux				
provins				
sens				
soissons				
senlis				

Figure 24. Mills Mentioned for the First Time. This grid graphically portrays the early development of milling in some cities (11th century) and its relatively late development in others (13th century).

The First Period of Urbanization: 950–1083

This was the period of urban hydraulic improvements. The canal networks appear to have been organized for the benefit of the mills, their nodal points. Seven cities—Rouen, Châlons, Etampes, Beauvais, Amiens, Reims, and Caen—very early distinguished themselves from all the others by the number of their mills. Of the eighty-two mills in the district, sixty-three were in these cities. It is safe to conjecture that at this period these cities were already centers of grain-producing regions whose yields had been rapidly increasing since the Carolingian era. The property belonging to the established authorities, who also owned these mills, thus appears to have been extensive. Power was concentrated in these cities in the hands of a single authority, whether lay or religious; the case of Troyes and Provins in the following period corroborates this observation. The revenue from these mills permitted the maintenance of a much larger court: the duchy of Normandy (Rouen and Caen), or the kingdom of France (Etampes); or a more elaborate cathedral chapter house (as in Amiens, Reims, and Châlons); or the construction of abbatial foundations (Toussaints in Châlons; Saint-Quentin in Beauvais); or else profitable collective enterprises (Grand-Pont in Amiens, Pont-Marne in Châlons).

Of all the mills counted in these cities at the end of the thirteenth century—an era of demographic saturation—half of those in Rouen, Beauvais, Reims, Châlons, Etampes, and Caen were in existence by the year 1083, and four-fifths of those in Amiens. But a question must be raised: was the number of mills in fact proportionate to the number of inhabitants at the end of the eleventh century? If so, Rouen, Reims, and Amiens (intra- and extramural) would each have had fifteen thousand inhabitants around 1080. This hypothesis must, of course, be very heavily nuanced. In the middle of the eleventh century, the handmill was still used by large numbers of peasants, which leads to the idea that the watermills of the nobility functioned sporadically, according to demand, contrary to the situation in the thirteenth century. The demand came from nonproducers—the aristocracy—who distributed flour and meal to their *familia* ("dependency"): slaves and military personnel (*milites*), but also Jews, merchants, and those artisans who no longer tilled the soil. The period under consideration was marked by vast urban reconstructions requiring a labor force not available for cultivating the land. The food for these workers, in the form of gruels and bread, came from the flour produced at the mills belonging to master-overseers. Hence the state of urban milling at the end of the eleventh century would be a reflection of the size of the *familia* of the builders. Rouen and Caen were capitals, and in the process of becoming kingdoms. Business concerns there had as much to do with arming knights as ships. On the eve of the battle of Hastings, these two cities included large garrisons, which had to be fed. Etampes, as early as 1025, was host to the royal court.

In Beauvais, Bishop Roger was a member of the rich landed gentry, and was in consequence the head of a large *familia;* this probably contributed to his making better use of the urban area, which covered a hundred hectares. The episcopal see of Amiens remained in the hands of the Foulque family, uncle and nephew, for sixty-seven years (991–1058); they held all ecclesiastical, military, judicial, and administrative powers. They had sixteen mills constructed on the branches of the Somme, near the walled part of the city. In Châlons, Bishop Roger

Table 6.
Major Urban Constructions, First Half of the Eleventh Century.

City	Foundations	Reconstructions	Palaces	Waterway Projects
Etampes	Notre-Dame, 1022 Saint-Basile, 1022		Royal Palace, 1025	Chalouette, 1015–1020
Rouen	Sainte-Catherine, 1023 Saint-Amand, 1030	Cathedral, 1045 Saint-Ouen, 1066	Ducal Palace, 970	Port
Beauvais	Saint-Pantaléon, 950 Saint-Barthélémy, 1037 Saint-Quentin, 1063	Saint-Laurent, 997 Cathedral, 1019 (burned, 1018)	Bishop's Palace, 1019	Thérinet, 1015–1030
Châlons	Saint-Germain, 1004 Saint-Nicolas, 1020 Toussaints, 1043	Saint-Jean aux Monts, 1020		Mau, 1020–1028
Amiens	Saint-Nicolas, 1075	Saint-Martin aux Jumeaux, 1073		Chemin de l'eau, 1030?
Reims		Saint-Rémi, 1005 Saint-Nicaise, 1060 Trinité, 1052		
Caen	Saint-Etienne, 1063 Trinité, 1066		Ducal chateau, 1030	Nouvel Odon, 1060–1070

I, following the example of his counterpart in Beauvais, acquired a monopoly over both power and prestige. Finally, in Reims, the power of Archbishop Ebles, with help from the king, allowed the city to oust its lay count and his followers (1024). The archbishop monopolized political and economic power, while the Saint-Rémi borough underwent extensive development in the second half of the century: in 1110–12, a time of lively tensions between Saint-Rémi and Saint-Nicaise, the population of the borough was estimated at ten thousand by a contemporary, but this number might also be an indication of the size of the *familia* of the abbot. In contrast, in the other cities studied, power was divided between the bishop, the count, and viscounts, which resulted in multiple conflicts between their diverse followers: in the eleventh century, these cities still had not built any new mills.

If the effective power of the mills indicates the size of the suzerain's *familia*, we can establish a hierarchy of cities in the eleventh century. Upon the death of Richard II (1027), Rouen, with ten mills, undoubtedly had the largest *familia* in the Paris basin. The inhabitants of Rouen numbered in the thousands, possibly ten thousand or more, taking into consideration the large military strength concentrated by the duke for his wars against the English and Scandinavians. In second place was Châlons, with seven mills on the Marne during this same period, and Reims also, with seven mills. Next, with six mills, came Etampes, capital of the modest Capetian kingdom, and finally Beauvais, with five mills. Each of these four cities could have numbered several thousand inhabitants within the walls—four or five thousand at the most. The population of Chartres, with two mills, was probably much lower at this time.

Some thirty years later, upon the death of Bishop Foulque II, the population of Amiens would appear to be more numerous than that of Rouen: sixteen mills belonged to the bishop. We must, however, take caution before concluding that the population of Amiens numbered well into the thousands. Since the disappearance of Quentovic, Amiens had become the second largest port on the English Channel, and Flemish and Scandinavian merchants came there in order to resupply Danish warriors. The panegyrist of Saint Firmin of Amiens, at the beginning of the eleventh century, wrote of the city: "Rich in lands, shaded by trees, provided with commerce and exchange, thou art protected on one side by a famous river whose diversions furnish fish in abundance to all thy citizens. [Thou art] also known for the high protection of thy walls." This was written before the Foulque family had decided upon the construction of mills on the Somme. Many of the mills of Amiens could thus have been used for export or for the supplying of fleets.

From a demographic point of view, watermills reveal heavily differentiated urban growth patterns for the first half of the eleventh century. Rouen, a powerful and opulent city, practically overpopulated, dominated the entire Paris basin, thus all of northern Europe. Along with Caen, on the verge of expansion, the duchy thus closely resembled a state, and one that wished to develop its technologies. Etampes, Amiens, Reims, Châlons, and Beauvais appear to have been large, well-populated cities, much like Paris and Arras. The first four cities had succeeded in ousting their lay rulers: the strength of milling highlights the advance of the church in the domain of energy exploitation. In the other cities, with the exception of Orléans, a royal city, and perhaps Noyon and Le Mans, the absence of hydraulic equippage implies a population that must have been only weakly urbanized and, at the very least, disunited vis-à-vis the political poles of lay and religious rulers.

The results of this investigation and the hypotheses I have tried to verify suggest an eleventh-century urban population that has been underevaluated by demographic historians. They have proposed a linear and continuous model of development: it was supposed that between the eleventh and the thirteenth centuries urban population developed uniformly, with no temporal or spatial jolts—a different pattern, by the way, from what is accepted for the late Middle Ages and the Renaissance. And it was thought that populations stabilized at the beginning of the thirteenth century, to decline around 1290–1300. The watermill index, on the other hand, suggests a differentiated pattern: certain cities seem to have known a demographic boom between 950 and 1050, to the point of reaching nearly ten thousand inhabitants for the largest cities, nearly five thousand for the average-sized ones, around 1060.

There were ninety-four mills in existence in 1082; but before 950 there were only a dozen known mills, centered around Auxerre, Noyon, Orléans, and Sens, all owned by large extraurban Benedictine monasteries. Four date from the sixth or seventh centuries; the others appear in texts at times of crisis during guerilla warfare (887 and 901) in confirmation of possessions (these mills could have been of Carolingian construction). This means that six times more mills were built during the 950–1082 period than before. If this ratio is applied to the data of the *Domesday Book*, nearly forty-eight hundred mills must have been built in England between 950 and 1086, the date of the writing of the register, and the limiting date for the first large phase of urban mill construction on the Continent. It remains to compare these statistics with the number of mills erected on English waterways before 1250, but the absence of precise information precludes such an analysis.

Decline: 1083–1106

Between these two dates, practically all mill construction ceased. Underutilization of existent mills appears to have been the principal reason for it. The conquest of England had moved the court from ducal capitals and had curtailed the number of military engagements between Danes and Normans. These factors resulted in a considerable decrease in flour consumption in Rouen, Caen, and Amiens. Major urban reconstructions were almost finished, and the labor force gathered to build them must have found employment in other artisanal activities—as early as the middle of the century in Beauvais, Reims, and Châlons, and about 1080 in Caen and Rouen. Finally, Etampes was less often host for the royal court, which now preferred to stay in Paris or Orléans.

Mills now played a secondary role in national economics, having ceded to a more profitable waterway enterprise—the construction of bridges: the Ysoard bridge in Le Mans (1067), the Marne bridge in Châlons (1107), the bridge of Orléans (1110), and Grand-Pont in Amiens (1121). Tolls from these bridges, in direct relationship with the city's commercial undertakings, would double the revenues of the nobles. In addition, new mills were placed under the arches or at the base of defense towers of these bridges.

To this politico-economic profile was added the bad climactic conditions of this period: St. Anthony's fire (erysipelas) caused by rye ergot, a fungus that proliferated when one rainy year succeeded another, decimated the population around 1082–85.[4] Heavy annual rainfall had a direct influence on cereal production, thus on the use of mills and on household consumption. The cessation of mill construction most likely indicates a demographic decline, aggravated by the departure of the princely courts in Rouen, Caen, and Etampes. Finally, the revolts of city dwellers and the emergence of the new social class of *burgenses* ("burgesses") suggest a metamorphosis in social life—namely, the dissolution of the large *familia*.

The mill had now acquired another meaning. Where it had earlier been an asset in the *familia*-based structure, it had now slowly become a profit-making venture for its owner. Independent citizens, willy-nilly, had to come to the mill for the grinding of their grain.

New Spurt of Growth: 1120–1275

This was a period of prosperity in urban development: more than half the watermills were built during this time. Cities with mills in existence since the eleventh century completed their milling infrastructure. The impetus given to Troyes and Provins by the counts of Champagne led to the construction of thirteen mills on the rivers of Troyes and seventeen in Provins. Chartres developed especially after the county had been granted by Henry the Liberal to his brother Thibaud. The increase in the number of mills remained steady during this phase, but accelerated between 1135 and 1215, coinciding with the last major drainings of marshes and the temperature rise (1180–1200), which in turn brought about an increase in cereal production. After 1215, only Provins, Chartres, and Sens continued to build mills and grow at the same pace; their development came much later than that of the other cities which now built no more mills. Urban milling had now reached a saturation point where it would remain for six centuries, subject only to internal modifications, such as increases in the number of wheels, reduction of trundles, or adaptation for other uses besides the grinding of flour.

It remains to be seen whether the utilization of the mills was permanent. Some were destroyed, sometimes to be immediately rebuilt, sometimes to remain in ruins for many years. The number of wheels and the height of the waterfalls gives a more precise idea of driving

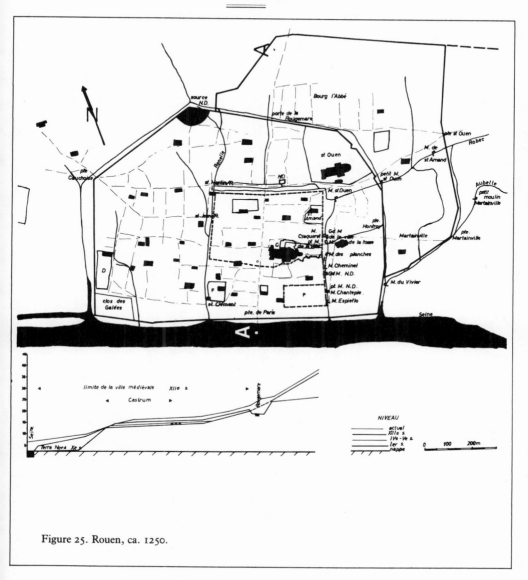

Figure 25. Rouen, ca. 1250.

power, but these criteria are documented only in the fourteenth or fifteenth centuries. In 1175 Troyes had eleven mills, totaling twenty-six
wheels in 1381; the number was probably the same for 1175.[5] Chartres
had eleven intramural mills in 1464, but only twelve wheels. Twenty-
four mills operated in Rouen in the middle of the thirteenth century,

89

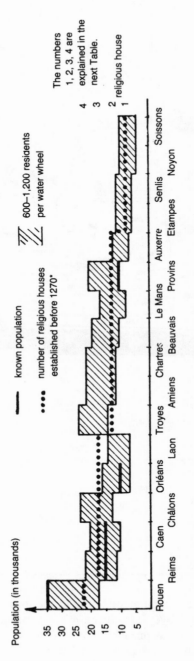

*J. Le Goff, "Ordres mendiants et urbanisation dans la France medievale," *AESC*, 1970, pp. 924–98.

Figure 26. Urban Population Calculated in Terms of the Number of Water Wheels.

with probably twenty-eight wheels, slightly more than in Troyes. We know that the driving force of a mill depends on the number of paddles or troughs attached to the turning wheel, but no text gives us the exact number. Medieval drawings show that the average was between eight and ten paddles per wheel, which, all things considered, would have given an effective yield varying from 10 to 30 percent.

To complicate the uncertainties in actual count, there were also projects that were never carried out, or had only a temporary existence. Thus, in 1173, the abbot of Saint-Quentin made an agreement with his bishop to construct thirty fulling mills within the city limits.[6] But it is clear that the gradient and the flow rate within the walls was insufficient for the energy required. These mills were undoubtedly located three kilometers downstream in the community of Albonne, where we find such place-names as Les Moulins ("the mills") and Terre à Foulon ("fuller's clay"). It is at this point that the diversions of the Thérain and the Avelon converge, and the land was probably uninhabited at the time. It is possible there were thirty mills, but it is more likely that this figure refers to the number of wheels or grinding hammers. A flow rate of eight cubic meters per second, a gradient of less than 3 pecent, and an effective yield of 20 percent are factors that nullify any hypothesis of mills or wheels. It would thus appear that the agreement between the abbot and the bishop concerned the number of fulling hammers to be housed in a small number of wheels. This contract must be understood in minimal terms.

The risk of error is thus not inconsiderable in this inventory of urban milling data. Although the dates of construction may be reliable, the yield, numbers, and uses of wheels nonetheless remain uncertain. In the absence of these elements, can we use mills as a criterion of urbanization for this period? Some population statistics for the end of the thirteenth century do, in fact, permit this. Rouen had nearly thirty-five thousand inhabitants and twenty-eight waterwheels; Reims, fourteen thousand inhabitants and twelve waterwheels; Orléans had ten thousand inhabitants and twelve waterwheels. The ratio obtained is thus one waterwheel per 600–1,200 inhabitants (see Figure 26).

Milling statistics are even more representative of the population at the very end of the twelfth century or the beginning of the thirteenth. Using the same ratio of inhabitants per waterwheel, a slightly different hierarchy of cities results. Rouen is clearly at the head of the list. Châlons, Troyes, Amiens, Reims, Caen, and Beauvais follow, with populations I estimate at eight to fifteen thousand. Finally, other smaller cities follow: Soissons, Senlis, Noyon, and LeMans, with between two

Table 7.
Fourfold Classification of Cities, from the Beginning of the Second Century to the Mid-Thirteenth Century, according to Size: 1) Very Large; 2) Large; 3) Medium-sized; 4) Small. *Criteria:* at the beginning of the 2nd century, the volume of land excavated in the process of urbanization; at the beginning of the 4th century, the volume of landfill accumulated around the *castrum;* at the beginning of the 10th century, the surface area circumscribed by moats; in the mid-eleventh and mid-twelfth centuries, the number of mill wheels in and around the city; in the mid-thirteenth century, the number of mendicant houses in and around the city ca. 1270. (Data on the last-named criterion are taken from J. Le Goff, "Ordres mendiants et urbanisation dans la France mediévále," *AESC*, 1970, pp. 924–46.)

	Beginning of 2nd Century	Beginning of 4th Century	Beginning of 10th Century	Mid-11th Century	Mid-12th Century	Mid-13th Century
Amiens	2	1	2	2	2	2
Auxerre	3	2	4	4	3	3
Beauvais	4	3	3	3	2	3
Caen				3	2	3
Châlons		4	3	2	2	3
Chartres	4	4	2	4	3	3
Etampes				3	3	4
Evreux	3	3	4	4	4	3
Laon		4	2	2	3	4
Noyon	4	4	2	4	4	4
Orleáns	2	2	3	4	3	3
Paris	2	2	2	2	1	1
Provins					2	2
Reims	1	1	2	2	2	2
Rouen	3	3	1	1	1	1
Senlis	4	4	2	4	4	4
Sens	2	2	3	3	3	3
Soissons	2	3	4	4	4	4
Troyes	3	3	4	4	2	2

and four thousand inhabitants. Chartres, Provins, and Evreux, at the bottom and still developing, had moved into the next higher bracket by 1230–40.

Analysis of milling from the middle of the eleventh century to the beginning of the fourteenth thus suggests a rather diversified demographic evolution for these cities. Rouen was the most heavily populated city during this period: Reims, Amiens, Caen, and Châlons remained average-sized; Etampes declined after 1080, Laon after 1130, and Beauvais around 1250. Troyes underwent rapid development between 1140 and 1200, leveled off, and then declined, like Provins and Chartres, after 1280. The annexation of the Champagne region to the rest of the kingdom was a factor here. Orléans and Sens, which were small cities in the eleventh century, grew especially in the second half of the thirteenth. Noyon and Senlis, in spite of a large enclosure surrounded by ditches at the end of the ninth century, were not able to develop important urban activities; they remained in a somewhat embryonic state, much like Soissons.

Naming the Mills

As early as the period of expansion in the middle of the twelfth century, most of the mills had a name. Two types of nomenclature can be distinguished: nominative and locative. In the first case, the name was that of the owner: abbey, count, king, or bishop (25 percent). In the second case, the names of localities (7 percent) must be distinguished from ordinary names, which qualified the site or piece of property adjoining the mill (18 percent).

Thirteen percent of the mills bore a saint's name, a percentage which would be doubled if we take into account mill names that also designated abbeys as their owners. Four-fifths of the names appeared before the thirteenth century.

Some names designate characteristics of relativity: high-low, big-small, before-behind. Others point to individual mill characteristics: the *Vannes Grivottes* (Grivottes, a place name) in Auxerre; *Ratel* ("rake") in Beauvais and Amiens; *Cochefilet* ("passenger network") in Chartres; and *Coisel* ("peaceful") in Noyon. The name might also indicate the principal function of the mill: *Taillefer* ("iron-cutter") and *Tappeplomb* ("lead-tapper") in Amiens; *Fouleret* ("fulling") in Etampes and Chartres; *à Tan* ("tanning") in Beauvais, Evreux, and Senlis.

The noise of the grinding was used to name 7 percent of the mills: *Claquerel* ("clacker") in Noyon; *Choc* ("shock") in Rouen; *Toxar* ("knocker") in Amiens; *Cliquet* ("clicker") in Châlons.

93

Finally, numbers indicate the existence of groups of mills: the *Quatre-Moulins* (4) in Amiens; *Les Trois* (3) in Provins; and *Les Sept* (7) in Châlons. Such names suggest huge conglomerations.

These names reveal the importance of saints, machinery, nuisances, and numbers in the medieval mentality, and they also show that few mills were used for anything but grinding wheat for flour. Barely 5 percent were used to full woolen cloth or to make tannin. But it should be kept in mind that the mechanization of crafts was just beginning, and overemphasizing it would mean falling into historical positivism.

Ownership of Mills

Table 8 indicates the divisioning of the mills among their different owners before and after donations or sales of mills in the cities in this study.

At the outset, city authorities were in possession of nearly two-thirds of the mills, which confirms the importance of both lay and ecclesiastical feudalism in the matter of technical innovations. Ownership transfers, by way of gift or sale, affected only half the mills. A third of these transactions occurred before 1080 and the remainder after 1110. In other words, in the eleventh century, the nobles seem to have been attached to these assets; donations concerned essentially the chapter houses placed directly under their authority, or dependent on their *familia*. In the twelfth century, however, transactions were more divided among chapter houses, extraurban abbeys, houses of mendicant orders, Templars, and communes. Communes in Rouen, Senlis, and Sens bought mills. If feudal authorities now seemed to let go of their mills more easily, it was because their interest in this type of machinery had diminished or had been displaced since the end of the eleventh century: the dissolution of the familial clan probably had much to do with it.

The church was the largest beneficiary of these transactions, owning little more than half the mills at the beginning, and nearly three-quarters by the end. Chapter houses appear to have been privileged legatees (20 percent increase), along with suburban abbeys (12 percent increase), to the detriment of lay authorities (27 percent decrease) and episcopal authorities (19 percent decrease). The Templars—like the cities—did not build mills, but were able to put together a not rather inconsiderable milling patrimony (7 and 9 percent, respectively).

Private citizens also owned mills, but always as members of associations. The reason: watermill construction required a large outlay of money—for foundations, stone channels and spillways, buildings, oak or chestnut wheels and cogwheels, stationary and moving millstones, costing nearly 50 pounds the pair. The cost of an ordinary mill in 1250

Table 8.
Ownership of Mills.

Owner	Number		Percentage	
	Initial	Final	Initial	Final
Count	98	34	41	14
Bishop	59	15	25	6
Abbey	44	72	18	30
Chapter House	15	64	6	26
City	0	18	0	9
Hospital	2	7	1	3
Church	2	15	1	7
Others	18	13	8	5
Total	238	238	100	100

can be estimated at between one hundred fifty and five hundred pounds, but the investment was profitable: the fourteen mills in Provins brought in more than three thousand pounds per year for the count at the end of the thirteenth century.

This analysis of the number, names, and ownership of mills brings out the importance of one of the foremost bases of the medieval city's energy supply and overall economy. More than a third of the mills were built on canals that had been diverted some years earlier. Nearly a third of the urban mills turning in 1080 would continue to grind for nearly eight hundred years more; the entire milling system was thus set and fixed as early as the middle of the thirteenth century. This technology had interested monks during the entire Middle Ages; and as early as the end of the tenth century, it also aroused the enthusiasm of the aristocracy, lay and ecclesiastical, who held royal rights on the vast majority of the waterways to be improved or diverted. The feudal mill dynamized potential hydraulic energy, 90 percent of which was used for the grinding of cereal grains—that is, for food. The Renaissance and the Ancien Régime would take over this medieval heritage without modifying it. Their interest in it was no longer for the dynamics of water but rather for static water and steam.

Riverside Crafts

As early as the beginning of the twelfth century, the "river crafts" were in place for the transformation of primary resources such as wool, skins,

95

and, to a lesser extent, cloth fibers (flax and hemp). The finished products, primarily woolen cloth and leather, were at the origin of urban wealth. Historian-economists have already exhausted the archives concerning the production and regulation of these industries. But the technological innovation of the medieval processes has often been ignored, or else these procedures have been treated as throwbacks to the techniques of antiquity. However, mordanting and dyeing were now done after weaving, not before, as during the Gallo-Roman or Carolingian eras. As for dyes, the majority of them had been known since ancient times, but artisans of the twelfth century multiplied the combinations and considerably diversified weave types. Cities acquired their reputation from the color and nap of their cloth. Color depended on the intensity of dye and on the mineral content of the water—and dyers were well aware of this. Raising the nap required a high level of mechanization (the weaving loom, developed in the eleventh and twelfth centuries) and treatment to avoid long soaking of the cloth in water. The cloth, once finished, had to be stocked in a dry, well-ventilated place, away from any source of humidity that could alter the colors or rot the wool.

The question of water pollution has never been raised. It nonetheless merits attention so as to establish an initial assessment, to discover the impact on the environment, and to see how it was controlled by local authorities.

The medieval city, ever since Guizot first outlined its history, has had a reputation for having been filthy, noisy, and extremely polluted. This notion has been perpetrated through school books and in studies on urban institutions published by the students of the Ecole de Chartes, Paris, from the end of the nineteenth century on. However—and what follows in this study will amply demonstrate it—Guizot and his emulators extrapolated to the twelfth and thirteenth century from the documents at their disposal for the fourteenth and fifteenth, using their progressivist a priori assumptions to detect traces of medieval archaism in the artisanal situation of the nineteenth century. In reality, medieval society was careful to protect its urban population from the risk of disease, by issuing prophylactic measures and regulations, moving unhealthy buildings, organizing the topography of river crafts so as to promote the self-cleansing of the water, and building steam baths and bathing areas. This type of collective hygiene, only partly under the jurisdiction of urban authorities (for example, they had no part in the construction of steam baths) remains one of the most significant factors of medieval urbanization.

My purpose here is to present an overall account of sanitization, not of the pernicious effects of health hazards. Moreover, the lack of quantitative data seriously limits such a project, and renders useless the construction of a laboratory simulation model. Microbiological analysis of the archaeological strata of the urban milieu would yield valuable information on pollution in the Middle Ages, providing an initial bank of bacteriological data for the kind of research that is carried on today.

The most important riverside craft was textiles, and the most abundant information on this subject is available for the thirteenth century in the regions of Artois, Flanders, and Brabant. Legislative decrees closely supervised craft activities; for example, "no dyer may have a privy on the river"[7] and "no fuller may be so irresponsible as to throw ashes into the river, under penalty of ten pounds fine and banishment from the city."[8] Clean water was a fundamental necessity for the quality of these textiles, which were exported. As early as the end of the eleventh century, textile chemistry had been refined and perfected by experimenting with variations in temperature and the composition of dissolved minerals. The degreasing of wool was carried out by successive hot and cold water baths; the fulling of the cloth, which gave it its quality (more body and a more consistent texture) was done with fuller's earth mixed with water, in pits where the cloth was fulled for at least twenty-four hours. Dyes, with the exception of woad (blue), had to be added to the cloth by means of a fixing agent, usually alum (less often, tartar) diluted in boiling water into which the cloth was put. Once it had been mordanted, the piece of cloth was put into the dye bath (madder, roset, fuchsine, or other dyes). When these operations were completed, the cloth was again washed in running water before being dried on stretchers set up beside the canals. One piece of cloth required approximately two cubic meters of water, thus approximately one hundred liters of water per kilogram. Only a few statistics concerning production have come down to us: fifty thousand pieces of cloth produced in Provins in 1276; twenty thousand in Chartres in 1290; five thousand in Troyes in 1298; but output from domestic production needs to be added to these figures, which are eloquent testimony of the extent of this industry in the thirteenth century. In home cloth-making, chemical processes were not subject to strict regulation, and urine, wine dregs, lye, or suint were used to clean the wool; pot blacking, *lavoir* (a black liquid exuded by heaps of woad in fermentation), bark, gallnuts, iron filings, or gum were used for dyeing.[9] None of these substances could be used in the preparation of cloth to be sold, under penalty of heavy fines.

The materials used for domestic production were not highly polluting. Bacteriogenesis was weak, and the most that can be said is that the residues of dyes that washed into the rivers may have noticeably increased anaerobic fermentation. But this must not allow us to ignore the purgative effects of alum and tartar (both were used for this purpose in the decantation pools of water-purification stations at the beginning of the twentieth century), which increased the precipitation of suspended particles. In addition, the velocity of river currents, by facilitating the dissolution of oxygen in the water, considerably reduced hydric pollution. In short, from the point of view of environmental deterioration, the textile industries of the twelfth and thirteenth centuries seem to have been relatively neutral, for both air and water.

The same conclusions emerge with respect to leather treatment, even though little is known of the procedures used for soaking and depilation of hides before the middle of the fourteenth century, and there are no indications of ferments before the sixteenth century. The final tanning operation was that of letting the leather soak in pits for at least two years; these pits were filled with water with a slight but continuous current, to which tannin was added. This product was extracted from the bark of oak trees, which was then ground in tanning mills. Tannin, or tannic acid, has good antipollution properties, so it can be supposed, as in the case of alum, that tannin helped clarify the city's water and prevented contamination. As for glove-making, parchment-making, and currying in the thirteenth century, baths of hydrated lime were used to make the hides swell; they were then soaked in an alum solution.[10] The lime facilitated the decantation of suspended solid matter, and the water was chemically neutralized as it was softened.

Flax and hemp occupied only a secondary place in medieval urban industry. It would seem that Troyes and Reims played the leading roles in this domain. Retting—that is, the organic decomposition of the plant stalks in ditches dug for this purpose alongside streams—was highly pollutive, as much for underground and surface water as for the air. But in the twelfth and thirteenth centuries retting took place more in the countryside than in the city itself, where the spinning and weaving of cloth was carried out.

Water pollution of artisanal origin was thus very moderate during this period. The chemistry involved was not neutral, but either acidic or alkaline, favoring the precipitation of solid organic material in water, which river currents carried beyond city limits. The self-purification of rivers was such that fish life was not threatened: fish was one of the staple elements of the urban diet at this time.

Complementarity of Crafts

A study of medieval artisanal topography shows the complementarity of these crafts. The tanners worked along the Avre in Amiens, the Auges in Provins, and the cross channels of Troyes. The dyers, however, were on other rivers: the Somme, the Durtein, and the Grand Canal—and this was generally the case. It was a logical arrangement: tannin, when it is oxydized, can discolor water, damaging the color of the cloth being dyed. In contrast, skinners, glove-makers, and curriers were often downstream from the dyers, as in Troyes, Rouen, or Paris. They were in fact able to take advantage of the excess alum dissolved in the dyeing mixtures, or simply thrown as waste into the river once it had been used as mordant for the working of cloth. By precipitating alkaloids (flocculation), alum enhanced the usefulness of water in the treatment of skins.

Chemical synergy was not limited to these industries. The association of tanneries and slaughterhouses appears to have been common. This underscores at once their interdependence and their coevality. They were frequently located alongside the same ditches of the city of the high Middle Ages. At the end of the twelfth century, most slaughterhouses were located upstream from the tanneries: in Amiens, Auxerre, Beauvais, Caen, Sens, and Troyes, for example. This was no doubt because slaughtering animals required large quantities of clean water, whereas the preparation of skins needed little water, and even dirty water could be used.

During the thirteenth and fourteenth centuries, in the interests of hygiene, authorities sometimes succeeded in moving the slaughterhouses to other locations. They were then put downstream of the tanneries, on the outskirts of the city. In each case, this logical association diminished the polluting effects of refuse; it kept tannin running continuously into the river from the ditches. The presence of fishponds downstream from these work places speaks for itself of the quality of the water.[11]

The river industries avoided chemical and microbic pollution. Everything suggests that the topographic organization of work was not haphazard, but rather the result of predetermination, or a tacit agreement, vis-à-vis the placing of crafts alongside the river. Urban authorities had clearly understood that, along with the regulation of products, water purity and the synergy of certain chemical products were indispensable for the wealth of the city. But by staking the profits of the textile industry on the quality of water, they made their production dependent on

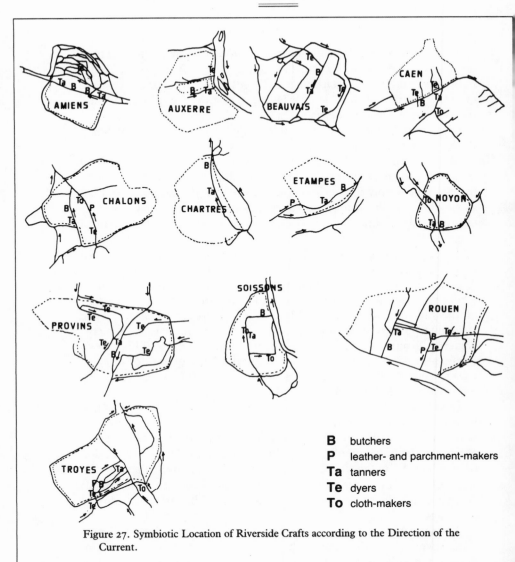

Figure 27. Symbiotic Location of Riverside Crafts according to the Direction of the Current.

B butchers
P leather- and parchment-makers
Ta tanners
Te dyers
To cloth-makers

the hydric ecosystem. We know today that the deterioration of the hydric milieu is in general inversely proportional to the flow rate of river currents.[12] The current had only to slow down slightly, in other words, for the quality of the textiles produced in it to deteriorate. Or if the alum were to disappear, the self-cleansing properties of the river water would be eliminated. This is exactly what happened in the fifteenth century. In the meantime, urban authorities looked for ways to maintain the purity of the air and water of their cities by creating sewers or by moving the public hospitals to the periphery of the city, when enclosures were enlarged.

Hospitals

Texts on air or water regulations are rare before the twelfth century. However, the authority of Jewish doctors attendant on nobles during the tenth and eleventh centuries would lead one to believe that the aristocracy was not insensitive to the concern for preserving the purity of drinking water. The Old Testament and the Talmud contain numerous precepts on this subject, and Jews drank only well water. Moreover, the medical documents compiled since the high Middle Ages attest to the fact that authorities, especially ecclesiastical, were very much preoccupied with bodily hygiene and the prevention of epidemics. In the tenth century, the *Aphorisms* of Hippocrates were to be found in the Abbey of Sainte Godeberte in Noyon, and Richer de Reims went there to consult them. The *Etymologies* of Isadora of Seville were kept in the abbeys of Saint-Pierre-aux-Monts in Châlons and Saint Pierre in Laon; the *Synopsis* of Oribasis was present in the chapter libraries of Paris, Laon, and perhaps Chartres. Thirteenth-century treatises on hygiene, such as the one by Aldebrandino of Sienna, were widely distributed among the upper classes. But the creation of hospitals by bishops remains the concrete manifestation of the physical separation of the sick and diseased; in consequence, the hospitals became prime places for infection. These "hôtels-Dieu," little known before the ninth century, were reformed in 816 by the Council of Aix-la-Chapelle. During the eleventh century, they were built near the cathedral in each episcopal city.

In the course of the twelfth century, the expansion of the episcopal palace and the major church in more than half of these cities necessitated transferring the hospital out of the *castrum*.[13] From then on, the public hospitals held a privileged place within the medieval enclosure— a place they would continue to occupy until the end of the eighteenth century. The choice of the site for the hospital clearly demonstrates that authorities strongly wished to avoid the spread of foul odors. The new hospitals were sometimes built to abut the new city wall, as in Noyon and Beauvais; immediate access to the moat allowed for the removal of wastes. Elsewhere, in Auxerre, Amiens, and Troyes, they were moved onto uninhabited plots of ground with access to water. Provins, around 1160, transferred its hospital outside the old ramparts, halfway down

Table 9.
Establishment and Relocation of Public Hospitals

City	First mentioned	Relocated	Date	Close to which rampart?*	Close to a moat?	Close to an aqueduct?	Prevailing winds from the west?
Soissons	11th century?	?		?	sewer?	?	no
Chartres	ca. 1070	no		HMA	no	yes	no
Reims	7th century?	no		HMA	yes	possibly	no
Sens	1204?	no		HMA	no	no	yes
Le Mans	830	no		(extramural)	yes	no	yes
Orléans	1122?	no		HMA	yes	no	yes
Senlis	9th century?	yes	1208	HMA	yes	no	no
Châlons	ca. 920	yes	1180–1200	HMA	yes	no	no
Rouen	10th century	no		outside the HMA	?	no	no

Paris	ca. 829	yes	1200	HMA	yes	wells	yes
Laon	ca. 1019	yes	1200–1210	HMA	yes	no	yes
Caen	ca. 1070?	no		EMA	yes	springs	yes
Etampes	ca. 1050	yes	ca. 1191	MA	yes	no	yes
Auxerre	9th century?	yes	1250	MA	yes	no	yes
Amiens	9th century?	yes	1236	outside the HMA	yes	?	yes
Beauvais	?	yes	1201	MA	yes	no	yes
Evreux	?	yes	1150–1160	MA	yes	no	yes
Troyes	1157	yes	1157	HMA	yes	no	yes
Provins	ca. 1050	yes	ca. 1160	outside the HMA	yes	no	yes
Noyon	9th century?	yes	1178	MA	yes	no	yes

*HMA = High Middle Ages; EMA = early Middle Ages; MA = Middle Ages

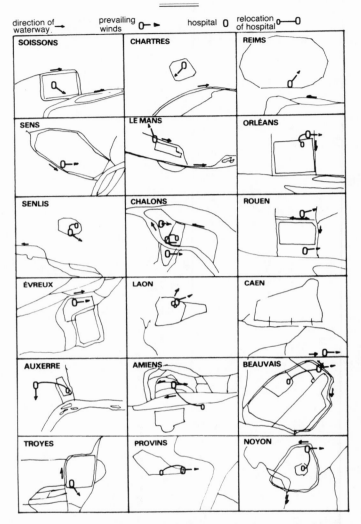

direction of waterway. →   prevailing winds O→►   hospital O   relocation of hospital O—O

Figure 28. Location of Public Hospitals. The great majority were located near moats; when the hospitals were relocated, it was with a view to the prevailing winds.

the slope, not far from a spring. Caen, around 1220, put its hopsital at the southern extremity of the Ile Saint Jean, near the Orne and a spring, about five hundred feet from the wall. Inasmuch as the prevailing winds come from the west over the Paris basin, building the hospital in the eastern part of the city lessened the risks of air pollution.

The transfer and reconstruction of these hospitals took place between 1150 and 1230, at a time when migration toward the cities was at a peak. Lay authorites encouraged these displacements by donating land or by financing their construction. At the same time, the first leper colonies were being built outside the city limits, a sign that authorities were not totally unaware of certain prophylactic measures.

Sewers

Even domestic pollution was controlled by regulations: the evacuation of hospital wastes into the ditches of the fortifications was one indication. There are documents which also lead us to conclude that the nobility had certain of the canals transformed into sewers.

Drainage ditches named Merderon, Merdançon, and Merdron (*merde* is the familiar term in French for excrement) appeared as early as 1208 in Troyes, and had spread to the other cities before the middle of the fourteenth century. The term designated a portion of the waterway along the city of the high Middle Ages, as in Troyes, Sens, Auxerre, Amiens, and Beauvais, or one that crossed a heavily urbanized zone, as in Provins and Noyon. In each case, the term applied to a canal with a slow current. In spite of the hesitation of etymologists,[14] merderon indeed designated a mode of evacuation for human excrement: latrines at the base of the city walls in Sens, or over the ditch (1246); stone chambers on the Merdançon in Beauvais (1251) and Troyes (1208), "droppings ditches in front of the Augustinians" in Reims (1328). Everything would lead us to conclude that these canals were depositories for human fecal matter, to which was added animal offal: the Merdereau of Amiens, Provins, and Noyon flowed alongside the slaughterhouses, as did a street of the Merdrons in Chartres. In general, these waterways were the late-empire ditches that, in the thirteenth century, no longer played a defensive military role: new walls, much larger and farther out, now protected the city.

It seems that these ancient canalizations were especially intended for this particular use by the urban authorities. In Beauvais in the fourteenth century, the fief of the Chaise ("chair") was in charge of the annual cleaning of the Merdançon under the Châtel bridge. In Soissons, in 1305, the Merdereau was explicitly mentioned as a sewer collecting the waste from the butcher shops and the count's palace. The Franciscans of Rouen, in 1257, received a royal authorization to build latrines above the Renelle, over the Merdereau. These examples show that officials were anxious to have it known that their authority covered the utilization of these ditches as drainage sewers.

What is really striking is the long period of time that separates the different mentions of these ditches. One after the other, at the end of the twelfth century, Philip Augustus in Paris and Henry the Liberal in Troyes ordered the construction of canals so that certain quarters—that of the butchers, for example—could be cleaned. There are two mentions from before the thirteenth century, which were not repeated before the beginning of the fourteenth century—a century and a half of silence, broken only by mentions of *merdereau* in the texts. Everything indicates that these sections of waterways were not primitive, uncontrolled dumping grounds, but sewers properly so called, operated as such, and created for the most part in the oldest ditches, whose currents had greatly diminished since their waters had begun to flow around the new urban enclosures. The creation of these sewers would necessarily have preceded their first mention in documents, by a few years at least; for example, the *merdançon* of Beauvais, which had borne the name "waters of Sainte-Marguerite" in 1219—thirty years earlier. The same was true in Soissons, where a *merdançon* was named "ditch along the slaughterhouses" in 1280—twenty years prior.

These sewers were almost exclusively reserved for the use of the episcopal and countal palaces, the houses of mendicant orders, and the slaughterhouses. The palaces were in fact located alongside these canals in Orléans and Soissons (the count's palace). With the wells and cisterns that belonged to them, they had the advantages of practically continuous drainage systems. The religious houses were next to the sewers in Reims (Augustinians), Sens (Dominicans), Rouen, Auxerre, and Provins (Franciscans). The mendicant orders also built aqueducts to provide water for their establishments; in the middle of the thirteenth century they were very certainly ahead of their time with such facilities. A perfected system for providing and expelling water marks them as urban inheritors of the monasteries of Cluny. The Merdereau was used almost exclusively by those in the privileged positions of power and by their protégés, the mendicant orders and certain hospitals.

But the aristocracy was also anxious to clean up the areas around the butcher shops and even more so around the slaughterhouses, considered to be putrid. The creation of a sewer in Troyes in the middle of the twelfth century, and in Soissons at the beginning of the fourteenth, show that the count wanted to reduce the noxious effects of these work places. In Sens, Etampes, and Provins, the count did the same thing, forcing the butchers to put the refuse from their shops into the sewers or downstream from the city. As to the ultimate source of these regulations, nothing has survived in written form, but the example of the first two cities would seem to indicate that here again Jewish preventive practices influenced the count. These five cities in fact had large Jewish communities, which were influential in the court of the count. In any

Table 10.
Merdereaus ("Filth Drains").

City	First mentioned	Near the river?	Near the late-empire ditches?	Flow (m³/s)
Troyes	1208	yes	yes	0.1
Amiens	1224	yes	yes	6.0
Sens	1246	no	yes	0.1
Beauvais	1251	no	yes	0.0?
Provins	1269?	yes	no	0.1
Soissons	1305	yes	no	0.1?
Reims	1328	no	yes	0.0

case, the regulations do not appear to have been decreed by municipal bodies, which included rich butchers concerned with protecting their own private interests. At the end of the thirteenth century, when the king imposed the transfer of slaughterhouses downstream from city centers, he was successful only in Amiens, Meaux, and Senlis, where municipal power was more or less in the hands of his bailiff; elsewhere it would take the French Revolution to get them to move.

These measures can indeed be qualified as prophylactic. The object was to move away from the palace these centers of putrefaction, which had been there for one or even two centuries, having originally been installed at a time when only the court of the count or the cathedral chapter house had any demand for fresh meat. The quality of air was an important issue at that time. Good air was a sign of good health, it was said. The clothmakers required good air for stocking their cloth, in well-ventilated warehouses, free of humidity.

Steam Baths

The same preoccupations guided the creation of steam baths, which have been considered the starting point of medieval social hygiene.[15] It is true that at the end of the thirteenth century, the price of a bath was modest: four *deniers* for a warm bath, two *deniers* for a steam bath, in Paris, according to Etienne Boileau's *Livre des Métiers*. But a close look at the matter reveals that access to these public baths was reserved for the wealthy, and more particularly for the aristocracy: knights, canons, ladies.

It can be estimated that there was one bathhouse per six thousand inhabitants at the beginning of the fourteenth century. Reims had three

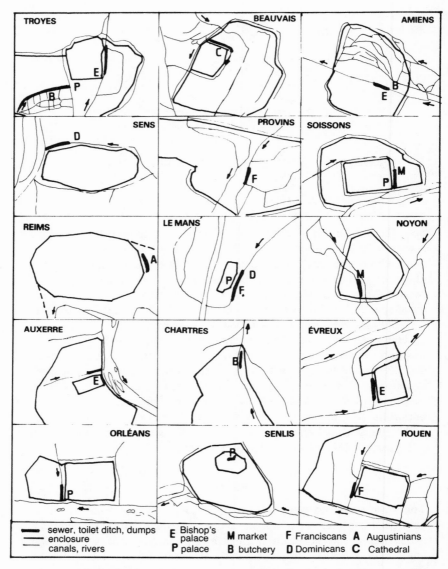

Figure 29. Location of Public Toilet Places. Most of them adjoined the late-empire moats.

in 1328 for a population of fifteen to eighteen thousand; Provins had two for twelve thousand inhabitants in 1270. In spite of this, the bath house operators in Paris, numbering twenty-nine, paid among the lowest taxes of any social group. We may thus conclude that the baths were not very popular.

The origin of the steam bath remains shrouded in mystery. They had little in common with Roman thermal baths, which were huge buildings supplied with underground conduits carrying large amounts of water. The Roman baths were attractions: residents went there to relax, read, chat, or work out; Suetonius called them a "passion." They had five parts: the *laconicum* or dressing room; the *sudarium*, a hot room, much like a sauna; the *caldarium* or hot bath; the *tepidarium* or lukewarm bath; and the *frigidarium* or cold water pool. During the period of the late empire, these baths fell into disuse, largely due to lack of equipment maintenance, in particular the aqueducts;[16] only private baths survived until the high Middle Ages. There was one in Athies, in the palace of Clothaire I, and in Aix-la-Chapelle where Charlemagne had one built. Any palace worthy of the name was supposed to have a thermal bath, fed by springs, according to a seventh-century manuscript from Laon.[17]

In the few references we have, there is no mention of public use. The building was reduced to one or two rooms. The thermal baths that Saint Radegonde had built at Poitiers in the sixth century had only one room, like the baths built two centuries later in Reims by Archbishop Rigobert for his canons. In Saint-Gall, the plan of the monastery shows only a *caldarium* and a *frigidarium*. In all cases, the pleasures of the bath were reserved to the nobility: Hincmar of Reims points out that Gottschalk could not have been an aristocrat, for he refused to take a bath.

In addition, beginning with the eleventh century, intense sexual repression was to manifest itself among the religious aristocracy. As early as 803 the Council of Aix-la-Chapelle took up the prohibitions of Gregory the Great: "If lust and voluptuousness are the reasons for taking baths, then we will not permit them on Sunday or on any other day. If, on the contrary, baths are taken because the body needs them, then we do not forbid them, even on Sunday." This council decreed as well that those members of religious orders whose health required it could bathe at the beginning of Lent, that an adequate number of tubs should be provided, and that the members of the community should bathe themselves especially there, "helping each other by giving all necessary services." The bath had become simply a hygienic necessity.

In addition, bathing became private. At Murbach a rule of the order provided for replacing communal baths with individual tubs. The

Table 11.
Public Steam Baths before the Fifteenth Century.

City	Number	First known mention	Street	Quarter	Near the Jewish quarter?	Prosti- tution?	Mendicant orders within 200 m?	Activity of the quarter	Access point
Troyes	1	1104	?	Cité	yes		yes		crossroads
Provins	1	1236	?	High	yes				
	1	1309	?	Low	possibly		yes	merchants	Bridge of the Fish
Paris	1	1248	Pelleterie	Cité	yes		no	skins, hides	well of the Circumcision
	1	1290	Croix Blanche	Blancs Manteaux	no		no		Barbette gate
	1	1290	Trois Chandeliers	Sainte-Croix	no		no		Barbette gate
	1	1290	Rosiers	Sainte-Croix	no		no		Barbette gate
	2	1290	Saint-Denis	Cité	possibly		no		
	1	1290	Temple	Temple	no		no	woolen cloth	gate of the Temple
	1	1290	Saint-Paul	Saint-Paul	no		no	woolen cloth	Saint-Paul gate
	2	1290	Thibotaudé	Saint-Germain	no		no	woolen cloth	road

City	#	Year	Street	Parish				Trade	Landmark
	1	1290	Vieilles Et. Saint-Honoré	Saint-Honoré	no		no	merchants	Saint-Honoré gate
	1	1290	Saint-Martin	Saint-Martin	no		no		Saint-Martin gate
	1	1290	Simon le Franc	Saint-Joce	no	?	no		road
	2	1290	Hirondelle (through the old city)	Saint-André	no		yes	butchers	
	1	1290		Cité	possibly		no		
	1	1290	Mégisserie	Saint-Germain marketplace	no		no	glove-makers	dock
	2	1290	Pl. Marché Neuf		no		no	merchants	
	1	1290	Marivaux	Saint-Jacques	no		no		road
	2	1290	Bucherie	Saint-Julien	no		no	butchers	
	2	1290	Vieille Lanterne	?	no		no		
	1	1290	Poulies	Saint-Paul	no		no	woolen cloth	Béguines gate
	1	1290	Roi de Sicile	Saint-Gervais	no		no	woolen cloth	
	1	1290	Vieilles Et. Saint-Martin	Saint-Martin	no		no		Saint-Martin gate
Châlons	1	1272	Bassinerie	Bourg Neuf	possibly		yes	merchants	Nau bridge
Sens	1	1310	Vieilles Etuves	Jewish	yes		no		
Orléans	1	1330	Vieilles Etuves	Jewish	yes		no	carpenters	well of the Circumcision

Table II. (continued)

City	Number	First known mention	Street	Quarter	Near the Jewish quarter?	Prosti-tution?	Mendicant orders within 200 m?	Activity of the quarter	Access point
Beauvais	1	1316	aux Charretiers	Sainte-Marguerite	no		no	linen and hemp	bridge of the Merle Parole
Senlis	1	14th century	?	Saint-Aignan	no		no		gate of the Donkeys
Reims	1	1328	?	Jard	no		yes	millers	
	1	1328	Buirette	Jard	no		no	weavers	
	1	1328	Buirette	Jard	no		no	weavers	
Soissons	1	1332	Bauton	Neuf	possibly		no	merchants	
	1	15th century	Vieilles Etuves	cathedral	no		yes	steam shop	

Auxerre	1	1339	Marine	Saint-Germain	possibly		no	merchants	
Chartres	1	14th century	Corderie	Saint-Eman	no		no	rope-makers	
Amiens	1	1389	Engoulvent	Neuf	no	yes	no	tanners	bridge of the Bras Coupé
Noyon	1	1355	Buat	Saint-Nicaise	no		no	butchers	
Rouen	1	1363	Ruissel	Martainville	no	yes		tanners	Honfroy gate
Rouen	1	1380	?	marketplace	no		yes	merchants	market
Caen	1	1352	Des Etuves	Fossés	no	?	yes	tanners	ditch
Le Mans	1	1455	Gourdaine	Notre-Dame	no	?	no	tanners	
Laon	1	15th century	?	?	no		no		

monastic rules of 817 emphasized that their use would be determined by the prior. The architect of Saint-Gall placed the baths next to the heater room and the infirmary, as was logical, and isolated them into individual rooms linked by a corridor. At Cluny twelve rooms for individual baths each contained a wooden bathtub. The rules of Lanfranc (eleventh century) stipulated how bathing was to be carried out: an older monk was to prepare the baths at dawn. He then informed the other monks, who could take a bath between prime and compline. After shaving, each monk was to return to a small place closed off by a curtain.

The art of the Roman bath was in decline and would disappear altogether in the ninth century; the medieval steam bath was not its successor.

Nineteenth-century historians believed that the use of the bath was introduced by the Crusades. The Arab *hammam* had borrowed its architecture partly from the Roman bath,[18] but there is no resemblance between it and the "steam house" of the beginning of the fourteenth century in Europe, whose furnishings were limited to a few wooden tanks placed in a large room, carpeted in some cases, on the second floor; on the ground floor or in the back courtyard, water was boiled in large kettles.

The French word *étuve* ("stew") was known in Old High German as *stupa* or *stuba*, in Old Scandinavian as *stofa*, and in Old English as "stove," indications of a long Germanic tradition. But the few mentions we have at our disposal would indicate that the practice of the bath was quite different from that of the medieval *étuve*. In the sixth century, Gregory of Tours mentioned a room for baths, heated by steam, where Theodoric's daughter was boiled to death. Later, in 973, Abraham Jacobsen, accompanying an embassy from the calif of Córdoba to Mersebourg, to the court of Otton I, speaks of steam baths enclosed in wooden huts, whose windows were stuffed with moss in order to keep in the heat and humidity. The procedure consisted of heating stones white-hot, then pouring water on them—the basic method of the steam bath.

The location of steam baths is interesting: the first ones appeared in the twelfth century and at the beginning of the thirteenth in cities under lay princes. The baths were next to the walls of the high Middle Ages, and adjoined the Jewish quarter, or at least the former site of that quarter after the Jews had been expelled by Philip Augustus in 1183.

Before the middle of the thirteenth century, baths are mentioned and their locations clearly indicated in Paris (1248), Provins (1236), and Troyes (1104), to which must be added Orléans and Sens, where the steam baths were classified as "old" at the beginning of the fourteenth century.[19] Unlike other baths built later, these baths had no immediate relationship with either commercial or artisanal functions, and would seem to have had nothing to do with urban development. They were established close to the court of the nobles and the Jewish quarter, and in Paris the earliest known steam baths were called *Judaeorum*.

We know that ritual bathing occupies an important place in the Jewish religion. Jews must wash before the daily study of the Law, and must bathe entirely before celebrating the Sabbath, and women must be "purified" after their menstrual period. "The public baths, to which was added the *mikveh*—women's bath—were maintained by Jewish communities as an integral part of the institutions of social life," stated Katan at the beginning of the nineteenth century, translating the precepts of Simliah de Vitry (twelfth century). Under these conditions, a community, if large enough, had to have bath facilities available not far from the Jewish quarter, and in the immediate vicinity of a source of running water, as required by *mikveh*. This is always the case of the first known steam baths. Elsewhere, in the middle of the twelfth century, Rabbi Joseph of Troyes, answering a question put to him, suggests that "it is not advisable for a Jew to hire out a bath or steamroom to a non-Jew . . . such establishments having traditionally been identified with the name or the nationality of their owners, and the public might get the false impression that the Jewish owners were using them on the Sabbath."[20] These Jewish baths were mentioned in Nîmes at the end of the tenth century, at Cologne in 1170, and in London in 1228.

Owners and users, Jews could thus be at the origin of the medieval steam bath. This would prove yet once more to what extent they fully participated in the creation of lucrative commercial activities in cities during the twelfth century. The development of urbanization, or the wishes of the ruling prince, would remove them from the city, more or less by force.

In the second half of the thirteenth century, baths flourished in those cities where service industries were predominant. Some had been repossessed from their Jewish owners; others were new creations located on the river banks. It would seem that collective hygiene was emerging, but in any event, it affected only a small part of society—namely, the aristocracy (the ritual bath of knights-to-be), and little by little the affluent bourgeoisie.

The rest of the population received only indirect benefits from this prophylactic equipage—namely, sewers, steam baths, and hospitals. To be sure, it is difficult to evaluate the domestic sanitary habits of city dwellers of the thirteenth century. We are reduced to looking for references here and there to "basins" and "tanks" in the wills of rich merchants, or else trying to find images of bathers in medieval works of art.

The spent water from household kitchens was emptied into the garden behind the house—or thrown right into the street when urban density had forced vegetable gardens out of the city limits. Individual latrines emptied into cesspools dug in back courtyards.[21] The ramparts and ditches of the high Middle Ages were equipped with "comfort stations" along the merdereau, reserved for the inhabitants of the surrounding neighborhood, the canons, rich merchants, and their people. Domestic wastes and fecal matter fed everybody's piglets and goslings, which were in fact the street cleaners of the times. Daily pollution in the thirteenth century was thus limited to animal excrement, and, from this point of view, the environment of the medieval city was a far cry from the nauseous picture that has been painted of it. Artisanal pollution was negligible, and even played a role in keeping the city clean.

Everything would suggest that the medieval city, in the period before the long crisis that was to shake the West, was a healthy-looking city. As regards underground pollution, especially pollution of the water table, the cemeteries attached to every urban church must, of course, be taken into account. But the determination of pathogenesis would depend on a knowledge of mortality rates and the types of disease the deceased had suffered. There is scanty information about the former; infant mortality was especially high. As for contagion and epidemics, we know that until the beginning of the fourteenth century, the West was not subject to serious, widespread, infectious diseases, except for leprosy, which authorities tried to isolate as early as the twelfth century. We can consider that microbial pollution of the water table was relatively minor in the thirteenth century, at least with respect to what it would be in the fourteenth and fifteenth; and malarial-type fevers do not develop in the absence of stagnant water. Well water, like river water, retained its pristine qualities: "the river is necessary and beneficial for humankind; it is used by all. It removes dirt from the body and from clothing, cools the overheated, and slakes the thirsty."[22]

Water flowed over the urban embodiment, marking it with its power. Water multiplied crafts and trades, turned the blades of the mill wheels, and altered the shape of the city. Dynamic water was the strength of the Middle Ages, which saw in cleanliness a symbol of wealth, reflected as much in its cultural values as in the minute care that artisans consecrated to their work, especially the weavers. If the reputation of the cloth of these cities spread as far as the Mediterranean, it was largely due to the quality of the city's water, which fixed the color or modified the texture of the cloth. Such rivers were the Thérain, the Robec, the Avre, the Mau, the Durtein, and the Tréffoir, which teemed with river crafts. The success of medieval "artisanalization" was in the water, and cities without calcium-rich waters had to turn to other types of activities if they wanted to develop. In Reims, the bishop solicited coopers, and encouraged the growing of flax and hemp, because the waters of the Vesle River were too silt-laden for the treatment of wool.

5

No-Man's-Land

Peace reigned in northern France until the first third of the fourteenth century. In the meantime, military technology was being hammered out on the battlefields of Languedoc and the outer reaches of Christianity.

In 1338, war surprised the kingdom, and would continue to rage for three centuries thereafter, until the Treaty of the Pyrenees in 1659. The city was threatened, besieged, pillaged, and little by little it closed in and retreated behind ramparts, which became thicker as poliorcetics made further advances. The shapely wall of the thirteenth-century ramparts came to be flanked with boulevards, bastions, buttresses, and ravelins. The moat was also modified, disproportionately widened; the result was a slowing of the kinetics of extraurban rivers. Local stagnation of water was thus begun.

The threat of war as much as the evolution of defense wiped out the suburbs, which were totally evacuated. In their place, little by little, a no-man's-land took shape, gorged with water, saturated with humidity, cutting the city off completely from its countryside.

Beginning of the Hundred Years' War

The thirteenth century was a century of peace, during which the ramparts played a role more political than strategic, more esthetic than functional. At the beginning of the fourteenth century, certain cities had not yet completed their fortifications, in particular in the marshy, thinly populated parts of the city where there were no gates and the unstable soil necessitated the building of ramparts on pilings. In Troyes, for example, the stone enclosure did not completely surround the city until the beginning of the fifteenth century. Before that time the defenses were constituted by an earth wall topped with fences and planking, especially to the southeast; but a continuous line of ditches, double in dry places, encircled the urban space to the north and east. In Reims, the new wall that was to join the city to the Saint-Rémi suburb was barely laid out at the beginning of the fourteenth century. Other cities, like Noyon and Soissons, which had financial problems that forced them to ask for help from the royal administration, had let their walls crumble into decay.[1]

In 1338 the hostilities declared by Edward III against Phillip IV immediately threatened the cities near the frontiers of the kingdom. They were hastily reinforced: the weakest parts of the ramparts were strengthened, and the religious establishments located on the outside approaches to the walls were also fortified. The battle of Crécy (1346), which gave the advantage to the English troops, accelerated work on urban defenses. Noyon restored its gates and drawbridges. Amiens extended its walls to include the suburbs. Rouen doubled the size of the Cauchoise gate to the north, and reinforced its wall on the Martainville side. Reims worked on its gates; palisades were put up at weak points, and the ramparts were improved with wooden hoardings and catapult towers. A second dry ditch enclosed the north of the city, as in Chartres and Troyes, so as to impede the approach of heavy battle machines. Beauvais, with the Craoul tower, indeed gave the appearance of the model fortress-city, according to John the Good.[2]

After a period of calm, due in part to the ravages of the Black Plague (1348–50), fighting began again in 1355 between John the Good and Edward III, allied with Charles the Bad. The annihilation of the French royal troops at Poitiers (1356) put the country into the hands of the Anglo-Navarrais troops. New fortifications were built to reinforce urban defenses. Troyes built two redoubts or *bertauches*. Noyon enlarged the width of its moat from eighteen to twenty-four meters. Sens diverted a part of the Mondereau River into the Saint Pregt suburb and detoured the springs of the Gravereau into ditches to the south of the city. Reims built up its wall between the Vesle gate and the mills of Saint Rémi along the river. Chartres decided to "reinforce the fortress of the said city and the surrounding country, where all the people come for refuge with their goods; thus diverse necessary repairs for the said fortress will be carried out, to put the city in a state of surety and defense."[3] The dry ditch was widened and deepened, and a third watercourse line—the New Ditch—was dug at the base of the ramparts between the Eure and the tenth-century ditches. Inside the walls, a nine-foot-wide road was laid out between the wall and the houses and gardens; and finally the main gates were supplied with artillery.

The cost of these renovations, shouldered by the communities, was covered by new city taxes levied by the king. A milling tax was put on grain to be converted into flour by the mills in Troyes and Reims; a tax was put on incoming wine and wheat in Chartres; there was a sales tax on furniture in Amiens, to which was sometimes added a tax on revenue from fishing in ditches conceded by the king. These new financial burdens accentuated the impoverishment resulting from a state of economic crisis rampant since the beginning of the century. The taxes would increase, following progress in arms and ballistics, which required thicker and thicker ramparts. Large-scale works were, for the most part, carried out by city residents, and to a lesser extent by rural inhabitants living within a radius of three to four leagues around the city; in exchange for service, these latter could take refuge within the city in case of attack.

This period was also marked by the first destruction of buildings on the far city limits. Defense was no longer simply a matter of reinforcing walls and ditches, but also of razing everything that could ease the approach and sustenance of attackers and their artillery: even if gunpowder did not always have the deadly effects claimed for it, other kinds of war machines, such as springalds, catapult machines moved by mechanical tension, were in fact very effective, perhaps even more redoubtable. Proof was the taking of Amiens by Charles the Bad in 1358 when a number of houses were destroyed on both sides of the walls. These "engines" had an effective range of two hundred meters. Defensive strategy, which until then had been satisfied with protecting the city wall with one or two moats, was now obliged to go much farther out from the wall and eliminate anything that could serve as shelter for the enemy. Religious establishments in the outlying suburbs, standing on hills or along major roads, were the first to go.[4]

Thus a wide empty space was dug around the cities, which would grow even wider as arms techniques developed. The walls were reinforced, the ditches were deepened and enlarged, and with the closing of the main gates, the city girded itself with an ecological barrier, a form of insulation that encouraged periodic epidemics.

From 1370 until 1400, restoration of defenses practically ceased in the cities. The king was in the meantime taking and using for his own interests the revenues from the different taxes levied for upkeep of fortifications, such as the sword tax and the hearth tax, levied in 1363 by John the Good and applied by Charles V the following year to all the communities in proportion to the number of homes they contained.

Adapting Defenses to New Arms

A resurgence in city fortification occurred again at the beginning of the fifteenth century, in 1404, when the truce between France and England

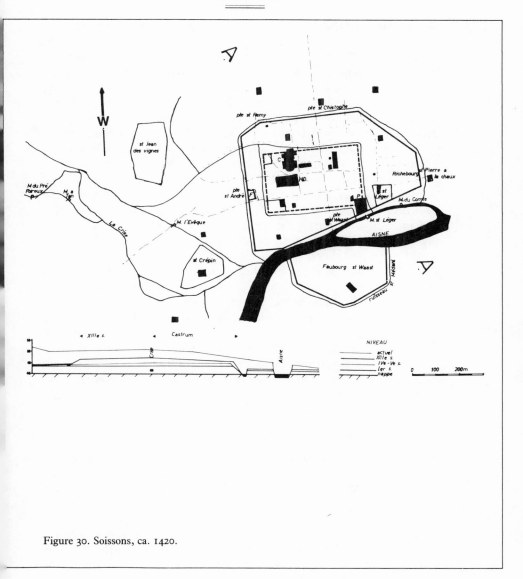

Figure 30. Soissons, ca. 1420.

was broken. Fear of attack led the municipalities to protect themselves as quickly as possible by undertaking reinforcements. The ramparts were enlarged along the Yonne River in Auxerre. Behind the Robec in Rouen, between the Martainville and the Columbier gates, a long wall, furnished with small towers, was built on pilings in the marsh, to expedite warnings of attacks coming from the river. It was the fourth and last enclosure, and it took in the Saint-Nicaise and Saint-Hilaire suburbs. The city thus increased its surface area by 15 percent. Enlarging the enclosure was not motivated by desire to protect these highly urbanized neighborhoods, but came rather from the necessity of having orchards and pastures within the walls, to provide for cattle and thus for the subsistence of the population during a siege.[5] In order to prevent the dispersion of defenders and the multiplication of weak points in the wall, certain gates were permanently closed and walled up: four in Amiens in 1412, two in Beauvais, two in Senlis in 1411. Certain towers were lowered in order to be equipped with a new artillery device, the bombard.[6] Troyes finished digging ditches to the north and east of the city; they were twenty to twenty-five meters deep, forty meters wide, and brought water from the Seine through the Croncels lock to the Preize gate lock over a distance of nearly one and a half kilometers; nearly one million cubic meters of earth were excavated.

At the beginning of the fifteenth century, it was imperative for defense strategies to adapt to the progress being made in firearms. The high ramparts built in the twelfth century and reinforced in the fourteenth were now ineffective and too fragile. Their thickness was no longer sufficient protection against the force of artillery; the path on top was not wide enough to accommodate the recoil of the cannons used for defense; their shape made it too difficult to position heavy machines on them. As early as 1415, most cities had two or three bombards placed at the gates, the weakest point in the city walls.[7] But the efforts at defense were insufficient: the civil war touched off by the assassination of Louis of Orléans (1407) subjected these cities to sieges.

Soissons is an example. In 1411 the municipality sided with the duke of Burgundy, but the bailiff remained loyal to the king. So the stronghold of le Chatel was besieged by the Burgundians, who attacked its entrance with cannon. The Maître-Odon gate and three towers were peppered, without much damage, but the garrison nonetheless surrendered after three months. The conquered city was made subject to the duke, and like Noyon and Compiègne, was given all the latest innovations in defense. The old walls were repaired and strengthened. The enclosure was widened in several places. The suburbs were all razed, as were the remainders of the Albâtre castle, a monument dating from the Roman era. To the southwest, the Saint-Jean Abbey managed to escape destruction; the monks, to defend their monastery, had taken the initiative of surrounding it with ditches, fortified ramparts, and towers. In contrast, the Franciscans, who had been located at the Saint-André gate since 1235, took refuge inside the city in the former synagogue; their friary was razed in 1414. The new ramparts enclosed three churches whose approaches were fortified with bastions. The ditches, in part fed by the Crise River, were extended to the west and widened.

These works, finished in less than a year, made Soissons a stronghold capable of withstanding any attack—or so it was thought. In spite of this—or perhaps because of it—Charles VI decided to reconquer the city in 1416. As a precautionary measure, the governor of Soissons, Louis de Bournonville, had the last remaining buildings in the suburbs razed; all large trees that might hide the enemy were chopped down, and the wood used to reinforce the city gates. Then fires were lit to prevent surprise attacks (at night). The king, arriving from Compiègne, reached the Saint-Jean Abbey in front of the city on May 10. The abbey, isolated from the city by two hundred meters of flat terrain intersected by a double line of ditches and poorly fortified in spite of what the abbot had promised, offered no resistance, and surrendered to the royal troops. The city decided to resist. The king, camped in the abbey, battered the rampart between the Saint-Rémi and Saint-André gates, and a breach was opened. On the northern side, the projecting rampart was also bombarded. The city, though it had some ten cannon and other artillery, was not able to hold the breaches, and was thus taken. Several hundred citizens were raped, decapitated, or hanged. Many of the houses were put to the torch. The churches of Saint-Victor and Saint-Pierre-à-la-Chaux were destroyed, and the other churches were heavily damaged.[8] The city would only just begin to recover from this catastrophe at the beginning of the sixteenth century, nearly a hundred years later.

It was especially after the Peace of Arras that Duke Jean, in control of the kingdom to the north of the Loire, organized the systematic defense of his cities and had them fitted out with the latest in strategic equipment: bastions, curtains (the part of a bastioned front that connected two neighboring bastions), cavaliers (a fortified structure usually rising from the middle of a bastion), and ravelins (two embankments forming a salient angle in front of the curtain of a fortified position).[9] The defensive ditch was neglected, and it was on this weak point that the attacks on Senlis, Evreaux, and Rouen turned; they were all taken by King Henry V of England in 1418.[10] The theoretically impregnable city was thus obliged to provide itself with a line of trenches sufficiently wide and deep to prevent undermining and attacks at the front of its ramparts; it also became indispensable for the city to maintain clear visibility through its suburbs. These exigencies shaped the new works to be carried out. From the time of the assassination of John the Fearless at Montereau in 1419, under threat of more serious hostilities, the city hastened to modify its immediate surroundings.

Protecting the Moats

Beauvais leveled its suburbs to a distance of three hundred meters.[11] Troyes sacrificed the largest part of the Croncels suburb; the Croncels and tannery mills, along with nearly four hundred houses, were all destroyed. A third ditch was cut between the Vienne and the old ditch to the south of the city. Noyon demolished the church belonging to the public hospital, built in 1176, in order to erect a platform in its place, and to improve the ditch in front of the Cocquerel tower. Evreux finished enclosing the inner city within walls. A *batardeau* (a wall built across a fortification ditch, with a sluice gate to regulate the water level) was constructed near the Planche mill, and two others were built at the foot of the towers in order to prevent the enemy from taking them and cutting off the water supply for the moat. Amiens worked on its riverbanks to bolster its isolation; a canal was cut on the side of the Duriame bridge in order to bring water into the city; the Cange bridge was rebuilt in stone, and fortified. Rouen, promoted to the role of Continental capital for the English king, built his palace downstream from the city. This key fortress, with walls four and a half meters thick at the base, dominated the mouth of the Seine with four towers, twenty meters wide and fourteen meters high.

The overhauling of the extraurban ditches and canals allowed the cities to successfully ensure their defense, faced with the sieges led by Charles the Reckless in 1471–72. In Beauvais, the duke attacked the city from the northwest. He captured the Saint-Hippolyte church, but the beleaguered defenders succeeded in setting fire to it. Charles, installed in the Saint-Quentin quarter near the Saint-Nicolas church, then tried to dig a tunnel under the approaches to the city. But the terrain was too spongy. Next it was decided to drain the moat under the ramparts. "The Burgundians broke two or three sluice gates on the Thérain River, about a half league from the city, in order to cause the river to lose its water or divert its course, and so dry out the ditches of the city, which are always kept full by means of the said river."[12] But the attempt was in vain: the current of the Thérain was too strong. And the ramparts were difficult to reach: the gate of the Hôtel-Dieu to the north was protected by the bastion of the Gré tower. The section of the ramparts that opened onto the Bassett suburb was protected by a large tower fitted squarely across the moat of the ramparts; and this tower contained

dées qu'on ne les puisse desmonter.

Cap. Il est bien vray qu'il n'y a nulle batterie qui soit exem-
pte de ce danger. mais entre toutes il n'y en a aucune qui en
soit plus asseurée, comme on peut remarquer en la figure.

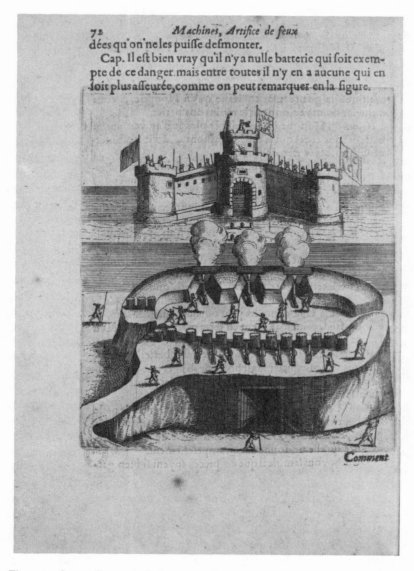

Figure 31. Cannon Battery in Action along a Waterway (J. Appier, *La Pyrotechnie*,
Paris, 1630). Reproduction courtesy Bibliotèque Nationale, Paris.

works to hold back the waters of the northern ditch, probably built in the middle of the century. From the Madame tower to the Bresles gate a long stretch of water and a marsh protected the city. In 1451 it had been decided to destroy the Saint-André mill and build a new one closer to the inner city. The aim was twofold: to provide the city with a mill for grinding flour in case of siege, and to protect with an aquatic barrier the extramural city. Finally, from the Bresles gate to the hospital, the land had been cleared several years earlier in order to widen the "Abyss," a ditch about ten meters deep and some fifty to sixty meters wide, cut in the tenth century. At the end of the siege, the stone and earthen ramparts were in ruins. It was a powerful coursing of water, as much as the courage of the inhabitants, that saved Beauvais and Amiens from the Burgundians. It was also the water around the walls, coming from the Verse and Goële, that turned them away from Noyon in 1472.[13]

The Defense Policies of Louis XI

The important role played by water in the defense of cities did not go unnoticed by Louis XI, after the defeat of Charles of Burgundy. He used all his energy, after that, to raise ramparts and innovate defensive structures in terms of military hydraulics. Thus, in Amiens, the count of Dammartin, sent there shortly after the siege, had the boulevard of the Montrescu gate built, along with three locks to hold the water at its most vulnerable points. The main bridges were fortified and surrounded with deep moats; the ditches were recut and widened by about fifty meters. More than seventy-two hundred pounds were spent on these fortifications.

Beauvais also arose from its ruins. There was even a plan to build a new, more defensive, hydraulic network, which would increase the expanse of the waters at the base of the ramparts and reduce the width of the Merdançon. But the projected costs and the opposition of the master of fortresses put an end to this proposal.[14] Instead, the ditches of the Craoul tower were widened. Three years later, in 1476, Louis XI decided to fortify the Bresles gate, which was fitted with a demilune and a moat with perpendicular sides, thirty meters wide, over which a stationary bridge with four arches was put in place. Finally, the Boileau tower, which dominated the mouth of the Avelon, was built according to the latest specifications of military art: two stories high, ten meters wide, with crenels intended for cannon muzzles, it was approached over the Thérain River by a wide boulevard flanking the Paris gate and its mills.[15] The riverbed was enlarged upstream. The entire fortress was complete in 1489.

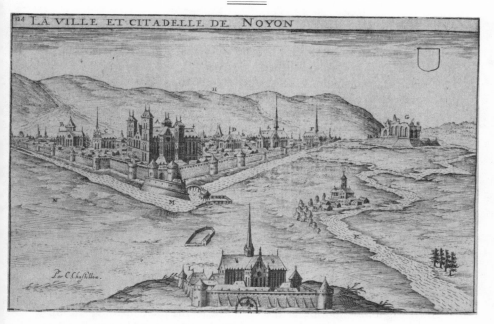

Figure 32. City and Citadel of Noyon, Mid-Seventeenth Century. G = Saint-Eloi and the citadel of King Henry IV. K = the Verse River. Reproduction courtesy Bibliotèque Nationale, Paris.

In Noyon, the ditches were modified in 1475 as the English were debarking at Calais. Louis XI ordered the building of the "enclosure of Monsieur Saint-Eloy-de-Noion, with ditches, walls, and other appurtenances, and likewise the dredging, widening, and deepening of the ditch between the Wez gate and the Cocquerel tower and others." Stonemasons from the Limousin and March regions, 370 in number, were hired to hasten the defenses.[16] In Reims, the king ordered the "dredging and deepening of the ditches as high as two men, with straight sides and in such a fashion as to be secure and out of reach of attack."[17] In Chartres he asked the city to enlarge the wall by deepening the dry ditches[18]—excavations from the latter were used to build up the former. In Orléans, a third enclosure was built between 1472 and 1490 to include the western and northern suburbs; it was endowed with thirty large towers and a ditch forty meters wide.[19]

Everywhere defensive measures were taken so as to withstand attack. The bases of ramparts were enlarged, and walls were lowered; a clear line of fire was provided for cannon across what had been suburbs. The enlargement of the ramparts used earth provided by the widening of ditches. In front of the ditches, what was left of the landfill was used to form a protective mound. The ideal ditch, fifteen to forty meters wide and three meters deep, had perpendicular sides and was preferably filled with water, controlled by valves.

The policy of aquatic defenses was abandoned after Louis XI, whose admiration for the Republic of Venice was well known. But the consequences of widening and deepening the ditches, begun in the middle of the fourteenth century, irreversibly marked the urban hydraulic network. Indeed, although the extension of the moats offered better protection for the walls, it also dissipated part of the hydraulic kinetic energy intended for the feeding of industrial canals within the walls.

Assuming that the length of the ditches remained unchanged and that the section of moat with water in it increased from ten square meters to seventy square meters on the average, then the capacity of these reservoirs increased, in less than a century, from 20,000 to 140,000 cubic meters in Noyon, Senlis, and Chartres, and from 35,000 to 250,000 cubic meters in Beauvais, Amiens, and Châlons. The new ditches in Rouen and Troyes must have held more than 100,000 cubic meters. Under these conditions, the current of the extraurban rivers slowed down to almost nothing at the entrance to the city, flooding the upstream suburbs, in the absence of more steeply sloped canals allowing the water to be carried downstream. The capacity of the ditches was continually enlarged with the rebuilding of fortifications, thus leading to the development of an extraurban filiform network.

By weakening the current upstream from the city, the "reservoir" effect of the ditches most certainly helped to absorb the spring floods, which the cities did not yet know how to control, but it also increased the amount of stagnant water in the city.[20] Thus, intramural humidity was increased, which would contribute to an increase in the production of saltpeter; Louis XI was the first to organize systematic experiments with this substance, beginning in 1477.

The sieges of Charles the Reckless had also made it clear that the model of fortifications inherited from the second feudal age entailed weaknesses in terms of defense, and uselessness, even danger, when fortifications crumbled inside the city. Louis XI took advantage of the situation: the old ramparts had to be pulled down, what was left of the late-empire ditches had to be filled in, and then the whole thing had to be rebuilt. This would in effect reduce the budget deficit of those cities heavily burdened by war. The ditch of the *castrum* of Senlis, and perhaps that of Soissons, thus disappeared between 1472 and 1478. In Beauvais the opposition of the captain of the city prevented its destruction, but in Amiens true urban renewal took place, between 1477 and

1483, in spite of the opposition of the municipality. The old ditches, filled in with the ruins of the wall, gave way to systemitized constructions "for the good, the adornment, the increase, and profit of the city."[21]

With Louis XI, the city left the Middle Ages once and for all. A new type of society was emerging, which, on the technological level, would abandon running water to replace it with stagnant, and would turn to the subterranean world in the search for the metals necessary for weaponry. This would bring about the isolation of the city behind its large ramparts and water-filled moats.

Zones *Non Aedificandi*

The policy of conquest led by Charles VIII in Italy provided a reprieve for the defense of the cities of the kingdom. But the crushing defeats inflicted on him in Italy demonstrated the advance of Italian poliorcetics—the art of siege warfare. Louis XII, Francis I, and Henry II made efforts to introduce these advances in France. The tower-centered defense strategy came into general use—the Boileau tower in Beauvais, the Bigot in Rouen, the Belle in Reims.[22] Wooden constructions on unstable terrain were replaced by massive works that controlled the entrance to the canals.[23] The boulevard adopted by Louis XI came into general use with Francis I, and was paved over with stone, on which cannon balls could ricochet. Arms continued to develop in power and destructive capacity. The feasibility of cannons no longer had to be demonstrated. Their number increased considerably throughout the first half of the sixteenth century, to such a point that Francis II standardized them in 1559 (the six-caliber French model). Defense bowed to the requirements of the times and weak points were reinforced according to Italian military art.[24] The first wave of Italian military engineers arrived in France: Bellenavo worked in Orléans in 1512; Francesque proposed various improvements for Amiens in 1519. But the major modifications in urban defense were carried out by the second generation of Italian engineers, who followed the teachings of Sanmicheli— even if only partially—on the borders of the Pontifical States.[25] Spurs, pentagonal bastions, and counterscarps made their appearance in the urban landscape. The main gates received a terrace surrounded with ditches. The approaches to the cities became huge building sites where the poor and beggars were obliged to come work for a handful of bread.[26] The cost of these renovations exhausted the community treasuries; more than thirty thousand pounds at Senlis in 1545, more than two hundred thousand in Amiens.[27]

The landfill evacuated from the ditches was used to strengthen the base of the ramparts, which was their weakest part. After the middle of the fourteenth century, gravel from the demolition of buildings was also added. Bombardments were not the only cause of ruins: the drop in population resulting from plagues left numerous dwellings abandoned, and the slightest rumor of an epidemic often persuaded municipal authorities to burn an entire part of the city. In addition, new constructions in stone were little by little substituted for wattle and daub buildings thrown up during periods of economic depression.[28]

To the rubble deposited on the outside of the ramparts was also added a daily amount of filth of all sorts,[29] because war had made the outskirts of the city unsafe. As early as 1408 the Longuemaisière gate in Amiens was "almost stopped up by the garbage and sweepings that were thrown there outside the city," and a new gate had to be opened in the walls in order to solve the problem.[30] At the end of the fifteenth century the garbage in Laon was transported to the "gullies" of the city, on slopes.[31] In Rouen, in the middle of the sixteenth century, the wide extramural ditches had been so filled in that the enemy could simply cross them on foot to enter the city.[32] Among the debris, there was much human and animal excrement.[33] It was common for residents to "relieve themselves" on top of the city walls, or on the edge of the moat, individually or in groups.[34] Military science recommended as well that latrines be built.[35]

The fortifications of a city were a sign of its opulence and power; in the same way, the filth deposited on the ramparts, visible from outside the city, was a sign of its stench.

The city was more and more isolated and separated. First the enlargement of the walls had necessitated the destruction of all the edifices near the ramparts. A pathway separated the inhabited space from the wall by a distance of about ten meters. Beyond, the moat and its counterscarp had pushed the extraurban space out some hundred meters or so. It was this strip of land, frozen into place for defense use, that would be used in the eighteenth and nineteenth centuries for the construction of peripheral boulevards and railroads. Moreover, secondary gates had been eliminated, and in front of the main entrances platforms had been installed. Finally, the almost permanent state of war had called for the definitive destruction of extramural buildings in a 500-meter radius around the city. Building materials were retrieved for the restoration of the ramparts—cut stone was very expensive.[36] Anything built in the suburbs was, therefore, intended only for temporary existence. The only thing built outside the city gates during truces were wooden shacks where diverse sorts of commerce were carried on, or where drinking and prostitution took place.[37]

The extraurban space had been deserted. All that was left were water-saturated fields and meadows where flax and hemp were planted. The ditches, when dry, were used to pasture cattle; very early on, gardens crept over the slopes and false ditches.[38]

The continuous fabric of houses, which had linked the city with the surrounding country, crossing over the walls, had disappeared and a *non aedificandi* zone now served as a buffer between urban and rural space.

Henry IV's Defenses

The wars of religion that raged throughout the second half of the six-teenth century were to accentuate even more the ruin of the extraurban countryside. The cities walled up their gates, leaving only two or three well-guarded openings protected by wide platforms.[39] The cities of the Paris basin did not accept the Protestant Reformation, and Huguenots were minorities there.[40] The accession of Huguenot Henry IV to the throne rallied them around the Duke de Guise, and Spanish troops sup-ported them from the Low Countries. In order to establish his sover-eignty, the king of Navarre (Henry IV) thus had to defeat, one by one, the cities leagued against him; from 1589 to 1596 most of them were put to siege.[41]

The tactics of Henry IV and his strategists, like Errard de Bar-le-Duc, who planned the siege of Amiens, was to surround a city, ap-proach its ramparts through the trenches, and then open a breach with as many and the most powerful weapons available, as much to frighten by noise as to destroy.[42] The rupture of the wall, which then crumbled into the moat, and the use of fagots (to fill in ditches) eased the assault by footsoldiers.[43] The defeat of these cities was due, in part at least, to the insufficient width of the moats.

A victorious Henry IV was anxious to protect his presence right up to the gates of the cities he had conquered. He imposed on them the construction of citadels on the walls. The one in Noyon was built be-tween 1591 and 1593 on the site of the former Saint Eloi Abbey, which had been razed, along with about a hundred houses; that of Chartres in 1591 near the Drouaise gate. In Amiens the king had the first rectangu-lar citadel built in front of the Montrescu gate to the southwest. But in 1598 he chose the north of the city. The church of Saint-Sulpice, the Hôtel de Bolly, two mills, and more than five hundred houses were razed on an area of nearly twenty-five hectares. This citadel, equipped with five bastions, took on a pentagonal shape. Each bastion bore a title to the glory of the king.[44] This toponomy was meant to reinforce a new ideological order, as were the coins minted with the bust of the king—to consolidate his absolute power.

It would seem that political reasons alone did not determine the site of the citadel. All fortresses were built inside the existing hydrographic network, the level of which was raised by using the ruins of demolished buildings. In places, more than four cubic meters of landfill were brought in. Water seems to have dictated the strategy of Henry IV, just as it dominated his transportation policy.[45] Water remained indispensable to defense: spread out in marshes, it hindered approaching cavalry; its stillness and horizontality lowered the relief of the landscape (thus eliminating hiding places), and allowed watchers to spot the enemy farther and farther away, especially when the height of the citadel or watchtower was raised a few meters. During the last quarter of the sixteenth century, a reduction in the extraurban relief transformed it from variegated and natural to monomorphic and flat. Mount Saint-Simeon in Noyon, Mount Saint-Symphorien in Beauvais, and the Saint-Jean hill in Soissons were all razed; trees were chopped down and the earth was used to fill in terraces around the gates.[46] The extramural part of the city dissolved into the huge swarm of water of the ditches and moats, out of which rose the imposing mass of the ramparts, more significant than ever.

Defense strategy included a high degree of ground saturation around the city, to prevent the digging of trenches. This, at least, was the opinion of strategists of the time[47] and of Henry IV, who had ditches widened.[48] Any large-scale movement of water was blocked; downstream outlets were blocked by the construction of heavy *batardeaux*.[49] The filiform canal network, which had been slowly developing since the middle of the fifteenth century around the cities and was used for the bleaching of cloth, now had another raison d'être. This hydraulic framework, added to the huge ditches continuously being recut or widened, absorbed the current of smaller rivers and considerably reduced that of average-sized ones. The stagnating water around the city brought with it a permanent state of high humidity.

The city of the beginning of the seventeenth century thus appeared "isolated" and cut off from the countryside, which it overlooked from the imposing mass of its sloping earthen ramparts, equipped with cavaliers and buttresses, and surrounded by immense moats. This topographical and social urban pattern would continue until the beginning of the nineteenth century.

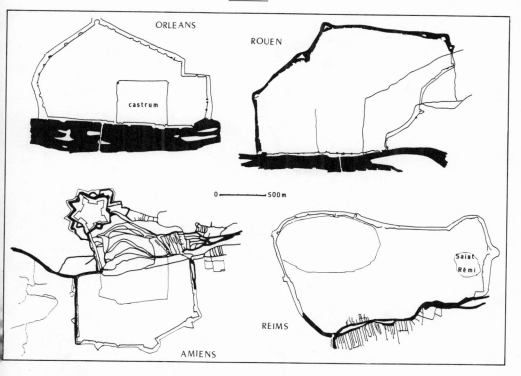

Figure 33. Urban Fortifications, ca. 1650.

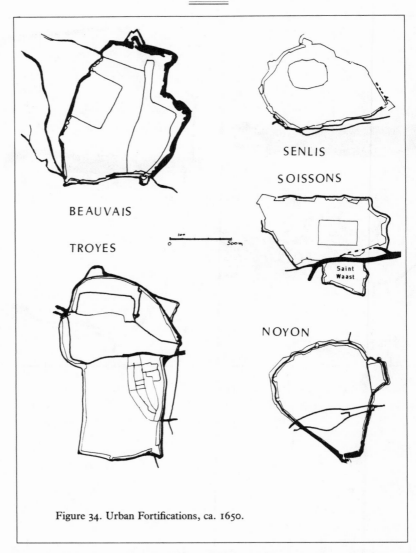

Figure 34. Urban Fortifications, ca. 1650.

As early as 1600, fortification building slackened off, or was transferred to the frontiers of the kingdom. However, with the Spanish
threat (1636) and the Fronde, danger of invasion continued, which
would not be definitively removed until the Treaty of the Pyrenees
(1659).[50] It was not safe in the outskirts of the city; thus demolished
monasteries and abbeys were reconstructed within the walls. The city
of the Counter-Reformation also gathered within its walls new religious

orders, which wanted to protect themselves from possible devastations outside the city. After 1659, with the exception of Amiens and Soissons, which remained fortresses, the cities gradually abandoned their ramparts, looking for ways to turn a profit from them, and thus to take some of the pressure off city treasuries. Certain cities succeeded in dismantling the citadels that Henry IV had placed on their main gates.

By bringing about the destruction of churches and monasteries in extraurban districts, the permanent state of war had desacralized the outskirts of the city. But, inversely, the movement of religious to the interior of the walls had accentuated the religious character of the big cities. Fear, exacerbated by the threat of war or plague, continuing unabated throughout this entire period, was moderated by the presence of the religious orders. They kept vigil, prayed, chanted, and led long processions that threaded through the streets on feast days. The more imminent the danger, the more a sense of religion enveloped the city. It was a question, at one and the same time, of imploring divine mercy in order to remain among the living, and of preparing for death, which could decimate in a few months up to half of a city's population. The city sanctified itself in proportion to the disappearance of the living and the consequent slowing of urbanization.

In other words, in the fourteenth, fifteenth, and sixteenth centuries, urban religiousness grew with "de-urbanization"—that is, with depopulation, corrosion of the built-up frame of the city, and the widening of ramparts. But in spite of this, urbanity remained a permanent fixture of this society, from all points of view: economic, political, and cultural. What did change was urbanization, which declined, and urban religiousness, which increased—both factors enmeshed in urbanity, itself unchanged.

By dwelling on these details of wall construction, I have wanted to show the slow, step-by-step evolution of the outlying area of cities. The continuous expansion of fortifications had brought about the isolation of the city, curled up behind a dense curtain several dozen meters wide (anywhere from 30 to 100 meters) through which hardly any noise filtered. An ecological barrier had been created, proof of which were the deposits of filth and rubble that did not extend beyond the limit of the moats. The ditch constituted the first line of defense, and it was enlarged only when defenders had suffered defeats. Weakened defenses were readapted to attack in the same way: adding on to the ramparts, then recutting the ditches, whose waterlogged soil strategists considered to be the best material for reinforcing the walls.

Enlargement of the ramparts, excavations of the ditch, cutting and filling in: such were the defensive dialectics that had transformed the outskirts of the city into an immense reservoir, to which was added the filiform network of the innumerable canals traced in the nearly uninhabited valley. The suburban rivers, which had been so dynamic in the twelfth and thirteenth centuries, were swallowed up, three centuries later, in a stagnant, static, extraurban abyss, regaining their velocity only downstream from the city. Thus, in the fifteenth century, an extremely cloudy microclimate—a "moist shield"—formed around and over the city. It would not disappear until the middle of the nineteenth century.[51] In addition, the stagnant water promoted the proliferation of mosquitoes and, in consequence, intermittent fevers, a factor of miscarriage. Water saturation also encouraged pulmonary diseases. The topographical term *assiette* (here meaning "soup bowl") is a good figure for representing the city: upper and lower in opposition.[52]

The relative passivity of cities has been repeatedly noted with respect to the size of the defense works to be carried out. City budgets were not large enough to permit them, and it was through concessions—even through force—that the king meddled more and more in city affairs, sending his engineers and fortification surveyors, organized first by Louis XI then by Sully. In this way, as early as the middle of the sixteenth century, the power of the wall no longer reflected that of the community, but the glory of the king: his blazon was on the gates, and the bastions proclaimed his victories. The new walls, like the royal taxes, sounded the death knell for feudalism and presaged the emergence of the state.

6

Pervasive Moisture

The long period beginning in the fourteenth century and ending with the eighteenth was, with the exception of the sixteenth century, a period of demographic decline. Reduction in artisanal activity and commerce brought the Western city to the antechamber of death. Medieval urbanization had brought to perfection an intramural hydraulic network, equipping it with watermills and workshops; its dynamism was impressive. The city of the fourteenth to the seventeenth century was satisfied with it, neither changing its direction nor developing its potential. The city preserved the intramural energy patrimony inherited from the Middle Ages but, devastated by incessant warfare, it lost most of its mills. Stagnation, to the point of energy recession, gripped the city in a permanent state of underdevelopment.

Innovation, however, did not stand still. The fourteenth century invented gunpowder, the fifteenth printing, and the sixteenth perfected these new techniques and developed other, older ones, like linen and leather manufacturing, to the detriment of the woolen industry, which had brought wealth to the medieval cities. The majority of the urban industries faced the same technical exigencies: high humidity (hence slow circulation of water and air), long maceration of basic products, and putrefaction. These interdependent exigencies called for stagnant water. The exploitation of water, the basis of urban economies, was appreciably transformed; the city of the Ancien Régime no longer exploited the dynamics of water, which had been fully utilized by the watermills, but rather stagnation and nebulosity.

The state of war, a permanent fact throughout this period, can be considered the principal impetus behind the technical developments of the Renaissance. In order to provide for defense, city ditches were enlarged to exceptional dimensions. The stagnant water of the moats surrounded the city, forcing it to keep all its waste within the walls, and enveloping it in a cloud of moisture. This microclimate favored the manufacture of saltpeter, vital for the kingdom. War, again indirectly, by imposing the blockage of rivers upstream of the city, contributed to the flourishing hemp and linen industries, set up on the network of diversion drains to prevent floods.

But war does not explain everything, such as the development of the paper-related industries and leatherworking, both of which involved putrefaction. Nor does it explain the raising of street levels and the deposits of waste inside the city even in times of peace. Another, more general, factor, of a long-term nature, must be taken into account: mentality.

The humidity that soaked the city during this time was also the result of a fall in temperatures and an increase in rainfall, which affected the entire northern hemisphere from the middle of the thirteenth century on. This cooling spell of about one degree Centigrade affected agriculture; cereal harvests fell, resulting in the grain crises of 1304–1305, 1314–15, and 1345–47. Freshwater fishing was also affected; its yields decreased on the order of 12 to 18 percent.[1] The laws of 1289, 1291, 1293, 1317, 1319, and 1326, regulating the meshes of fishnets and the protection of species, were unable to stop the dwindling yields. The consumption of fish, which made up more than a third of the diet, decreased 15 to 20 percent on the average between 1200 and 1300. This was a serious loss. At the beginning of the fourteenth century it certainly aggravated undernourishment among the lower classes, and assuredly played a role in the extraordinary mortality rate that struck Europe in 1348–49 in the form of the Black Plague. The cold and humid climate, which lasted for more than five hundred years, also had an influence on international relationships. Plagues, dynastic wars, and new discoveries in what could be called the "fungous" economy that governed the city from the fourteenth century to the middle of the eighteenth were directly linked to this climactic factor. A new mentality emerged. It was fascinated by the "excremental" and filled with fear of the day-to-day, which the state of war only augmented.

Changes Brought on by Warfare
Manufacture of Saltpeter

Saltpeter, or "salt of stone" (Latin, *sal petrae*), is a mixture of nitrates, which would be synthetically produced in the nineteenth century. It was the primary component of gunpowder, thus a fundamental substance for warfare, once iron cannonry had given place to bronze weaponry and the harquebus had made its appearance in the fourteenth and fifteenth centuries. The harquebus became widespread after the battle of Pavie (1525), under the impetus of Francis I and Francis II. These two French kings organized a corps of *saltpetriers,* whose job it was to comb the kingdom and collect the precious material, "expressly charging all persons, whatever their quality, to open their doors and let the said *saltpetriers* have access to their houses, basements, cellars, and the walls of their houses, and not to prevent them from taking and carrying away the saltpeter crusts."[2] These kings required their "good cities" to make heavy saltpeter contributions: four thousand pounds per year for Beauvais in 1538 and Senlis in 1542, six thousand pounds for Troyes in 1551, eight thousand for Chartres in 1541—in other words, approximately one pound of saltpeter per household.

Gunpowder was known in the West as early as the second half of the thirteenth century, but it was only in the fourteenth that its manufacture was perfected, to remain unchanged until the nineteenth. The formula given by La Framboisière (1613) is clear: "Natural niter is no longer available. In its place, saltpeter is now used, which is to be found on old walls, among rocks and stones. This putrified earth is saturated with animal urine, mixed with water, and run through a boiled cloth, after which it thickens and is fixed."[3] Approximately one hundred thirty tons of earth were necessary to produce one ton of saltpeter. In other words, in the middle of the sixteenth century, Beauvais and Senlis, to meet the needs of the king, had to excavate some two hundred sixty tons of earth per year; Chartres, twice as much.

Saltpeter mines were thus created in humid places subjected to the putrefaction of excrement: stables, basements located near ditches used for human waste, the rubble and debris from demolitions. The city, and especially the lower city, more humid and more densely populated, became the principal saltpeter quarry; to ensure production, a powder mill was installed there. The cannon potential of the state thus depended on the cities, more precisely on the putrefaction of the urban underground. Inasmuch as the production of saltpeter was proportional to the density of habitation and underground humidity, it must be supposed that the municipalities, responsible to the King for this production, had to maintain the state of putrefaction in their cities. An act dated 1777 is eloquent: "Everything that tends to accelerate putrefaction, also tends equally to accelerate the production of saltpeter."[4] The deposits of garbage and dirt in the streets and in front of the fortified gates and piles of mud along the banks of waterways also bear witness to this.[5] It is even probable that the owners of basements or courtyards in marshy neighborhoods made some money by selling these "salts of the earth."[6] The Convention of the French Revolution would permit everyone to use "this means of making a profit from his property."

Saltpeter, stocked in the royal or municipal arsenals, was subject to the vagaries of supply and demand, especially at times when war broke out. Periods of noncombat and the demolition of old walls or buildings helped to reduce a gunpowder deficit.[7] By the same logic, the conservation of a stock of ruins within the city or on its limits—that is to say, the maintenance of an excess of strategic raw material, so to speak—turned out to be of prime necessity, notably for cities close to combat zones, as long as transportation networks remained underdeveloped.

Until the beginning of the nineteenth century, the city was thus the primary producer of saltpeter. Its production was furthered by everything that the crafts and small industries could not use in their production methods: debris, excrement, dirt. Deposits of garbage along the ramparts or in the streets, or even the presence of old buildings, became useful by helping cities to maintain defensive self-sufficiency in case of a siege, and by ensuring the kingdom its independence, to a certain extent. The state of war encouraged the "putrefaction" of the city.

Demolishing the Mills

Protection of the outskirts of the city decreed the demolition of mills capable of facilitating enemy penetration. The first mills to be knocked down were the ones built over the thirteenth-century ditches, which hindered water stagnation, like the Fossés mills in Noyon and Evreux, the Saint André and Saint Laurent in Beauvais, the Croncels, Tannerie, and Monts in Troyes: all were destroyed in the first half of the fifteenth century. Only the Saint André mill was rebuilt within the walls on the Thérinet (1451). Some of the others were reconstructed over nonstagnant ditches, once peace had been restored—the Croncels (1424) and Sancey (1477) in Troyes—but most of them were replaced by windmills or hand-operated mills, which were easier to build and less costly. The Moulin Neuf (new mill), which replaced the Saint André mill in Beauvais, cost a thousand pounds; the windmills in Troyes cost from six to sixteen pounds each in 1523. Windmills, less reliable than watermills, were built on platforms: Chartres had seven of them in 1553, Troyes had five in 1565, whereas the number of watermills had diminished by three.

To the destruction caused by defense must be added the harm done by attack, which deprived the besieged of their flour: the Mareshal mill in Evreux was destroyed by the English in 1418, the Choc mill in Rouen was set on fire in 1374 and again in 1418, the Courcelles in Noyon in 1552. Henry IV had two mills razed in Amiens, two in Senlis, one in Rouen, one in Noyon, and one in Chartres; the Allard mill in Beauvais owed its survival to the intervention of the cathedral chapter. Decrease in population and a decline in cereal production also contributed to reducing the number of flour mills, some of which were converted into mills for weaving or for grinding other products. But it was not just cereal fluctuations, analyzed by Guy Bois, that brought about these transformations or abandonings: the width of the ditches and the multiplication of drains around the city increased the loss in energy potential of the currents and reduced the power of the wheels accordingly. It is easy to understand why sixteenth- and seventeenth-century mill owners looked for any way to intensify flow rates in their millraces;[8] archives are filled with records of litigation against millers by riverside residents.

Development of the Linen Industry

The military importance of moat enlargements has already been pointed out. These very large volumes of water resisted the flow of incoming streams, thus causing the more or less abandoned lands upstream of the city to become completely waterlogged. These spongy lands, although constituting a supplementary protection against invasions by enemy cavalry or heavy artillery, were, in the course of the twelfth and thirteenth centuries, partially drained by canals circling around the city, diverting their waters downstream. This technique, developed during the late Middle Ages, crisscrossed these war-ruined valleys with a grid of shallow canals barely one meter wide, where flax and hemp were cultivated.

Flax, sown at the beginning of spring, thrives on shallow, chalky, and slightly humid soil. Hemp, sown at the end of winter, needs deep, rich, and very wet soil instead. Both are harvested at the end of summer and need little labor, but these crops rapidly exhaust the soil—flax in particular cannot long be cultivated in the same place unless the soil is continually fertilized. The outskirts of the city were suitable for these plantings because farmers could gather materials rich in nitrate and phosphate in the sewage ditches or in the streets. Once the plants had been harvested, the stems were dried for about two weeks before being put into retting tanks at the beginning of autumn. The hemp and flax fields were located upstream in Noyon, Chartres, Troyes, Reims, Senlis, Rouen, and Caen; downstream in Orléans, Châlons, and Beauvais. Retting facilitated the softening of the stalks and separation of the woody fibres, which were then spun, and finally bleached or dyed.

Flax, much more than wool, due to easy cultivation, a slow but simple transformation process, and ease in weaving, belongs to a subsistence-type economy. Its production developed in competition with wool throughout the late Middle Ages. Linen dominated the urban economy during the sixteenth century, spreading to outlying areas afterward. Certain regions—Maine, Anjou, Soissonnais, and Etampois—specialized in the production of undyed linen.

Bleaching remained an urban activity because of the long daily operations required during summer and autumn: successive washings in ash, lime, potash, or milk; rinsing in clear water; drying under moonlight in fields. The linen cloth gradually took on its whiteness because of the slightly acidic quality of the running waters and the selenic vapors. Bleaching required an enormous amount of water, which only slow, regularly flowing rivers, feeding into a multitude of canals, could provide. The *aires*, marshy terrains covering about fifty hectares, located above Beauvais, were turned into bleacheries at the end of the fifteenth century. In Amiens refugees from Cambrai following the wars with Henry IV set up the first bleaching works on the outskirts of the city, in Prailleux and Hotoie. Serge weaving reached Beauvais around 1535. Between Darnetal and Rouen bleacheries filled the valley of the Robec. The valuable study by Chaumonnont allows us to better grasp the setting up of this extraurban network in Troyes.

Troyes. The waters of the Seine flowed into canals through forty-one sluice gates beginning at the Pétal mill, 1.7 kilometers upstream, and continued down to the Tauxelles 800 meters downstream. A list drawn up in 1617 mentions thirty-nine of these canals; they had probably been in existence since at least 1567, when, upon the "remonstrances, complaints, and grievances of the tanners, parchment-makers, dyers, bakers, and millers," the city council decided that the sluice gates that led into the city, "starting with the Pétail and Hardel mills, up to the moats of the city, would be dismantled and taken away, with a prohibition to all persons to build new ones under pain of fines and banishment." These canals were an obstacle to the proper functioning of the mills at the low-water mark, and were periodically the subject of bans—in 1603, 1616, 1619, 1627, 1630, 1632, 1644, 1667, 1705, 1731, and 1742. But they were still in existence in 1869. They can be classified into four groups:

1. Within the walls, there were the sluices of the Séminaire, probably cut at the beginning of the thirteenth century, to drain the fields and build Notre-Dame-en-l'Isle; and the sluice of the Arquebusiers, opened from the Planche-Clément canal in 1448, to be used to flush the sluggish waters from the firing range of the harquebusiers. These two watercourses provided water for six hectares of meadow.

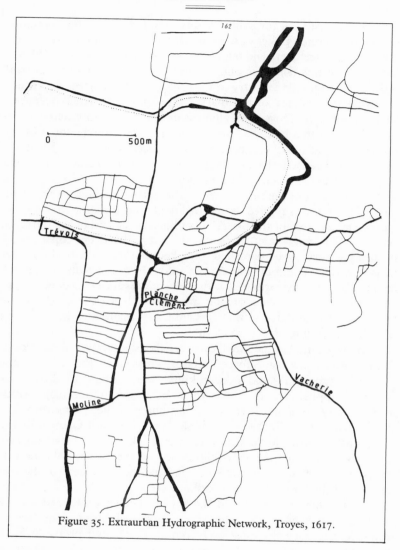

Figure 35. Extraurban Hydrographic Network, Troyes, 1617.

2. Outside the walls, between the Moline and Trévois canals, there were nearly four kilometers of canals irrigating thirty-five hectares of meadows and gardens, most of which were used for bleaching at the end of the sixteenth century. But these drains seem older, going back probably to the thirteenth century, even the High Middle Ages. The elongated form of the plots would seem to indicate that this land, near

the Croncels gate and the spinners' quarters, perhaps on the commons, was used to stretch pieces of woolen cloth at the end of the twelfth century, like the stretchers laid out along the Durtein in Provins. The new use to which this land was put can also be explained by the renewed activity of the textile industry in the middle of the fourteenth century, following the collapse of the market fairs of Champagne. A century later, the linen of Troyes had attained national, even international, repute. In 1616 this land was uniformly redivided among some fifteen property-holder bleachers. Next to the Croncels gate lay the Bleachers Mall, where nearly twelve hundred meters of small streams wound their way over an area measuring two hectares.

3. To the east of the Moline, up to the Vacherie, about twenty kilometers of drains supplied water to about one hundred hectares of meadowland, used for the bleaching of linen at the end of the sixteenth century. This huge tract of land, which had been episcopal in the twelfth century, was parcelled out between ecclesiastical chapter houses, hospices, and the barons of Vouldy. Here the plots were much larger (about ten hectares each), the network less organized and, to all appearances, of later construction, perhaps early sixteenth century, at the time of the building of the Rave mill, first mentioned in 1504, and used for the fulling of woolen cloth.

4. Between the Moline and Trévois canals, beyond the mills of Notre-Dame, there were some forty hectares, crossed by the canal of the Papeterie (paper mill) and a dozen kilometers of drains used by truck farmers (suppliers for the abbey) and bleachers. Three major landowners were prominent there at the beginning of the seventeenth century: Master de la Rothière, counselor on the Grand Council of the City; Master Nico; and the widow Nivelle. Each owned a bleaching mill that drew water from the Trévois intended for the intramural canals. It was probably against these three persons that the complaints of the corporation of the lower city were raised in 1567.

The bleachers first occupied the ancient network intended for the washing of woolen cloth. The watercourses had been considerably slowed down since the moat had been widened, and probably more were added in order to drain excess water from the soggy soil. Then, as the linen industry gradually grew, these bleacheries spread farther upstream from the city, onto fields on the flood plain where the Seine, as it overflowed, deposited alluvium beneficial for the cultivation of flax.

In all, more than thirty kilometers of narrow canals with weak currents crisscrossed the south of the city downstream from the paper mill. Its spent water, resulting from the fabrication of paper pulp, acidified the water and thus enhanced the whiteness of the linen for which Troyes was so famous. At the end of the sixteenth century, mechanical fulling mills made use of a total of ten mill wheels—one quarter of the available hydraulic power, as much as was devoted to paper-making[9]— but fullers occupied only 10 percent of the hydraulic network. The rest of the canals were used for the soaking of cloth, which was then laid out on meadows: evaporation was a prime factor in bleaching. This practice spread from the outskirts of the city as far as the distant valleys of the Barse and Aube.

Reims. As early as the middle of the twelfth century, the linen industry in Reims enjoyed an international reputation. A *rue des Téliers* (in modern French, *toiliers*—cloth-makers) appeared in the city at this time. A century later, documents locate the first workshops of bleachers along the Vesle, between the Abbey of Saint-Rémi and the Vesle bridge. These buildings were generally residences with an oblong meadow where cloth of all kinds was dried and stretched. These plots had only a narrow frontage on the waterways, the banks of which belonged to the church. The archbishop, the Notre-Dame chapter house, and the Abbey of Saint-Rémi drew substantial revenues from these earliest linen-producing installations, added to the abundant hay-making activities of this marshy city whose hydrographic network had not yet been definitively traced out. But in the second half of the fourteenth century, war brought about the decline of the industry in Reims. At the end of the fifteenth century, its linen reputation, unlike that of Troyes was lost.[10]

In contrast, muslin—which had played a minor role in textile production at the beginning of the fourteenth century—rebuilt an international reputation for Reims. From the sixteenth to the eighteenth centuries, this city would hold the first place in Europe. Muslin, which was first used for the sifting of flour, began to be used in clothing after the first half of the fifteenth century. Muslin is a loosely woven cloth that could be woven on unregulated looms (easier to install). Muslin was light and cheap, and thus appropriate for an economy in crisis. It was made from a blend of linen and hemp, which were again being cultivated around the city.[11]

It is to this time that the development of the filiform hydraulic network in the marshes bordering on the left bank of the Vesle must be dated. The vast meadows of the Middle Ages, especially those belonging to the archbishop, were divided into more than three hundred plots, only a few meters wide and about a hundred deep, and surrounded with superficial drainage ditches at right angles to the principal bed of the

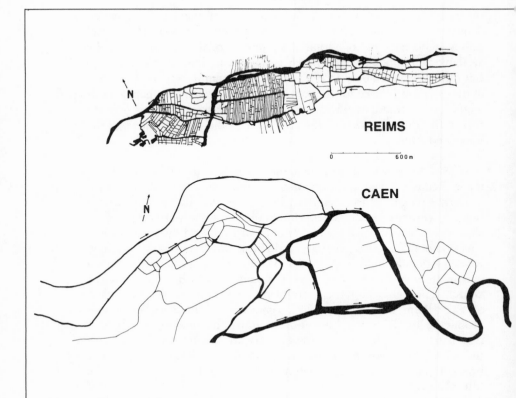

Figure 36. Extraurban Hydrographic Networks, ca. 1750.

Vesle. The muslin was washed there, which tightened its texture; soaking gave it more body. Then it was stretched out on the grass, as for other white cloth. Upstream, on the meadows of the chapter house and the abbey, the water network was less dense; it seems to have been used more for truck farming and the growing of flax and hemp, fertilized with the garbage collected in the Jard, Venise, and Neuve streets, where gardeners went to collect it. More than fifty kilometers of canals bordered the city at the beginning of the eighteenth century.

Beauvais. The divisioning of the lands and canals around Beauvais was similar. To the west were the meadows owned by the Abbey of

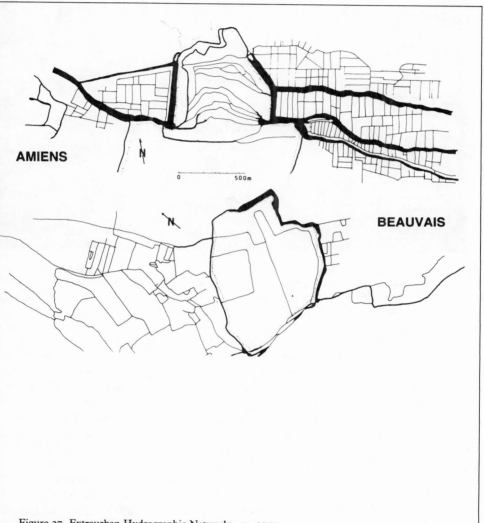

Figure 37. Extraurban Hydrographic Networks, ca. 1750.

Figure 38. Drying Dyed Cloth, Beauvais, ca. 1670. 1. Craoul tower. 2. Saint-Lucien Abbey. The view is taken from the north of the city, near the ramparts. In the center, the Saint-Quentin Abbey. Reproduction courtesy Bibliotèque Nationale, Paris.

Saint-Quentin since the middle of the twelfth century, laid out at that time for wool-makers and converted in the sixteenth century for linen-making, under the leadership of large bourgeois families. Pierre Goubert has discussed their importance, especially that of the Danse and Motte families, who set up their washing and bleaching operations along the Saint-Jean canal and around Saint-Gilles. To the east were the Saint-André and Marissel suburbs, a huge swampy area drained by the Wage (an overflow from the ditches), divided into lots occupied by less affluent bleachers as early as the beginning of the sixteenth century. Finally, to the southeast of the city, in the large valley of Thérain, a few important bourgeois families from Beauvais divided up among themselves the hydraulic network and the adjoining meadows, thus taking advantage to a certain extent of the acidification of the Thérain, slowed down at the exit from the city by the clayey waters of the Avelon.[12] Here again, nearly twenty kilometers of crisscrossing canals formed the outskirts of Beauvais into a "micronesia" shared with truck farmers, as in other textile centers: Caen, Rouen, Saint-Quentin, Reims, and Amiens. The conversion of the woolen into the linen industry needs to be analyzed in greater detail.

These three examples show the importance of the extraurban network developed during the late Middle Ages, starting with the building of ditches. The cities with the largest moats and ditches were also those with the largest canal network: Troyes, Reims, Beauvais, Rouen, and Amiens, which would become the great textile centers of the seventeenth and eighteenth centuries.

An element of urban defense—a portion of the no-man's-land circling the city—the extraurban swamp, during intermittent times of peace, was adapted to a precarious and discontinuous artisanal activity, not needing heavy equipment—linen and hemp production. This climaxed the older agro-pastoral activities present on the same sites since the twelfth century. The development of a hydrographic network within these marshes made vegetable-fiber textiles possible and improved military protection.

The production of linen and muslin, an indirect consequence of the defensive strategies of the city, sprange up on the edges of large masses of water. Techniques inherited from the thirteenth century—especially the preparation of wool, paper manufacturing, and the curing of hides—also underwent modifications, adapting themselves to the new environment of moisture and decay.

New Techniques

Textile Processes

Until the middle of the fourteenth century, woolen-cloth production constituted the bulk of urban exports. Raw materials came from England, which between 1320 and 1330 was still delivering more than six thousand tons of wool per year to the Continent. But little by little, as early as the end of the thirteenth century, this wool was exported to Flemish textile centers, to the detriment of the Picard and Champenoise cities. The cities of Flanders were better equipped and had access to Italy through the Rhine Valley. The French cities reacted by developing their own woolens; it was assuredly less fine, but it was more varied in color and texture. The wool used for weaving was local, of inferior quality, or blended. This new woolen industry stopped producing luxury fabric for clothing as early as 1340–50, concentrating instead on upholstery fabrics like serge and other weaves.

The decline in wool imports from England due to the war, and poor water management, which had disturbed the self-purifying properties of the canals, were now aggravated by the problem of the nonavailability of traditional additives. Since 1357 the extraction of fuller's earth in the Rougemare Forest near Rouen had come under strict control of the city aldermen. In order to supplement the meager supplies in Amiens, suet was added to fuller's earth. The number of dyes also diminished: from around thirty in Amiens at the beginning of the fourteenth century, to fourteen at the beginning of the sixteenth, to stabilize at around twenty.[13] Red dyes, more and more in demand, were obtained by using wine dregs and blood, which were added to madder, still undercultivated in the fifteenth century. The fawn-colored tint known as "tanned," made by using a mixture of woad and madder, was produced in Saint-Denis starting in 1373 using walnut roots, which were not expensive.[14] Alum, the chief fixing agent for dyes (with the exception of woad), came from alum pits of the eastern Mediterranean. The price rose sharply in the middle of the fifteenth century after the Turkish conquest, and even the discovery of the Tolfa mines near Rome, in 1465, did not bring the price down.[15]

Cheaper and easier to procure were iron filings soaked at length in tanks, wood ash, and especially vinegar, which until this time has not been used in this way; all three were substituted for alum. "Tartar, arsenic, saltpeter, salts of niter, rock salt, salts of ammonia, ordinary salt, mineral salt, agar-agar, wine spirits, urine, tin, bran, flour from peas or wheat, starch, or lime—all these drugs are used to fix the color of cloth, and to render the dyes more beautiful and distinct."[16] These materials became current in the sixteenth century, but we do not know exactly when they first made their appearance. These indigenous products had been used early on for domestic cloth production; medieval prohibitions did not apply to cloth produced for personal use. The permanent state of economic crisis in the fourteenth century, and, to some extent, the fifteenth, encouraged familial independence and the use of these products, easy to come by.

Fermented urine mixed with vinegar was substituted more and more often for fuller's earth: "in the draper's shops where wool is carded and where woolen cloth is made, there are always barrels where the workers urinate, and in which the urine is left to putrefy to be used in this state," wrote Ramazzini in 1700.[17]

Roland de la Platière explains:

Rather than choosing earth to remove the lanolin, it is better to use just urine, or to mix urine with some pig or sheep droppings. The fatty viscous liquid penetrates the material, soaking it, and easily forming a new combination with the fatty and oily substances encountered. First, a light fulling is carried out, just enough to moisten the fabric well, and then it is left to heat as long as necessary for fermentation to act strongly on the fatty substances, without deteriorating the fabric of the cloth to which these fatty substances adhere.[18]

In Reims at the beginning of the eighteenth century, each house had barrels available for this purpose, placed in front of the door or in the corridor leading to the shop. "Some are of the opinion that urine gives long life and strength to the cloth," recalled Duhamel du Monceau in his *Art de la draperie, principalement pour ce qui regarde les draps fin* (1765) ("the art of woolen cloth, especially fine woolen cloth").

Textile chemistry had thus been profoundly modified, going from mineral in the Middle Ages to biological. In the twelfth century the textile industry had stimulated the self-purification of rivers; now, due to the enormous amount of waste matter dumped into rivers, this purifying function was considerably reduced, and urban ecology was altered on a long-term basis.

The use of new products for dyeing can be explained in the same way. Sunflowers, sorrel, wild saffron, roucou (annatto), chimney soot, Avignon grains, grapes, pot-blacking, rust, and lichens, all of which had been banned during the Middle Ages, were the ingredients used for light tints as defined by Colbert in 1667. These products, unlike woad or madder in the Middle Ages, did not require labor-intensive cultivation, drying, mill grinding, fermentation, and compacting.[19] A minimum of handling sufficed. Thus, archil, which gave a red color, was invented around 1300 in Italy, and "was composed of a kind of moss called *perella* (*pérelle*), quicklime, and urine, which are fermented together, being moistened from time to time," as the *Encyclopédie* explained. These dyes were plant extracts, from easily grown or semiwild plants that anyone could find and collect. This was a subsistence economy, whose market developed according to circumstances, all the while maintaining autonomous production.

Fixing these dyes, like fulling cloth, required large quantities of warm or hot water. The shops became true sweat-shops in which workers, "surrounded by the noxious odors of rotting urine and oil, frequently half-naked, become consumptive and asthmatic."[20] The textile fibers had to soak in constant wetness right up to the last phase of manufacture. No humidity meant no good cloth, no pay, no fame. Humidity ruled despotically over textile production, for colorfast as well as for all other dyes. The maintaining of humidity necessitated water saturation, complete absence of drafts, and almost no shifts in room temperature, which only basements could provide.

Linguet, in his *Canaux navigables ou Developpement des avantages qui resulteraient de plusieurs projets en ce genre pour la Picardie, l'Artois, la Bourgogne, la Champagne, la Bretagne* (1769), wrote:

> When one enters into one of these renowned shops, where luxury is spread out in all its forms, one admires the brightness of the colors of the multitude of cloths laid out. One does not think of the putrid urine, or of the thousand other noxious ingredients whose absence, however, would mean that the colors would not be so bright. One is dazzled by the magnificence of these shops, where the cloth sits waiting for the buyer; one forgets that they are produced over a dungheap and that the wealth of the merchant has its roots in the poverty of the worker.

The woolen industry was in decline from the fourteenth century on, even though directed toward upholstery by integrating textile fibers: silk, gold thread, goat or camel hair, linen. Nonetheless, linen-making became more and more important in urban industry. Profits were even made from the state of war, because plant fibers were cheap and easy to cultivate, in contrast to woolen cloth whose fiber supply suffered from animal diseases and raids on stocks of yarn.

We have little information on the subject of spun cloth production before the seventeenth century. It was based on the retting of fibers, and "everybody knows how bad the disgusting odor of flax or hemp, retting in the waters, smells in the autumn, and how far this odor carries in the air," wrote Ramazzini. Retting was particularly harmful to water: "Care must especially be taken not to drink water in which hemp has retted. It contracts an odor so strong and unpleasant that it provokes disgust, nausea, vertigo, diarrhea, and chronic illnesses. This water kills the fish that swim into it."[21] There is no question that the location of retting pits upstream from the cities played a major role in deterioration of water quality, especially when the current of waterways slackened. Noyon, where the situation was aggravated even more by the blood-filled ditches of the barber-surgeons along the Verse River and less than three hundred meters from its walls, held the record for water pollution until the end of the Ancien Régime. But other cities on the Seine or at some distance from a river, like Senlis, suffered relatively little from noxious pollution: prevailing winds helped carry vapors away from the city.

Once the retting had been completed, the carded stalks were woven in cool, damp places. Pouchet of Rouen wrote:

> Threads can be produced successfully only in basements. Everywhere the workshops of the spinners, as much for linen as for cotton, are at least half-buried. I have heard an enlightened manufacturer praise the shops of Troyes because they are all basements. The spinners rarely have underground shops, but they work in places that are nonetheless cool, on the ground floor of low houses, where daylight filters in only through glass peepholes that are never opened.[22]

The best linen was bleached white, and this probably means that most linen was bleached. Cloth containing wool was treated very differently from pure woolen cloth; and linen that was to be dyed was also treated differently. Dyed linen flourished again in the second quarter of the eighteenth century, when the ban on its production had been lifted (after 1675). According to Macquer, "wool and all other animal materials are, of all the substances that can be dyed, the most apt for dyeing; whereas linen and all purely vegetable materials are, on the contrary, the most difficult to dye: they take the least color, and, in addition, they take the colors that are the less beautiful and the less solid."[23] It is easy to understand why the bleaching of linen and other plant-fiber cloth was so important, and also why using alum became less important in the mordanting: strongly diluted acids were more effective. Solutions made of hen or pig droppings, sheep manure, or cow dung were used in the fulling and mordanting of cloth.[24] Finally, to promote the soaking in of the dyes, the linen had to be sized, "pasted," beforehand with a mixture of flour and water; it enhanced the final quality of dyed linen. The prepared and sized linen had to be maintained in the constant humidity of the dye works,[25] most of which were in cities: Rouen, Caen, Beauvais, Reims, Amiens.

From the end of the Middle Ages to the beginning of the nineteenth century, humidity thus constituted a fundament of the textile industry. Evaluation of quality by overseers was based to a large extent on the humidity maintained in a workshop. There could be only slight variations in temperature, and only a minimum of light. Closed-in places, buried in the ground and bathed by underground humidity, satisfied all these conditions: basements and ground floors, access to which, in the thirteenth century, after a half-millennium of debris, was by means of a descending stairwell built into the wall. Manufacturers looking for new terrain suitable for textile production looked on the outskirts of the city, in the marshes: the Saint-Sever or Darnetal quarters in Rouen, the right bank of the Vesle in Reims, Saint-Nicolas and Avilly in Senlis, and the Ham and Hotoie quarters in Amiens. The most far-sighted among them suggested to the king, often in vain, that these neighborhoods needed to be protected and developed.

Stagnating water and a water table near the surface of the ground were important factors for this industry, which used nearly three hundred thousand tons of hemp per year at the end of the eighteenth century.[26] Most shops were set up in cities: five thousand looms worked in Amiens in 1746; nearly two thousand in Beauvais, Rouen, and Reims at the end of the seventeenth century; and probably a thousand each in Caen and Troyes. All these cities had a hydraulic network of good quality within the walls, and another, filiform and extensive, outside the walls, unlike Chartres, which had only eighty looms in 1708; Auxerre, which could not keep up its production, encouraged by Colbert in 1666, on the banks of the Valan stream; and Noyon, which was satisfied with the manufacture of coarse grayish-brown cloth.

The development of wool-making cities also depended on minute quantities of matter diluted in the running water: copper salts to fix blue tones, or iron salts that accentuated reds; finally, uric, nitric, or picric acid to enhance bleaching and the brightening of colors—a flood of particles, all coming from urban pollution. The richness of the dyes of the Gobelins factories cannot otherwise be explained, but it was not until 1863 that Chevreul would demonstrate this in his work, *L'influence de l'eau distillée, de l'eau de Seine, de l'eau des puits de Paris sur la couleur de la laine, de la soie, et du coton* ("the influence of distilled water, Seine River-water, and Parisian well water on the coloring of wool, silk, and cotton").

Moreover, the study of the decline of the textile industry in Provins in the late Middle Ages could shed much light on the question. It is probable that the hardness of the waters of the Voulzie and Durtein rivers, though excellent for the fixing of dyes, was an impediment for the bleaching of linen. To this was undoubtedly added discoloration due to tannic acid and the *lévosine* coming from the tanneries, and the impossibility of developing a sufficiently dense hydraulic network on the outskirts of the city. Nor does this take into account the disappearance of the merchant bourgeoisie linked to the decline of the Champagne fairs at the beginning of the fourteenth century, which had a significant impact on the textile industry in Provins: from three thousand looms in 1250 to barely a hundred in 1402.

Putrefaction was another, no less important, factor that characterized the transformation crafts located upstream from drapers: retting, fulling with urine, preparation of dyes—which could not be done without humidity. Putrefaction remained a basic expression of the subsistence economy: it required no investment and no transportation; its biomass was its only energy. To be sure, fermentation was understood in antiquity and the Middle Ages, but it was during the fifteenth and sixteenth centuries that it began to play a more and more important role in the transformation of raw materials: the leather industry is a good example.

Curing of Hides

As early as the end of the fourteenth century, the leather industry had been revitalized, due largely to the lightening of military uniforms (leather was replacing metal) and to the growing size of armies;[27] thanks also to fashion, which now preferred furs to woolens, and later still to the development of printing (leather bookbinding). Demand for leather remained high until the beginning of the seventeenth century,[28] and cities were obliged to lay down regulations for the new tanneries: Reims in 1380, Beauvais in 1416, Etampes and Noyon in the sixteenth century. Attempts were made to fill leather shortages in Amiens in 1464 by using dog skins; new methods were invented to reduce the time-consuming treatment of hides (Evreux, 1387). Leatherworks counted more than nine hundred pits and employed four hundred workers in Rouen in 1581; just as many in Sens and Soissons around 1590. Henry IV introduced into France the method of leather treatment used in Hungary for making tack for horses, and French *hongriers* began to form guilds. However, the pollution produced by tanneries irritated the municipalities, which took preventive measures against the irritation. Tanners left the cities by their own decision after the heavy taxes imposed on leather in 1627 and 1652:[29] the number of tanners in Troyes went from four hundred in 1640 to sixty in 1657, and there were only ten or so in the eighteenth century. In Caen there were only ninety-two left in 1725, twenty-two in 1748, and ten in 1789. Similar numbers probably applied to Rouen, Orléans, and perhaps Evreux.

From then on, hides would be tanned in the countryside, in small leatherworks with one or two pits. In the city, only the glove-makers, furriers, parchment-makers, and a few tanners (attendant on butchers and the urban consumption of meat) remained behind. The city was used for the marketing of the skins. Orléans still had a few tanneries concentrated along the Loire River, but its reputation was essentially based on trade in fine chamois skins. The greater part of the 144,000 hides that were marketed each year at the beginning of the eighteenth century came from central France.

Tanning is the penultimate step in the treatment of leather. It consists in soaking pretreated hides in a bath of water and tannin, which is extracted from the bark of oak trees. This process varied little until the middle of the eighteenth century (improvements at that time reduced the duration of the soaking bath, and thus the consumption of tannin; the suppleness of the leather was increased). [30] Before tanning, the skins were swelled to facilitate the penetration of tannin. This process of pore dilation may have been a recent technique, but more probably dated from the late Middle Ages. It varied according to region: in Normandy and Picardy, calcium-rich regions, hides soaked for four months in pits filled with lime water. In Brie and Burgundy, wheat-producing regions, skins were soaked in an acid juice produced by the fermentation of wheat and barley. In the west of France, broom flowers were used, to which were added dog, chicken, or pigeon droppings. In England, pigeon droppings were used. Each region used the most common, least expensive, local material, and in its absence, the excrement of domestic animals. These methods indicate subsistence economies—they used their own waste products for maceration.

In the Middle Ages, alum in a more or less pure state was used to cure hides. But when this salt was unavailable, or when it became too expensive, a substitute was found: dog or hen droppings: "Three or four buckets of dog dung are put into a large tank. A bucket of water is put in to soak it, after which the worker gets into the tank and works it all about with his clogs, and adds water to half-fill the tank; then he puts in hot water, and then the hides, which are stirred around, . . . then the water is heated." [31] Ramazzini describes the rude working conditions of these laborers:

> They look pale and cadaverous; they are puffy-faced, out of breath, and subject to diseases of the spleen. How indeed in such a humid place, in such air infected with putrid vapors, where these workers must almost always remain, could their organs stay intact? I have many times seen horses balk at the reins and not want to pass in front of such shops." [32]

Kennels in cities or on their outskirts were important. Dogs were not so much "man's best friend" as stock animals whose fat was mixed with beef suet and used in candle-making. Dogs were present everywhere in the iconography of the Ancien Régime.

The use of animal excrement was common; it was even indispensable during periods of crisis. The nuances of colors, the velvety smoothness of cloth, the suppleness of leather were the direct result of the quantity and degree of fermentation of the digestive juices contained in animal droppings. They added to the value of manufactured products. It was thus a fungal economy that kept urban industries alive. This meant that wastes had to be stocked, both to allow their fermentation, and to cater to variations in demand. Hence the pits for droppings and urine along the waterways, and the manure deposits in front of house entrances, against which the municipalities and the king railed unceasingly, threatening repressive measures. For the record, it was not so much the odors as the vapors emanating from these wastes, capable of spreading contagion, that were the object of these decrees. But piles of refuse and filth were sources of income for manual workers.

If a domestic animal was killed for the meat, everything was used, nothing was wasted. The hide went to make leather, and the fat was used for making candles:

> It is the butchers who generally render animal fats, at least in the big cities, because in the little cities of the provinces, where butchers do not kill enough animals to make a profit from rendering their fats, they sell them to chandlers, who collect fats from several butchers and melt them down for their own use.[33]

> There is not an infernal abyss or poisonous lake that could harm workers more than the places where candles are made. . . . The pots where tallow from goats, oxen, and pigs are boiled spread such an infectious vapor that it pollutes the entire neighborhood. Chandlers, leaning over their pots, are made to suffer. I have many times heard women who live near these shops complain of hysterical fits because of the bad smells; . . . the smoke and odor can cause miscarriages.[34]

> The scrapings from hides and leather, the feet, the skin from the heads, and the tails of various animals, even the bones, if dissolved in a large cooking pot, can make glue.[35]

In short, an artisanal chain complemented the nutritional chain. Regions that produced mutton in great quantities also did business in products derived from slaughtering and dismembering. Troyes "has a considerable commerce in wax and tallow candles, known for the whiteness of their wax and the good quality of the tallow." A monopoly was formed among the butchers who melted fats near their slaughterhouses, in the low quarters close to the Vienne River.

During this long period (fourteenth to eighteenth centuries), the city of northern France not only survived by ingesting its wastes; it also reinforced its economic independence by branching out into new spheres of manufacture, like the making of gunpowder from saltpeter, discussed above, and paper-making, for a market that greatly expanded after the spread of printing.

Paper-making

According to de La Lande, France was the largest paper producer in Europe until the beginning of the eighteenth century. Making paper from rags had been done since the twelfth century, but the development of a large-scale industry followed upon the widespread demand for printing. Paper took the place of parchment, which had known its apogee in the middle of the thirteenth century (the preparation of hides with alum and powdered calcareous stone was no longer compatible with the self-purification of rivers, as in the thirteenth century). The industrialization of paper derived from cloth was linked with the development of linen and other plant-fiber textiles. "In the cities, there is no lack of rag merchants who carefully scrounge for old cloths; they buy them and store them away." [36]

Paper-making entailed a series of operations, the major one taking place in a tank called the steeping vat (*pourrissoir*). The sorted rags were put into tanks, then filled to the brim with water; this was repeated for ten days, eight to ten times a day, without stirring the rags. Then the rags were turned over so as to accelerate fermentation, which would last for about a month, after which the internal heat would "become high enough so that the hand could be held for only a few second within." The rotting place had to be vaulted, and it was essential to maintain even temperature, in order to minimize the manufacturer's risk of error in timing fermentation; it should neither be interrupted nor overhurried. The rags were then ground up and reduced to pulp in paper mills, notably in Troyes, Rouen, and Caen. Fermentation continued in special tubs in which the water slowly drained out of the pulp:

> It is believed that the wetness of this shredded pulp, which is kept in tubs, brings about a kind of fermentation that finishes the softening. Moreover, one should use the heavy winter and summer rains to good purpose as a precautionary measure; when the dry season arrives, the tubs should be opened only a crack. . . . As soon as the hot weather sets in, the pulp must be

handled carefully, for not only might it yellow, but also worms are engendered in it and putrefaction sets in.[37]

This description, to which could be added de La Lande's *L'Art du cartonnier*,[38] describing the same processes, needs no commentary on the use of fermentation and humidity, basic to this industry. Little by little paper-making would decline at the end of the seventeenth century, following the revocation of the Edict of Nantes. Its nullification forced the best paper-makers of the kingdom to flee to Holland. Moreover, a decree by the Council of the King in February 1748 put heavy taxes on paper and cardboard. The paper mills of Rouen shut down as the workers left for Holland. The paper mills of Troyes, which in the sixteenth century had used a third of all the hydraulic energy, were for the time being converted to use in the textile industry.

But, as early as 1750, interest in paper-making revived. Réaumur observed that paper could be made from rotten wood,[39] and Guettard showed that the ponds of Dourdan, near Etampes, transformed tree leaves into a pulp similar to that of rag pulp.[40] The era of making paper from rags extended from the middle of the fifteenth century to the beginning of the eighteenth. Riverside paperworks and their mills were built upstream from urban centers because they needed very pure water, not "waters subject to railing by rainfall and those that run off miry lands," according to de La Lande. The Trévois canal in Troyes, the banks of the Robec to the Darnetal near Rouen, and those of the Orne in Caen were suitable for this industry at the beginning of the sixteenth century. The parchment-makers of Etampes, Sens, and Chartres disappeared.

Pollution from the manufacture of paper was very high: to the wastes from the pulping tanks was added that of glueworks. But although they polluted the water, they also, because of their mildly acidic solutions— fermented urine, for example—lowered the pH upstream from the dyers, which favored the scouring and treating of linen for bleaching. Here again the symbiosis of two industries helped to produce linen of better quality, notably in Troyes where "simple wood soapings are more effective than are lime, potash, or milk elsewhere." Heavy rains and floods in winter and spring—when most of the putrefaction took place—had a moderating effect on pollution, accelerating the dilution and evacuation of wastes. On the other hand, the fabrication of paper pulp did not cause much pollution. It was done during the summer and the beginning of autumn, the low-water period. But all in all, "the paper-maker's season" added to the stagnation of the rivers: in winter the paper mill needed power to shred the rotted rags, thus lowering hydraulic energy downstream from the mill; in summer the mechanical tables for the fabrication of sheets of paper used all the power of the low waters.

Textiles, leather, paper, and saltpeter were the major products transformed in and by the city up to the beginning of the eighteenth century. Production processes depended on humidity and putrefaction—that is, the quantity of excrement produced by the city. Water and droppings, in artisanal economics, were raw materials that had to be available, even held in reserve. In this sense, in a mercantilist theory of economics, wastes and water were to the craftsman what gold and silver were to the state. Water no longer had to be dynamic, but on the contrary had to flow with a minimum of current, remaining in a liquid and gaseous state, and within the walls of the city. This explains the importance of wells and reservoirs; the semiburied shops described at length in Young's *Travels;* the development of the extraurban capillary network, in the fifteenth and sixteenth centuries especially; and the utilization of marshes. "God created humidity and heat to be the principal causes of generation. This is why from the most ancient times the banks of remarkable rivers and the edges of large forests have been chosen for the construction of great cities; by reason of these blessings, persons can live there comfortably and multiply," wrote Olivier de Serres, an eyewitness of his times,[41] like Barthélémy de Granville three centuries earlier. Moisture, "thanks be to God," was part of the nation's wealth.

Barber-wigmaker-bathers displayed their patients' blood in front of their doors, and municipal authorities had a great deal of trouble getting them to empty their receptacles outside the city. Dyers put barrels at the entrance to their shops, so passers-by could urinate there. Butchers killed animals at home, burying the blood in the back courtyard or throwing it into the street where it "stayed and gave birth and nourishment to worms and other hideous bugs and infection, and caused pestilence, mortality, and epidemics."[42] No one was upset except municipal authorities answerable to urban patricians who had slaughterhouses built on the city limits in Amiens (1341), Evreux (1407), Troyes (1420), Rouen (1432), and Chartres (1520). Nonetheless, butchers continued to slaughter animals at home, like most other city residents, for their own consumption. The scraps were thrown into the street, to feed chickens and pigs, the carrion-eaters of the city. Decaying wastes did not appear to ordinary citizens as a problem of any kind. "From time immemorial the weavers [of Troyes] have had the right to deposit their excrement in front of their doors."[43] In fact, the visible accumulation of these wastes in and around entryways betokened a worker's success and constituted a means of attracting new customers.

This economic system peaked in the fifteenth and sixteenth centuries, at the time of the greatest demand for leather, linen, and saltpeter. War necessitated the outfitting of ever more numerous troops; cities had to ready themselves for sieges and self-sufficiency. The system continued until the middle of the eighteenth century, encouraged by the Physiocrats, who considered putrefaction "a gift of nature,"[44] and hence something to be made use of, with supervision. Fungal economics would disappear only with more concern for hygiene and the development of industrial and synthetic chemistry, which little by little spread to all the provincial cities at the beginning of the nineteenth century.

Although humidity and putrefaction fostered industry, its development could not take place without a high potential labor force and without exportation. Pierre Goubert and Jacques Perrot have shown how Beauvais and lower Normandy, respectively, coped with fluctuations in the textile industry. This was no doubt true of the other cloth-producing cities. Troyes had to convert to hosiery, which used more than twenty-four hundred looms in 1782. In Amiens serge weaving lost more than a thousand working looms after the 1762 authorization to make serge in the countryside without supervision. Nevertheless, a large velvet-making workshop was set up in the Hotoie neighborhood of Amiens in 1765. But almost everywhere, textile manufacturing spread into outlying districts or into the countryside, little by little moving out of the city, which in turn became cleaner. In the same way, as we have seen, the urban production of leather broke down in the middle of the seventeenth century, except in Sens and Rouen, and died out in the rural world. Paper-making, the speciality of Rouen and Troyes, declined at the beginning of the eighteenth century. As for saltpeter after 1750, urban production dropped off considerably.

In short, in the eighteenth century, once the state of war had ceased to be the major urban preoccupation, and the extraurban districts began to rebuild, the large manufacturing cities lost their most pollutive activities, which were also, most likely, the least profitable. This is shown by its opposite, the development of lace-making in Caen in the second half of the century. These cities started up service industries, following the example, it would seem, of the small cities that had not recovered from the crisis of the late Middle Ages, such as Soissons, Auxerre, and Provins.

This economy of humidity and excrement left its mark on urban topography. For us it is now a question of recognizing its traces and learning how they were transformed. There was first of all the almost imperceptible raising of the ground level, which facilitated the penetration and retention of humidity, especially when underground levels were marshy. This mounting up buries ever more deeply the vestiges of the day-to-day activities of history, which archeologists seek to bring back to light. Then there was the distribution of fecal deposits in and around the city, which seems to be linked to a topography of marginality, especially prostitution and crime, particularly in the fifteenth and sixteenth centuries.

Urban Topography
Raising of the Ground Level

Ever since the end of the thirteenth century, the city had been sinking into the ground: buildings were demolished or collapsed, leaving debris and rubble in the street. The improved building projects had left debris and rubble in the street; rarely were they moved outside the city limits. Preventive measures against plagues had necessitated, from the beginning of the fifteenth century, the removal of the furniture and clothing of the sick, to be burned in back courtyards or in public places. The siege of cities, especially under Henry IV, had damaged not only the walls, but also nearby dwellings. All this refuse accumulated, and only the saltpeter collectors paid it any attention. To all this was added the sticks and straw thrown onto major thoroughfares to soak up the winter mud. Paving temporarily fixed the street level, but this too gradually rose with time, whereas interiors of houses remained the same, raised at the most by a few centimeters when floor tiles were laid. In order to keep mud and water from coming into the houses, thresholds were put at the doors, slightly above the street level. Little by little the ground floor had "sunk" beneath the street level, and steps had to be added. Sometimes it was buried two or three meters lower, and thus became a basement or privy pit.

The ground floor of the twelfth century had been level with the street, well-lit, and airy; by the fifteenth and sixteenth centuries, it had become dark, humid, and lighted only by peepholes—to everyone's general satisfaction, it must be said, for technology required ever more humidity and dampness. Those who were conscious of the unhealthiness of the air—that is, those who were rich and educated—abandoned old ground floors and lived instead on the floor above, which was now on the street level. The others, more particularly the inhabitants of a marshy underground, were subjected to the uncongeniality of their en-

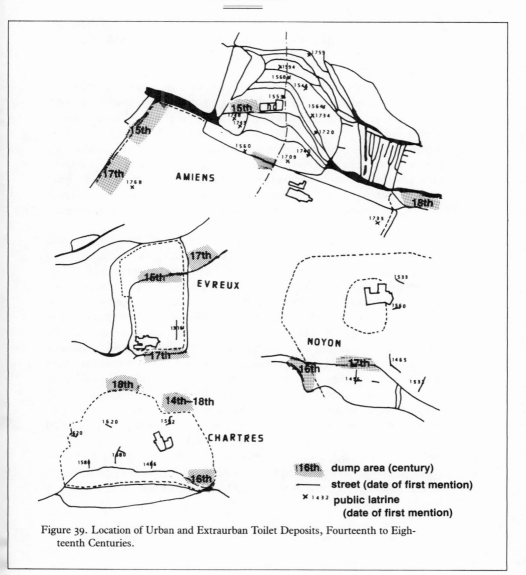

Figure 39. Location of Urban and Extraurban Toilet Deposits, Fourteenth to Eighteenth Centuries.

vironment: buildings made of mud and straw, or wood, rotted more quickly; household wastes were not removed as often as in the upper city, and the streets were not paved.[45] The lower city was buried faster than the upper. The religious and commercial zones of the city vertically crushed the artisanal zones, which had made of humidity and fermentation a modus vivendi adapted to the terrain. This vertical differentiation, which became more and more marked as time went on, would serve as the model of "social layers" at the beginning of the nineteenth century.

This urban phenomenon was reflected in a theological parallel. In 1274 the Second Council of Lyons taught the existence of purgatory, and associated it with the netherworld.[46] Now thought to be peopled by human spirits, the underground world was no longer just the habitat of devils, but an intermediate zone between heaven and hell, where human spirits could be helped by the offerings of the living. It was commonly believed that the well-to-do could gain access to paradise by buying indulgences. Hence the earth received into its depths only the souls of indigent persons. This was a close reflection of the urban pattern, magnified in the infinite beyond.

The underground world was thought to be the refuge of evil spirits, and knowledge of them was attributed to sorcerers. The "discovery" of the underground seems to me to have been just as important as the contemporaneous discovery of the New World. History has not attached much importance to the former, perhaps because the "superstitions" of the masses did not merit notice by the mighty, or perhaps because the underground was never colonized. However, the first probings into the underground—mining in the sixteenth century—sparked numerous inventions: the divining rod, steam engines, and the perfecting of water pumps and sounding instruments. The underground would long be an immeasurable universe, the object of lengthy scientific polemics, as was the sidereal universe. But the first voyages into the caverns of the earth were made by artisans and miners of the Renaissance, preconditioned by the obscurity and humidity of urban undergrounds, habituated to their own "burial," unlike the city dwellers of the twelfth and thirteenth centuries, accustomed to living just above the water, on the river banks, in a water dynamics witnessed to by the number of mills built at that time.

Refuse Dumps and Privies

During the thirteenth century, most monasteries, convents, palaces, and large bourgeois houses had latrines or toilet pits (in Paris, Bretons had a monopoly on waste disposal recycling). In the fifteenth century, most houses still did not have any toilet facilities. Fecal matter was no longer used, as in the thirteenth century, to fertilize vegetable gardens behind the house; the gardens had been replaced after the late Middle Ages by courtyards or outbuildings. The few remaining *merderons* of the city were not enough to handle all the wastes not utilizable by industry. The ramparts and ditches, now more easily accessible thanks to the progress of poliorcetics, were used for part of these wastes; toilet pits and the streets took all the rest.

Privies multiplied in the sixteenth century, especially in Paris where Francis I made them obligatory for all new buildings. Elsewhere, the toilet pit remained an exclusive privilege of the well-off bourgeoisie and the urban aristocracy; religious houses had huge ditches, several dozen cubic meters in volume, which permanently exuded foul odors. Four solutions were adopted to avoid this problem: "Make air vents in the conduit of the privy; in winter use snow to dissolve and filter the material into the earth; extend the ditches into waterways, to drown, so to speak, the exhalations that cause the bad odors."[47] The fourth solution was the siphon method, invented by Bullet, architect and student of Blondel; it prevented the reflux of odors into the ditch.

These ditches were not made watertight, despite the known risks of contaminating nearby wells. "Privies or water closets emptied into ditches through earthenware conduits. These pipes were often clogged, because of insufficient drainage. Those who did not have latrines—the great majority—threw their slops out the window, or went out to the street. Citizens in the south of France did just the opposite: they climbed onto the roof to take care of their needs.[48] This practice, suited to dry climates, offered the advantage of avoiding anaerobic fermentation, and thus the formation of obnoxious smells; but it also had the disadvantage of washing excrement into the street whenever it rained. Still others used a waterway if their property adjoined one. In cities where the water current was rapid enough, as in Beauvais, Caen, or Evreux, the filth was taken far out of the city; but in Troyes, Châlons, and Noyon it stagnated and contributed to the air pollution.[49]

Filthy Streets

Rue Orde ("ordure street"), *rue Basse-Fesse* ("lower backside street"), *rue Bougerue* ("pigsty street"), *ruelle des Aisances* ("easement alley")—these were Renaissance names for streets used as public toilets. These street names appeared in the middle of the fourteenth century; other streets were used for the same purpose, but without having their names changed. Each city had at least one *rue des Aisances* ("easement street") near the main marketplace: a narrow, often dead-end, street, with a seamy reputation, opening onto the main street with a tavern at the corner. At night these dead ends were places of "ugliness and villainy" committed by younger persons: Jacques Rossiau has studied their role in fifteenth-century society.[50] These streets were near the prostitution district: the municipal brothel, the steam baths, the "love street." A whole subculture established itself around the intramural fecal deposits, the ditches, and the city gates. Links between prostitution and public toilets were a constant in this society. The Saint-Abraham Hospital in Troyes was founded for repentant prostitutes; it had the responsibility of collecting manure and excrement on the Place du Marché-aux-Blés ("wheat market"). In the middle of the nineteenth century Parent-Duchatelet wrote on the relationship between prostitution and street-cleaning in Paris.

The health dangers of these streets sometimes worried municipal authorities, who tried to close them in order to mitigate the problem, especially during times of plague. But these streets would continue as before, until the middle of the eighteenth century. In addition, they were used as sewerways, like the *merdereau* of the thirteenth century. Residents who had neither the money nor the desire to install a water closet at home went to other streets as well, especially in the lower city, to defecate, as is shown by the prohibitions "to all to make their filth in the streets, alleys, corners, and gutters" of Reims, Troyes, Beauvais, and Amiens. These prohibitions were handed down by municipal authorities who most likely had sanitary facilities themselves. The bans were rarely respected by the masses, for whom excrement was part of everyday existence; neither its sight nor its smell provoked disgust. These deposits in the street also helped to raise the ground level. Latrines emptied into intramural waterways; the surface hydraulic network tended more and more to become the receptacle of the excrement of inhabitants living along its banks.

Dirty water and piles of filth pervaded the city, which only rain washed clean. Of course, sometimes peasants took these piles away, as in Paris, Troyes, Chartres, and especially Amiens, where marsh gardens planted with onions required rich, well-fertilized soil. But more often the city council was obliged to threaten those who voiced hesitations about their removal—with no result; urban jurisdictions dating from as early as the eleventh and twelfth centuries were in perpetual conflict over who should remove the filth. The city, when it had sufficient financial means, awarded contracts for refuse collection: twenty pounds in Amiens in 1579, four hundred pounds in Laon in 1737–38. These were relatively small sums for a community budget. This type of sanitation was rarely done at fixed intervals, at least in the sixteenth and seventeenth centuries (it slowly became regularized during the course of the eighteenth century: every ten years in Laon, monthly in Reims, quarterly in Beauvais), but was linked to the threat of epidemics, especially the plague. In the sixteenth century, one city was endowed with public latrines: Amiens. They were installed around the market, on the Avre and the branch of the Somme; at the same time, the city forbad "infecting the city streets with excrement."

The cleaning of intramural rivers followed the same logic. Cities with a sufficient gradient opened the upstream valves once a year during the summer. Residents then put their collected filth into the river. But these measures were frequently inefficient. Moreover, this form of cleaning was very superficial. It could not carry away artisanal sludges or the excrement that had solidified at the bottom of streams for more than a year. In order to take care of this, certain cities, like Etampes, "closed the river"; it was dried out every three years; every nine years in Evreux. But in general this deep cleaning was carried out only at the time of an epidemic or when silt had filled the riverbed to the point of blocking navigation or flooding and infecting the property bordering on it—about once every century. And then, digging out the mud in summertime, spreading it out on the banks, with all the heat, brought on intermittent and often fatal fevers. Thus it was preferable to leave the canals and their mire alone, rather than scrape them out and increase the virulent, or even lethal, condition of the air. After all, the canals' load was only moderately infectious. And, even more than the deposits of filth on the roads, the mud of the river bottom was especially sought after by gardeners on the edges of the city, at least in Amiens, Reims, and Châlons.

Streams (like the Renelle in Rouen) or canals with too weak a current (like the Mau and the Nau in Châlons, or the cross streams of the lower city in Troyes) could not be used to clean themselves. Filth accumulated in them, transforming them little by little into quagmires. They were still used by a few curriers and tanners, and their waters benefited from the tannin wastes, which encouraged the flocculation of solid matter, but the pollution of the water from organic wastes was such that self-cleansing had all but vanished. It could easily be thought that all the excrement, together with the spent water of workshops, irremediably polluted the canals. But this would be to forget a role played by the hydric ecosystem: the slowness of the current, plus the widening of the ditches, encouraged anaerobic purification, and the ditches turned into high-yield decantation basins. This technique, utilized by the *merdereau* of the thirteenth century and today called lagooning, could eliminate 70–90 percent of the organic pollution in four or five months in basins with a depth ranging from three to five meters, equivalent thus to those of the ditches dug in the course of the Middle Ages.

Development of the organisms (algae, protozoans, bacteria) that digested the solids was dependent on the prevailing temperature; it was not very effective during the winter, allowing a build-up of acidic discharge. But we know that during this season artisanal activities were limited, and the acidity of the water facilitated the bleaching of linen and hempen cloth. Another system of self-purification, based on the precipitation of floating solids and the swiftness of the currents, was thus substituted for the medieval method. Its disadvantages were that it bred mosquitoes and emanated gases: methane, hydrogen sulfide, carbonic gas. And it was these odors, more than suspended solids, that bothered the inhabitants of the riverbanks, because they did not drink the river water but dug down to reach the water table in the river far upstream, but without always being able to find better water.

Contamination of the water table varied according to the city and the neighborhood, and daily activities were more responsible than was industry: sludge sealed the sides and bottom of watercourses; microbial infection, coming from the deposits of filth in the streets and in the cemeteries (which had become, since the middle of the fourteenth century, what with epidemics and sieges, mass graves), reached the water table directly. It was located not far beneath the surface of the lower city and was the source of drinking water for the population.[51] Pollution did not spare the well-to-do of the upper city either: toilet lines, with ventilation holes to expel odors and facilitate the flow of urine, contaminated the water table from which all drew water. The only source of good water, "nice to look at, clear and clean, without odor, without taste," was far upstream from the city, in rivers or springs. All citizens were equal with respect to the pollution of underground water, but quite unequal with respect to air pollution, for the upper city enjoyed good air whereas the lower city suffered from bad air.

Sanitation

Efforts of public authorities to reduce unhealthy conditions in the city were notable during the reign of Louis XII, and especially Francis I. In Chartres in 1525 and Etampes in 1556, butcheries were moved downstream. In Chartres and Senlis it was ordered that all households maintain a supply of water at the front door in order to put out fires and wash the thresholds. These two were hilltop cities and washing the streets was easy. Sens diverted the *mondereau* inside the city, using large wooden troughs set near the Formeau gate in 1531, replaced by a stone canal in 1556, "to throw water in the said streets and ditches, as much to clean and preserve from fire, which is much to fear since all the houses are built in wood, as for keeping all security and defense." This method of washing the streets became common only in the second half of the nineteenth century when cities had fire hydrants supplied by a network of underground conduits. In 1503 Louis XII authorized the city of Châlons to divert a part of the Marne so as to increase the flow of the Mau, the stagnant waters of which had brought about a serious cholera epidemic the year before, decimating the population of the lower quarters. Finally, in Rouen, "the Renelle carries much filth and infection, and it would be well if it passed under the ground to prevent the said infections." The following year, 1519, it was covered over and its current reduced for the exclusive use of the numerous tanners installed on its banks; a sluice gate was installed at the crossroad of the street of the glovemakers. Water was diverted through the Ecuyère and Herbière streets, which were particularly polluted. The admiralties of the Ruissel and the Renelle probably dated from this time; they were responsible for supervising the waterways.[52] In 1589, in Amiens, orders were given "to make the said river [the Hocquet canal] flow, or fill in the canal with earth to prevent infection." Here, as elsewhere, the threat of epidemics dictated these prophylactic measures, advised by Renaissance doctors who counseled the municipalities.

But although the city councils had streets cleaned and filth carried outside the walls, it was not so much to protect the water table as to purify the atmosphere—the "bad air . . . infected with ugly vapors that rise from the dead bodies deprived of burial, from the stinking streets, from obnoxious pits, from cloacal filth, and from stagnating water."[53] All treatises on sanitation published from the sixteenth to the eighteenth century proposed solutions for this problem, and the sites chosen for "places of health" for the plague-stricken show the essential role attributed to air quality. Established in 1520 in Amiens, 1521 in Rouen, 1582 in Chartres, 1586 in Auxerre, and 1606 in Troyes in marshy areas away from frequented places, they did not threaten the city, thanks to the direction of the prevailing winds. The same reason had dictated the siting of public hospitals in the twelfth century. Even in ordinary times, the city exuded a foul odor—a by-product of economic necessity.

The Influence of a Mentality

Excrement also won a place for itself in the scientific realm, in medicine especially, which flourished during the Renaissance. Analysis of urine and feces was the basis of pathology: color, odor, and consistency were linked with different types of disease. Many dissertations on this subject were defended in the medical schools of universities. Droppings of all sorts were used in medicinal preparations, as Luther noted:

I am surprised that God has put into dung such important and useful remedies. We know from experience that trout droppings stop bleeding and horse manure is used for pleurisy. Human excrement heals wounds and black pustules; donkey droppings, mixed with others, are used in cases of dysentery; cow dung mixed with roses is a highly effective remedy for epilepsy in children.[54]

The Healing Pharmacy of Filth, or, How Almost All Diseases, Even the Most Serious, Can Be Cured with Dung and Urine, by Paullini, went through three editions in German between 1696 and 1748.[55] Brandt (1676), Kunckel and Kraft (1677), Robert Boyle (1679), and, more generally, chemists interested in medicine extracted phosphates from urine. As Macquer wrote, "the alchemists . . . have done much experimentation with the excrement of man and the other animals."[56]

Chemistry, which since Boyle had been searching for scientific status, leaned heavily in its early development on the organic, the vegetable and animal kingdoms. For Bucquet, "the decomposition of something simply by the change of its parts in [someone's else's] intestines, with the help of heat and humidity, allowed the formation of products that had not existed before: these essential characteristics are found in putrefaction."[57] Macquer noted:

But if the complete theory of putrefaction is the most difficult, it is also perhaps at the same time the most important matter of physics; it appears to be the true key to the most essential and most hidden secrets of animal life. Indeed, just as the proper substance of all the parts of the animal body differs from vegetable materials, with which all animals are directly or indirectly nourished. . . . it is obvious that the changing of vegetable matter into animal matter takes place principally by a kind of fermentation or even by the slow and unnoticeable beginnings of putrefaction. It is certain from this point of view that perfect animalization [life] depends on fermentation.[58]

Putrefaction served not only to help understand life, but also to make useful products: fermented urine provided phosphoric acid and ammonia; fermented sugar produced alcohol; soda ash could be derived from saltwort.[59] As for nitrous acid, according to the chemists of the seventeenth century, it was contained in the air of the atmosphere and deposited in calcareous soils at hand; with this soil and the latent humidity, it formed the different types of niter. The niters that formed saltpeter were, moreover, produced by vegetation, from which they passed to animals. "Putrefaction is the means nature uses to develop and differentiate" niters.[60] From the fermentation of plants and animals could be extracted a quantity of related oils, in the theory of phlogistics—which dominated chemistry from 1730 to 1760—even phlogiston itself.

If humidity or vapor were the prime transformers of nature, water was the *materia prima*. Water formed the earth, as the experiments of Van Helmont, Boyle, and later du Hamel confirmed: plant a bush in a pot; it grows from the addition of water alone, which means that at the end of several years, water has been transformed into vegetable matter, which distillation reduces to the state of its salts. Thus, all solid bodies, including the earth, were generated from water by the action of seeding and fermenting; even gases were only a form of water, of vapor.[61] De Milly wrote:

> In order to perfect Art, we must consult Nature and try to imitate her; this important truth would be the compass of all those who wish to make any progress whatever in the physical sciences. If we consider thus the surface of the globe, we see that, in the decomposition of materials, nature is not as violent as the fires of our boilers; Nature uses only the gentle heat of the atmosphere to produce fermentation; all bodies are subjected to it, as an immutable and primitive law of nature, which applies to all things. Finally, fermentation is the principal agent nature employs for the destruction and formation of beings, *destructio unius, generatio alterius.*[62]

In this context, we can understand the publication of the long *Mémoire sur la putréfaction* by Thirioux d'Arconville, and Réaumur's research in his *Histoire des mouches à deux et quatre ailes* ("the history of two- and four-winged flies"). The fungal domain contributed to the flourishing of Occidental civilization. And it was especially an urban factor, ever since the new industries had appeared during the course of the fifteenth century. An economy founded on fermentation took shape during the fourteenth century, and was complete at the end of the eighteenth.

Putrefaction clung to the city like the humidity that marked this long period of climactic cooling. Both had determined the wealth of the city; the worse a city smelled, the richer it was. The putrid was one of the pillars of urbanization, as the sacred had been in the late empire. Its privileged moments were the fifteenth and sixteenth centuries, when textiles and leather occupied urban industry, and war and plague spread destruction. At the end of the seventeenth century, maceration would play a less important role in urban activities: the putrefaction of leather-making was relegated to the countryside; cotton, less polluting, was substituted for hemp and linen. Paper left for the region of Auvergne, and, little by little, the affluent sought to limit the humidity of their environment. Paving streets and the building of privies contributed to reducing filth deposits within the walls, and the populations of the large economic centers concentrated on industries that were less polluting, leaving the preparation of raw materials to the countryside. The urban elite again savored the good air of public walkways and gardens.[63] The big cities cleaned themselves up, and parted company with their mire. The putrefaction that had engendered the wealth of the city and the nation would now be pushed away, reduced, and eliminated.

The eleventh- and twelfth-century hydraulic network had become waterlogged in the late Middle Ages. From the fourteenth to the sixteenth century the extraurban waterways had multiplied into galaxies of canals, the majority intended for cloth-bleaching, and secondarily for the irrigation of meadows or for gardens. This filigree grid corresponded to the inertia of the huge moats cut during this same period for the needs of military defense. These scores of kilometers of streams, a few decimeters deep, mitigated the spring floods, bolstered the low water of summer, and raked up the humid soil of valleys in the autumn. This network acted as a blotter for the increasing rain brought on by the climactic cooling at the same time. The large pre–industrial age city flowed over its walls in order to set up new crafts along the valleys. Small cities, with smaller hydraulic networks, were less dynamized by a fixed and centralized corporative system than were the big cities. Indifferent, they were satisfied to survive within their enclosures, storing farm surpluses before floating them down the rivers toward the big textile, leather, or paper centers.

Stagnating water and humidity, part and parcel of the "ideal city" of utopians,[64] played a fundamental role in urban economies during these four centuries. Water vapor was the chemical agent essential for fermentation and the mechanical agent necessary for the loosening of fibers or for dressing and finishing skins, cloth, and paper. Indispensable for the fine quality of cloth, it was the economic catalyst of Occidental urbanization. Unmoving and heavy water vapor clung to the lower city as to the rags of the paper-makers. Only a little ingenuity was needed to promote steam to the ranks of the great inventions. Many tried, of whom history has retained only a few names: the Marquis of Worchester, Papin, Savery, Newcomen, dillettantes or engineers, all educated in the new discipline called dynamics. The steam engine would be born in

these circumstances. As Pierre Mantoux has clearly shown, the first en-
visioned an "atmospheric engine," one that did not use the kinetics of
steam, but rather its pressurizing potential. It was not until 1764 that
James Watt used steam "not as an auxiliary force, as a means of making
a vacuum in the body of a pump, but as an active force generating
movement."[65]

The city of the Ancien Régime re-covered or spilled over the medieval city limits, according to its economic wealth. The large cities—
Rouen, Amiens, Reims, Caen, and Orléans—had been at work during
the course of the economic renaissance of the sixteenth century to fill in
the empty spaces in their walls. Average-sized cities, like Beauvais,
Troyes, and Châlons, had not grown at all. Small cities had remained
closed up within their walls, which, built in the eleventh and twelfth
centuries, had definitively traced out on the earth the limits of their
wealth, now only a legend. The economic priorities of cities from the
fifteenth to the eighteenth centuries had accentuated the differences between neighborhoods:

1. The old city of the High Middle Ages was now reserved for the
church.

2. The riverside and the market quarter came into place during medieval expansion. The former, made up of cul-de-sacs and narrow
streets, was where the poorest residents lived, soaked in the nauseating
odors necessary for the crafts; the latter, more airy, was where the merchants lived.

3. Extensions dating from the Renaissance, with more greenery and
less densely populated, were where the new religious orders of the
Counter-Reformation took up residence.

4. In the largest cities, a zone of manufacture was now to be found
on the outskirts.

Beyond the boulevards, in the valley, a vast hydraulic network
spread out, the source of the bleachers' wealth. Extraurban space was
dedicated to the production of whiteness (cloth and paper), whereas the
city center was taken up with colors and the putrefaction of matter
(dyeing, leather). And everywhere the obsessive presence of water
affected all urban activities.

Was war alone responsible for this urban structure founded on humidity and putrefaction? It was certainly a significant element; it codified
a new organization of space: life was pushed back within the walls, and
a no-man's-land was occupied by the vapors emanating from the wide
waste-digesting moats and the complementary network of canals and
ditches. A new poliorcetics had made the city the major producer of
saltpeter, vitally needed for war. But war was not the only cause of

changes. Like the plague and the change in weather conditions, war contributed to the birth of a new mentality that left sanitation aside and found its widest social and economic dimensions in moisture and the unvarying temperatures of the basement and the underground. Upon closer examination, all the technical procedures developed throughout this long period, which began in the late Middle Ages and ended with the eighteenth century, were the concrete, tangible realization of the mentality of the era: the time of the macabre, of fascination with dead bodies, which has been detailed in the research of Huizingua, Jean Delumeau, and Philippe Ariès.[66] The imaginary was linked with the economic, the technological, even the scientific—all focused on putrefaction. And why should we not use the word "culture" to denote this ensemble, the culture of putrefaction, the culture of the fungal? This would entail demoting the elitist criteria used by the history of art—the culture of the Renaissance and the culture of Classicism.

7

Burying of the Water Networks

All the technological innovations of the preceding period had faithfully echoed the prevailing collective imagination. But scientists ("philosophers") and then technicians would react with disgust at the fascination with death—the interest in decomposition and putrefaction—that held sway in the West at the end of the eighteenth century. Repugnance at representing or imagining death and its cadaver," as Ariès put it, corresponded to a new urban technology founded on the dynamics of water, the acceleration of chemical transformations, and more generally the development of synthetic chemistry, which would allow humankind to control matter in vivo, not allowing nature to dictate human conduct. "Water is the favorite agent of nature," said Lavoisier and Dubuat. To control water was to control nature.

In one century, the hydraulic network of the cities would virtually disappear, filled in or covered over; urban ecology would once again be completely changed. On the eve of the French Revolution, this network, though it still retained all its vigor, had become the object of incessant criticism from men of letters. Army officers, doctors, geographers, agronomists, chemists, and even members of the European Royal Academies, all denounced the dangers of water, engineered by nature and condoned by artisans. "Everyone argues about water management, but few listen," wrote Dubuat in 1786. The turbulence of the revolution would for a time turn a deaf ear to these caustic critics, but they would start in again just as strongly with the Restoration (1815–30). The intellectuals were joined by the first industrialists and the politicians, enthusiastic about recent progress made in technology: advances in ballistics, development of the steam engine, increase in mill productivity, the emergence of inorganic chemistry. From then on, any pretext sufficed to nullify the urban watercourses: first the moats themselves, then the use of hydraulic energy, and finally the water-related crafts. By the middle of the nineteenth century, the network, no longer functional, was, in the eyes of medicine, nothing but the breeding ground of diseases that infected the water table from which drinking water was drawn. Engineers took care of all the rest.

The network was put to death in two stages. The first was to the rhythm of scientific thought, starting in Italy and spreading to northern Europe in the course of the eighteenth century. There were two theories about the cycling of water—through underground passages or by evaporation and precipitation. The latter notion was the one finally accepted. With it came awareness of how polluted water could cause infections. The quality of water and its consequences on health became a matter of concern. Humidity and stagnating water, until then so precious for crafts and military defense, were now feared as a source of *méphitisme:* "the condition of any locality, by which it ceases to be safe for human and animal respiration, and by which it is or becomes capable of attacking life more or less quickly and energetically." [1] The raging waters of torrents were thought to be the sole cause of soil erosion. Secrets of the internal structure of fluids were finally revealed: its chemistry, mechanics, and especially its resistance, which had to be minimized at all costs. This first stage mobilized primarily intellectuals in the largest European cities—especially Paris—and secondarily those in provincial cities.

The chronology of floods inventoried in historical records shows that Paris was by far the most affected by them, especially between 1780 and 1825, in the very middle of the "scientific revolution," in chemistry as also in hydraulics. This environmental deterioration was more obvious in Paris than anywhere else in the region. The "fungal city" had to be set free, by whatsoever means.

In the debate between those who clamored for the elimination of stagnant water and those who claimed that, on the contrary, the rivers ought to be slowed down, the opinions of engineers carried more and more weight. Engineers were ready to be at once the doctors and surgeons for water. At the request of political authorities, they sponged, curetted, and cauterized the open wound that the surface water network had become. And they were more and more successful, especially because, to unreliable practices inherited from the Renaissance were now added the more reliable methods of hydraulics, Enlightenment science par excellence, pursued in all engineering schools.

In the nineteenth century, positivism supplied the second rhythm of the burial of the network. Water, now canalized and controlled, was indispensable for urban development, it was asserted, and agricultural treatises argued that natural water resources were limited in quantity. In order to avoid a shortage crisis, ways of finding this natural resource

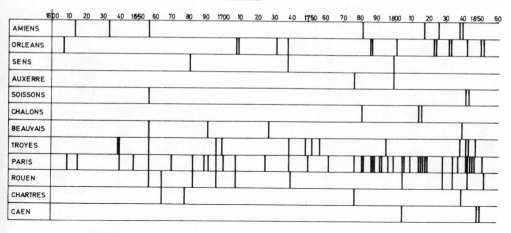

Figure 40. Floods in Twelve Cities, from 1600 to 1860; Each Line Indicates a Flood
(Champion, *Les Inondations en France*, Paris, 1858–1864).

would have to be multiplied, and wasteful uses and harmful excesses would have to be stopped. The Academy of Sciences and the Central Society of Agriculture organized competitions with prizes in these fields. Sanitation findings penetrated to provincial cities by way of the publications of the *grandes écoles* of Paris. The more the city was industrialized, the more it hastened to bring about the disappearance of its canals, and for good reason: there more than anywhere else the labor force had abandoned riverside crafts to work in factories where machines required pressurized water of absolute purity. The big city, with its many resources, could resist the influence of millers, who needed canals. Engineers from the prestigious schools of Paris, placed at the head of the technical services in other major cities, could systematically transform the canals into underground sewers, following the example of Paris and London. The smaller cities were more hesitant; small crafts retained their importance there, and the miller remained a person who was listened to in municipal council meetings. Municipal technical services, if in existence, were confined to locally recruited agents who did not have large budgets at their disposal. The burial of the canals was postponed in these cities until later, in the twentieth century.

First Stage

The Cycling of Water

The history of the study of the source of water is intimately linked with that of geomorphology. During the seventeenth century, this his-

177

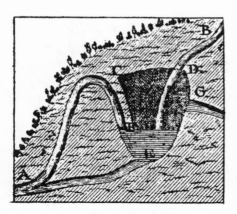 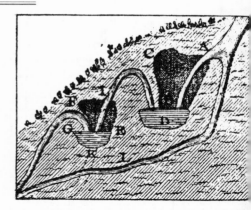

Figure 41. The Formation of Underground Waters, according to Brisson, *Dictionnaire raissoné de physique*, Early Nineteenth Century). As late as the second quarter of the nineteenth century, the distribution of subterranean veins of water was still a matter of inquiry. See, for example, Bidone, "Expériences sur la forme et la direction des veines et des courants d'eau lancés par diverses ouvertures" ("Experiments on the form and direction of veins and currents of water that spring from diverse openings"), *Mémoire*, Academy of Turin, 1829.

tory shared in the Galilean revolution; in the eighteenth century, in astronomical and astrological speculations. The now universally accepted theory of water circulation ("atmospheric") was controverted until the seventeenth century; only Vitruvius, and much later Alberti and Palissy, defended it in earnest.

The subterranean cycle theory was supported by Aristotle and Plato. Albert the Great's *De causis proprietatum elementorum*, the commentaries of Thomas Aquinas on Aristotle, and the *De proprietatibus rerum* of Barthelemy de Granville upheld this theory. Based on the biblical flood, this theory asserted that the ocean was the origin of all water; it bathed the innermost, overheated depths of the earth. By evaporation and capillary action, water rose up to the ceiling of the grottoes in the underground; the rivers thus formed flowed on to the ocean. The lack of movement of underground waters was the ad hoc argument for the contiguity of the oceans and water wells. The Book of Ecclesiasticus provided another proof of the validity of this theory; it speaks of "flood waters stored on high" (43:10). The ocean could thus feed wells by interconnecting channels, even wells located at the highest elevations.

This idea of a centralized source of water becomes more and more widespread as we advance into the seventeenth century. First of all, it had the advantage of a unanimous tradition: Greco-Latin antiquity, the Old Testament, the Middle Ages. It was also one of the fundamentals of the new astronomy that propounded the sphericity of the earth, whose center was supposedly occupied by the biblical abyss or the Tartaros of Homer. Kircher (1641), Papin (1647), Gaffarel (1654), Van Helmont (1670), Rohaut (1671), Woodward (1685), and especially Descartes (1644) defended the objectivity of ancient wisdom. Socrates, Moses, Archimedes, and Copernicus all agreed: subterranean waters must have been at the origin of the biblical deluge:

> The earth's crust, dried out, ends by cracking. The water underneath expands and exerts pressure against the vault of the orb, which will break into pieces and fall into the abyss. The cracked crust, weakened, breaks up; water gushes violently out, in proportion to its mass and the space it had just occupied. Thus, with the rains falling from the heavens, came the universal flooding and upheaval. The rain stops, evaporation begins, and dryness sets in.[2]

This theory also provided an explanation for the presence of fossils in mountainous regions.

Nevertheless, doubts persisted: master well-diggers dug to very great depths without ever encountering salty water. Mariotte and Perrault were not convinced that water occupied the center of the earth. They preferred the Aristotelian theory of fire at the center of the earth, which had come into favor since the middle of the seventeenth century. Contrary to the theory of water at the center, the fire theory could be verified by experiment: "heat a vessel containing salt water; the vapor collected at its neck will condense and even form a small spray of fresh water."[3] Perrault, for his part, showed that water could evaporate at any temperature. Schott's theory of capillarity (1663) was also seriously undermined. The theory, inherited from Anaximenes, that air was the primary element, along with the theory of the four elements of Aristotle, was definitively overturned following Rohaut's experiments (1671) against Schott and Ritthaler (1684). "All physicists will agree to the usefulness of measuring exactly the quantity of water that falls every year in every country, and how much evaporates."[4] To the discredited Mariotte, Perrault, and Rohaut were added the Jesuit Father Cabee, the astronomer Sedileau, and Wren, member of the French Royal Academy.

Steam obsessed the entire second half of the seventeenth century. The Marquis of Worcester speculated (ca. 1660) on the pressure of steam under containment. Around 1683, Morland proposed to Louis XIV that water could be raised to higher elevations by means of steam. In 1698, Papin and Savery visualized a fire-operated engine. Their design was based on the prevailing theory of subterranean waters: springs conduct water from the sea; it is then changed to the gaseous state by the heat of the central fire. Kircher (1641) had proposed a simpler model.

In the water-centered system, rain and snow played only minor roles. Scholars held that precipitation could not penetrate more than a few meters into the earth.[5] It was thought that there were three types of soil—"sandy soil, which does not retain water; the clayey type, which holds water like misers; the third is spongy or porous, which, like liberals, holds one part and lets another go." The water for springs was thought to come from the center of the earth by means of rising humidity—"the decrease in heat is proportional to the elevation in height of the place" (*Transactions*, 1666). The huge reservoirs contained in mountains thus fed the rivers.

However, in spite of these speculations, the construction of wells followed common sense for the most part, judging fluctuations of underground waters in terms of seasonal precipitations. This is what Perrault established around 1670–72 in Dijon. He demonstrated that the volume of water that falls each year into a river basin was six times more than the volume of the river. Mariotte also calculated the average quantity of water that fell in one year on the Seine River basin and concluded that "it is thus evident that when a third of the rain waters have evaporated, a third will keep the soil moist in the large plains, and a third will still be sufficient to feed springs and rivers."[6] For proof there were the experiments carried out from 1670 to 1680 by Vauban on his fortifications: a sloped embankment several meters high, laid out on ground with a slight downward gradient, would increase the downward flow rate. And English miners claimed that they could smell the perfume of clover in their shafts long after the period of flowering (*Transactions*, 1682).

Not much more was necessary to convince Colbert, who was supervising the construction of Versailles, with Mariotte as chief well-builder: according to their calculations, a surface area of six square leagues (100 sq. km.) would supply all the water the palace would need. An enormous number of channels were then cut in the Satory, Saclay, Trappes, and Arcy plains. But hardly more than a few hundred cubic meters of water per day could be collected. The Marly waterworks and the Maintenon aqueduct had to supply the deficit. This was the first setback for Colbert's administrative economics: systematic patterning (of a drainage basin, a workshop, or an area of arable land) does not always turn out to be appropriate for obtaining an expected quantity (of underground waters, manual labor, or agricultural products, respectively). And it was the first setback for the theory of water circulation that was trying to escape from the Platonist model.

But the rift finally came from elsewhere, and first of all from the astronomer Halley, who conjectured an empty terrestrial center for his
theory of magnetism. His demonstration was convincing: calculating
the total surface area and the annual evaporatin of the oceans, he proved
that the volume of precipitation remained clearly superior to that contained in rivers during the same period of time. By the same stroke, he
established the atmospheric cycling of water, reducing to silence those
who thought that the permanent flow of rivers into the oceans was com-
pensated by an equivalent absorption of the oceans into the central
abyss. But in the *Principia,* published at Halley's expense, Newton confirmed that the earth was composed of concentric homogeneous layers.
The earth attracts exterior bodies as if all its mass were concentrated in
the center: a sine qua non for universal gravity. Doubts thus lingered
concerning the consistency of the terrestrial center, all the more so
when MacLaurin, Newton's disciple, hypothesized a heterogeneous
earth whose center could be empty or full, light or heavy, without
making any significant difference.

As for the origin of subterranean water, thinkers in the first half of
the eighteenth century still hesitated between two explanations. On the
one hand, there was that of the central abyss filled with water, supported by the medical doctor Boerhaave (1732) and the geographer
Rilliet (1735), or full of "a quantity, a beauty, that escapes us," a theory
that captivated Fabricius (1741). On the other hand, there was the explanation that it came from rain, toward which the engineers Leupold
(1724), Belidor (1737), Zendrisi (1741), and the geographer Pluche
(1735) were inclined.

Unanimity came in 1743 with the publication of Clairaut's *Théorie de
la figure de la terre, tirée des principes de l'hydrostatique* ("theory of the
shape of the earth, drawn from the principles of hydrostatics"), which
showed that the weight and centrifugal force of the earth necessarily
flattened out the poles: "If we suppose that the depth of the ocean is not
in any place more than the height of the mountains, it is evident that we
can without noticeable error look at the earth as a spheroid with no in-
equalities, covered by an infinitely thin sheet of water."[7] "If we want to
understand this spheroid, we must suppose the crust to be hard, and
covered only with an infinitely thin sheet of water."[8]

To the brilliant demonstrations of Clairaut were added the arguments
of Buffon, who argued that a terrestrial crust of only a few leagues'
thickness could not explain such a regular rotation of the globe. Hence,
the interior vault did not exist. The water cycle could only be atmospheric, if not orological: rainwater penetrated the earth down to the
impermeable layer; it stagnated there or flowed out to form springs and

rivers. The water that evaporated from the oceans and seas formed the clouds, and Buffon and Pluche confirmed it, despite the reservations of Fabricius and Bertrand, who looked instead to the biblical deluge and the existence of large underground lakes interconnected by channels.

Clairaut and Buffon were correct, and triumphed around the middle of the eighteenth century, notably with the calculation of the earth's density, which no longer left any doubt about the composition of its center. From now on, "each river is a large lake that stretches out far underground."[9] The idea of a subterranean water table appeared for the first time in 1776 in the "Essai sur une application des règles des maximis et des minimis à quelques problèmes de statique relatifs à l'architecture" ("essay on rules of maximums and minimums applied to certain problems in statics relative to architecture"), by Coulomb, in his *Mémoires de mathématique et de physique.*

However, the presence of water at very great depths still remained to be explained. Three theories confronted each other: the first was based on the existence of underground lakes; the second on plant biology; and the third on "animal magnetism."

The huge reservoirs, formerly thought to have been fed by Tartaros or the central abyss, were now underground lakes supplied by natural tunnels deep in the earth. Hassenfratz was convinced that "Africa and Asia are in the shape of a cone dug out at the summit. The waters flow out in part into the center; they are reunited into the great lakes or interior seas from which they are transported to the sea, either by evaporation, or by underground conduits."[10] D'Aubuisson de Voisin (1828), Héricart de Thury (1829), and Huot (1839) shared these ideas. This explanation of course reflected the model of the underground water cycle. But it also took inspiration from medicine, especially from gynecology: the menstrual blood defined by the *Encyclopédie* as "an overabundant blood that serves for the formation and nutrition of the fetus in the womb, and at other times is eliminated every month . . . must be close by in some reservoir where it stays, motionless, as long as it is not flowing out." It flows out of the body like water from the underground.

Those convinced of atmospheric water circulation came up against a problem in the explanation of reservoirs of water at very great depths—wells, and especially artesian wells, which went to a depth of more than thirty meters—because of the theory that water did not penetrate the earth for more than four meters. But there were plants whose roots attained a depth of several dozen meters, and it was argued that they could put moisture into the ground.

Ever since the discovery of evapotranspiration by Halès (1727), experiments "proved that leaves are furnished with suckers and absorbant vessels . . . that pump moisture out of rain, dew, and even that which is spread out in the air in a less perceptible way."[11] Physicists and agronomists attributed to trees the ability to appropriate gases from water, which they returned to the earth and the atmosphere:

> The lowliest plants enjoy the capacity to attract the watery parts of the atmosphere, the vapors that travel in their spheres of attraction, to condense them and transform them into dew. . . . They are almost always in a place where humidity can be found, one of the most active elements of plant life. But it is especially in their influence on the clouds that one must consider the extent of their power. These superb trees, which rise to the summit of mountains, seem to be interposed between the heavens and the earth, in order to establish continuous contact between them. Clouds always drift toward the highest summits, by reason of the laws of attraction. [The summits] divide them [the clouds], so as to make up an equal division. They constrain them to submit to their power and to dissolve in beneficial rain. . . . Let us cover our hills with a dense layer of vegetation and we will have shelter against undesirable influences of the north; we will also have powerful means of reverberation and concentration of solar rays; we will have dews, fresh and pure air; we will attain the goal of dividing up the clouds, to control the rains more uniformly, preventing ravines and soil erosion, perhaps also to procure springs for ourselves, but especially to consolidate within our realm this salutary humidity that plays such an important role in the workings of vegetation.[12]

Forests came to be prized for the conservation of underground waters: "the woods will produce this effect [the penetration of water into the earth] even more when they are denser." This theory, whose promoters belonged for the most part to the Central Society for Agriculture, thought of the forest as a "hydraulic siphon,"[13] even an "economic siphon," capable of increasing the hydric potential of the nation, because it was then feared that the water evaporating on the earth's surface was decreasing in quantity. Any clearing of forests would cause a weakening of the water table; in the long run, the systematic destruction of forests could provoke a water-shortage crisis. Water—the prime source of energy, chemical solvent, and basic resource for humanity— no longer seemed inexhaustible. Only systematic reforestation and

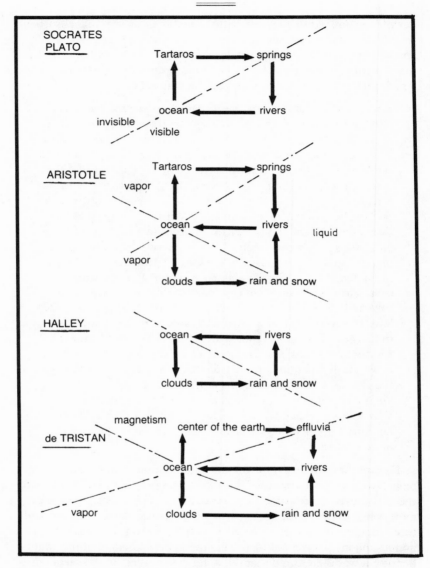

Figure 42. Representations of Water Circulation, from Antiquity to the Nineteenth Century.

draconian management measures of the nation's natural resources would avert a crisis. The usefulness of artesian wells, and the development of the railroad after 1830, somewhat calmed this furor.[14]

Although the existence of underground lakes remained doubtful for many scientists, the presence of forests alone did not satisfactorily explain the presence of water at great depths. For some scientists, the underground contained paramagnetic effluvia that humans could attract to themselves; the animal magnetism discussed in the works of Mesmer, and confirmed by those of Fourcroy and Laplace during the French Revolution, and Azais under the empire, explained this phenomenon. Thouvenel (1781) persisted in believing that "traces of internal water are the conductors of underground electricity, like clouds in the air for airborne electricity"; this magnetism was thought to contain terrestrial electricity (positive and negative). De Tristan (1826) took up this research, and concluded that the divining rod could excite a hydric charge due to its two branches, the right-hand one positive, the left-hand one negative, similar to a U-shaped magnet. Paramelle (1856) and Chevreul (1861) followed this theory to the end, which then fell out of favor with scientists.

The adoption of the atmospheric model of water circulation at the end of the eighteenth century carried with it a preconception about the quality of underground water. In the underground cycle, water was thought to be purified by the fire in the earth's center, and protected from surface pollution by the impermeable layer that extended several meters in depth: water pollution at that level was unthinkable.

Pollution could intervene only in the other cycle: traveling through the soil before reaching the water table, rainwater collected miasms, which corrupted it. All water, "even the purest, absorbs the germs of a host of animalcules that develop with time, given variations in temperature, movement, the nature of the collectors, etc.," asserted Berthollet in his *Essai de statique chimique*. Of all the samples of water he analyzed, it was obvious that rainwater—the rarest water in the underground cycle—was the most polluted, whereas water from wells and water filtered through bone charcoal were the least offensive as to taste and smell. In fact, water became, in the eyes of doctors and chemists, the privileged medium for spontaneous generation: the cholera epidemics of 1832 and 1847 were the "obvious proof." It would require all Pasteur's skill to prove that pure water was incapable of producing microbes. In the meantime, water had to be stored at a distance from habitations, and not allowed to remain long in contact with the air: its vapors were fatal.

Noxious Vapors

The damage caused by the frequent overflowing of the Arno in Florence and the Tiber in Rome, and the deposits of sludge that accumulated in the canals of Venice, very early motivated Italian civic authorities to reduce the pernicious effects of water. It was not so much the health of the citizens that was at stake as the fate of the buildings of these cities. In the sixteenth century, with the rehabilitation of Greek and Latin medical treatises, the question of the unhealthiness of marsh air was raised, but it was not until the end of the following century that the medical school in Padua put the blame on the fumes that arose from stagnating water and the noxious exhalations coming from urban industrial workshops. The *De febribus epidemicis romae falso in pestium censum relatis* by Heyne (1710) and the *De noxiis paludum effluviis eorumque remediis* by Lancisi (1717), showed that "the healthiness of a place comes from dry soil and drained marshes; unhealthiness springs from foul odors." The investigations carried out by Lancisi around Venice and Rome proved that the foul air of the marshes had a direct effect on animal and human mortality. In the Pontine marshes, or in the delta of the Po River, inhabitants rarely lived to the age of fifty. Fevers appeared in the summer during dry spells, weakening and killing the strongest individuals along with the weakest. The *Treatise on the Diseases of Tradesmen* by Ramazzini (1700) raised fundamental questions about the causes of urban mortality. All forms of employment entailed health hazards: fullers, chandlers, and linen-workers suffered from lung problems; curriers from spleen ailments; bleachers from rheumatism; canal-cleaners, weavers, and soap-makers from eye problems. The remedy? To air out the shops and let in more light.

The excellent work of the Academia del Cimento had only a minor impact on France, at least until 1760–70, after which the situation changed. The publication of the *De aquarium fluentium mensura* by Domenico Guglielmini, in 1710, which consecrated an entire section to malaria, was enthusiastically received. Fontenelle, in his address to the Academy in 1710, and d'Alembert in the *Encyclopédie*, were interested exclusively in the "theory of rivers." By contrast, in Germany and especially in England, Italian research was used as early as the second quarter of the eighteenth century in the hope of protecting troops and colonists from the fevers of American marshlands. Pringle's *Observations on the Diseases of Armies in Camps and Garrisons* (1753) stressed the harmful role of vapors rising from miry lands and the influence of humidity and terrain on the gravity of illnesses. From then on, the marsh was no longer an ineluctable given in nature, but a wound that could be treated and cured by men of science and art: in this earthen dermatology, doctors dealt with the most urgent need—the survival of individuals— whereas engineers worked on preventive measures for summertime, when bodies of water were low.

Investigations revealed an extremely high mortality rate among marshland laborers and peasants who lived nearby (the Academy of Bordeaux raised a protest in 1764; the Academy of Medicine in 1788). In the second half of the eighteenth century, there were disastrous reports on the health of inhabitants of marshy areas in the provinces. The *Constitutions épidémiques*, published by doctors to support the theses of the school of Padua, were alarming:

> Observation and calculations have demonstrated that the average life span is shorter in marshy districts—five or six years less than the known life span for regions or cities where the mortality rate is not regulated by the host of moral and physical circumstances that obtain in capitals and principal cities, where life entails a staggering diminution of the average life span.[15]

Responsibility for this mortality rate was attributed to the mephitic vapors emanating from stagnant water. Lafosse maintained that it was the peaty layer between clayey bottoms and topsoil that let the miasmas escape through cracks in the superficial layer.[16]

We find this same vertical cross-section approach in the description of privy pits: the most pernicious odors came from the greenish liquid located between the impermeable bottom of the container and the superficial "crust."[17] The term *méphitisme* was applied to the vapors from swamps as well as from privies. The marsh and the privy pit were now two of a kind. Plants and aquatic animals rotted and decomposed in the marsh, and the worst sorts of diseases were generated there.

City cemeteries were crammed with cadavers, many of them rotting just beneath the surface. From common graves rose noxious vapors befouling the air. All around, "the silty mud of the streets contains rotted or half-rotted animal and vegetable substances, which gives to the air an infection level of 1.2 on the eudiometric scale. This infection diminishes in proportion to the drying out of this mud, which is all the more pernicious in that the weather is always damp and warm." De La Condamine estimated that entire cities had disappeared because of diseases coming from swamps. The high mortality rate in the lower quarters of Arras, Frontignan, and Chateau-Thierry threatened irreversible depopulation if the municipal authorities did not take measures. "If one were to ask for more precise information on the progression of depopulation in marshy regions, we should say that a population of six

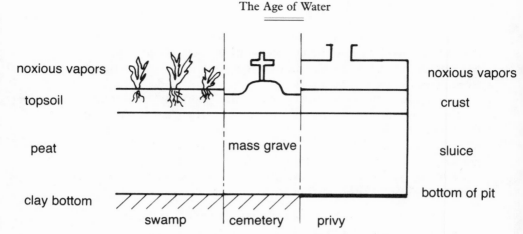

Figure 43. Schematic Representation of the Biosphere (End of the Eighteenth Century).

thousand in a marshy district will have been reduced to one thousand over a period of eighty years—five-sixths of the total population," Baumes maintained before the Royal Society of Medicine in Paris in 1789.[18] A century would suffice to depopulate the area.

Around 1770, a new form of chemistry would find answers to the threat presented by noxious exhalations. This was a new current of thought in chemistry, which broke with the doctrine of phlogiston and went beyond the fermentation-exploiting organic chemistry. In France, the precursors were Rouelle, who carried out numerous experiments on minerals in his courses in Paris in the Jardin du Roy; in England, Cavendish, who in 1766 published a series of works on his experiments with air—a series received with great enthusiasm by Parisian intellectuals; and in Sweden, Scheele. Lavoisier, Berthollet, Guyton de Morveau, and Fourcroy represented a new generation of chemists, who wanted to push back the frontiers of putrefaction, death, and everything static. With this new chemistry came disgust for and prohibition of putrescence. Lavoisier wrote on the animal kingdom:

> The possibility of converting animal matter into oils could lead one day to important discoveries of benefit to society. Animal wastes are principally composed of carbon and hydrogen; they thus closely resemble the state of oil, and in fact they provide much oil when distilled with a naked flame. But the unbearable stench that accompanies all such derivative products does not really permit us to hope to use them for a long time for anything but fertilizer.[19]

The only kingdom "not possessing any oily substance"—that is, susceptible to fermentation—is precisely the mineral, or inorganic,[20] that of the underground kingdom that so interested physicists at the time.[21] In addition, announced Berthollet, "animal and vegetable substances are so changeable and variable"[22] in comparison with mineral substances, whose acids and salts were easy to obtain and measure, and whose laboratory reactions were rapid. Practically everything could be obtained from minerals. Even saltpeter could be found in a natural state just about everywhere in France. The "mineral machine" was not only efficient, like all simple machines, it was also clean and healthy.

Research on gases began when the general public, in the larger cities, became incensed when it came to understand the dangers of putrid emanations. In Paris, since 1760, the upper middle classes living next to cemeteries and slaughterhouses demanded that measures be taken against the pestilential odors. The *Mémoire pour se garantir de la puanteur des puisards* ("report on how to protect oneself from cesspool odors"), by the engineer Deparcieux,[23] pointed an accusatory finger at *mofette*—a "highly toxic" gas produced by the decomposition of animal and vegetable matter. Lavoisier and Priestly succeeded in isolating this gas in 1772. "*Mofette*" was nothing other than nitrogen. As for oxygen, Lavoisier in 1774 named it "vital air," at Condorcet's suggestion, who was worried about the high mortality rate prevailing in marshy districts. It was thus in a dialectic of life and death that the research of the new generation of scientists took place: Lavoisier, Dubuat, Fourcroy, Silberschlag, Coulomb. They worked within a "paradigm of oxygen"—to use Kuhn's terminology[24]—only part of a much larger schema, that of life itself. The preceding generation, that of Rozier, d'Alembert, Guettard, Réaumur, de La Lande, the "phlogiston generation," had been firmly grounded in the paradigm of death. They discovered a number of scientific laws, but their *modus procedendi* was not the contestational, reformist approach that their successors would adopt, as Alain Corbin has pointed out.

The Mineral Kingdom

Between the organic and the mineral, between artisans and manufacturing, the choice was obvious for this new generation of thinkers. Since as early as the middle of the eighteenth century, the Parisian scientific community had become disenchanted with the virtues of artisanal activities. Artisans were now reproved for their passive utilization of nature, and their adherence to procedures that were useless, if not indeed harmful, and very time-consuming. Desmarets, in his *Premier mémoire sur la papeterie* ("first treatise on paper-making"), in 1771, in praising the superiority of Dutch products, denounced French paper-makers. They "were so intent on using rotten rags to make paper that they paid attention only to the beneficial effects of putrefaction on their papers; the Dutch methods, in spite of the beauty of the finished products, were offensive to them precisely because they represented exceptions to their cherished principles." [25] Lavoisier in his *Rapport à l'Académie sur le Rouissage* ("report to the academy on retting"), in 1783, criticized the hemp- and linen-makers: "Retting in stagnant water, putrefaction, infection, the release of inflammable hydrogen—must not these things harm the surrounding habitat?" [26] Coulomb wrote about millers that "they each believe themselves in the possession of secrets that they are most unwilling to disclose to the knowledgeable. This love of exclusion and secretiveness is encountered at every step in their mills and in all their commercial transactions. It has often led astray the policies of enlightened nations, precipitating them into wars. And even though it is equally the enemy of enlightenment and general prosperity, of liberty and political wisdom, it holds the sway of an empire, against which the truly enlightened protest again and again." [27]

But Berthollet, in his *Eléments de l'art de la teinture* ("elements of the art of dyeing"), pointed out that "fortunately, a revolution is taking place among us. It is no longer to ignorant workers that our places of manufacture are being turned over; we find there instead, in the main, very enlightened men, well-educated physicists, and it is to them that we must address ourselves if we wish to bring about the progress of the useful arts and remove the obstacles that might oppose them." [28] For these scientists, then, only a new system of education, based on confidence in science, technology, and life, could bring about an industrial revolution in France. The *Réflexions sur l'instruction publique* ("reflections on public education") by Lavoisier (1793) and Fourcroy's work for a new system of education show this clearly. Elementary teaching should begin with the practice of sanitation and respect for new techniques. This line of thought was even more evident during the First Empire. For example, there was the *Rapport demandé à la classe des Sciences Physiques et Mathématiques de l'Institut, sur la question de savoir si les manufactures qui exhalent une odeur désagréable peuvent être nuisibles à la santé* ("report submitted to the department of physical and mathematical sciences at the Institute [of Sciences], on the question of whether crafts that exude disagreeable odors are harmful to one's health"), written by Guyton-Morveau and Chaptal in 1805. It was to be used in the passage of a law on *commodo-incommodo* investigations (decrees dated 15 October 1810 and 14 January 1815):

> [The solution to this problem is] all the more urgent inasmuch as the fate of useful establishments and the existence of several arts have until now depended upon elementary policing regulations. Some [manufacturers], removed at a distance from their source of supply, from the labor force, or from consumers, by prejudice, ignorance, or jealousy, continue to fight against many disadvantages, against innumerable obstacles placed in the way of their development. . . . Thus it is that we have seen the manufacturers of acids, ammoniac salts, Prussian blue, beer, and leather preparations relegated far outside the city limits; and each day, these same establishments are yet again denounced to the authorities by anxious neighbors or jealous competitors. . . . This state of uncertainty, this continual battle between manufacturer and neighbor, this unending indecision on the outcome of an establishment, paralyze the efforts of manufacturers, slowly attenuating their fortitude and energies.

The Institute of Sciences then judged it indispensable to "take a look at" the industries that polluted the most, according to its own set of criteria. First, industries were divided into two groups:

The first will include all those whose workings allow to escape into the atmosphere by means of putrefaction or fermentation any gaseous emanations that could be considered repugnant by reason of their odor, or dangerous by reason of their effects: the retting of flax and hemp, working on animal entrails, slaughterhouses, starch manufacturers, tanneries, breweries—all those establishments where a large quantity of animal or vegetable matter is submitted to putrefaction in a humid atmosphere. Emanations re-

The second will include all those that, operating by means of fire, develop and release, in steam or in gas, diverse exhalations more or less unpleasant to breathe and reputed to be more or less harmful to health: the distillation of acids, wines, and animal fluids, the art of gold leafing, the preparation of lead, copper, mercury. These are much more profitable than the first, and much more intimately linked to the prosperity of national industry. There are few of these that will render the neighborhood unfit to live in.

leased by fermentation and
putrefaction are really harmful to health.

Magistrates must carefully distinguish what is merely uncom-
fortable and disagreeable from what is harmful and dangerous;
they must recall that for a long time coal was forbidden on the
unfounded pretext that it was dangerous for health. They
must, in a word be full of truth, . . . so that we will gradually
come to eliminate from cities the blacksmiths, carpenters, millers, pot-makers, coopers, smelters, and weavers. For it is certain that workers in those crafts tend to form neighborhoods
that are more disagreeable than those of the other types of
manufacture of which we have spoken; and the only advantage
that the blacksmiths and their like have over the others is that
they have been in business for a longer time.[29]

In the reforms it recommended, the institute did not mince its
words, nor did the state, which followed through with laws based on
those recommendations—and this position would be reinforced in the
years to come. Differentiating two classes of industrial activity aimed at
separating two classes of workers: those who worked for national development, and who thus deserved all the attention of the state and its institutions, and those who prevented national development. The former
represented progress, cleanliness, health, stoutheartedness; everything
should be done to help them: ventilation of work places, construction of
public baths, standardization of privileges. The latter were anathema-
tized: they symbolized the mental backwardness of primitive peoples,
carried with them the grime of the past, and lived in the mire of the
city. For them there could be no salvation without conversion, which
would necessitate the destruction of their environment. Not only must
nature be closely watched, but those who encouraged its worst excesses
must be heavily penalized. The "repression" that Michel Foucault has
shown to be representative of the end of the eighteenth century applied
to all sciences and techniques.

Stagnant water was now *the* enemy. To the voices of Ramazzini
(translated into French in 1777), Pringle (1760), and Platner (1765),
were now added those of Condorcet (1775), Lavoisier (1782), Chaptal
(1787), Fourcroy (1788), and Baume (1789), all denouncing noxious vapors. Guyton-Morveau (1801), Berthollet (1803), Chaptal (1805), and
Gay-Lussac (1808) condemned *méphitisme* irrevocably, and with them,
other members of the Institute of Sciences and professors in the *grandes
écoles* in Paris—Lamblardi, Girard, Fourrier. The ideological message

came out in their teaching: engineers and doctors would be the first missionaries. But in the meantime, the most urgent matters had to be dealt with.

"What would be the best means of procuring a healthy atmosphere for the city of Batavia [Indonesia], whose air is so polluted by the river vapors?" asked the Haarlem Society in 1778. "Is it healthy or noisome for the constitution of humans to plant trees in cities or in their environs? Do the gases they give off purify or infect the air?" asked the Academy of Toulouse in 1782. "Animal respiration, fermentation, combustion, and finally effluvia of all sorts will soon corrupt the air of the atmosphere and render it fatal to all animal life, had nature not found means at her disposal for turning used air back into ordinary air . . . these means are plants," seems to have been the answer by Lavoisier in 1788. In the overall order of life, the vegetable kingdom made up for the neutrality of the mineral kingdom, reducing the problems caused by the animal kingdom. Hence the trees and shrubs planted along the boulevards in cities, providing them with "suction and force pumps moved by the air,"[30] thus regulating the vertical circulation of vapors. It was not just forests that would control smog.

It was thus a question of eliminating all excessive consumption of oxygen—that is, of eliminating unproductive putrefaction, that of street muds and of "stagnant water, or water exposed to the summer sun, in which cattle are watered, and which contain the germs of unhealthiness or putrefaction," as Rozier wrote.[31] In the urban slums, a crowd of common folk, washerwomen, bleachers, dairymaids, pig drivers, and the hungry gathered along the waterways. The established powers could not control them, and they could be ripe for rebellion. That water might deprive better-off citizens of clean air and their freedom.

Although water was indispensable, it was to be used only in its dynamic form. All other water must disappear, and those who were concerned with the problem at the time studied those immense bodies of water that ringed the city on all sides: the fortification moats.

The Moats

Until Stévin (1630), the water-filled moat was unanimously approved by strategists. For Dürer, Lanteri, and Perret, "water prevents the enemy from tunneling under the walls, and it impedes offensives"; it eliminated surprise attacks, especially at night. But the defeats inflicted upon the French armies in Italy, and the Spanish armies in the Netherlands, as well as the sieges of Henry IV in his conquests had exposed the weaknesses of the water-filled moat. The destruction of moats was both lengthy and expensive in terms of labor for besiegers, but they could also overcome the obstacle by constructing boat-bridges. In warm regions, water gave rise to a permanent state of bad air, which was noxious for besiegers as well as for the besieged; in cold countries the moats could freeze over and thus nullify their value for defense.

The dry moat also had its detractors: although it could be used as a refuge and allow close counterattack and the supervision of the approaches to the city, it also facilitated access to the enemy, who could tunnel under or climb over the city walls. The absence of a water barrier also fostered desertions. Intermediate solutions combining features of the two systems were proposed. Machiavelli originated the *cunette,* a wide canal, two or three meters deep, excavated in the bed of the dry moat and filled with water. Stévin, hydraulics engineer in the service of the prince of Orange, suggested around 1618 the construction of dikes and locks. With this method, the running water detoured from the moats in times of peace could better serve the craft activities within the city. The multiplication of putrid fumes would thus be avoided, because the moats were dry, and yet accumulated filth could be flushed away. At the approach of an enemy, opening the sluices allowed for the flooding of the approaches to the city. As an alternative to the continuous and static system of Machiavelli and the dry or water-filled moats favored by others, Stévin proposed a system of discontinuous and dynamic flow. In this, his innovation brought him closer to the ideas of Galileo and Fermat, his contemporaries, all three of them forerunners of kinetics and differential calculus.

At the end of the seventeenth century, during the wars with Holland, moat locks were a good means of protection against the French, especially in view of the ignorance of hydraulics shared by Louis XIV's strategists. It was responsible for the failures and defeats of French armies, which bogged down in marshes or drowned in moats fitted out at the time of Stévin or designed by Cöerhom. In light of these experiences, Vauban was opposed to the projected fortification of Clairville in Dunkirk in 1668. He opted instead for bastions that could be lock-flooded, operated by hydraulic engineers whom he called "Archimedes' band." Complex hydraulic improvements thus came to protect the cities on the borders: *batardeaux* four to five meters thick built at strategic points; sluice locks and protected runways at the top of ramparts, like those in Metz; a siphon aqueduct built between the marketplace and the citadel of Lille. To this, Vauban added a system of entrenched encampments, which provided the fortress-city with a new line of defense, at a greater distance from the city, flanked by advance troops and cavalry. The lengthening of firing range and the ever-increasing accuracy of weaponry necessitated ever more distant defensive measures. For Vauban, as for Mariotte and Newton, water was no longer an inert mass, but a natural force that had to be controlled and adapted.

The teachings of Vauban did not bear immediate fruit: until the end of the seventeenth century, the relative success of French armies abroad left the fortresses within France to their own devices. But in the second quarter of the eighteenth century, Louis XV had them reinforced, and founded the School of Military Engineering of Mézières (1748–50). There strategists tried to demonstrate how the absence of water control could be fatal for defense, whereas storing water and a good use of locks would render a place impregnable during war and healthy in times of peace. Belidor in his *Architecture hydraulique* (1737–39) claimed that "the manner in which places are attacked has undergone extraordinary progress since the beginning of the century, whereas defense seems to have lagged behind. . . . The only defense tactics that appear to have made any progress are those that make use of the motility of water." Water, so precious to defense, must be held back by *batardeaux*, allowed to flow out only to a small extent into only a part of the moat, recovered and stored elsewhere in order to strengthen the tenailles (outworks in the main ditch between two bastions of a fortification):

> The best moats for defense are those which are naturally dry and can be flooded when necessary and then emptied. . . . We can accomplish this by having large water reserves within easy access to dry ditches, in order to be able, when it is time, to submerge besiegers with suddenly released floods of water. . . .
> It is less the number of structures that will contribute to good defense than the good use that can be made of ditches and water.[32]

The besieged city was now no longer a sealed monolith, uniform and passive, but a many-armed body, mobile and active, equipped with unpredictable factors difficult for assailants to grapple with, such as the depth and velocity of the waters in the ditches, the quantity of powder stocked in the citadel, and the number of men responding to the siege.

At Mézières, not only was a new military science being taught but, especially with Abbé Bossut and d'Alembert, an economic policy for water management was also being worked out, which Stévin had already foreshadowed. In the ditches of the citadel, the future military engineers—Dubuat, Coulomb, and Carnot, to name only the most famous—analyzed and reproduced with minute accuracy the hydraulic models of the defense of sites and the resistance of fluids. The Corps of

Engineers School became the principal European center for hydrodynamic calculations, and economic factors were also taken into account.

The rampart and the moat thus lost some of their importance; their upkeep had become much too expensive for the small advantages they offered. Carnot wrote on the eve of the French Revolution:

> The present [military] system envisages few sieges, and a place might remain for an entire century without being attacked; but during this time the rampart has to be taken care of, and at great expense, in spite of its lack of use. If war were to break out, this fortification is still of little use, because if it did not exist, one could easily make up for its lack with trenches built then and there; their layout would be chosen according to the particular case. One cannot change the position of a fortification during war and if it is advantageous in one set of circumstances, it might not be worth anything in another.

The upkeep of fortifications was the major question strategists had to answer in the last quarter of the eighteenth century; most of them opted for taking the ramparts down.

From static water, continuous and standard in the sixteenth and seventeenth centuries, the defense of cities had come, little by little, through the course of the Enlightenment, to a dynamic state, discontinuous and "irregular," as Leblond wrote in 1775. Elaborated by statisticians like Vauban, mathematicians like Euler, and architects like Blondel or Cormontaigne, poliorcetics had followed the evolution of scientific thought, which wanted to make good use of the movement of water.

Fluid Resistance

The important hydraulic works undertaken in the Netherlands and Italy in the sixteenth century for the reclamation of arable lands, the development of river traffic, and the containment of floods were generally entrusted to the same architects and engineers who worked on urban fortifications. The success of their enterprise depended essentially on the solidity of their constructions, which had to be capable of withstanding the worst weather conditions, floods being the least foreseeable and the most dangerous. To understand and reduce the violence of water was the primary preoccupation. Castelli, at the beginning of the eighteenth century, inaugurated the "study of water movement," which was divided into "theory of rivers," "hydrodynamics," and "fluid resistance." Each of these new disciplines stressed the dangers of the excessive velocity of running water, and attempted to find ways of containing and controlling it.

Guglielmini's *De fluminum natura tractatus physico-mathematicus* (1712) addressed the nature of rivers. It studied the velocity of currents and its influence on the bed and banks, riverborne silt deposits, and the gradient of rivers. Five hundred pages of valuable research on the theory of rivers were received with great enthusiasm by the Academy in Paris, which lost no time in having them published in France, along with other Italian texts relating to floods. The three volumes of the *Recueil d'auteurs Italiens qui traitent de la vitesse de l'eau* ("collection of Italian writers dealing with water velocity"), published in 1722–23, were completed by six more volumes in the second edition of 1784–86. The *Architecture hydraulique* by Belidor, the major French work, was very influential: there was not a course in hydraulics taught at the Ecole des Ponts et Chaussées that did not make reference to it.

The most convincing conclusions of the Italian scholars concerned the straightening of rivers in the Italian peninsula, whose sinuosities and violent floods had caused terrible flooding and damage to urban centers. Castelli's disciple Galileo, going against the teaching of his master, claimed that water velocity was independent of the gradient of the river. But Viviani and Torricelli did not agree with him, and reconsidered Castelli's theories. They advised building dikes, as well as widening and straightening the beds of the Bisenzio and the Arno upstream from Florence. The results were positive. Straight prevailed over curved, and Italian science and technology overcame the impetuousness of nature, just as they had mastered the indolence of the Italian swamps. According to the Italians, the best way to prevent floods was to accelerate a river's current, but this idea was strongly criticized by engineers of the time, and in France the headwaters of rivers would continue to be dammed until 1750, to prevent flooding; static water was still preferred over dynamic.

Once remedies had been applied, it remained to analyze the causes of floods. For Guglielmini and Belidor, the two most authoritative experts, rivers overflow their banks because of the continuous eroding effect of surface waters. Dubuat wrote in support of Guglielmini:

> Valleys were little by little dug out by running waters, and if their beds appear stable now, it is only because of the enormous work already accomplished by the waters that have flowed without interruption. Thus the hills have been lowered, the valleys filled in, and mountains expose the rocks of their innards; and the low-lying lands, raised up and nourished for a

little while by the substance of the highlands, will one day, but much later, also flow out into the ocean. The earth of the future, reduced to a shocking level, will resemble an immense and uninhabitable swamp.[33]

This apocalyptic vision was held by the most eminent hydraulic engineers at the end of the eighteenth century, who believed that the world was no more than five thousand years old. In other words, if a river had taken four or five millennia to reduce its longitudinal profile, one or two centuries more would suffice to eliminate the gradient altogether.

The doctors of the swamps were thus joined by hydraulic engineers, geographers, and agronomists in criticizing the cutting down of forests. Cadet de Vaux wrote in 1798:

> The elderly claim that the seasons are reversed . . . that the mistral did not exist before the construction of the Languedoc Canal and the cutting down of the trees on the surrounding hills. . . . The heat of the earth is decreasing. Americans plant

Figure 44. The Dynamic Power of Water (Guglielmini, *Opera omnia*).

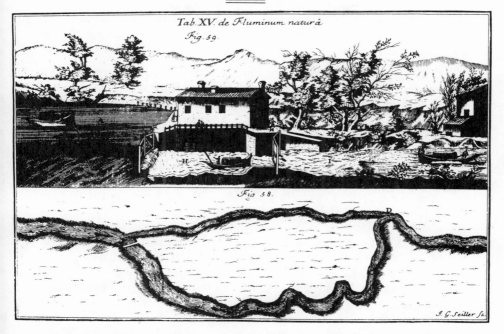

Figure 45. The Art of Diverting and Regulating Waterways (Guglielmini, *Opera Omnia*). Reproduction courtesy Bibliotèque Nationale, Paris.

trees when their children are born; we cut down forests to endow our offspring with misfortune.

In order to put a stop to the deterioration of nature, the beds of waterways had to be stabilized. One approach was by controlling the permanent silting up of rivers, resulting from the normal current and periodic flooding, because of rain or melting snow. This in turn led to the development of meteorology under the direction of Coulomb and Laplace at the beginning of the nineteenth century. Another approach was that of developing the riverbanks: "the river bottom cannot be considered stable until it is capable of letting all extraordinary flood waters flow out with a velocity suited to the holding capacity of the soil, its bottom, and its sides." [34] From this followed the widening of the bed for ordinary flooding, the construction of levees for extraordinary floods, and the leveling and straightening out of the bed:

> In general, a river should be considered a good friend, which, at one moment or another, can become our worst enemy. Just as fortresses built in times of peace are the strongest, so must the banks of the rivers be fortified so that they do not war

against us; that is, the banks must be righted and planted thick with brambles and willows, and reinforced with bulrushes and grass.[35]

The work of the technicians did not stop at terrain improvements. Since the beginning of the eighteenth century, those with a good background in mathematics became interested in what Daniel Bernoulli called the "statics of running water," or "hydrodynamics," the science of the Enlightenment.

Unlike air, water is a visible, homogeneous fluid whose viscosity can be measured; it can be stored and divided into as many parts as desired. It can thus be easily used in experiments. In addition, time conferred upon the science of water its letters of nobility. All this contributed to link water intimately with the development of the concepts of mathematical formulations. Water contributed not only to the formulation of important physical laws, but even more to the experimental verification of the first hypotheses of infinitesimal and differential calculus. Thus Parent, Euler, Ricatti, the Bernoullis, and d'Alembert elaborated, each in his own way, the general principles of fluid movement. But not only the pure sciences brought about progress in hydrodynamics. Academic esteem solicited technological innovation, and hydraulics seemed to be one of the disciplines capable of increasing the wealth of nations. Water interested those in key sectors of the economy: transportation and manufacturing.

Under the general heading of transportation, "maneuvering vessels" came first. It was necessary to understand the workings of the tiller, the state of equilibrium of a ship and its stability, masting, and oar action. At the end of the seventeenth century, Renau studied coasting (1689), Hoste applied trigonometric calculus to maneuvering (1692), and Bouguer evaluated the resistance of water in his *Traité complet de la navigation* ("complete treatise on navigation") (1698). New insights were introduced during first half of the eighteenth century. The *Essai d'une nouvelle théorie de la manoeuvre* ("essay on a new theory of maneuvering") by Jean Bernoulli (1714) and *La théorie de la manoeuvre reduite en pratique* ("theory of maneuvering made practical") by Henri Pitot (1732) were the first works to use the methods of infinitesimal calculus. Euler worked as early as 1738 on the movement of floating bodies, in particular "on vertical oscillations and their application to research in the weight of vessels," and on wind forces; his *Scientia navalis*, published in Berlin in 1749, was a decisive step forward in the acceleration of maritime transportation, along with the *Essai d'une nouvelle théorie de la resistance des fluides* ("essay on a new theory of fluid resistance") by d'Alembert (1752). D'Alembert wrote in his Introduction:

Knowledge of the resistance of fluids is an absolute necessity for the construction of ships. The invention of differential and integral calculus has put us into a position to examine the movements of bodies right into their elements or ultimate particles. It is with the help of calculations alone that we have been able to penetrate these fluids and discover the interplay of their parts, the action that their innumerable atoms exercise upon each other, and see what constitutes a fluid, which appears simultaneously united and divided, dependent and independent, single and manifold.

In his hydrodynamic research, d'Alembert deduced three types of fluid resistance. The first, constant, results from the cohesion of the particles of a fluid; it is independent of the form and speed of the solid body resisting it. The second is proportional to velocity and "is the result of the rubbing that the fluid particles experience as they slide over the surface of the resisting solid body by virtue of their respective velocities. The third is proportional to the square of the velocity and comes from the force of inertia." From these results, he concluded that fluid resistance is least when the speed of a floating body is identical with that of the fluid, and, if this latter is zero, as in the case of a sea or canal, when the inertia of the floating body is reduced.

These conclusions were taken into consideration and developed experimentally under the direction of Choiseul, and then Turgot, who named Condorcet, d'Alembert, and the Abbé Bossut joint directors of navigation in 1775. A laboratory was set up in the gardens of the Ecole Militaire; Bossut and Condorcet carried out several hundred experiments there. They proved that "it is essential to make navigational canals as wide and deep as possible, but without throwing ourselves into useless expense." In addition, in order to reduce water resistance, "it is necessary that the boat be longer than it is wide, and an elongated poop will noticeably increase the speed of the wake. . . . The objective in naval transportation is not simply to shorten the distance that a vessel must travel, but also to go from one point to another in the shortest time possible."[36] In support of the formulations of d'Alembert, it was demonstrated that between a river and a canal of slight gradient, the canal offered, in the case of two-way river traffic, the least resistance. In order to increase the average speed of boats, the velocity of rivers thus had to be diminished, or, when this was not possible, a parallel system of canals had to be cut. Experts in hydrodynamics and proponents of the theory of rivers were in complete agreement with these conclusions.

In order to analyze the resistance of fluids to solid bodies, mathematicians first used simple surfaces, the square and the circle. The first

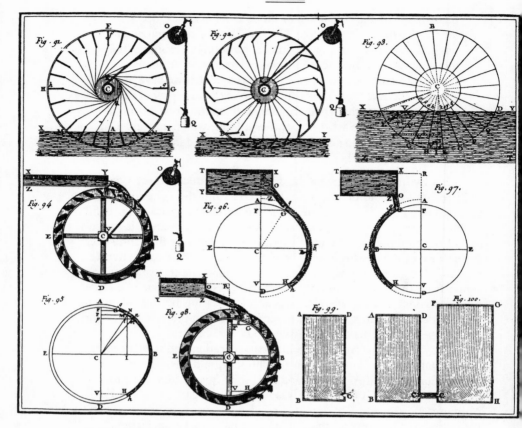

Figure 46. Experiments on the Force of Waterwheels (Bossut, *Traité d'hydrodynamique*, Paris, 1786–1787).

experiments were conducted by Mariotte; in the annexes of Versailles and Chantilly, he tried to measure the impulse given by a current to a square pallet. He concluded that it depended on the speed and depth of the current. His apparatus featured a lever that maintained the force of the current in equilibrium with a weight equivalent to a column of water, whose base surface was identical with that of the pallet: a simple, linear system, in which statics explored the dynamics of forces.

Across the English Channel, Newton was experimenting with the oscillations of small lead balls in water. He found that the resistance of fluids as compared with the speed of a pendant varied according to the metric force of that speed: proportional to its speed for a slow movement of the pendant and squared for a rapid movement. Newton's was an oscillating, kinetic system, based, like that of Huygens, on astronomy and the measurement of time.

For an entire century, surveyors and mechanics vacillated between these two laws, trying different experiments. The results, frequently controversial, were often applied to the hydraulic machine whose simple design most closely approximated the pallet: the watermill. Mariotte, the precursor of hydrodynamics, mentioned in the margins of his *Traité du mouvement des eaux et des autres corps fluides* ("treatise on the movement of water and other fluid bodies") (published posthumously in 1686) a method of measuring the power of wheels by "comparing the velocity of river water to the velocity of the water flowing out of a reservoir."[37] At the beginning of the eighteenth century, Parent, taking up

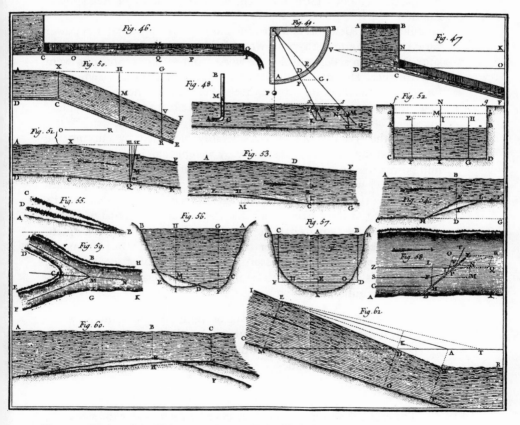

Figure 47. Reclamation of Waterways (Bossut, *Traité d'hydrodynamique*, Paris, 1786–1787).

the static studies of Mariotte, and using the dynamics of Newton, was the first to apply the theory of the percussion of fluids to the question of mill yield. He thus observed, in 1704, that the impulse given to a paddle wheel is proportional to the square of the difference between the velocities of the current and the wheel. He established that machine power is maximal when the velocity of the center of impulsion of the paddle wheel is equal to a third of the current velocity. Belidor, Daniel Bernoulli, and d'Alembert took up these results but maintained different hypotheses favorable to one or another of the founders of fluid resistance. More precise experiments on mill wheels permitted all initial contradictions to be resolved. In Germany, Euler encouraged his son Albert; in France, d'Alembert urged Deparcieux to publish his early results; in England, Smeaton was encouraged by the Royal Academy of London.

Euler and d'Alembert demonstrated in 1754 that maximal mill power varied according to the type of wheel being used, and that the best results came from scoop wheels, the worst from turbines. Smeaton went even further. He first of all defined "mechanical power," which he found to be maximal for scoop wheels. For paddle wheels, he showed that the maximum was obtained when wheel velocity equaled about half the speed of the current (1757). He supposed, in addition, that the impulse of the water could be considerably increased by curving the blades, that the water acted far more by weight than by force, and that mill power was proportional to the diameter of the wheel.[38]

Two other works, by Chevalier de Borda (1767) and by the Spaniard Jorge Juan (1771), showed that fluid resistance is proportional to the natural speed of the current, and that the power is maximal when the speed of the wheel equals half the speed of the current. Smeaton opted, in a much later dissertation, for two-fifths; in 1779 Dubuat proposed 0.42. All were unanimous in asserting the superiority of scoop wheels, and in promising a brilliant future for turbines. All criticized the underutilization of mills. Bossut wrote in 1787:

> In practice, [mills] are given six or eight blades, sometimes even fewer for mill wheels located on small rivers. This number is too small; the wheels would work more efficiently with twelve or eighteen blades.

Smeaton added in 1796:

> The effect of scoop wheels, if we imagine them under the same circumstances of charge and water consumption, is on the average double the effect of paddle wheels. . . . The greatest effect

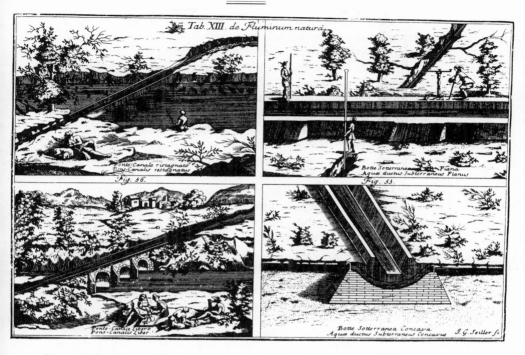

Figure 48. Transporting Water by Bridge-canals (J. Leupold, *Theatrum machinarum hydrotechnicarum*, Leipzig, 1724).

possible is a speed of three feet per second for the largest as for the smallest scoop wheels.

Fabre claimed:

> Too many mills attain only the smallest effect. . . . Runners should be placed in all the machines, even in those which are located on rivers. . . . The use of locks must be avoided as much as possible. . . . One must always allow for the water exiting from a wheel to attain at least the same velocity as that of the wheel.[39]

"Examine the banks of rivers and you will find that badly-located mills, on points that are too narrow, are the cause of floods; remove the causes and you will eliminate the effects," recommended Silberschlag. After 1770–75, millers were accused not only of inflating the price of flour, but also of being the ones responsible for the slowing of rivers; they stood accused by public opinion with the support of science.

Thanks to the formulas deduced from differential calculus and laboratory experiments, the active resistance of water could now be better employed. The turbine or "hydraulic machine moved by its reaction with water" was without question the most elaborated model used by fluid mechanics in order to put this resistance to good use. At the beginning of the eighteenth century, the turbine, especially in Languedoc, used only a small number of straight blades; its effective yield would have been less than 30 percent. Euler, looking for a way to apply his method of maxima and minima, devoted himself entirely to this during the 1750s. He showed that the effect is optimal when the feed channel is at right angles to the blades, and when the blades have a curved profile. Bossut and Smeaton improved the curvature and multiplied the number of blades around 1775. At the end of the century, the theoretical yield was around 70 percent; fluid resistance had been practically overcome. The general formula, which had escaped Dubuat, was announced by Prony in 1804, proving both Mariotte and Newton correct.[40]

But the solutions proposed to reduce this resistance remained, as yet, too theoretical. Fabre wrote in 1783:

> The results that would be obtained on a machine built according to these formulas would still depend as much on luck as on principles. The real principles of good construction are still unknown: but we have the necessary means to find them.

A century had thus been sufficient for the "philosopher" physicists to dominate the third element of nature, to build up as many good as bad theories on the origin, utilization, disadvantages, and forms of resistance, and to assert that, at all costs, resistance and its excesses must be limited: "running water is another, less violent cause of change, but more common nowadays than volcanoes," mused Cuvier in 1808.[41] It was thus necessary to activate or cover over stagnant water, and to slow down and closely supervise torrents. The regulation of water and its vapors was thus an interplay between dynamic statics and static dynamics, the goals of hydraulics. As for the air, "we have reached the point of being able to purify it by chemical means, of making it more healthy, of disinfecting prisons, dungeons, and other unhealthy places, and to generate, if we can say so, a healthier and more breatheable air than even that of the atmosphere," claimed Lavoisier around 1790.[42]

Dubuat, the Lavoisier of hydraulics, wrote:

> Each kingdom, each province, each city has its hydraulic needs; necessity, convenience, or luxury cannot do without the help of water; water must be brought into the very center of our dwellings; we must protect ourselves from its ravages, and

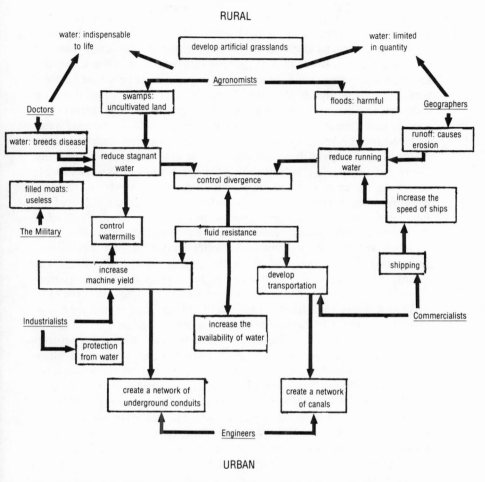

RURAL

Figure 49. Control of Water (Late Eighteenth Century, Early Nineteenth Century).

make it work the machines that will ease our discomforts, deco-
rate our dwellings, embellish and clean up our cities, increase
or preserve our holdings, transport from province to province,
or from one end of the earth to the other, everything that need,
refinement, or luxury have made precious to us; large rivers
must be contained; the beds of smaller rivers must be changed;
we must dig canals and build aqueducts.[43]

At the end of the eighteenth century, water no longer appeared to be
exhaustible. It was subject to atmospheric recycling and could be mea-

sured by rain gauges and hygrometers; abundant vegetation provided the means to capture and regulate water. This same vegetation decontaminized the soil by allowing it to take advantage of the benign gases of the deep underground, and by generating oxygen, necessary for life. Limited in quantity, running water had to be made to serve the key sectors of the economy: agriculture, the backbone of the nation; fledgling industry, anxious to capitalize on the energies of water and steam; commerce, which needed a large-scale hydraulic network. In a word, water had become the key element of development, and its future lay in the hands of the Corps of Engineers and of the engineers of the Ecole des Ponts and Chaussées ("school of bridges and roads") who were capable of taming the most infected swamps and the most impetuous torrents by appropriate measurements and controls, as Prony, the director of the Ecole des Ponts et Chaussées, reported to Napoleon. Almost a third of the courses of the *grandes écoles* were then devoted to hydraulics.

Moreover, the highway network, neglected during the French Revolution and the Empire, was in ruins; getting it back into shape and maintaining it in the future promised to be very expensive. The hydraulic network set up prior to 1789 retained all its assets, and the cost of its upkeep was minimal. Its development on a large scale would permit an increase in agricultural potential by draining swamps and irrigating land. At the dawn of the Restoration, the realization of these projects presupposed an enormous quantity of water that had to be stored, channeled, and economized. Because water was now in short supply, agronomists, whose knowledge was vital for the national economy, emphasized the constant loss of water on the earth's surface, aggravated by the disappearance of forests to attract clouds. The historian cannot ignore the panic that overtook political circles (and even took on the aspect of an energy and chemical crisis around the years 1820–25) in order to comprehend the desire to reduce the loss of water and to manage its distribution:

• in space: A systematic crisscrossing of the country could be achieved by developing a network of interconnecting canals. Not only could merchandise be transported almost costfree, but the irrigation of lands would encourage the extension of artificial pastures, thus of cattle-raising, and combat the pernicious effects of drought.

• in time: Reforestation would establish natural control of the seasons, of rainfall and floods. It would also increase the flow rate of springs, and hence augment the sources of artificial and natural waterways. Meteorology could predict recurrent floods, while waiting for nature to heal itself.

• in cities: A network of conduits could be created in order to provide drinking water for all residents according to their means. Low-lying areas, the breeding grounds for disease, were to be filled in. Riverbanks subject to flooding were to be raised. The number of mills would be reduced, or their mill races severely regulated. Commercial warehouses were to be set up in the outskirts and along navigable waterways. Industrial implantation would be encouraged.

Water was not only an element necessary to life, but the very basis of the capitalist economy, which gave terms used for the measurement of water velocity its own referents: the continuous "flow" of merchandise, by analogy with the volume of water that flowed per unit of time. The term *débit*—"flow," "outflow"—appeared in the vocabulary of water engineers around 1830 after its initial use by Say in 1818, in relation to canals. In the eyes of deterministic economics, urban artisanal activity, embedded in the lower parts of cities, was careless about conserving this precious resource; it exhausted the rivers by transforming them into sewers, and increased urban putrefaction, which used up oxygen.

Second Stage
Filling in the Ditches

After the first half of the seventeenth century, urban fortifications lost all their immediate usefulness. A long period of internal peace and the power of the French army caused these vast spaces to be forgotten; municipalities filled them in with greenery. Walkways lined with elms and lindens decorated the ramparts. Residents came there "to rest and enjoy recreation in the shadow of the trees." Archers and artillery regiments came there to practice; below, on the flanks or in the dry ditches, were the firing ranges for harquebusiers. Sometimes swans could be seen on nearby ponds. The boulevards became the favorite spot for the Sunday promenade; the term, by the way, took on its present meaning in the nineteenth century; "Residents often promenade on the rampart in order to breathe clean air, . . . on the other side of the rampart, one is delighted by the charming view of the countryside at the peak of the season." [44] This description of the outskirts of Amiens at the end of the eighteenth century undoubtedly applied to all the cities studied here.

"The governors and chief officers of fortified places allow the town dwellers to plant gardens surrounded with shrubbery and ditches, to plant trees, and even sometimes to build houses in the vicinity of the forts," to Vauban's immense dismay. Beauvais rented out certain portions of the boulevard for the growing of madder and drying of pieces of cloth; Soissons and Noyon authorized the setting up of private gardens. In Le Mans, even earlier, Richelieu had ordered the chateau to be demolished, and the city had authorized inhabitants to make openings in the wall for their convenience, against the payment of a fixed fee of sixteen pounds (1643). In the area of the gates, along courtyards and counterscarps, all sorts of small shops proliferated: butchers in Chartres, wine vendors in Orléans, rope-makers in Evreux and Auxerre, drawn there probably because city taxes were not applicable. As for the interiors of towers, the cities used them for jails, asylums, or for other uses—for example, as powder magazines, in cases where the towers were not leased out to individuals to be used for lodging, or for lime-kilns as in Châlons-sur-Marne. In exchange, renters were held responsible for eventual deterioration, but the commitment little by little became a dead-letter. In the absence of regular maintenance, entire sections of the wall caved in, and the edges of ditches crumbled, undermined by roots and eroded by the continual cattle crossing. Municipal budgets could not cover the cost of upkeep, and sometimes it took the authority of a master fortification-builder to have well-chiseled stones picked up from conspicuous piles on roadways.

Sometimes orders were given to reduce the height of one part of a rampart in order to decrease the cost of maintenance and to put a stop to further deterioration. In Noyon, Evreux, and Auxerre, the rampart was thus lowered from ten to three meters at the beginning of the eighteenth century. But more often authorities were satisfied with simply tearing down terrepleins and fortification curtains.

When earth had been used to fill in part of a ditch, it was earmarked to be used for the large intercity roads then under construction. This mixed material, composed of peat excavated from the ditches and of gravel, rubble, or other debris from the city, was porous, and the engineers of the Ecole des Ponts et Chaussées chose it for surface drainage projects. The walls of Senlis were used to build the Paris-Compiègne road in 1764; those of Etampes, the Paris-Orléans road in 1768; those of Auxerre permitted the construction of a road on the riverbanks (1775). The immediate proximity of this landfill thus enjoyed a twofold benefit, economic and technical. The wide public thoroughfares that crossed the city from one end to the other pushed aside the monumental gates, whose demolition supplied cheap cut stone, useful for the urban renewal advocated by city administrations, and excellent for architectural works of art. In Senlis and Beauvais, the Paris gates were used for bridge decorations; the Peinte gate in Evreux (1764) and the Guillaume tower in Chartres (1780) were used for adding on to the city hall; and an annex to the episcopal palace of Châlons was built with stones from the Jard gate (1780).

By the end of the eighteenth century, demolition was no longer lim-

Figure 50. Troyes: Ruins of the Fortifications—The Challouet Tower and the Pouce ("Thumb") Diversion Leading to the North of the City. Engraving by Fichot (1851). Reproduction courtesy Bibliotèque Nationale, Paris.

ited to just doing away with a few portions of the wall. On the advice of doctors, urban authorities wanted to fill in the ditches of their cities. In Rouen, Thiroux de Crosne, between 1780 and 1783, destroyed "the ramparts and enormous ditches that separate the city from open land; they had become useless, inconvenient, and even dangerous."[45] The stones were used to enlarge and repair the quays. In Reims, major undertakings in 1787–88 covered over the pond and the drainage ditch located on either side of the Ceres gate, and enclosed the waters of the Dieu-Lumière gate in an underground drain, the Rivière Neuve. Finally, in Amiens, the ditch fed by the Hotoie spring was reduced to a simple stone-lined reservoir, intended for the water supply of the city.

During the First Empire, the movement spread to the smaller cities, first those near Paris. "The destruction of these walls and ramparts will procure for the city of Senlis an advantage in that new constructions will be added to the suburbs of the city; they will be more airy and will have wider and more agreeable promenades." The law of 27 July 1808 decreed the demolition of the ramparts and the filling in of the city ditches. Beauvais followed suit under the city government of Nully d'Hercourt: 14,113 francs were spent in 1804 for the "establishment of boulevards," the transformation of moats into a narrow encircling canal, and the razing of the Craoul tower. Similar projects were undertaken in Etampes, Orléans, Chartres, Troyes, and Evreux, all declassified as strongholds by Napoleon. In the larger cities, health concerns took an interest in the easily flooded lowest and seediest parts of the city, both within and without the walls, the places where the working-class population was densest and where new industrial workshops were building up.

The city architect of Rouen in 1806 gave the advice: Of all the towers in Rouen, the location of the Vieille most readily lends itself to embellishment, and for the lowest cost. At present, now that we are no longer encumbered by the walls of the city, it will be a matter of demolishing the section of old houses that separates the tower from the quays. The Martainville quarter, the lower part of the city, is the marshiest, the worst built, the least healthy, and nevertheless the most populous. The marshy land will have to be raised by at least two feet. In Amiens, the Hotoie park was filled in and laid out again.

These works slowed down somewhat during the Restoration; here and there, work was limited to transforming into botanical gardens some of the marshes previously kept in place for defensive purposes (Châlons and Auxerre, 1817). But the cities were more preoccupied with the setting up of a transportation network similar to the one in England. Each city made plans to make its main river navigable, if it was not so already, or to cut canals to the closest access to river transportation. Cities on major waterways multiplied their port improvements: Orléans protected itself from the floods of the Loire by raising its quays along the ramparts; Rouen raised and reinforced the riverbanks; Caen deepened its port and equipped its eastern rampart with new warehouses.

The cholera epidemic of 1832 signed the death warrant of the fortifications. New political authorities, anxious to project a progressive image and to absorb at little cost the unemployment that had resulted from the economic crisis, went forward in the name of social hygiene and ordered their complete destruction. The second epidemic, in 1849, would result in the disappearance of the last traces of the ramparts.

In Etampes, between 1833 and 1840, in Noyon between 1835 and 1845, in Troyes between 1835 and 1860, in Chartres from 1838 to 1847, and in Amiens from 1835 to 1870, the walls were nearly all knocked down and used to fill in ditches and moats. In their place now stood the large trees of the boulevards—the lungs of the city.

But cholera epidemics were not the only cause: the canalization of territory—the mouth of the Aisne-Vesle canal in Reims; the Angoulême canal along the Somme in Amiens—and especially the railroads, required large open spaces outside the cities. The railroads followed precisely the same paths as the circumferential boulevards. Stations were built on plots of ground whose prices had been frozen for centuries; they were now sold to the railroad companies at bargain prices. Only Soissons kept in its role of fortified city, retained its seventeenth-century moats. The goal of the reformers of the end of the eighteenth century had finally come to pass: the city breathed and was dynamized thanks to the clean air of its lovely boulevards, and malarial fevers had slowly disappeared. But the reverse side of these municipal improvements was the disappearance of the bodies of water that had digested a large part of the city's wastes. Imperceptibly, water pollution thus increased with the disappearance of the moats.

Abandoning the Network

Until the Restoration, the urban water network had retained its usefulness in toto. The discoveries in mechanics and industrial chemistry, perfected at the end of the eighteenth century or at the very beginning of the nineteenth, had no effect on it, with few exceptions, until after 1830. It was at that time that the river crafts began to disappear as production costs were gradually brought down. The network both inside and outside the city, abandoned by economic activity, retained only one final function: the cloacal.

The Watermills. The works of Smeaton and the French scientists were taken up by Fabre in France and especially by Evans, the "American Watt," at the end of the eighteenth century. *The Young Mill-Wright and Miller's Guide*, published in Philadelphia in 1795, went through fifteen editions in sixty-five years (twelve for 1818–53 alone). Its French translation, *Guide du meunier et du constructeur de moulins*, by Benoist, miller of Saint-Denis, suggested clear improvements as to the diameter of grindstones, the number of lantern pinions, and the number of scoops or paddles according to the height of the waterfall. It followed the methods of simple calculus—not those of integral or differential calculus, as in the austere work by Coriolis, *Du calcul de l'effect des machines* (1829). The *Guide* used easily understandable diagrams (very few complex geometric figures, such as abounded in works published by Poncelet in 1825 and 1827) and elementary drawings with tables of correspondences between the different parts of a mill. There were no elaborate theories like Rousset-Galles' "Memoire sur la théorie des roues à augets, des machines à réaction et de celles à colonne d'eau" ("memorandum on the theory of scoop wheels, reactor machines, and machines worked by a column of water"), published in the *Annales des Mines* in 1828. Case studies were to be found in annexes to the work, with a description of the mills of Saint-Denis: improvements had doubled the theoretical power furnished by the waterfall. This important and popularized work was not advertised in technical journals, but the publicity given to it in departmental directories, which listed fairs and reviewed various agricultural and industrial productions of the region, along with customs and regulations, guaranteed it wide circulation among millers.

The results were not long in coming: as early as 1832, the two largest mills in Beauvais, the Ratel and Saint-Laurent mills, owned by the same person, were reequipped; their yield went from 30 to 60 percent of total theoretical yield. The Huez and Roi mills in Noyon benefited from the same kind of improvements in 1833. The "English process," which replaced gears with ball bearings (invented around 1796), was adapted for the Andreux mill in Noyon in 1834, mills on the Juine in Etampes in 1836, and the Saints-Pères mills in Chartres in 1838. Effective yield rose on the average from 40 to 70 percent, for an investment of 4,500−5,000 francs per pair of millstones.

Between 1830 and 1832, Burdin made decided improvements on the turbine engine studied by Euler. He brought its effective power to 67 percent of the theoretical maximum. Morin, in 1838, raised it to 75 percent, using wheels with a smaller diameter than that of paddle wheels, and for the same cost. These turbines were set up in Chartres in 1840, at the Saint-Jean mill in Beauvais in 1843 (with an effective yield of 80 percent), and at the Sempigny mill in Noyon in 1847. Everywhere, the goal of technical improvements was the profit to be realized on flour, and competition advantages over other millers. It is most likely that at Beauvais, for example, the owners of the Limaçon and Porte de Paris mills would have waited longer before adopting the "English" methods for their mills in 1844, except for the rivalry of three other millers, who, in order to bring their prices into alignment with Paris market prices, had already improved their equipment and, in order to amortize their costs, had increased their production. Some millers in Etampes, having only small waterfalls available, readily harnassed their mills to steam engines. There was no longer any question of illegally raising sluices to increase the water charge, ever since on-site inspections had been imposed by the government. The fact remained that paying for these mechanisms depended upon the productivity of the mill, and few millers could invest several thousand francs into their works and then risk seeing cheaper or better-quality flour arrive on the local market. An ancillary network of rural roads was slowly added to the essentially interurban highway network. This factor cannot be ignored: during the second quarter of the nineteenth century, half of the mills of the Robec ceased to operate despite the doubling of the population of Rouen; the city was at the center of a web of departmental roads and byways that had increased from five hundred to thirty-six hundred kilometers between 1838 and 1850. The flour was transported overland and on the Seine.

Between 1832 and 1845, the average yield of the mills of Beauvais and Noyon went from 40 to 65 percent. By increasing by half the effective power of the mills, technological innovation had found a way to increase cereal production, 30 percent on the average during the Restoration. But by this same token, mills that were not improved were condemned to destruction, like the mills of Saint-Blaise, the Coisel, and Tarlefesse in Noyon, even though they had been built only in 1800; the Bayard in Amiens; and still others. Between 1830 and 1860, a third of the urban mills were abandoned; less than 10 percent in Beauvais and Troyes, nearly 30 percent in Noyon, 50 percent in Rouen and Châlons, whereas the effective yield of the others was increased by more than half. The final assessment was thus in favor of increasing the power of urban milling. Decrease in the number of mills does not reflect the stagnation of water, but on the contrary, a dynamization: the mills that failed were those that were weak, set up in the Middle Ages at the mouth of ditches or on intramural canals: the Versette in Noyon, the Robec in Rouen, the Nau in Châlons, the Plache-Clément in Troyes, the Odon in Caen. The only mills that survived were those located on riverbanks.

The Riverside Crafts. The discovery of chlorine and the industrial expansion of cotton were the death blow to artisanal textile production. Calcium chloride and chlorine bleach, perfected by Berthollet in 1796, revolutionized the procedures for bleaching cloth: the process now required only eleven days, whereas before, using ash, it had taken several weeks. The quantity of water needed was reduced proportionally, and the flocculation of ashes was eliminated. Until 1825, the making of

Figure 51. View of the Entrance to Evreux near the Planche Mill (Mentioned as Early as 1298) and Its Watering Trough, 1842.

bleach was limited to Paris and Rouen, and used essentially in local industry. At the beginning of Louis-Philippe's reign, the use of bleach tended little by little to become general in other textile centers, first in Amiens, then in Beauvais, Reims, and Troyes, where bleaching was carried on in shops with pressurized water. The minute-by-minute timing of baths, concentration of fluids, and washing in abundant water, as recommended by Berthollet and Chaptal,[46] required expensive equipment, close attention, and a division of labor not to be found in the slow traditional methods. Passive resistance to industrialization was in vain, in the face of its reduced production costs and competition in the form of cotton introduced through the coastal cities of Rouen, Caen, and Amiens. Raw cotton was as cheap as flax or hemp, with better intrinsic qualities (in the raw state it contained only 5 percent undesirable colorants, as opposed to 20 percent for flax), and bleaching was reduced to eight operations, as opposed to seventeen for other materials. The long network of small extraurban canals little by little lost their chief artisanal function; retting tanks for flax and linen would last for only a few decades more.

In 1804, Bralle, in Amiens, succeeded in retting hemp in two hours, using a chlorine-based solution. This method was the object of a ministerial decree, but it was soon noted that the cloth deteriorated after only a few washings. In 1816, "an anonymous offer was made to the Academy of Sciences in the amount of three thousand pounds to be given to the inventor of a machine capable of loosening the fiber of flax and hemp, and reducing it to filaments without having to have recourse to the unhealthy operation of retting." Several processes were proposed, none with success. The prize, offered year after year, was finally withdrawn in 1853. Four years later, Leoni and Coblenz's machine finally satisfied manufacturers: their machine was rapid, nonpolluting, and cost only a thousand francs. But the sum was still out of the reach of small craftsmen. In Troyes and Reims, some craftsmen were still using the traditional methods along the Seine or the Vesle at the beginning of the Third Republic, but in Amiens, Beauvais, and Noyon the dried harvest was delivered directly to manufacturers.

In fact, the extramural hydraulic network had been little by little converted to truck gardening and pasturage, along with the development of urbanization. The smallest plots of land, those closest to the city, less irrigated as a result of the controls on flooding, became workers' gardens. The others, regrouped, enlarged, and partially dried out, had been converted into pastures with the encouragement of the minister of agriculture; each year France imported more than 50 million francs' worth of cattle. The hydrographic network was beginning to blur; the water vapor rising from land under drainage began to diminish.

Inside the city, the battle against foul odors went hand in hand with industrialization. In the manufacture of cloth, for example, Dubuc, a citizen of Rouen, received, in 1829, the Montyon prize, offered for inventions that would improve the lot of the worker. He had worked out a new process of facing and gluing with a calcium-chloride and wheaten flour-based product, which kept all the moisture in the cloth in a relatively dry atmosphere:

> The desire to be of use to this numerous class of weavers, and
> to exhume them, so to speak, from the so frequently unhealthy
> slums where they are forced to stay for a portion of their lives
> by the nature of their work, determined me to occupy myself
> first of all with the composition of dressings now in use; sec-

ondly to find a slightly hydrometric glue, which would have no effect on the weaves except in basements and other similar places.[47]

The process was adopted in Amiens and Rouen by enterprises that could build dry, well-ventilated buildings. The small craftsmen of the lower city—alone, without capital, unable to move their shop or to invest in newer techniques—were condemned to disappear. Their methods varied "from shop to shop, and were modified according to the locale, the water, . . . the seasons, and the climate."[48] In fact, "sanitization," as understood by Dubuc, signaled the independence of new industry from the small crafts.

Another example of a disappearing craft was the tannery. The process perfected by Seguin in 1794 permitted the preparation of skins in three weeks. The two hundred forty thousand skins prepared annually in his factory on the île de Sèvres filled a quarter of the annual national consumption. The process did not become widely accepted, first of all because it utilized a bark concentrate that required a somewhat more sophisticated technology; secondly, because it produced a lighter leather; finally, because it required continuous production, which the small rural and urban tanners could not accept without completely destabilizing their way of life. In 1800, Sens was the only city using the new method, which needed much less water than the older techniques. After the First Empire, this method was implanted in the largest cities, in workshops situated near the slaughterhouses relocated for sanitary reasons outside the city and downstream. As long as towns remained more or less isolated through lack of interconnecting highways, the traditional family-operated tanneries managed to survive, though their leather was recognized as of lesser quality by their peers. But leather was also subject to competition from other substances that were more supple and much cheaper, such as new waterproof fabrics (the MacIntosh method, 1836) and boiled cellulose products. As a consequence, the last tanneries disappeared in Provins, Evreux, Auxerre, and Noyon after 1840. Deprived of their bleaching shops, tanneries, and slaughterhouses, the intramural canals of Troyes, dating from the twelfth century, were finally suppressed in 1836; the municipality accused them of breeding disease and of propagating misery in general.

Again in Troyes, paper-making, which provided a living for a hundred rag dealers, adopted new methods in 1840: the "continuous" machine invented by Louis Robert in Rouen in 1798, and bleaching with chlorine, perfected around 1835, which made less use of rotting tanks. These new methods accelerated production and reduced water consumption, a boom for the Papeterie mill in Troyes. But around 1850, the cellulose extracted from wood, ground up, soaked, and centrifuged, was used in place of rags, thereafter used only for making deluxe paper. The paperworks in Troyes failed as a result.

In the middle of the eighteenth century, the consumption of saltpeter increased noticeably: a larger and larger quantity was allocated for the manufacture of nitric acid, indispensable for dyeing and used in pharmacy. Because extraction did not increase and the stock of powder was in decline, the nation very quickly found itself depending upon foreign imports. The government became concerned about the matter, especially when the public raised an outcry against the vandalism of saltpeter collectors, who forced open basements in the name of the king or who took bribes from peasants. In addition, many citizens preferred to throw the ashes from their woodfires into the stream rather than give them to the saltpeter collectors. The Academy of Sciences became concerned with the problem, and offered a prize for "finding the quickest and most economical means of procuring a more abundant production and harvest of saltpeter than those that are at present available in France," in the hopes also that *salpêtrier* scavenging raids into private homes would be abolished. The prize was won in 1782 by the Mesmerian Physiocrat Thouvenel, who introduced artificial nitrate beds, already in use in Sweden, Switzerland, and Prussia.[49] But production was not developed in France until after 1800 when it was set up in the countryside on "plantations," or artificial nitrate beds. Here again, the city lost the monopoly on a primary resource.

Fermentation, which had now been eliminated from all industrial production methods, and condemned for its foul odors, was definitively exiled from the city. The cemeteries had been exiled outside the walls at the end of the eighteenth century. The slaughterhouses and hospitals went the same way under the First Empire. There remained wastes of all kinds, which inhabitants continued to throw into privy pits, canals, and even the street, or around the ramparts, when these had not been razed.

Unlike Paris, which according to Cazeneuve had seventy thousand privies, the cities in the provinces had very few: several dozen in Chartres, barely a hundred in Rouen. And journalism had not yet campaigned to reduce these "storehouses of corruption and expel the hydra, which from its stinking volcano, ceaselessly throws out into our atmosphere the marks of corruption."[50] Only an anonymous *Projet pour la parfaite salubrité de l'air dans la ville de Rouen, proposé aux amis de l'humanité* ("project for the perfect salubrity of air in the city of Rouen, presented to friends of humanity") proposed the "construction of a general sewage canal at a half-league at least from the city, to be called the Health Ditch. Carriages, to be called 'chamber pots,' the name of the sewage carts in Paris, will go back and forth without interruption, to carry away wastes at no charge. Between the canal and the city, the authorities will grow sweet-smelling plants." This revolutionary project—it dated from the years 1790–95—was unfortunately never put into operation. The "ventilator process," which had made the fortune of its inventor in Paris, was hardly even mentioned in Rouen at the beginning of the French Revolution. Several years would have to pass before Parisians sought out the provincial market. In 1801, Pierre Le Manissier suggested to the city of Beauvais that he take away human excrement without charge, and convert it into powder "for the great benefit of agriculture." He offered his services to Orléans in 1804. But the mayors did not follow up. Only a few "moveable and odorless ditches" invented by Cazeneuve in 1818 were sold in Rouen and Amiens. The other few privies were emptied by nearby peasants and vintners.

In fact, the razing of the ramparts and the closing of cul-de-sacs by police measures forced the large majority of city dwellers to discharge their wastes into the canals, or, when it was still there because it had retained some usefulness for local craftsmen, into the moat. With the disappearance of the mills, the intramural hydrographic network was now used only for the function of absorbing human excrement. The mild auto-purification maintained by the waste products from artisanal activities having entirely ceased, the canals now became public sewers, as in London and Paris, if not worse; in some cities—Amiens, Caen, Troyes—the volume of ditch water left after the city supply was diverted to navigable waterways was insufficient to flush away all the filth. The ancient network, sooner or later, had to be covered over. The technological model of underground sewage conduction was the only one acceptable to the Ponts et Chaussées engineers: watertight, odorless, and with negligible current loss if flushed out often enough.[51] Health had finally triumphed!

In Châlons, the Nau was covered in 1862; in Troyes the ditches of the old city were buried in 1865; in Rouen the Robec and its tributaries were covered over between 1874 and 1878. Elsewhere—in Etampes, Beauvais, Noyon, Evreux, and Auxerre—technical services were in the hands of the by-road services, which were more attached to techniques and traditions that could be called "soft." In their rivalry with the engineers, the byway agents prided themselves on not using the same methods.[52] To the health boards in the various departments,[53] which urged them to cover over the canals, they answered that frequent cleaning out

Figure 52. Side View of the Cathedral of Amiens, 1832, and the Entrance of the Somme into the City at the Queue de la Vache ("Cow's Tail") before the Riverbanks Were Raised. Reproduction courtesy Bibliotèque Nationale, Paris.

was just as efficient for the same maintenance cost. The municipal councils agreed with their advice, and it would be necessary to wait until after World War II to see the final and definitive burial of the hydrographic network. In the end, the Ponts et Chaussées won the battle with the municipal services.

The long period of burial of the hydraulic network, begun at the end of the eighteenth century, was finished only during the twentieth. Different sciences, by their evolution and their popularization, were participants in this process.

Water was a key element in scientific development. Water gave of itself to science. It was on water that the experiments of mathematicians, astronomers, physicists, chemists, and agronomists were based, to explore infinitesimal calculus, the sphericity of the earth, fluid resistance, inorganic chemistry, and the transpiration of plants. Science, by definitively establishing the atmospheric cycling of water, showed that deforestation and the drying of wetlands would bring about a loss for the entire nation if other measures were not taken, especially because the economic development of the country required ever more water in its canals. At the same time, questions were asked about the dangers of stagnant water, and it was decided that vapors and still water, though useful for craftsmen, had to be removed from the city, where they served only to spread the ravages of epidemics.

This "anxiety crisis" increased as the sciences became more popular, and also as a desire to mold the city according to a new esthetics became manifest. It called for airiness in public places and along the ramparts. This crisis also increased as poliorcetics evolved, for which water had no value other than as a reservoir perfectly controlled with locks or pilings. The enormous ditches abandoned since the middle of the seventeenth century were the first to be filled in, with the help of the dismantled walls; the peat extracted three or four centuries earlier was now put back into its original place. The boulevards clothed with greenery were the pride of the municipalities. Leisure now upstaged warfare. The microclimate set up around the city began to disappear, and with it, malarial fevers—the first sign of purification.

There was a movement afoot to eliminate putrefaction from the city. At the end of the eighteenth century, inorganic chemistry was put to work on the Parisian waste ditches, to reduce their noxiousness; the bad air of the city, brought on by poisonous vapors, was decried. Traditional urban crafts, using putrefaction as a means of production, were condemned to disappear: intellectuals, engineers, doctors—all educated Parisians—criticized them for their pollution and the slowness of their techniques. Now only the hygienical, the mineral, and the mechanical were desirable.

A new rhythm began to take hold in the eighteenth century, a rhythm espousing acceleration. Water, too, was to undergo this acceleration. Water would amplify movement to the extent that it contributed to the knowledge of mechanical yield and to the reflourishing of commercial activities in the interior of the country. Free, undomesticated water was harmful not only because of evaporation, but also because of its inactivity. Water could be precious to humankind only as canalized, supervised, and captive. This captivity focused attention on the dynamics and kinetics of water. Water vapor was pressurized, subjected to the dynamics of steam engines: the dynamic played with the static. The velocity of water had to be brought to a uniformity of movement in order to facilitate navigation and to regulate the blades of mills: statics supervised dynamic water. The statics of dynamics and the dynamics of statics, taking advantage of kinetics, wiped out, to some extent, the natural force of water. Fluid mechanics was thus paradigmatic; from now on it had at its disposal all the instruments of water control. Along with research on construction materials—solid mechanics—the way was open to the elaboration of the mechanics of continuous media in the second quarter of the nineteenth century.

Water, now dominated on all sides by sciences and techniques, had become a sound economic value.

Conclusion

Let us escape for a moment from the constraints of time and space. This study covers sixteen centuries of regional history, which saw two periods of urban growth—the Middle Ages and the period of the Industrial Revolution—two periods of urban decline—at the end of the Roman Empire and in the late Middle Ages—and three mutations of urban technologies—medieval, post-medieval, and industrial. It is therefore tempting to go into historical and geographical comparisons in evaluating the common or divergent forms of city and technology.

Urban growth, around a built-up center, is always preceded by profound changes in the structuring of political power. Whether it is a question of the Roman conquest, which wiped out the power of the Druids; feudalism, which arose from the crumbling Carolingian dynasty; or bourgeois order refusing royal absolutism—each of these phases masquerades behind the innovating aspects of its political revolution the firm will to bring together populations that until then had been more or less dispersed, so as better to be submitted, nay exploited, in the name of new principles. Post-Carolingian township-building and the Industrial Revolution gave rise to new forms of urbanization, which incorporated themselves into the preceding urban fabric thanks to vestiges of the past and inherited economic and political infrastructures. Protourbanization, characteristic of the tenth and eleventh centuries, was comparable to what was elaborated at the end of the eighteenth—which historians call protoindustrialization—and what followed the war of the Gauls. These three movements accompanied demographic growth, which increased the potential labor force necessary for the carrying out of the new objectives of the powers in place: the construction of a network of roads and public monuments in the course of the first century; the creation of a hydrographic network and the building of churches in the eleventh century; the multiplication of communication networks at the end of the eighteenth.

This first phase in the process of urbanization modified traditional social behavior and turned the city into the hub of these transformations. There followed a period of economic development signaled by the grafting of new activities onto the network in place, and by the settling down of previously transient populations. In a similar way, the network inherited from the preceding period was abandoned, retaining only its main, indestructible axes. Thus with each successive phase the past was symbolically erased.

Out of these economic upheavals, the true dynamos of urban growth, came a sanitation phase. The new political order adopted the firm position of protecting the two vital elements of air and water by removing from the city all breeding grounds of miasmas. The clear, sparkling water of the Middle Ages, the water furnished by the aqueducts of the Roman era, the clean air and pressurized water of our own era, have become symbols of cleanliness, health, and urban prosperity. Bodily hygiene is parallel to urban hygiene. The city must control its own ecosystem.

But urban expansion seems always to be limited. It lasted little more than two centuries in the Roman era; hardly three in the Middle Ages. Demographic growth came to a halt; death unbalanced life. The city creates within its own midst a reaction to sanitation: dirtiness became a sign of holiness in the third century, and the medieval steam baths were transformed into brothels. The decline of interregional commerce and the cooling of the climate then played a decisive role in the breaking up of the delicate state of equilibrium that the city had been able to maintain. The spread of urban decline was encouraged by wars and epidemics, which thus forced the city to close back in upon itself; a moat, supported by a wide rampart, was built to isolate the city more effectively from the surrounding countryside. The imagination turned toward the macabre, and the times were attuned to the rhythm of the sacred; technology discovered putrefaction and standing water. Meanwhile the city continued to take advantage, willy-nilly, of the heritage of the past. The very houses sank into the earth, into the damp ground, along with the dead: recent digs of Merovingian sites carried out in France and England allow us to picture this for the High Middle Ages. The malarial fevers engendered by the stagnating water of the marshes or ditches, the famines caused by the bad harvests due to poor weather, or by the ravages of war, plagues—everything worked together, during half a millennium, to make the city a center of poverty, from which only a few managed to escape. The city was dominated by its environment.

Conclusion

Urban growth, urban decline: Can we say that urban history itself is cyclical? The forms I have just described conceal economic and political structures that are quite different: the first period of urban growth was colonial, and established a political economy founded on Roman ideology, as Paul Veyne has brilliantly demonstrated. The second period was the result of feudalism, and brought about a revolution in small crafts. The last period was based on the power of the state, and triggered the Industrial Revolution. Much the same was true of urban decline: although the two periods in question placed an emphasis on spirituality and religiousness at the expense of materiality, they differed fundamentally: the first occurred during the decline of the Roman state and the rebirth of regional particularities; the second—more relative—followed the decline of feudalism and the emergence of the public sector and the state as economic agents. In reality, urban history varies considerably from one region or one country to another. Urban growth had not totally disappeared from the Italy of the High Middle Ages, and England, which did not have to withstand attacks from abroad, did not fortify its cities in the same way in the late Middle Ages, with the result that its urban micro-climate was totally different from that of French cities.

Urban history and the history of techniques should be, above all, unitary and regional histories, by the analysis that can be made of the introductions, transfers, delays, and blockages of new techniques or of forms of urbanization—notably the sacred. Techniques and the city are intimately entwined in the geographical area that stimulates them.

If we study England from the fifteenth to the eighteenth century, for example, we find that an entirely different technological system developed. England was now keeping and using the wool it had formerly exported to France. Textile technology (using Roman alum) was developed, whereas on the Continent flax and hemp prevailed. What were the means of production worked out in England? The history of technologies shows that textile mechanization was more widespread, and hydraulic energy much better used than in France, whereas the techniques of maceration and putrefaction seemed much less important, and fortifications inside a city behind a wall of stagnant water were less effective.

Holland, the leader in paper production at the beginning of the eighteenth century, did not use the process of steeping rags. Desmarets examined the question in two papers read before the Royal Academy in 1771 and 1774. In Holland, the Protestants driven out of the Angoumois region by the revocation of the Edict of Nantes did away with rotting and substituted first the washing of cloths in order to degrease

227

them, then a mechanical grinding using hammers and cylinders. The paper they produced was of much finer quality. Dutch cloth was also whiter and of better quality. As in England, coagulated milk was used: its acidity more readily eliminated discolorations. The fermentation of hemp was also carried out more rapidly.

Everything would lead us to conclude that in Protestant countries the attitude concerning death and decomposition was different from the French. In any event, English and Dutch cities, in the eyes of French scientists of the second half of the eighteenth century, were indeed much cleaner. And, taking a lead from Max Weber, it is probably through analysis of the "differential" of the religious experience, and more generally of attitudes regarding death and decomposition, that we will be able to analyze the vast technological differences, and to know why England gained such an economic advance over France between 1750 and 1830. Indeed, of the most recent analyses, only those that presuppose the existence of a proscientific subculture convincingly answer this question.[1]

In northern Italy from the fifteenth to the eighteenth century, public authorities committed themselves to a war against the death rate. Without the research that they encouraged, would eighteenth-century France have taken up the challenge? What were the deep, underlying reasons that urged the Italian state to pursue this combat, whereas in northern France the question would be studied only a century later? Could the answer be that there was a stronger desire to maintain a high life expectancy of the laboring population in Italy, whereas in France a kind of "death wish," analyzed by Huizingua, prevailed? And resistance to technical innovations was much stronger in northern France because craftsmen were attached to their putrefactive methods even if these same methods were decimating them.

Urban techniques follow, in the long run, the evolution of social behavior. Given a choice of several technical solutions, a given era and region will choose the one that most closely conforms to the mental structures and collective imagination of its population. The nineteenth century could have perfected fungal chemistry, as the alchemists of the sixteenth and seventeenth centuries had tried, those who thought they would find the philosopher's stone in dung, as the research of Réaumur and Thiroux d'Arconville in the middle of the eighteenth century had suggested. But putrefaction had become a taboo. Only a few technicians were still looking for ways to use excrement in textiles or in leather-manufacturing at the beginning of the nineteenth century. In the late Middle Ages as well, craftsmen could have invented more dy-

namic chemical processes, such as tannin concentrate for leather manufacture, like the dyers of the thirteenth century for woad and madder;
or at least they could have reacted more vigorously to the import taxes
imposed by the king of France on the Roman alum so necessary to the
making of manufactured products a century before. It can be observed
as well that, as early as the fifteenth century, technicians knew how saltpeter was formed. They thus had the means of producing it and of
creating artificial nitrate beds. But four centuries would have to pass
before new procedures would be carried out.

The development of chemistry thus reveals an identification of form
with energy. The putrefactive era favored stagnant water, intense humidity, and the nullification of energy. The dynamics of water, fundamental for the urban technologies of the twelfth and thirteenth centuries, together with mechanization that impeded contact between
artisans and their materials, became useless for the techniques of the
Renaissance. And vice versa, with the heightened consciousness of the
philosophers of the eighteenth century, a new attitude toward nature
was responsible for the creation of a new technology: everything that
could corrupt, rot, or destroy life had to be forbidden and eliminated.
"That which is concerned with the preservation of life belongs most
particularly to the domain of physics," wrote Fontenelle.[2] The domes-
tication of water—in liquid or gaseous form—became a vital necessity:
the dynamics of the static and the statics of the dynamic were two vec-
tors of the sciences of the Enlightenment. Synthetic chemistry, easier
to master, gradually replaced the natural chemistry of fermentation,
which had drawn all its energy from stagnant water. To enter the era of
a truly organic chemistry, it was necessary that the death taboo be overcome, as is perhaps the case today with the development of the bionic.

From all this it follows that technological or scientific innovation
comes first and foremost from upheavals in mental structures, and does
not deviate as long as these structures have not been modified. Thus, at
the very beginning of the eighteenth century, as Robert Mantoux has
shown, Newcomen, Savery, and Papin, following the example of craftsmen, used only the passivity of steam to make a vacuum in the body of
the pump or in order to counterbalance atmospheric pressure. The passage of the atmospheric machine to the steam engine, "the generator of
movement," would not take place until the passive mentality vis-à-vis
the power of nature—the hydrostatic—had been overcome by a mentality that believed more and more in the control and exploitation of
living forces of this same nature—the hydrodynamic. Thus, Gallic society had all the necessary elements for the construction of the watermill, but it would take form only in the high Middle Ages with the Bene-

dictines in order to increase their spiritual autonomy (spend less time on daily, material activities) and develop in the eleventh century in order to regularize the feudal tripartite division, which arranged the submission and exploitation of the *laboratores*. A society can "stock" technical information, but it will be liberated only when society has undergone an internal revolution. This revolution came to life in the Paris basin at three distinct periods: the second half of the eleventh century, the first half of the fourteenth, and the second half of the eighteenth: periods of time contemporaneous with social restructurings, as revealed by urban history and the history of technology. It was precisely during these periods that the totality of techniques in use converged in another productivity: the technology of statics and fermentation came into place only when hydraulic energy was monopolized and the provisioning of key materials had become a problem. The technology of Lavoisier and hydraulics could materialize only when the entire city had been saturated with foul vapors, and it is probable that medieval technology was inscribed in a similar manner on the city of later centuries. What now remains is the task of studying the genesis of the "artisanal revolution."

If economics is the servant of invention even during times of crisis, it is probably because economics as well is affected by underlying movements concerned about the future, which give direction to the composite of urban techniques—and without doubt also that of rural and mining techniques[3]—according to a paradigm shift balanced between the two extremes of life and death.[4] The city becomes aware of its own environment: sometimes it masters it, and sometimes it adapts itself to it.

The city of the Middle Ages used the self-purifying effect of its artisanal wastes and the dynamics of its rivers to limit water pollution. The city of the Ancien Régime used its huge ditches and its static waterways to digest urban wastes. The city of the Industrial Age, having buried the surface water network, had no way to reduce water pollution except by moving it outside the city. Each type of urban technology had its own regulative system, adapted to its own society, which tended to limit the deterioration of the environment.

Notes

Works listed below without full bibliographical details are to be found in the Bibliography.

Abbreviations

ACNSS	*Actes du Congrès National des Sociétés Savantes*
AD	*Archives Départementales*
ADG	*Annales du Gâtinais*
AESC	*Annales, Economie, Société, Civilisation*
AM	*Archives Municipales*
AN	*Annales de Normandie*
BA	*Bulletin Archéologique*
BAMR	*Bulletin des Amis des Monuments Rouennais*
BCASI	*Bulletin de la Commission des Antiquités de Seine-Inférieure*
BEC	*Bibliothèque de l'Ecole des Chartes*
BHPCTHS	*Bulletin Historique et Philologique du Comité de Travaux Historiques et Scientifiques*
BLSAS	*Bulletin de Liaison de la Société Archéologique de Sens*
BM	*Bulletin Monumental*
BSAASADO	*Bulletin de la Société Académique d'Archéologie, Sciences et Arts du Département de l'Oise*
BSAEL	*Bulletin de la Société Archéologique d'Eure-et-Loir*
BSAL	*Bulletin de la Société Académique de Laon*

BSAM	*Bulletin de la Société Archéologique de la Mayenne*
BSAME	*Bulletin des Amis du Musée d'Etampes*
BSAP	*Bulletin de la Société des Antiquaires de Picardie*
BSAS	*Bulletin de la Société Archéologique de Sens*
BSHAP	*Bulletin de la Société d'Histoire et d'Archéologie de Provins*
BSHN	*Bulletin de la Société d'Histoire de Normandie*
BSLSI	*Bulletin de la Société Libre de Seine-Inférieure*
BSNAF	*Bulletin de la Société Nationale des Antiquaires de France*
BSSHNY	*Bulletin de la Société des Sciences Historiques et Naturelles de l'Yonne*
CAF	*Congrès Archéologique de France*
CRAIBL	*Comptes-Rendus de l'Académie des Inscriptions et Belles-Lettres*
CRMCAHSN	*Comptes-Rendus et Mémoires du Comité Archéologique Historique et Scientifique de Noyon*
CRMCAS	*Comptes-Rendus et Mémoires du Comité Archéologique de Senlis*
CRSSAASADO	*Comptes-Rendus des Séances de la Société Académique d'Archéologie, Sciences et Arts du Département de l'Oise*
EHR	*Economic History Review*
JHS	*Journal of Historical Sciences*
MA	*Le Moyen-Age*
MAB	*Mémoires de l'Académie de Berlin*
MARS	*Mémoires de l'Académie Royale des Sciences* (Paris)
MASABLC	*Mémoires de l'Académie des Sciences, Arts et Belles-Lettres de Caen*
MFSSA	*Mémoire de la Fédération des Sociétés Savantes de l'Aisne*
MGH	*Monumenta Germaniae Historicae*
MSAASABLDA	*Mémoire de la Société Académique d'Agriculture, des Sciences, Arts et Belles-Lettres, du Départment de l'Aube*

MSAASADO	*Mémoire de la Société Académique d'Archéologie, Sciences et Arts du Département de l'Oise*
MSACSADM	*Mémoire de la Société d'Agriculture, Commerce, Sciences et Arts du Départment de la Marne*
MSAEL	*Mémoire de la Société Archéologique d'Eure-et-Loir*
MSAHO	*Mémoire de la Société Archéologique et Historique de l'Orléanais*
MSAN	*Mémoire de la Société des Antiquaires de Normandie*
MSAP	*Mémoire de la Société des Antiquaires de Picardie*
MSASBLAO	*Mémoire de la Société Académique des Sciences, Belles-Lettres et Arts d'Orléans*
MSHPIF	*Mémoire de la Société Historique de Paris—Ile de France*
MSNAF	*Mémoire de la Société Nationale des Antiquaires de France*
NRCB	*Nouvelle Revue de Champagne et de Brie*
OSP	*Observations sur la Physique*
PATASBLAR	*Précis Analytique des Travaux de l'Académie des Sciences, Belles-Lettres et Arts de Rouen*
PTRA	*Philosophical Transactions of the Royal Academy* (London)
PL	Migne, *Patrologia Latina*
PTENC	*Position des Thèses de l'Ecole Nationale des Chartes*
RA	*Revue Archéologique*
RC	*Revue Celtique*
RCB	*Revue de Champagne et de Brie*
RDN	*Revue du Nord*
REA	*Revue des Etudes Anciennes*
REJ	*Revue des Etudes Juives*
RH	*Revue Historique*
RHEF	*Revue d'Histoire de l'Eglise de France*
RHES	*Revue d'Histoire Economique et Sociale*
RHGF	*Recueil des Historiens de Gaule et de la France*

RN	*Revue du Nord*
RTSLASABLE	*Recueil des Travaux de la Société Libre d'Agriculture, Sciences, Arts et Belles-Lettres de l'Eure*
TANR	*Travaux de l'Académie Nationale de Reims*
TC	*Technology and Culture*

Introduction

1. Lynn-White, *Medieval Religion and Technology: Collected Essays* (Los Angeles, London, Berkeley, 1978), pp. 92 ff.

2. Daumas, *Histoire générale des techniques* (Paris, 1962); Gleisberg, "Geschichte," pp. 44–78; Singer, Holmyard, Hall, and Williams, *A History of Technology*, 5 vols. (Oxford, 1954–58); Lynn-White, *Medieval Technology and Social Change* (Oxford, 1962); Cardwell, "Technologies," pp. 192–207; Mantoux, *The Industrial Revolution in the Eighteenth Century* (London, 1959). For the point of view of the economic history of techniques, see Ashton, *The Industrial Revolution, 1760–1830* (London, 1969); Cipolla, *Industrial Revolution;* David, *Technical Choice, Innovation and Economic Growth* (Cambridge, 1975).

3. Dugas, *Histoire;* Taton, *Histoire;* Hall, *Revolution;* Beer, "Relations"; Mathias, et al., *Science and Technology, 1600–1900* (Cambridge, 1972); Fox and Weisz, *Organization.*

4. *Essais*, pp. 110 ff.

5. Kuhn, *The Structure of Scientific Revolutions*, 2d ed. (Chicago, 1970); McCann, *Chemistry.* For criticism of Kuhn, see Hesse, *Structure;* Lakatos and Musgrave, *Criticism.*

6. Paris, Aubier, 1982; Cambridge, Mass., Harvard Univ. Pr., 1986.

7. For the second half of the twentieth century, see Landsberg, *Climate;* UNESCO, *Hydrological Effects of Urbanization* (Paris, 1974); Sykes and Skinner, *Pollution.*

8. Thus, in 1789, as the eighty-two *départements* were created, three-fourths were given the name of their principal river.

9. Lemoine, *Géologie;* Abrard, *Géologie;* Pomerol and Feugneur, *Guides géologiques régionaux: Bassin Parisien, Ile de France* (Paris, 1968); Pedelabore, *Climat;* Bournieras, *Guide des groupements végétaux de la région Parisienne* (Paris, 1968). Historical unity is demonstrated by Longon, *Atlas*, p. 48; Ennen, *Frühgeschichte*, p. 42; Ganshof, *Etude;* Russel, *Regions*, pp. 146–54; and, more recently, Duby, *The Three Orders: Feudal Society Imagined*, tr. Arthur Goldhammer (Chicago, 1980).

10. "Ordres mendiants," and more generally, Emery, *Friars;* Duby, *Histoire de la France Urbaine*, vol. 2 (Paris, 1980), pp. 214 ff.

11.   I have taken Paris into account only for the period preceding the
        twelfth century and for the eighteenth century, inasmuch as this city
        has already been the object of major scientific research. In 1300 the
        population of Paris was close to two hundred thousand—that is, the
        total of all the other cities studied here.

Chapter 1

1.   Dodds, *Pagan and Christian;* Barb, "The Survival of Magic Arts,"
        in Momigliano, *Conflict,* pp. 100–25.

2.   *Panégyriques latins* (Paris, Galletier, 1949, i, v, 19, 4): Erimenus's
        panegyric, dating from 298.

3.   The first is the older; Turgot had already repeated it in his "Second
        discours sur les progrès successifs de l'esprit humain prononcé le
        11 décembre 1760," *Oeuvres complètes* (Paris, 1808, II, p. 75) and it
        is found in most of the manuals, such as Jullian, *Histoire,* etc. The
        second was developed by Roblin, "Cités ou citadelles: les enceintes
        romaines du Bas-Empire d'après l'exemple de Paris," *REA,* 53
        (1951), pp. 301–12; idem, "Cités ou citadelles? Les enceintes ro-
        maines du Bas Empire d'après l'exemple de Senlis," ibid. (1965),
        pp. 368–91; and more recently by Fevrier, *Histoire de la France Ur-
        baine,* vol. 1.

4.   The extent of the regional capitals of *civitas* in the north of Gaul is
        relatively well known as regards cemetery borders at the time of the
        Pax Romana. For Paris, see Duval, *Paris;* for Reims, Boussinesq
        and Laurent, *Histoire de Reims depuis les origines jusqu'à nos jours*
        (Reims, 1933, vol. 1); for Senlis, Matherat (with many reservations),
        "Sur le plan d'Augustomagus (Senlis)," *BSNAF* (1942), p. 198; for
        Le Mans, Verdier, *Plan archéologique du Mans* (Le Mans, 1935,
        4 maps); for Amiens, Will, "Recherches sur le développement urbain
        sous l'empire romain dans le Nord de la France," *Gallia* (1962),
        pp. 79–101; for Auxerre, Louis, *Autessiodurum christianum—les
        églises d'Auxerre des origines au XIe siècle* (Paris, 1952); for Beauvais,
        Leblond, "La topographie romaine de Beauvais et son enceinte du
        IVe siècle," *BA* (1915), pp. 3–39; for Evreux, Mathière, *La civitas
        des Aulerci Eburovices (pays et ville d'Evreux) à l'époque gallo-romaine*
        (Evreux, 1925), pp. 140 ff.; for Orléans, Debal, "De Cenabum à Or-
        léans," *Actes du 95e Congrès National des Sociétés Savantes* (Reims,
        1970), pp. 175–94; for Sens, Hure, "Le Senonais gallo-romain, IIe
        partie: la ville ouverte d'Argenticum," *BSSHNY,* 90 (1936), pp. 207–
        84. Little has survived regarding Chartres, Noyon, Laon, Troyes,
        Châlons-sur-Marne, and Rouen. See Frezouls, "Etudes et recherches
        sur les villes en Gaule," *Atti de Colloquis sul tema la Gallia Romana*
        (Rome, 10–11 May 1971), pp. 153–66 and 186–87; Chevallier,
        "Cité et territoire: solutions romaines aux problèmes de l'organisa-
        tion de l'espace," *Mélanges Vogt* (Berlin, 1974), vol. 2, pp. 745–62.

5.   For the names of these rivers one would need to consult, besides

ancient texts, the *Dictionnaires topographiques départementaux* (summations concerning the whole territory still need to be made—for the Oise, for example). See also Lebel, *Principes;* Dauzat, *Glossaire;* Krahe, "Flussnamen"; Holder, *Alt-celtischer Sprachschatz* (Leipzig, 1893–1903); Pokorny, *Wörterbuch.* For the Thérain, see Longnon, *Noms,* vol. 9, p. 272.

6.   On Indo-European trifunctionality (first function, that of the priests, attributed by the Romans to Jupiter; second function, that of the warriors, attributed to Mars; third function, that of the workers, attributed to Quirinus), see Dumezil, *From Myth to Fiction,* tr. Derek Coltman (Chicago, 1973), and Benveniste, *Indo-European Language and Society,* tr. Elizabeth Palmer (Miami, Fla., 1973). For the Celtic world, see Duval, "Notes sur la civilisation gallo-romaine, IV—Teutates, Esus, Taranis," *RC,* 8 (1958–59), pp. 41–58.

7.   Louvet, in his *Histoire et Antiquitez du païs de Beauvaisis* (Beauvais, 1635, II, p. 237), mentions a large rock pulled from the foundations of the ancient city of Beauvais in 1633, upon which was engraved, "Diomedis monumentum." This rock was set in the water as the monument to the Diomedes mentioned by Saint Augustine (*De Civit. Dei,* XVIII, XVI).

8.   Vita S. Luciani, *Acta Sanctorum,* 8 January (vol. 1, pp. 459–68).

9.   On the Mediolanum or Mediodunum, see especially Guyonvarc'h, "Mediolanum Biturigum, deux éléments du vocabulaire religieux et de géographie sacrée," *Ogam,* 13 (1961), pp. 137–58; for Evreux, Mathière, *Civitas,* pp. 18 ff.

10.   Lucan, *Phrasale,* lib. I, 445–46 (Paris, Bourgery, 1926, p. 21): ". . . the hideous Esus in his savage sanctuaries, Taranis on altars no less cruel than those of Scythian Diana." Lucan was speaking about Trevires and Ligures.

11.   Vita S. Taurini, *Acta Sanctorum,* 11 August (vol. 2, pp. 635–56); Mesnel, *Les saints du diocèse d'Evreux–Saint Taurin, premier évêque d'Evreux* (Evreux, 1914), pp. 42–54.

12.   Laurendeau, "Du canal de dérivation de la Crise," *BSAS* (1867), pp. 128–82; idem, "Topographie de Soissons, Cours de la Crise," ibid. (1868), pp. 77–82.

13.   De Barthelemy, in *Revue de Numismatique* (1885), pp. 143–50; Blanchet, *Traité,* pp. 114, 376, and 486.

14.   Their *vitae* are from the eleventh century: *Acta Sanctorum,* 25 October (vol. 11, pp. 495–540); Duchesne, *Fastes,* vol. 3, pp. 141–52.

15.   It is said that Saint Eloi, bishop of Noyon and a formidable preacher, found their bodies in a crypt at Soissons, but Gregory of Tours mentions the sixth-century basilica in *Histoire des Francs,* V, 35.

16.   Andre, "Sources," p. 329; Dumezil, *Mythe,* p. 28; Toussaint-Duplessis, *Description,* vol. 1, p. 327; Deville, "Essai sur les médailles gauloises de Rouen," *MSAN* (1837–39), p. 63.

17.   Vita S. Romani, *Acta Sanctorum,* 23 October (vol. 10, p. 74). This temple and the pools for the wells have been located in the amphi-

theater; see Delamarre, "L'amphithéâtre gallo-romain de Rouen," *BCASI*, 15 (1909–11), pp. 232–63.

18. Sens, capital of Lyonnaise IV, went to the extent of building four kilometers of canal works to divert water from the Vanne at Malay-le-Grand (Masliacus subterior [519]); see Quantin, *Cartulaire général de l'Yonne* (Auxerre, 1860), vol. 1, p. 3. *Vanne* means "white"; cf. Irish *fann;* Breton *gwan, gwenn*). The monastery of Saint-Pierre-le-Vif was built on the riverbanks around 520; the monastery of Saint-Colombe, a legendary martyr, was built between it and the river Yonne. The name "Colombe" is related to the root *col-*, which signified a pale color, almost white in Latin; see Ernoux and Meillet, *Dictionnaire étymologique de la langue latine*, art. "Columba." In Troyes, the Seine was diverted for more than 300 meters. The Moline canal was cut at the foot of a Mt. Gargan, in the immediate vicinity of the Blaise, "Belisama," "the Most Brilliant"; see Guyonvarc'h, "Etudes." At Châlons, the Nau (Nautae) did not derive from the Marne (Materna, "the Divine Mother"; see Vendryes in *Mélanges Albert Dauzat* [Paris, 1951], p. 381), but rather from the Moivre, its tributary.

19. *Epitoma rei militaris* (Leipzig, Editions Teubner, 1869), IV, I, p. 129.

20. Guyonvarc'h, *Etudes*, p. 157; Martin, *Histoire de France* (Paris, 1885–90, 4th ed.), vol. 1, p. 464.

21. Dumezil, *Idées*, pp. 175 ff.; Leroux, "Celticum."

22. By the same token, questions can be raised about the motivations behind the fires set by the Bagaudes, to destroy cities. Might they not have been sacrifices to the divinity of this incendiary function? We know that the Bagaudes elected a king and put themselves under the protection of a deity.

23. Lestoquoy, "Abbayes"; Lesne, *Histoire*.

24. Vogt, *Orbis*, pp. 150 ff., has shown how the *urbs*—that is, Rome—was presented as a light of the world by Cicero, Saint Jerome, Fortunatus, and others, and that this expression was taken up by the popes and Christianity to signify the grandeur of the church; see also Breguet, "Urbi et Orbi: Un cliché et un thème," *Mélanges L. Renard* (Latomus, 1968), vol. 1, pp. 140–52.

25. Cabrol and Leclerc (*Dictionnaire*, art. "Rogations") conclude, after having presented diverse theories, that this feast was something new, and not traditional.

26. "Taranous et Thor (2ᵉ partie)," *RC*, 10 (1889), pp. 265–86 and 385–413.

27. *Acta Sanctorum*, 11 May (vol. 2, p. 631). This event has generally been dated ca. 470. Vigils were held on 8 April 467, 30 March 468, 12 April 469, 4 April 470, 27 March 471, 15 April 472, and 31 March 473. The key for determining the Rogation Days is the 15th of April; and this date is verified in the year 472.

28. *Vie des Saints*, p. 214. The same declaration can be found in the

décrets of Buchard de Worms, lib. XIII, cap. 7, "De jejunis Rogationum," Migne, *P.L.*, t. 140, col. 886.

29. *Paulys Realencyclopädie der classischen Alterstumwissenschaft*, art. "Taranis."

30. Flemming in *Pro Alesia*, 1908, p. 391 ff.; Desnoyers, "Les fouilles de la Loire en 1894 autour de l'île aux Poissonniers," *MSAHO*, 27 (1898), pp. 41–58 and 389–92; Chedeau de Sarcus, "Mémoire sur les découvertes archéologiques faites en 1864 dans le lit de la Mayenne au gué Saint-Léonard," *BSAM* (1865), pp. 1–11; see also Gandilhon, "Découvertes d'armes dans la Marne," *BSNAF* (1944), pp. 395–400.

31. Durand, *Rational*, art. "Rogations," vol. 4, p. 279.

32. Le Roux, "Aspects de la fonction guerrière chez les Celtes," p. 187.

33. Cabrol and Leclerc, *Dictionnaire*, art. "Ascension," col. 2936–37.

34. Schilling, "Dea Dia"; Dumezil, p. 382; Roscher, "Ausführliches Lexicon der griechischen und römischen Mythologie" (Leipzig, 1884–90), art. "Dea Dia," col. 964–75.

35. Preaux, "Vertus." This apotheosis was in effect as early as the first century, but for emperors who were deceased. Diocletian instituted it for himself during his lifetime.

36. *Gloria confessorum*, c. 2; ed. and trans., Bordier (Paris, 1860), pp. 346–47. This lake is certainly Saint Andéol's Lake, whose superstitions were kept alive until 1860.

37. Another echo of this can be found in a sermon by Césaire d'Arles (beginning of the sixth century), contemporaneous with the inauguration of the Rogation Days: "Let us turn to the arsenal offered to us by God's mercy, by fasting, vigils, prayers. . . . Do not shed the blood of animals. . . . Rather pray and sing psalms for spiritual comfort for your souls rather than the gross satisfaction of your appetites in feasting. Spit out, like a deadly poison, futile and worldly conversations."

38. Martinet, "Les pratiques païennes à Laon à l'arrivée de sainte Salaberge au VIIe siècle," *MFSSA*, 14 (1968), pp. 51–60.

39. Divine aid, for example, was called upon for the building of a city's walls: *C.I.L.*, VIII, 2095 and 4799; Christ gave the order to build: ibid., 10498. At Sens, the vita of Saint Savinien, dating from the ninth century, reports that the martyr entered into the city and carved crosses on the city walls—a legend that hagiography still retains.

40. The fundamental role played by the Council of Orléans in the elimination of Jupiter-Taranis should be noted here, as much on the level of ritual as of topography: Saint-Pierre-le-Vif of Sens was founded less than ten years later; Saint-Crépin in Soissons and Saint-Lucien in Beauvais were founded during the same period of time; Viator, the predecessor of Laudulfe in the episcopal see of Evreux, had participated in this council and was trying to find vestiges of Saint Taurin. In spite of this, Jupiter persisted during the Middle Ages under the name of Jupin, in the *chansons de geste*, in Guibert de Nogent,

etc. See Langlois, *Table des noms propres contenus dans les chansons de geste* (Paris, 1904), p. 387.

Chapter 2

1. Demographic growth was due to changes in the climate (Le Roy-Ladurie, *Territoire*) and to transformations in the methods of agricultural production (Duby, *The Early Growth of the European Economy: Warriors and Peasants from the Seventh to the Twelfth Century*, tr. Howard B. Clark, Ithaca, N.Y., 1978).

2. Fournier, *Château*, p. 61; de Bouard, *Manuel d'archéologie médiévale—de la fouille à l'histoire* (Paris, Sedes, 1975), p. 93; Vauville, "Mémoire sur plusieurs enceintes antiques du département de l'Aisne," *Mémoires de la Société des Antiquaires de France*, 1889, pp. 295–320.

3. In 946 Otton I; in 949 Arnould of Flanders and Louis IV d'Outremer attacked in vain; in 978 Otton II avoided it entirely and preferred to attack Paris; in 986 Louis V went there to retire (Lot, *Carolingiens*, p. 192; Carolus-Barre, "Une charte originale de Constance, évêque de Senlis [15 avril 983]," *Mélanges Félix Grat*, vol. 2, p. 60). Between 859 and 868, the Normans laid waste to the entire region, but it seems that this city was spared.

4. The cathedral of the tenth century abutted the late-empire ramparts. See Seymour, *Notre-Dame of Noyon in the Twelfth Century: A Study in the Early Development of Gothic Architecture*, New Haven, 1939, p. 18.

5. Flodoard, *Historia*, p. 52.

6. Lair, "Le siège de Chartres par les Normands (911)," *CAF-Chartres 1900*, pp. 176–225; Chedeville, *Chartres et ses campagnes (X^e–XIIe siècles)* (Paris, 1973), p. 406.

7. Thus the Abbey of Saint-Démy of Reims, ca. 925 (Flodoard, *Historia*, 19); the town of Saint-Waast near Saint Médard of Soissons (Bourgin, *La commune de Soissons* [Soissons, 1908], p. 5); in Flanders and in Brabant, nearly all the *castra*, or *castella*, were built in the tenth century: Gand and Douai ca. 920, Bruges before 879; Ypres, Messines, Lille are mentioned for the first time under the reign of Baudoin V (1037–67) (Ganshof, *Etude*, p. 15). Consider also the 1.3 km.-long "earth hedge" built on the borders of the duchies of Normandy and Brittany, "in the fear that half-starved plundering hordes would come to carry out their pillaging at the expense of defenseless churches and populations," under Richard I, ca. 930 (Guillaume de Poitiers, *Histoire*, p. 106).

8. On this point, see Soehnee, *Catalogue des actes de Henry Ier, roi de France* (Paris, 1937), § 70; Flodoard, *Historia*, p. 49; Grignon, *Topographie historique de la ville de Châlons-sur-Marne* (Châlons, 1889), p. 6.

9. See chap. 3, below, p. 59.

10. Helgaud, *Vie du roi Robert*, Pognon, ed. (Paris, 1947), pp. 237,

261; Fleureau, *Antiquitiés de la ville et du duché d'Estampes* (Paris, 1693), p. 20; *Cartulaire de Notre-Dame d'Etampes*, Alliot, ed. (Paris-Orléans, 1888), § LXIX.

11. Nahon, in *REJ* (1976), p. 126.

12. Schwarzfuchs, *Juifs*, p. 19.

13. Chazan, "1007–1012," p. 112: "in each case the attack was led by a combination of lay and religious authorities—among whom the King and Duke were pre-eminent. The outcome had to be renunciation of the faith and the acceptance of the major church. In each case, Jews and Christians refused and were massacred."

14. Duby, *Les trois ordres ou l'imaginaire du féodalisme* (Paris, 1978), esp. pp. 157 ff., concerning heresies; Le Goff, "Les mentalités: une histoire ambiguë," *Faire l'histoire* (Paris, 1977), vol. 3, pp. 76–94.

15. Châlons would continue to develop above the Mau throughout the twelfth century: a charter from the archbishop of Reims in 1185 stipulated that "the part of the ditches that separated the *ban* of Saint-Pierre from the city will not be re-cut"; a judgment from 1221 states that "the Marne will fill up the ditches of Sainte-Croix and those that the *ban* of Saint-Pierre now surrounds" (Barbat, *Histoire de la ville de Châlons-sur-Marne et de ses monuments depuis son origine* [Châlons, 1855], vol. 1, p. 165). The enclosure was finished in the second half of the thirteenth century (Guilbert, "Les fortifications de Châlons-sur-Marne à la fin du Moyen-Age," *Actes du 95ᵉ Congrès national des Sociétés Savantes* [Reims, 1970; Paris, 1974], pp. 195–203). Rouen would expand under Philip Augustus, who built his palace on the site of the ancient Roman amphitheater. A third enclosure was built at the beginning of the fourteenth century. As early as 1209 in Reims a ditch was dug around the site of the future fourteenth-century enclosure (Bruhl, *Palatium*). Marlot *(Histoire de la ville, cité et université de Reims* [Reims, 1846] vol. 4, p. 101) dates it from 1219. Around 1236 the king destroyed the parts of the wall that the city had built in spite of Archbishop Henry de Dreux (Marlot, *Reims, ses rues et ses monuments* [Reims, 1844], p. 29; Desportes, *Reims and les Rémois aux XIIIᵉ and XIVᵉ siècles* [Paris, Picard, 1979], pp. 526–28).

16. The Paris gate in Rouen, Senlis, Beauvais, Orléans, and Amiens—that is, the cities that depended on the kingdom. On interregional dependencies, see Russel, *Regions*.

Chapter 3

1. In Sens, for example, it has been estimated that 200,000 cubic meters were excavated.

2. Guillerme, "Contribution."

3. Helgaud, *Vie du roi Robert* (Paris, Pogmon, 1947).

4. Fauroux, "Recueil des actes des ducs de Normandie de 911 à 1066," *MSAN*, 36 (1961), p. 93.

5. Musset, "Les actes de Guillaume le Conquérant et de la reine Mathilde pour les abbayes caennaises," *MSAN*, 37 (1967), pp. 59 and 102.

6. Ibid., p. 103: "The abbot Guillaume . . . has received from Geoffroy le Maréchal land where the monks have cut the bed of the New Odon and permission to pass across his lands to maintain the bed."

7. Guy founded the Abbey of Saint-Quentin around 1066. Before that he had been the dean of the collegiate church of Saint Quentin in Vermandois, and archdeacon of the church at Laon. For having wanted to extend the holdings of the abbey, he was disgraced; and he was exiled for having allowed the holdings of the count to deteriorate without the authorization of the king (Louvet, *Histoire*, pp. 194–97). The people must have sided with the king; we know that Guy put the city under an interdict. He could not resume his functions until he had made honorable amends to his subjects (letter from the pope to the chapter house of the cathedral). Yves de Chartres seems to have played the role of mediator. At that time he was provost of the Saint-Quentin Abbey. It is thus highly probable that it was in 1074, upon the return of Guy, that the authorization to drive pilings into the river was accorded to the burgesses. See Yves de Chartres, *Correspondance*, ed. Leclercq (Paris, 1949), pp. 70–76, 123–36; Labande, *Histoire de Beauvais et de ses institutions communales jusqu'au commencement du XV ͤ siècle* (Paris, 1892), pp. 72 ff.

8. As early as 1037; see *AD*, G 11. The municipal archives were destroyed by fire in 1940. It is thus impossible to obtain further details.

9. Leblond, "Topographie," p. 7.

10. It was not until 1305 that the burgesses decided after an uprising that all citizens could set planks over the Thérain as they saw fit (Giry, *Documents*, pp. 161–62).

11. The diversion of the spring onto Domitian's Way took place after 814, the date when Louis le Débonnaire mentions the forum (DeVic and Vaisette, *Histoire du Languedoc* [Paris, 1733], II, ch. 12, col. 93), but before 1015, when the capitol and its annexes were sold as public goods (*Cartulaire du chapitre Notre-Dame de Nîmes* [Nîmes, 1892], § 99).

12. The parish of Saint-Martin, mentioned as early as the end of the eleventh century, was bounded by the Versette (Ponthieu, "Note sur l'ancien Noyon: la paroisse Saint-Martin," *CRMCAHSN*, 1910, p. xxi).

13. Much remains to be written concerning the way these prelates planned investments in their "economic" time frame, comparable to the "linear" time frame of twelfth-century merchants, as analyzed by Jacques Le Goff, "Moyen-Age," pp. 924–26.

14. Date of the first mention of the Pétal mill given by Henry the Liberal to the Hôtel-Dieu of Saint-Bernard, as well as of the mention of the Paresse mill (Chaumonnot, *Rivière de Seine, étude sur la dérivation de Troyes* [Troyes, 1868], pp. 67 and 76). The average gradient of the canal was 2 percent. The construction of the two canal bridges required an exact knowledge of the floods of the Vienne and the Seine.

15. D'Arbois de Jubainville, *Histoire des ducs et des comtes de Champagne* (Paris, 1861), I, p. 258.

16. This included the twelve-foot-wide Grand Ru ("big stream") and the seven-foot-wide Petit Ru ("little stream"), two other parallel streams four feet wide, and cross streams. The average depth was four feet.

17. Ditsch, "Rapport sur les découvertes archéologiques faites dans les fouilles de Provins," *BSHAP*, 1899, p. 13.

18. Bourquelot, *Histoire de Provins* (Paris, 1839), I, p. 270. The river flowed between two rows of pilings one or two meters high; the riverbed had oak pilings sunk into it, probably for the use of tanners and dyers (Forgeas, "Curage du Durteint; promenades et trouvailles," *BSHAP*, 1959, p. 80).

19. Stein, "Le maître d'oeuvre André, architecte des comtes de Champagne (1171–1222)," *NRCB*, 1931, pp. 181–85.

20. Bois, *Crise du féodalisme* (Paris, Fondation Nationale des Sciences Politiques, 1976), p. 120.

21. The *portus* was mentioned by Gregory of Tours ("Liber de Virtutibus S. Martini," *MGH, SS, Rer. merov.*, I, p. 598. It was the third-largest port on the English Channel in the ninth century, and exempt from tonnage tax for Saint Germain des Près (*MGH, DD Karol*, I, p. 170, § 122).

22. On the evolution of transportation, see Leighton, *Transport*, pp. 152 ff.

23. In 1145 it received *cayage* (quayage—a fee for use of a quay) from Mainier's son (Thierry, *Recueil de monuments inédits de l'histoire du Tiers-Etat* [Paris, 1850], I, p. 56). In 1149 it made an agreement with Jean de la Croix to develop the old and new docks built by him (ibid., p. 60). Two years earlier Jean de la Croix had lent 100 pounds to Saint-Martin-aux-Jumeaux (Massiet du Biest, "Les origines de la population et du patriciat urbain à Amiens, 1109–XIVe siècle," *RDN*, 1948, p. 126; de Colonne, *Histoire de la ville d'Amiens*, [Amiens, 1899], I, pp. 124–28).

24. Carus-Wilson, "La guède française en Angleterre: Un grand commerce du Moyen-Age," *RDN*, 1953, p. 93.

25. Massiet du Biest, "Les ports fluviaux et le chemin de l'eau à Amiens," *BSAP*, 1953–54, p. 247.

26. The bishop, who had participated in the development, received 195 pounds as *caiage* (see n. 23, above) in 1301," *BSAP*, 1912, p. 153).

27. The loading dock in Auxerre was located at the Saint-Nicolas postern, where Parisian merchants deposited their merchandise as early as 1200 (Quantin, *Cartulaire*, vol. 1, p. 150). As early as 1145 an agreement between Hugues, bishop of Auxerre, and William II, count of Nevers, clarified that the narrows of the Régenne mills had to be opened to let boats through. Louis IX, receiving complaints from mariners and navigators from Auxerre, had the river cleared of anything obstructing navigation (Quantin, *Recueil*, pp. 422, 1266; Leboeuf, *Mémoires concernant l'histoire ecclésiastique d'Auxerre*, [Auxerre, 1848], I, p. 428; Quantin, *Histoire des rues d'Auxerre*

[Auxerre, 1870], p. 354). In Sens the loading dock was in the Yonne suburb. Two *deniers* was the payment for each cartload or boatload (Lecoy de la Marche, "Les coutumes et péages de Sens, texte français inédit du commencement du XIIIe siècle," *BEC*, 27 [1866], p. 287). In Soissons a *portus* existed near Saint-Quentin in the eleventh century (Vercauteren, *Etude*, p. 130); modest traffic is mentioned in 1065 (Bourgin, *Commune*, p. 76). Châlons had two ports on the Nau—the Milet and the Chanteraine. The remains of large stone buildings can be found there; they were probably used as warehouses (Moignon, "Châlons souterrain," *MSACSADM*, 1986, pp. 81–82).

28. *Historia ecclesiastica* (Paris, le Prévost, 1840), II, p. 324.

29. *Phillipidos* (Paris, Delaborde, 1885), p. 211.

30. "Vita Adalberti," ed. Jaffé, *Bibliotheca rerum Germanicarum*, III, p. 594, v. 247–51.

31. "Vita S. Medardi," *Acta Sanctorum*, June (II, p. 90) (before 1098).

Chapter 4

1. Bloch, "Avènement et conquête du moulin à l'eau," *AESC*, 1935, pp. 538–63; Bautier, "Mentions"; Fagniez, *Etudes;* Lynn-White, *Medieval Technology and Social Change* (Oxford, 1962); de Poerck, *La draperie médiévale en Flandre et en Artois* (Bruges, 1951). A general study is to be found in Gille, *Histoire*, pp. 508 ff. The following list gives the names of mills, their first mention, and references, city by city:

    Amiens: Ratier, Bayart, Clencain, Taillefer, Bocard, Frementel, Grenier, Toxar, Becquerel, Tappeplomb, Passarrière, and Passavant (1060)—in Roux, "Cartulaire du chapitre de la Cathédrale d'Amiens," *MSAP*, 14 (1905), p. 30; de Calonne, *Histoire de la ville d'Amiens* (Amiens, 1899), p. 231. Hocquet, Noyon, Longpré, Happetarte, Le Roi, and the Quatre-Moulins (1176)—in Massiet du Biest, *La carte et le plan considérés comme instruments de recherche historique. Etude sur les fiefs, censives, et la condition des tenures urbaines à Amiens (XIe–XIIIe siècles)* (Tours, 1954), pp. 239 ff.

    Auxerre: Saint-Martin (665)—in Richard, "Les moulins de Preuilly et de Saint-Martin à Auxerre," *BSSHNY*, 97 (1957–58), p. 349. The Grands-Moulins or Moulins-sous-Murs (887), Batardeaux (1148), Mi-l'eau (1178), Brichoux, Judas (1150), d'Arnus, de Preuilly, and Bouffau (1220)—in Quantin, *Cartulaire*.

    Beauvais: Allard (997), Saint-Symphorien (1033–58), Saint-Laurent (before 1037), Saint André (before 1037), Saint-Quentin (1063), Limaçon (1063)—in Louvet, *Histoire*, I, pp. 290 and 552. Ratel, de la Fontaine (1109), Quarrier (1144), Courcelles, Becquet (1147)—in Labande, *Histoire de Beauvais et de ses institutions communales* (Paris, 1892), p. 167.

    Caen: Darnetal, Rainard, Saint-Ouen (1066–77), Crapaudière (1080), Montaigu, Gémare (1080–82), Vaucelles (1082)—in Musset, "Les actes de Guillaume le Conquérant et de la reine Mathilde pour les abbayes caennaises," *MSAN*, 37 (1967), pp. 57, 67, 71, 77.

Note to Page 78

Croisier, Estoupefour, Hôtel-Dieu (1150)—in Charma, "Monographie de l'abbaye Saint-Etienne de Caen," *MSAN*, 1855, p. 470, and Pont, *Histoire de la ville de Caen*, (Caen, 1866), pp. 242 ff.

Chalons: Bayart, Petit-Ton, Gros-Moulin, Beauvoisin, Rhodes, Cliquet, Moyen (1028)—in Pfister, *Etude*. Cinq-Moulins, Porte-Marne (1107), Cocherel, Ferry (1138), de La Ruelle (1211), Trois-Moulins (1214)—in Grignon, *Topographie*, pp. 35, 115.

Chartres: Comtesse, Herle (1029–37), Saint-Père (1070)—in *Cartulaire de l'Abbaye de Saint-Père de Chartres*, Guerard, ed. (Paris, 1840), I, p. 212. Reculet (1101–29), Tanneurs (1120), Désert (1168), Cochefilet, Ponceau (1180), Rogers, Chaume, Cinq-Ruelles, Brèche, Sept-Arches (1210)—in Chedeville, *Chartres*, p. 98. Filles-Dieu (1232), Saumon (1250), Bans-des-Près, Graviers (1270)—in *Archives DDE*, Box 989, File no. 409.

Etampes: Darnetal, Branleux, Petit Notre-Dame (1046), Sacas (1050), Deux (in Vieil Etampes) (1113), Fouleret (1185), Sablon (1190), Trinité (1200), Hospice (1243)—in Fleureau, *Antiquités*, p. 462, and Lefèvre, *Etampes et ses monuments aux XIᵉ et XIIᵉ siècles* (Paris, 1907), p. 47.

Evreux: Château (1094–1100), Tour (1150), Grocet (1160), Fares, Tanneurs (1170), Rainouard (1180), Evêque (1185), Gichainville (1279), Saint-Aquilin (1285), Planche (1298)—in Delisle, "Cartulaire Normand de Philippe Auguste, Louis VIII, Saint-Louis et Philippe le Hardy," *MSAN*, 1852, p. 288, and Lamiray, *Promenade historique et anecdotique dans Evreux* (Evreux, 1927).

Noyon: Wé, Andeu (901), Saint-Maurice (1175), Pulset, Saint-Blaise (1128), Saint-Rémy (1153), Coisel (1157), Fossé (1185)—in *Le Livre rouge, cartulaire de la ville de Noyon*, Mazière, ed., (Chauny, 1932), pp. 53 ff.

Orléans: Saint-Aignan (1000), Clos-le-Roi (before 1000)—in *Cartulaire de Sainte-Croix d'Orléans*, ed. Jarry Thuillier, (Orléans, 1906), p. 24. Cinq sous le pont des Tourelles—in Collin, "Le pont des Tourelles à Orléans (1120–1760)," *MSAHO*, 1902, p. 73.

Provins: Saint-Ayoul (1153), Saint-Quiriace (1160), Fontaine (1176), Neuf, Foulon, Temple (1166), Ruelle, Bordes, Trois-Moulins (1232), Moucelle (1232), Changes (1237), Vicomté, Richebourg, Coudoux (1275)—in Bourquelot, *Histoire*, II, pp. 231 and 270.

Reims: see Boussinesq and Laurent, *Histoire*, I, pp. 272 ff.; Varin, *Archives administratives de la ville de Reims* (Paris, 1839), I, p. 402; and Desportes, *Reims* (chap. 2, n. 15, above), p. 415.

Rouen: Escarchon (tenth century), Petit and Grand Notre-Dame (996), Petit and Grand Saint-Ouen, Chantepie, Cheminel, Fossés, Petit and Grand de la Ville (1012–16), Trinité (1030), Saint-Amand (1080), Claquerel (1120), Choc (1122), Petit Martainville, Pannevière (1195), Saint-Paul (1211), Espiègle, Martainville (1247), Nid-de-Chien, Sainte-Catherine, Brétèque (1242), Neuf (1260), Planches (1270)—in Cerné, *Les moulins à eau de Rouen* (Rouen, 1936).

Senlis: Chapitre or Sainte-Marie (1091), Saint-Etienne (1141), Evêque (1147), Saint-Nicolas (1211), Saint-Vincent (1215), Victoire

(1226), Gastellière, Le Roi (1242), Plessis (1260)—in Flammermont, *Histoire des institutions municipales de Senlis* (Paris, 1881), pp. 28 ff.

Sens: Saint-Jean (sixth century), Saints-Pères—in Quantin, *Cartulaire*, I, p. xxxix. Fossé, Renelle (1150), Paillard (1250), Feu-Galon, Saint-Didier (1239)—in Perrin, *Le ru Gravereau* (Sens, 1932), pp. 12 ff.

Soissons: Porte-de-Crise, Saint-Crépin, Pré-Foireux, Saint-Jean, Fossat, Saint-Léger (1139)—in *Cartulaire de l'Abbaye Saint-Jean-des-Vignes-de-Soissons* (Am Soissons, MS 5); Pecheur ("Les rues de Soissons," ibid., p. 85). Porte-Saint-Waast (1202), Pont, Comte (1216), Notre-Dame—in Bourgin, *Commune*, pp. 290 ff.

Troyes: Sancey, Bains, Tour, Jaillard, Saint-Quentin (1157), Challouet, Merdançon (1171), Paresse, Croncels (1174), Notre-Dame (1188), Pétal (1189)—in Bourquelot, *Histoire*, I, pp. 72 ff., and Chaumonnot, *Rivière*, p. 16.

2. Steinbert, *Farms and Mills in Denmark during Two Thousand Years* (Copenhagen, 1952), pp. 294–98.

3. Vendryes, "Les moulins en Irlande et l'aventure de Ciarnat," *RA*, 1921, p. 368.

4. Chaumartin, *Mal des Ardents*, pp. 72–74.

5. Chaumonnot, *Rivière*, p. 212.

6. Labande, *Histoire*, p. 272; Bauthier, "Mentions," p. 585.

7. Espinas and Pirenne, *Recueil*, I, p. 313.

8. Ibid., p. 242.

9. Ibid., I, p. 21; II, p. 308.

10. We have no precise documents concerning this craft. However, in the eighteenth century, the procedure that used animal excrement was called *alunage* ("application of alum"), which leads me to conjecture that prior to that time, when alum was cheaper, it had been used in glove-making.

11. Châlons, Pont-des-Viviers on the Mau; Provins, mound gate on the Buat; Beauvais, bridge of the Vivier near Saint-André.

12. Schneider, "Aspects of Hydrological Effects of Urbanization," *Proceedings of the American Society of Civil Engineers*, HY3 (1975), pp. 449–68; and more generally, *Report of the Subgroup on the Effects of Urbanization on the Hydrological Environment of the Co-ordinating Council of the International Hydrological Decada* (Paris, 1974).

13. Laon: Hôtel-Dieu founded in 1015 by the chapter house, transferred at the beginning of the thirteenth century a little more to the north (Broche, *La Cathédrale de Laon* [Paris, 1961], p. 11). Noyon: Hôtel-Dieu founded in 1178 to the north of the city (Mazière, "Noyon religieux et Noyon hospitalier," *CRMCAHSN*, 1894, p. 140). Provins: Grand Hôtel-Dieu founded by Thibaud I ca. 1050 on the site of the Saint James church (Veissière, "La collégiale Saint-Quiriace de Provins au XIᵉ siècle," *BSHAP*, 1958–59, p. 74), relocated ca. 1160 (Dupraz, "Les cartulaires de l'Hôtel-Dieu de Provins, édition critique," *PTENC*, 1973, p. 76). Amiens: in 1236, the Hôtel-Dieu

was relocated on lands freed from the fiefdom of Heilly (Mortet and Deschamps, *Recueil des textes relatifs à l'architecture* [Paris, 1929], text 123). Beauvais: hospital relocated before 1201 to the north of the city (*Cartulaire de l'Hôtel-Dieu de Beauvais*, ed. Leblond [Paris, 1919], p. xv). Troyes: Hôtel-Dieu-le-Comte founded in 1157, larger than the one built by the bishop (Pietresson de Saint-Aubin, "Essai sur la formation et le développement topographique de la ville de Troyes jusqu'à 1524," dissertation, Ecole de Chartes, 1917, p. 54). Senlis: hospital rebuilt in 1208, probably following its relocation (Muller, "Analyse du cartulaire, des statuts de Notre-Dame-de-Senlis," *CRMCAS*, 1904, pp. 65–66). Châlons: Hôtel-Dieu next to the cathedral ca. 920, relocated perhaps at the beginning of the thirteenth century (Héron de Villefosse, "Chartes relatives à l'hôpital Saint-Etienne de Châlons," *RCB*, 9, 1880, p. 5). Chartres: the hospital was founded ca. 1050–80 (de Lepinois, *Histoire de Chartres* [Chartres, 1854], I, p. 332). Reims: hospital known around 860 (Hollande, *Essai sur la topographie de Reims* [Reims, 1876], p. 127). Sens: Grand Hôtel-Dieu facing the cathedral as early as 1204 (Hédiard, "Du petit Hôtel-Dieu de Sens," *BSAS*, 6, [1854], p. 23), founded perhaps by Archbishop Magnus in 816 (Bouvier, *Histoire de l'église et de l'ancien archidiocèse de Sens* [Paris, 1906], I, p. 80). Auxerre (Demay, "L'hôpital de la Madeleine d'Auxerre, le grand cimetière et ses galeries," *BSSHNY*, 62 [1908], p. 8). Etampes: Hôtel-Dieu, rebuilt around 1191 (Fleureau, *Antiquité*, p. 413). Evreux: Hôtel-Dieu founded between 1140 and 1160 by Count Simon de Montfort (Langlois, *Notice sur l'hospice d'Evreux* [Evreux, 1866], p. 2).

14. "Place filled with filth" for *merdier;* "mire, sludge," for *merde* (Godefroy, *Dictionnaire de l'ancienne langue française*). "Stream that leaves all kinds of filth behind after a flood; muddy place" (Lebel, *Traité d'hydronymie*, p. 109).

15. Weyl, *Histoire*, p. 120; Heine, *Körperpfläge und Kleidung bei den Deutschen* (Stuttgart, 1903), pp. 48 ff.

16. Guillerme, "La Destruction des aqueducs romaines des villes du nord de la France," *Journées d'études sur les aqueducs romains, Lyon (26–28 mai, 1977)* (Paris, 1983), pp. 167–73.

17. Martinet, "Un palais décrit dans un manuscrit carolingien de la bibliothèque municipale de Laon," *MFSSA*, 1966, pp. 72–84.

18. Monneret de Villard, *Introduzione allo studio dell'archeologia islamica* (Venice, 1966), p. 142.

19. For Paris, see Jaillot, *Recherches critiques historiques et topographiques sur la ville de Paris* (Paris, 1772), p. 155. An André de Balneis was mentioned in 1203. For Provins, see Bourquelot, *Histoire*, I, p. 277; for Troyes, see *Cartulaire du chapitre cathédral Saint-Pierre-de-Troyes*, Lalore, ed., (Paris/Troyes, 1880), p. 28; for Sens, in 1310, they are mentioned as the *Vieilles Etuves* ("old steam baths") in Tarbé, *Recherches historiques sur la ville de Sens* (Paris, 2nd ed., 1889, p. 85). For Orléans (1330), rue des Vieilles Etuves (Vergnaud-Romagnezi, *Histoire de la ville d'Orléans* [Orléans, 1830], p. 416).

20. Quoted in Agus, *Urban Civilisation in Pre-Crusade Europe* (New York, 1965), vol. 1, p. 380.

21. In Senlis, in 1208, there is mention of private ditches to be built between the Hôtel-Dieu and a house (Muller, "Analyse," p. 315). In Soissons, the Notre-Dame Abbey was authorized to spill its used water into the streets (Germain, *Histoire de l'abbaye royale de Notre-Dame-de-Soissons* [Paris, 1675], p. 443). For Paris, see Roux, "L'habitat urbain au Moyen-Age, le quartier de l'université de Paris," *AESC*, 1966, p. 1199.

22. Barthélémy de Granville, *De proprietatibus rerum*, lib. 13, cap. 3. The same holds for this point of view for the rural world: "It will not suffice merely to contain water; it quickly becomes necessary to regularize water flow, to drain bottoms that have been unusuable up until now. But in order to carry out such works on spongy terrain, attacked by frost, floods or rodents, it was necessary to wait for the technical progress of the very end of the thirteenth century. Around 1170, to the south of Cambrai, a little later on the Somme and the Authie rivers, after 1220 around Amiens, appeared the first detours, the first detours, the first diversion canals. Running water had to be directed into pastures or fishponds, and the course of the river had to be diverted in order to drain unstable terrain; the ditches that were thus cut seem to have been considerable" (Fossier, *Terre*, p. 367).

Chapter 5

1. Noyon: in 1299 Philippe le Bel delegated the bailiff of Vermandois and the abbot of Compiègne to regularize the financial situation of the city (Lefranc, *Histoire de la ville de Noyon et de ses institutions jusqu'à la fin du XIIIe siècle* [Paris, 1897], p. 158; the settlement was carried out over a period of some fifty years (ibid., p. 176); in 1339, Philippe de Valois observed that the urban fortifications were time-worn and dilapidated (Maziere, *Annales*, p. 122). Soissons: the commune was eliminated in 1325 after having filed a statement of affairs (Bourgin, *Commune*, p. 158); in 1341 it was observed that the ditches and walls were deficient (Pecheur, *Annales du diocèse de Soissons* [Soissons, 1865], IV, p. 355).

2. Letter dated 25 April 1355, quoted in Graves, *Statistiques du canton de Beauvais* (Beauvais, 1852), p. 145. The continuous ramparts protected on the east by the vast Marissel marsh, on the west by the Saint Quentin meadow, and on the south by the swift current of the Thérain and the Avelon were now completed by the Craoul tower, built during the thirteenth century upstream from the episcopal palace. The strength of the tower came from its mass (16 meters at the base, 20 meters in height) and from its forward-projecting and crooked entrance, called *le Déloir* (Old French for *décrocher*, "to break off," or *disloquer*, "to dislocate"), the architecture for which came from Asia Minor.

3. Quoted in de Lepinois, *Histoire* (Chap. 4, n. 13, above), vol. 2,

p. 18, and in Bonnard, "Les fortifications de Chartres: essai historique et archéologique," *MSAEL*, 1936, p. 280.

4. Saint-Symphorien, 150 meters to the south of Beauvais; Saint-
Barthélémy, 100 meters to the north of Noyon; Notre-Dame-du-Val,
200 meters from Troyes to the Provins gate; Saint-Pregt, Saint-Rémi,
and Saint-Didier in Sens; Saint-Eloi and Saint-Hilaire in Reims;
Saint-Saturnin and Saint-Julien in Chartres.

5. Bouquet, "Deux restes des anciennes fortifications de Rouen à l'hospice général," *BAMR*, 1900–1902, p. 78. In 1431 in Troyes the
ditches were cut to protect the cattle (Boutiot, *Histoire de la ville de
Troyes et de la Champagne méridionale* [Troyes, 1872], II, p. 542). In
Caen the Ile Saint-Jean had been enclosed for the same reasons ca.
1360.

6. Amiens: *AM*, AA2, folio 73, treaty between the bishop and the city.
Caen: de Beaurepaire, "Compte des dépenses pour travaux de ma-
çonnerie, de charpenterie et de couverture exécutés au château de
Caen en 1399 et 1400," *BSHN*, 10 (1905–1909), pp. 80–82. Noyon:
Maziere, *Annales*, p. 175.

7. Caen had two in 1400 (de Beaurepaire, "Compte," p. 82); Noyon,
two in 1401 (Maziere, *Annales*, p. 176); Beauvais, two in 1413, one
at the Saint-Laurent gate to the north, the other at the Paris gate to
the south (Leblond, *Eléments*, p. 101).

8. Enguerrand de Monstrelet, *Chronique 1400–1444*, Douet d'Arcq,
ed. (Paris, 1857–62), III, p. 154. As late as 1418, the Dauphinois
surprised the city and pillaged it (Pecheur, *Annales*, p. 493).

9. Chartres, which for a short time became the capital of the Burgun-
dian kingdom, rebuilt the Guillaume gate, monumental and heavily
fortified (Jusselin, "La date de la porte Guillaume à Chartres," *BM*,
73 [1909], p. 72). Amiens repaired the walls of its suburbs in 1417,
gunboats were stationed at the Saint-Pierre and Gayant gates, and a
dam was built at the Cange bridge (Daire, *Histoire de la ville d'Amiens*
[Amiens, 1760], I, p. 228). For Senlis, see Vatin, *Senlis, récits historiques* (Senlis, 1876), p. 157. On the siege of Senlis, see Jean Mallet,
"Extrait en bref de ce qui s'est passé en la ville de Senlis et es en-
viron d'icelle, depuis l'an 1400, que Charles VI était roi de France
jusqu'en 1594," *Monuments inédits de l'histoire de France (1400–
1600)*, Bernier, ed. (Paris-Senlis, 1835), p. 8.

10. The arsenal set up within the enclosure of the Galées on the left
bank of the Seine was razed at the approach of the English in 1418:
Notre-Dame-des-Prés was destroyed (Périaux, *Dictionnaire indicateur
et historique des rues et places de Rouen* [Rouen, 1870], pp. xv and 40).
Evreux was taken in May 1418 by the duke of Exeter. The English
took the suburbs: "The English broke the gates [sluices] above the
said mill [the Maréchal] and attacked the said mill while it was
working, in such a manner that the wheel of the said mill was broken." The canals bordering the city were thus deprived of water.
The English were preparing to give battle when the bailiff and the
inhabitants surrendered (Blanquart, "Prise d'Evreux in 1418, remise

partielle de fermage," *BSHN*, 2 [1913–18], p. 378). Etampes was taken in 1417 in the same way by John the Fearless.

11. On January 25 "the order was given that all around the fortress of Beauvais were to be cut down all trees belonging to anyone whatsoever, up to the line of two *arbaletes* along the walls"; the scribe, after having written "up to the line of the cannons," replaced this with "two *arbaletes*" (Leblond, *Eléments*, p. 151).

12. *Discours véritable du siège mis devant la ville de Beauvais par Charles le Téméraire* (Beauvais, 1622), p. 12.

13. Tassus, "L'abbaye Saint-Eloi de Noyon," *CRMCAHSN*, 1893, p. 161. Charles simply had the suburbs burned down, notably the abbey and the Saint-Eloi borough. In Amiens the wall was so ruined that Louis XI exempted the city from taxation (de Calonne, *Histoire de la Ville d'Amiens*, [Amiens, 1899], I, p. 414). On the destruction of the extraurban monuments, see Denifle, *Désolation*.

14. Renet, *Beauvais*, p. 328 (27 Sept. 1473). The cost of the detour was 400 or 500 pounds, or the equivalent of the annual budget of the city.

15. Guillaume de Hangest, captain of Châlons-sur-Marne, proposed the same improvements for the towers of Châlons, destroyed during the flood of 1491 ("Coppie de la visitation des murs et murailles de Châlons," in Guilbert, "Fortifications," pp. 199–203). Orléans enlarged its surface area by constructing a third enclosure with protruding towers (*AM*, Orléans, EE 39, 1).

16. Vaesen and Charavay, *Lettres de Louis XI* (Paris, 1884), vol. 6, letter dated 5 July 1475; Le Vasseur, *Annales de l'église cathédrale de Noyon, jadis dite de Vermand* (Paris, 1633), p. 1093; Maziere, *Annales*, p. 316. These works, interrupted in 1476, were begun again in 1480–81: washing out the ditches, installation of dams at the gates; see Maziere, *Annales*, p. 322. In 1471, Louis XI had employed masons and carpenters from Paris for the fortifications of the reconquered cities of the Somme.

17. Vaesen and Charavay, *Lettres*, vol. 5, letter dated 21 Sept. 1473; Varin, *Archives administratives et législatives de la ville de Reims* (Reims, 1834), I, p. 797. The wall was finished at that time, and measured 10 feet at the base and 8 feet at the top.

18. In 1491 (Bonnard, "Fortifications," p. 289); in 1467, he had given the inhabitants the right to fish in the ditches, and to prune the trees planted along the banks, in return for their help in the construction of moats and the Imbout and Drouaise gates (Vaesen and Charavay, *Lettres*, vol. 5, letter dated 14 Dec. 1467; de Lepinois, *Histoire*, II, p. 116. Again in Rouen, Guillaume Picard, general of Normandy, tried in 1472 to have construction started on the "most beautiful moats ever made" (See, *Louis XI*, p. 96).

19. *AM*, Orléans, EE 39, document 1; in 1486 (document 5) an assembly composed of more than two thousand persons found that the enclosure would be far too spread out, and suggested limiting it to the Cordeliers and the Jacobins. But the project was maintained (docu-

ment 6). The wall along the Loire had been rebuilt between 1399
and 1429.

20. Stagnation along the course of a flowing waterway is explained by
the formula $Vm/s = (Qm^3/s)/Sm^2$ (where V = velocity, Q = quantity [of water], S = surface [of water], m/s = meters per second).
If a river has a current upstream, but Q = 0 at the city gates, there
must be a diversion before the city gates carry off the 0+ current.
For the same reasons there must be a *batardeau* or similar structure
downstream.

21. Vaesen and Charavay, *Lettres*, vol. 5, letter dated 24 Jan. 1475; the
cost of the undertaking was estimated at 50,000 pounds. In March
1467 the municipality was still discussing the pros and cons of such a
loss; the city would be "most desolate, ruined, and would lose its
beauty" (*AM*, Amiens, BB 13, folio 15v°, and de Calonne, *Histoire*,
I, p. 441). Louis XI made his decision soon after (VI, p. 104); the
works began in March 1477 around the Saint-Michel gate, destroyed
in 1479, and the Saint-Denis and Saint-Firmin gates, both demolished in 1483. For Senlis, see Vaesen and Charavay, ibid., letters
dated 19 July 1472 and 13 May 1477; Bernier, *Monuments*, p. 29; the
Hôtel des Quinze-Vingts disappeared. For Soissons, see Laurendeau,
Du Canal, p. 181.

22. Built in 1501–1502: "There will be three stories . . . , the front side
of the bottom of the ditch will be 20 feet thick . . . there will be four
stations for defense along the ditches, as many on the side of the
Augustinians as on the side of the Cérès gate. . . . The lower floor
will be 36 feet long and 36 feet on the side, and be 16 to 18 feet
thick; the second story will be 72 feet long, 37 feet wide, 20 feet
thick on the front, and 16 feet thick on each of the sides. The third
and last story will be like the second . . . safe repositories, well
vaulted in order to be able to store and enclose five or six powder
kegs" (quoted in Lebourq, "Les anciennes fortifications de Reims,"
TANR, 1885, p. 290).

23. The Saint-Antoine castle in Châlons had, however, been completely
redone in 1473 (Barbat, *Histoire*, II, p. 356). In Senlis, the old Saint-
Rieul gate was demolished and rebuilt with stones and a terrace in
1500 (Bernier, *Monuments*, p. 37).

24. In Amiens the works began in 1523 with the construction of the boulevard and the ravelin of the Monstrescu gate. The ditches were deepened by 60 feet and widened by 120 (de Calonne, *Histoire*, I, p. 488).
In 1536 work was begun again on the weakest points. Earthen cavaliers were constructed. The Guyencourt spur was raised in 1545.
The gates were provided with boulevards from 1551 to 1554; a new
rampart included the Saint-Jean Abbey; a mill and several houses
were "destroyed and demolished to be converted into ditches and
counterscarps" (Berlette, "Antiquités de la ville de Soissons re-
cueillis de divers auteurs et chroniques [1575–82]," *BSHAP*, 1888,
p. 142). The nave of Saint-Pierre-à-la-Chaux and the church of
Notre-Dame-des-Vignes were razed and buried under platforms; the
Saint-Christophe gate was provided with a demilune and a draw-

bridge. The moat was 24 meters wide. The city was given the responsibility of acquiring all these terrains. Particular attention was
given to the defense of Amiens and Soissons because they were located on the frontiers of the kingdom, and threatened by Charles
Quint.

25. Germanico in 1553; Fredance and Bartholomeo in 1558 in Amiens;
Baptiste at Senlis in 1552; Strozzi in Calais, Vergano, and La Ro-
chelle in the middle of the 16th century; Bellamarti, run out of Sienna in 1530, went to France to build Le Havre.

26. First mentioned in Rouen in 1524, where 300 poor persons worked,
527 the following year, and between 7,000 and 8,000 in May of 1557
(Panel, *Documents concernant les pauvres de Rouen* [Rouen-Paris,
1917], p. xxvi). In Noyon they were put to work in 1525 (Maziere,
Annales, p. 14). In Senlis there were 226 of them in 1534 (Bernier,
Monuments, p. 44). For Etampes in 1536, see Dupieux, "La défense
militaire et policière d'Etampes au XVIᵉ siècle," *ADG*, 40 (1930),
see p. 130. For Amiens in 1542, see de Calonne, *Histoire*, I, p. 494.
For Reims in 1555, see Lebourq, "Fortifications," p. 194.

27. Bernier, *Monuments*, p. 48; Daire, *Histoire*, I, p. 260.

28. Quenedey, *L'habitation rouennaise, étude d'histoire, de géographie et
d'archéologie urbaine* (Rouen, 1946); "Le prix des matériaux et de la
main-d'oeuvre à Rouen du XIVᵉ au XVIIIᵉ siècle," *BSLECISI*,
1924–25, pp. 331–56; Bois, *Crise*, p. 194.

29. *AM*, Amiens, BB 23, folio 64 v°, 1538: "Orders to all the carriers to
put their compost and refuse on the wall between the Hautoie gate
and the Guyencourt tower in order to fill in the city ditches." In
Senlis (1534) all the landfill and refuse of the city had to be taken to
the ramparts so as to enlarge them (Bernier, *Monuments*, p. 44). *AM*,
Beauvais, BB 14, 1538–44: an ordinance to have all the city refuse
carried to the ramparts, particularly for the platform of the Grès
tower.

30. *AM*, Amiens, BB 1, folio 46 v°, 20 April 1408.

31. *AM*, Laon, CC 28, 1497–98.

32. Panel, *Documents*, p. 15: (1524) 300 poor persons were put to work
to clean them up.

33. In 1526 the monks of Saint Jean of Chartres claimed to have the
right to pick up and carry away all the manure to be found in the
moat of the city ditches beyond the Saint-Jean gate (Lefevre, *An-
nuaire statistique, administratif, commercial et historique d'Eure et Loir
pour 1847* [Chartres, 1847], p. 437). The ditch next to the Augustin-
ian monastery in Reims had 37 privy ditches in 1328, six of which
belonged to the archbishop; in front of the Mars gate, next to the
archbishop's castle, there was also a ditch, and another one at the
Saint-Pierre-le-Vieux gate (Varin, *Archives*, I, p. 275).

34. For Evreux, see Lamiray, *Promenade historique et anecdotique dans
Evreux* (Evreux, 1927), p. 9, and Bonnin, *Opuscules et mélanges historiques sur la ville d'Evreux* (Evreux, 1845), p. 17. Under threat of
siege in 1491, the administration of Beauvais ordered "that no per-

son go to take his ease on the walls of the fortress under pain of a 60 sous fine" (Leblond, "Beauvais dans l'angoisse pendant la seconde partie de la guerre de Cent Ans, Extraits des délibérations de l'Hôtel de Ville de Beauvais [1402–1405]," *MSAASADO*, 1932, p. 155). For more on a rare document concerning collective behavior, but which says much about this custom, see Grosley, *Ephémérides Troyennes* (Troyes, 1720), p. 124.

35. Belidor, *La science des ingénieurs* (Paris, 1729), p. 96: "Sometimes latrines are made of a wooden frame over the ramparts between fortification curtains when there is no postern gate beneath. . . . When there is a river or a stream to be found in the neighborhood of the barracks, it is best to take advantage of it to make latrines." De Clairac, *L'ingénieur de campagne* (Paris, 1749), p. 189: "Concerning latrines: no matter where they are placed in the lines, they are always a problem. If they are placed without, desertion is encouraged; if within, they infect and disrupt the battlefield." See also Cataneo, *Capitaine*, p. 85.

36. In Châlons it was the duke of Nevers who carried out the destruction on orders from the king in 1520 (Barbat, *Histoire*, II, p. 167). In Noyon, it was the Hungarians of Charles Quint in 1552 (Moet de la Forte Maison, *Antiquités de Noyon* [Rennes, 1845], p. 170). In Senlis, on orders from the king (Bernier, *Monuments*, p. 61). In Beauvais in 1521, houses were pulled down to extend the rampart (Leblond, "Beauvais," p. 442). The same thing happened in Senlis in 1524 (Bernier, *Monuments*, p. 44). For Etampes, in 1536, see Bourgeois, *Quelques recherches sur le port d'Etampes* (Etampes, 1860), pp. 294–95.

37. *AM*, Amiens, AA 12, folio 34, ca. 1350: "Street women are not to go to the fortress." BB 23, folio 61 v°, 1538: "Public girls must go live behind the barrier." For Chartres, see Bonnard, "Fortifications," p. 289. For Noyon, see Maziere, "L'organisation administrative de Noyon," *CRMCAHSN*, 1893, p. 322. For the south of France, see Rossiau, "Prostitution, jeunesse et société dans les villes du Sud-Est au XVᵉ siècle," *AESC*, 1976, pp. 289–325.

38. In Reims in 1348, the municipality decided to forbid pasturage. It was necessary, so said the city officials, "to let the grass remain to hold back the soil, because it runs off to the detriment of the ditches" (quoted in Varin, *Archives*, II, p. 1209). Leasing out the grass brought in a few pounds for the community's treasury (*AM*, Beauvais, DD 8, in 1625). In Noyon in 1358 rental of the new ditches amounted to 24 pounds (minted in Paris) per year for the grass, fish, and "compensation for injuries and outrages, noise, beatings, and melees" (Maziere, *Annales*, p. 322). In Troyes they were rented out in 1404—but they had by that time become useless (Boutiot, *Histoire*, II, p. 114). In 1527 they were filled in (ibid., III, p. 342). For Soissons, in 1582, see Pecheur, *Annales*, X, 1900, p. 121.

39. In Amiens it was forbidden to open more than two of the gates per day in 1593 (Goze, *Les enceintes successive d'Amiens* [Amiens, 1854], p. 76). In 1458 the city had 48 gates (de Calonne, *Histoire*, I, p. 280).

In Etampes only three gates were opened in 1585 (Dupieux, *Les institutions royales au pays d'Etampes 1478–1599* [Versailles, 1931], p. 142); two gates in Noyon in 1562 (Maziere, *Annales*, p. 86); two gates in Senlis in 1588 (Bernier, *Monuments*, p. 390)—the Paris gate would not be reopened until six years later; the Creil gate, ten years later. Two gates were in use in Soissons in 1567 (*Journal de D. Lepaulat, religieux du monastère de Saint-Crépin-le-Grand de Soissons . . . sur la prise de cette ville par les Huguenots en 1567* [Laon, 1862], p. 42).

40.   Soissons was taken by the Huguenots in 1567. They destroyed the principal churches and abbeys of the city; the damage was estimated at more than 100,000 pounds in 1572 (*Journal de D. Lepaulat;* Pecheur, *Annales*, V, p. 289). But this example is unique. Beauvais, Provins, and Senlis remained relatively neutral. Senlis was beseiged by the Parisians in 1589; damages were estimated at 200,000 *écus* (Bernier, *Monuments*, p. 95). Provins was burned by Condé in 1580 and by the Catholic League in 1587.

41.   Rouen in 1589; Etampes in 1590; Rouen, Chartres, Noyon in 1591; Laon, Noyon, and Amiens in 1596.

42.   Eight pieces of artillery (cannon) pointed on the counterscarp of the Saint-Eloi moat in Noyon; four others on the curtain (Maziere, *Annales*, p. 193); forty-five pieces of artillery battered the ravelin at the Montrescu gate in Amiens (Vaultier, *Histoires et discours d'une partie des choses faites et passées en ce royaume, qui ont eu cours depuis le 13 mai 1588 jusqu'au 16 juin 1598*, ed. Bernier, *Monuments*, p. 376). The ravelin of the Drouaise gate in Chartres was knocked down by a battery of six cannon (Bonnard, "Fortifications," p. 306).

43.   Sully called the siege of Amiens exemplary. In addition to 13,000 foot-soldiers and 45 pieces of artillery, 6,000 cavalry participated in the siege, and 1,700 cannon shots were fired. "There were [in Amiens] several very good public places, streets, parishes . . . all kinds of occupations" (Vaultier, *Histoires*, p. 379). The cost of the siege, which lasted six months, rose as high as 6 million pounds, according to Daire, *Histoire*, I, p. 303. It is true that Henry IV spared no expense to chase out the Spaniards who, at only a few days' march from Paris, had put the entire kingdom in danger.

44.   To the north, the "Béarn," near the Saint-Pierre suburb; "Vendôme," near the Chaussée-au-Blé; "Saint-Pol"; and, on either side, "Montmorency" and "Chaunes" (de Calonne, *Histoire*, II, p. 245); the same thing in Châlons, where the bastion of Aumale was built, Barbat, *Histoire*, p. 168.

45.   Sully was named chief overseer of France and master-in-chief of fortifications. The Briare canal was begun under Henry IV (Pinseau, *Le canal de Henri IV ou canal de Briare, 1604–1943* [Paris, 1944]; Grangez, *Précis historique et statistique des voies navigables de la France et d'une partie de la Belgique* [Paris, 1855], pp. 40 ff.). And there was Bernard's imaginative proposal, *La conjonction des mers (au sujet d'un projet de canal entre l'Océan et la Méditerrannée par la Saône et la Seine)*,

1613. See also Buisseret, "The Communications of France during the Reconstruction of Henry IV," *EHR*, 1965, pp. 267–77.

46. In 1589 in Beauvais in order to carry out the excavations of the Saint-Jean gate, *Recueil mémorable d'aulcuns cas advenus depuis l'an du salut 1573 tant à Beauvais qu'ailleurs*, Leblond, ed. (Paris, 1909), p. 34. In Noyon in 1436 the municipality deliberated about bringing stones from the quarries of Mount Saint-Siméon in order to redo the boulevard of the Dame-Journe gate, but finally decided against it (Ponthieux, "L'Ancien Noyon," p. 118). In 1562, because of the "great perils and dangers [caused by] the troubles and divisions of the Huguenot heretics," the works were carried out in haste, especially next to the Garnot tower, where "a parapet and a wall twenty feet high were made to be out of the range of ladders"; the earth and stones had come from Mount Saint-Siméon (Maziere, *Annales*, p. 86); Henry IV continued to level the mountain in order to build up his citadel.

47. Lanteri, p. 31; Dürer, *Instruction*, p. 8; Perret, *Des fortifications et artifices* (Frankfurt-am-Main, 1602), p. 2; Machiavel, *Oeuvres*, book 7, chap. 1; Fabre, *Pratiques*, p. 187; de Ville, *Les fortifications . . . contenant la manière de fortifier toute sorte de places* (Paris, 1629), p. 116; Errard de Bar-le-Duc, *Fortification*, p. 218.

48. De Billon (*Les principes de l'art militaire* [Lyons, 1622], p. 89), Lupicini (*Discorso*, p. 82), Errard (*Fortification*, p. 202), and Cataneo (*Capitaine*, p. 68) suggest ten to fifteen fathoms wide. Perret (*Fortifications*, p. 8) suggests twelve fathoms measured at the shoulders. De Ville (*Fortifications*, p. 115) stipulates that "the best ditches are of average depth and width."

49. "Mauvillain" in Châlons built in 1614, "Pontereaux" in Etampes in 1606.

50. In Châlons the Saint Sulpice suburb was surrounded with temporary fortifications (Grignon, *Topographie*, p. 7). In 1653 the city borrowed 10,000 pounds in order to continue the work (Barbat, *Histoire*, p. 169). Etampes, besieged by Turenne and Louis XIV in 1652, temporarily set up stockades in front of the ditches and demilunes placed before the gates (Marquis, *Les Rues d'Etampes*, p. 318); Chartres enlarged its ditches in 1623 between the road of the Courtine and the Saint-Michel gate (de Lepinois, *Histoire*, I, p. 320). In 1636 in Senlis the trees along the ditches were cut down because of the Spanish threat, and the ditches were filled in with fagots (Broisse, *Recherches historiques sur la ville de Senlis* [Senlis, 1835], p. 96).

51. It must also be noted that sludge from decomposing vegetation accumulated at the bottom of ditches with still water. Volta in Italy, and Lavoisier and de Diétrich in Paris, extracted methane from it for chemical experiments ca. 1770.

52. "The site (*assiette*) of this city of Troyes is comparable to a soup plate, being partly low, and watery, and partly sterile and firm" ("Mémoire pour les fortifications" [1542], in Grosley, *Mémoires historiques et critiques pour l'histoire de Troyes* [Paris, 1811], II, p. 280).

Chapter 6

1. *Actes de la conférence intergouvernementale d'experts sur les bases scientifiques de l'utilisation rationnelle et de la conservation des ressources de la biosphère,* Paris, 4–13 September 1968 (Paris, UNESCO, 1970), p. 101; Le Gren, *The Application of Science to Inland Fisheries—A Review of the Biological Bases of Fisheries* (Rome, 1958), pp. 41–42.

2. Edict dated 13 February 1543, concerning the of 300 saltpeter-makers and 14 saltpeter lofts, and concession of rights and privileges for the saltpeter-makers (*Catalogue des actes de François I,* IV, p. 558, num. 13611; *Recueil Général des anciennes lois de France,* Isambert ed., XII, pp. 701–3, 28 November 1540). Large cities like Paris were exempted from this obligation.

3. *Oeuvres,* p. 38; see also *AM,* Chartres, c1a, 15 October 1557; Des Billettes, "L'art de faire de la poudre à canon," *MARS,* 1705, p. 217; see also Gilles, *Histoire des techniques,* pp. 639 and 647–48. Berthelot ("Pour l'histoire des arts mécaniques et de l'artillerie vers la fin du moyen âge," *Annales de chimie et de physique,* 1891, p. 482) gives the composition of bombardment powder: 16 ounces of saltpeter, 4 of sulphur, 3 of willow charcoal. It was probably at the end of the fifteenth century that the composition of cannon powder was fixed; see Sarton, *Appreciation,* p. 309.

4. *Instruction sur l'établissment des nitrières et sur la fabrication du salpêtre, publiée par ordre du roi par les régisseurs généraux des poudres et salpêtre* (Paris, 1777).

5. Sauval (*Histoire et recherche des antiquités de la ville de Paris* [Paris, 1724], I, p. 186) states that "the mud of Paris is black, smelly, and of an intolerable odor for foreigners; the saltpeter-makers find sulphur, saltpeter, and fixed salt in it."

6. *Instruction* (n. 4, above).

7. *Extrait du mémoire sur la fabrication du salpétre* (Paris, 1782).

8. Chaumonnot, *Rivière,* reports on several of these procedures in Troyes. Cerné, on Rouen, makes clear that entire cabinets are full of archives pertaining to conflicts.

9. The report of 1504 lists six mill wheels for fulling: two at the Rave, and one each in Sancey, Paresse (replaced in 1538 by a powder mill), Saint-Quentin, and Fouchy. We know that in 1617 there were also four bleaching mills. Thus ten wheels of the forty in use. Paper-making used eleven wheels, and flour mills nineteen.

10. Desportes, *Reims et les Rémois* (Paris, 1979), pp. 582 and 600. According to the tax returns of 1436–37, cloth now accounted for only 18 percent of the tax receipts; only 8 percent in 1438–39.

11. Ibid., p. 667. On the place du Marché-au-Blé there had been a muslin exchange since the end of the thirteenth century. At the beginning of the sixteenth century, the location was named La chanvrière, and hemp was sold there.

12. Goubert, *Familles marchandes sous l'Ancien Régime; les Danse et les Motte de Beauvais* (Paris, 1953).

13. Ibid., p. 27. See also Deyon, *Amiens, capitale provinciale* (Paris-The Hague, Mouton, 1967), p. 173. Aymard ("Production, commerce et consommation des draps de laine du XIIe au XVIIe siècle," *RH*, 246 [1971], p. 8) states that "in the first half of the fifteenth century, a new fashion, that of bright colors, red in particular, completely eliminated the older preference for blue and green." On the color scarlet, see Weckerlin, *Le drap "escarlate" au moyen âge, essai sur l'étymologie et la signification du mot écarlate et notes techniques sur la fabrication de ce drap de laine au moyen âge* (Lyons, 1905). Kermes oak or gale nuts disappeared from dyeing at the end of the sixteenth century, even though they were still being gathered in the middle of the eighteenth in the region around Narbonne; see Hellot, "Mémoire sur la teinture," *MARS*, 1741, p. 50.

14. Lombard, "Les mesures-étalons de l'abbaye de Saint-Denis," *BM*, 1979 (137), p. 144.

15. *AM*, Amiens, AA 13, folio 43 v°, 25 August 1458. Aldermen noticed that for some time cloth was being poorly dyed by using bark, whereas before alum had been used (Delumeau, *L'alun de Rome, XVe–XIXe siècle* [Paris, 1963], pp. 22–23).

16. Diderot, *Encyclopédie*, art. "teinte"; most of these drugs were not mentioned, even in the form of prohibition in the regulations, compiled by De Poerck or Espinas and Pirenne for the fourteenth century.

17. Ramazzini, *De Morbis artificum* (Modena, 1700), sect. 88 (translated into English by Robert James in 1746 and into French by Fourcroy in 1777). Urine was prohibited from fulling in Arras in 1377, in Douai in 1394.

18. *L'art du fabricant d'étoffes en laine, rases et sèches, unies et croisées* (Paris, 1780), p. 49.

19. Joris, "La guède en Hesbaye au moyen âge (XIIIe–XVe siècle)," *MA*, 1963, pp. 773–89; Espinas, *La draperie dans la Flandre française au moyen âge* (Paris, 1923), vol. 2, p. 88; Perroy, *Le travail dans la région du Nord du XIe au début du XIVe siècle* (Paris, 1962), p. 69.

20. Ramazzini, *De Morbis*, sec. 90.

21. Macquart, *Manuel sur les propriétés de l'eau* (Paris, 1783), p. 103. He adds that "the English have long forbidden retting in streams that empty into frequently used rivers."

22. Pouchet, *Traité sur la fabrication des étoffes* (Rouen, 1768), p. 46.

23. *Dictionnaire de chimie* (Paris, 1773), IV, art. "teinture," p. 26. In contrast, it remained difficult to obtain white woolen cloth.

24. Roland de la Platière, *L'Art du fabricant*, p. 49. See also Vitalis, "Procédé pour teindre le fil de lin ou de chanvre en rouge dit des Indes ou d'Andrinople," *PATASBLAR*, 16 (1814). This process was imported from Turkey around 1750: "bath of droppings, or dyeing bath. The intestinal juice of ruminants is used, or albumino-gelatinous juice, which is to be found rather abundantly in sheep droppings. These substances combine more easily with the parts to be colored" (ibid., p. 93). Duhamel du Monceau, *L'Art de la drape-*

rie, p. 78: "Because ewe droppings are very astringent, they are not to be used until the very end of the fulling process."

25.   Dubuc, *Traité,* p. 2: "It is a fixed notion among the heads of these establishments that the manufacture of their merchandise, in order to insure good quality, can be done only in places that are dark and cool, and by using a paste ordinarily made of flour and water." Another postmedieval "invention" for linen and hempen clothing should be mentioned: starch; see Duhamel du Monceau in *L'Art de l'amidonnier* (Paris, 1775, p. 4): "This remarkable art shows how to draw out of bran, by means of fermentation, the starch contained in that part of flour that the art of milling has not been able to separate; for this, bran, cuttings, and bad-smelling grains are used, which the starch-makers buy and grind up coarsely; this is then put into barrels, with a sufficient quantity of water, and allowed to soak long enough so that the part that forms the starch is separated."

26.   In 1783, according to Rozier ("Sur la culture et le rouissage du chanvre," *OSP,* 1788, p. 268), "more than four hundred million pounds were used for ropes, cables, and sails," to which must be added the hemp used for other purposes (sacks, canvas, etc.). For general information, see Wolf, *History,* p. 510.

27.   Charles VII created, on 9 January 1450, an office of the general inspector of battle gear (Gandilhon, *La politique économique de Louis XI* [Rennes, 1940], p. 199).

28.   Rural tanners forced off their property by war also flocked into the cities. Thus in Reims, ca. 1350, the urban population was augmented 30 percent by immigrants, a third of whom had professional qualifications. The most frequently mentioned occupation among them was that of leather-working (Desportes, *Reims,* p. 577).

29.   Dupont de Nemours (*Rapport sur le droit de marque des cuirs* [Paris, an XII], p. 29) stressed, and with good reason, the fact that the taxes did nothing to halt the manufacture of leather, but rather accelerated the exodus of tanneries to the countryside.

30.   The preparation of the *jusée* ("juice")—that is, the juice of old bark—was adopted at Bayonne and Dax in 1750, and generally in the southwest around 1760. In 1781 tanning "in the bath" was introduced, an English procedure (a prolonged soaking in tanning juices) that reduced the tanning time and made the leather more supple. In 1795 Seguin's method let hides be tanned in three weeks by using a concentrated extract of tannin; this method produced 240,000 ox-hides per year (Quef, *Histoire,* pp. 52–54). Tannin became harder and harder to find as fallow land was reclaimed; see also Savary des Bruslons, *Dictionnaire Universel de Commerce* (Paris, 1723), II, art. "tanner."

31.   De La Lande, *L'Art du Corroyeur* (Paris, 1767), p. 35.

32.   Ramazzini, *De Morbis,* sect. 104.

33.   Duhamel du Monceau, *L'Art du Chandelier* (Paris, 1764), p. 3.

34.   Ramazzini, *De Morbis,* sect. 109, 110.

35. Duhamel du Monceau, *L'Art de faire différentes sortes de colles* (Paris, 1771), p. 2.

36. *L'Art de faire du papier* (Paris, n.d. [ca. 1760]), p. i; see also Savary des Bruslons, *Dictionnaire*, II, art. "papier."

37. De La Lande, *L'Art*, p. 45. See also *Arrêt du Conseil du Roi portant règlement pour les différentes sortes de papier qui se fabriquent dans le Royaume*, dated 27 January 1739, reproduced in De La Lande, ibid., p. 9; this procedure had not been modified since the Middle Ages. See also Desbilletes, "Description de l'art du papier," *MARS*, 1706, pp. 34–38.

38. De La Lande, *L'Art du Cartonnier* (Paris, 1762).

39. Réaumur, *Mémoire pour servir à l'histoire des insectes*, vol. 6; *Suite de l'histoire sur les mouches à quatre ailes* (Paris, 1734–42), p. 154.

40. Guettard, *Observation sur les plantes* (Paris, 1747), I, pp. 5–6.

41. *Le théâtre d'agriculture* (Paris, 1600), p. 663.

42. Around 1420 in Troyes (Boutiot, *Histoire*, II, p. 442). The same in Chartres: the blood from slaughtered animals "would carry infection through the streets" (De Lepinois, *Histoire*, II, p. 194), and in Senlis in 1402 (Muller, "Analyse," p. 51).

43. Picard, "Mémoire sur la topographie médicale de Troyes et de ses environs en 1786," *MSAASABLDA*, 1873, p. 200.

44. Thirioux d'Arconville, *Essai pour servir à l'histoire de la putréfaction* (Paris, 1766), p. xi.

45. Thus in Beauvais in 1580, "many of the streets were paved, which had never been before, to discourage the residents from throwing their refuse in them" (*Recueil mémorable*, p. 5). For Rouen, see Le Pecq de la Clôture, *Collections*, p. 228: "the small streams of the Robec and the Aubette have become the home for myriads of manufacturers and dyers. . . . The center of the neighborhood is filled with persons seemingly foreign to the climate of Rouen. The men and women there have about the same habits; they go together to cabarets, drinking large quantities of aqua vitae; they have bad complexions, with dark skin, black hair, and are thin, which speaks of the misery that reigns in their dirty, damp habitations." Young, *Voyage en France* (Paris, 1783), I, p. 280, concerning Clermont-Ferrand: "There are streets that, by their color, filth, and bad smell, can be compared only with a path drawn through a dung-heap."

46. Purgatory as a state of bodiless souls appeared at the end of the twelfth century. It was made official at the Second Council of Lyon in 1274; see Le Goff, *The Birth of Purgatory*, tr. Arthur Goldhammer, Chicago, 1984.

47. Bullet, *Observations sur la nature et les effects de la mauvaise odeur des lieux d'aisances ou cloaques et sur l'importance dont il est d'éviter cette mauvaise odeur pour la conservation de la santé* (Paris, 1696), p. 13.

48. Bouchard, *Confessions, suivi de son voyage de Paris à Rome en 1630* (Paris, 1881), p. 42; he visited Aix-en-Provence, Marseilles, Arles, Fréjus, and other cities. Water-closets were invented in England at

the end of the eighteenth century and adapted in France at the beginning of the nineteenth.

49. Out of spite, many went to places of public authority to defecate; in Le Mans, "several persons, especially from the neighborhood of Les Halles [near the Palais de Justice], who have no latrines in their houses, are rash enough, and insolent enough, to take care of their needs in the said room [of the palace], which gives it a stinking and infected odor" (*AD*, Sarthe, 614, act of 5 May 1733).

50. Rossiau, "Prostitution." See also Bouchard, *Confessions*, p. 295.

51. Quenedy, *Habitation*, p. 101.

52. De Beaurepaire, "Le Clos Saint-Marc," *PATASBLAR*, 1906–1907, pp. 171–72.

53. De la Framboisière, *Oeuvres*, p. 114.

54. Brunet, *Propos de table de Martin Luther* (Paris, 1844), p. 377. Luther added a little further on: "I am surprised that man has not yet covered the entire earth right up to heaven with his droppings." A pharmacopoeia of excrement is also mentioned by Pliny, *Hist. Nat.*, books 20, 29, 30.

55. Paullini, *Dreck-Apotheke*.

56. Fonseca, *De Rominis excrementis* (Paris, 1613); Rulando, *Pharmacopae nova de hominis stercore* (Nuremberg, 1644); Boerhave, *Dissertatis de utilitate inspiciendorum excrementorum ut signorum* (Nijmegen, 1693); Buckio, *Dissertatio de medica stercoraria* (Hamburg, 1700); Juch, *Dissertatio de retrimentorum corporis humani coloribus varian in aegrotis significationem praebantibus* (Nijmegen, 1703); Homberg, "Observations sur les matières fécales," *MARS*, 1711; idem, "Phosphore nouveau ou suite d'observations sur les matières fécales," ibid., pp. 238 ff.; Schurig, *Chylologia* (Dresden, 1725), pp. 752 ff.; Paul, *Dissertatio de medicamentis excorpore humans desumitis merito negligendis* (Leipzig, 1821); Lavoisier, "Mémoire sur les différents gaz des matières fécales," *MARS*, 1782; Baumer, *Anthropologica anatomica physica* (Frankfurt, 1784), pp. 405 ff.; Tessier, *Rapport fait à l'institut de France sur les excréments humains* (Paris, An V [1796]).

57. *Introduction à l'étude des corps naturels tirés du règne végétale* (Paris, 1773), II, p. 227, and more generally, Metzger, *Les doctrines chimiques en France du début du XVIIᵉ siècle à la fin du XVIIIᵉ siècle* (Paris, 1923).

58. Macquer, *Dictionnaire*, art. "Putréfaction."

59. Du Hamel, "Observations sur les sels qu'on retire des cendres des végétaux," *MARS*, 1767, pp. 233–40; he adds that the "plants of our provinces supply tartar."

60. Lemery fils, "Premier mémoire sur le nitre," *MARS*, 1717, p. 50; Stahl, *Fundamenta chimiae dogmatico-rationales*, II, 3rd ed., Montpellier, 1861; Lavoisier, "Documents et mémoires relatifs au prix du salpêtre," *Oeuvres*, VI, p. 468.

61. Van Helmont, *Ortus medicinae* (Lyons, 1667), p. 23; Boyle, *Works* (London, 1772), I, p. 564; Du Hamel, *Physique des arbres* (Paris,

1749), II, p. 198; Yverdon, *Eléments d'agriculture* (Paris, 1766), p. 83. For Stahl, the founder of the doctrine of phlogistics, the four principles are water and three earth elements corresponding to the three principles of iatrochemistry; the second element is phlogiston (sulphur). See also Hall, *The Scientific Revolution, 1500–1800: The Formation of the Modern Scientific Attitude* (London, 2nd ed., 1962), pp. 312–14. Lavoisier ("Sur la nature de l'eau et sur les expériences par lesquelles on a prétendu prouver la possibilité de son changement en terre" [*MARS*, 1770], p. 73) disproved this proposition.

62. De Milly, "Essai sur une nouvelle manière d'analyser les substances du règne animal et végétal . . . ," *MARS*, 1781, pp. 39–40. De Milly adhered to the doctrines of phlogistics, even after the discoveries made by Lavoisier.

63. For Caen, see Perrot, *Caen*, I, p. 274; for Rouen ca. 1750, see Le Cat, "An Account of the Malignant Fevers, that raged at Rouen at the end of the year 1753, and the beginning of 1754," *PTRA*, 1755, pp. 24–30.

64. Choay, *La règle et le modèle: Sur la théorie de l'architecture et de l'urbanisme* (Paris, Le Seuil, 1980).

65. Mantoux, *Révolution*, p. 332.

66. Huizinga, *The Waning of the Middle Ages* (New York, 1924); Delumeau, *La peur en occident, XVIe–XVIIe siècles* (Paris, 1978); Aries, *Essais sur la mort en occident* (Paris, 1976).

Chapter 7

1. Fourcroy, in *Encyclopédie méthodique—chimie et métallurgie* (Paris, 1808), vol. 5, art. "air méphitique."

2. François, *La science des eaux* (Rennes, 1633), p. 27.

3. Kircher, *Magnes*, p. 594.

4. *Histoire de l'Académie des Sciences* (1692), p. 33.

5. Mariotte, *Traité du mouvement des eaux et autres corps fluides* (Paris, 1686), p. 23; Perrault, *Origine*, p. 322. Macquart (*Manuel sur les propriétés de l'eau, particulièrement dans l'art de guérir* [Paris, 1783], p. 129) states that there was no agreement on the depth of penetration of water, and records the same observation as Buffon (*Histoire*, I, p. 122) on the impermeability of the earth beyond a depth of four feet.

6. *Traité*, p. 33.

7. *Théorie*, p. 225.

8. Ibid., p. 259.

9. Silberschlag, *Théorie*, p. 4.

10. "Programme du cours des mines," *Journal de l'Ecole Polytechnique* (1806), p. 357.

11. Duhamel du Monceau (*Physique*, p. 155) refers to the *Vegetable Statiks* of Hales (London, 1727), which was enormously successful in France; see Guerlac, "The continental reputation of Stephen

Hales," *Archives Internationales d'Histoire des Sciences*, 1951, vol. 4, p. 394.

12. Dubois de Morambert, "Proposition," p. 63.

13. Bernard, *Principes*, p. 138.

14. Around 1830 it was shown that leaves could not be water-captors. The hydrological role of leaves was reduced to protection against erosion. However, adherents of this theory of the "forest-as-siphon" can still be found in all branches of science today. Several million dollars have been spent on the study of the influence of forests on the water table level, with very contradictory results: the Swiss claim that the forest has no effect on the water table, the Americans claim exactly the opposite, and the Japanese have taken a position between the two. It is true that research has been carried on for only half a century, which from a historian's point of view is not very long. However, from the point of view of topology, hardly any of the springs and fountains disappeared during the long periods of land reclamation in the Middle Ages, and the evolution of fallow land during the fourteenth and fifteenth centuries did not raise the level of the water table.

15. Baume, *Mémoire qui a remporté le prix, en 1789, au jugement de la Société Royale de Médecine de Paris sur la question proposée en ces termes: Déterminer, par l'observation, quelles sont les maladies qui résultent des émanations des eaux stagnantes, et des pays marécageux, soit pour ceux qui habitent dans les environs, soit pour ceux qui travaillent à leur dessèchement et quels sont les moyens de les prévenir et d'y remédier* (Paris, 1789), p. 23.

16. *Mémoire sur les exhalaisons des marais du Bas-Languedoc* (Paris, 1786).

17. Laborie, Cadet le Jeune, and Parmentier, *Observations*. See also Corbin, *Miasme*.

18. The two citations are from Baume, *Mémoire*, pp. 13 and 23. See also Fourcroy, *Rapport*, p. 12; Condorcet, "Table," pp. 52–55; Chaptal, *Mémoire*.

19. "Précis historique sur les émanations élastiques qui de dégagent des corps pendant la combustion, pendant la fermentation et pendant les effervescences," *Oeuvres*, III, p. 523. Lavoisier was named *Régisseur des Poudres* ("director of powder") by Turbot, and wrote a report to the Academy on retting in 1788 (ibid., IV, pp. 498–500).

20. Macquer, *Dictionnaire*, III, p. 320.

21. The Corps of Mines was founded in 1783.

22. *Essai*, I, p. 21.

23. *MARS*, 1767, pp. 133–37.

24. Kuhn, *Structure*. See also McCann, *Chemistry;* Guerlac, *Antoine Laurent Lavoisier, Chemist and Revolutionary* (New York, 1975).

25. *MARS*, 1767, p. 681.

26. *Oeuvres*, IV, p. 499. See also Moret, *Mémoire*, p. 12.

27. "Sur les machines mues par la force du vent," *MARS*, 1781, p. 43.

28. *Eléments*, I, p. vi.

29. *Annales de Chimie,* 54 (an XIII = 1804), 86–103.

30. Brisseau-Mirbel, *Eléments de physiologie végétale et de botanique* (Paris, 1815), I, p. 209. For Lavoisier, see his "Précis historique sur les émanations, etc.," in *Oeuvres,* II, p. 523.

31. *Cours complet d'agriculture théorique, pratique, économique et de médecine rurale et vétérinaire* (Paris, 1781–96), IV, p. 81.

32. Belidor, *Architecture hydraulique,* IV, p. 262.

33. Dubuat, *Principes,* p. 105; see also Bernard, *Principes,* p. 138; Michand d'Arçon, *Considérations militaires et politiques sur les fortifications* (Paris, an III), p. 128.

34. Dubuat, *Principes,* p. 115.

35. Silberschlag, *Théorie,* p. 32.

36. Bossut, *Traité,* I, p. 385; d'Alembert, de Condorcet, and Bossut, *Nouvelles expériences sur la résistance des fluides* (Paris, 1777), p. 193.

37. *Traité,* p. 221.

38. Deparcieux, "Mémoire dans lequel on démontre que l'eau d'une chute destinée à faire mouvoir quelque machine, moulin ou autre, peut toujours produire beaucoup plus d'effet en agissant par son poids qu'en agissant par son choc, et que les roues à pots qui tournent lentement produisent plus d'effet que celles qui tournent vite, relativement aux chutes et aux dépenses," *MARS,* 1754, pp. 603–14; Smeaton, "An Experimental Enquiry concerning the natural Powers of Water and Wind to turn Mills and other Machines depending on Circular Motions," *PTRA,* 1759, pp. 100 ff. See also Cardwell, "Technologies," pp. 192–208. It should be noted that Deparcieux, an engineer at the Ecole des Ponts et Chaussées, published in 1767 a "Mémoire sur un moyen de se garantir de la puanteur des puisards, quand on est contraint d'en faire dans le voisinage des maisons," *MARS,* pp. 133–37. He supported the theories of Lavoisier, and encouraged the teaching of the new chemistry at the Ecole des Ponts et Chaussées.

39. *Essai sur la manière la plus avantageuse de construire les machines hydrauliques et en particulier les moulins à blé* (Paris, 1783), p. 284.

40. $R = a\,u + b\,u^2$, where u is the speed relative to the body with respect to current, and a and b are the two parameters given by the abacus (*Recherches physico-mathématiques sur la théorie des eaux courantes* [Paris, 1804], II, p. 63). Prony applied the method of correction of anomalies developed by Laplace in his *Traité de mécanique céleste* (Paris, 1799–1825).

41. "Rapport du 6 février 1808 sur les progrès des sciences naturelles," in *Oeuvres* (Paris, 1881), I, p. 105.

42. "Note pour l'article chimie," *Oeuvres,* V, p. 299.

43. *Principes,* p. 115. A similar proposal was suggested by Fourcroy to eliminate putrefaction within the city: "Aerate places of habitation, and establish there frequent ventilation, cover sewers and move them far away, establish cemeteries outside the city, have only fresh, running water in the covered canals, and especially, let it spurt out

in jets or cascades" (*Encyclopédie méthodique*, IV, 1794, art. "Altération qu'éprouve l'air respiré" [1785], and in *Oeuvres*, II, p. 687).

44. Devermont, *Voyage pittoresque . . . dans la ville d'Amiens* (Amiens, 1784), p. 38.

45. D'Ornay, *Essai sur la ville de Rouen, Travaux faits et à faire pour le plus grande utilité et le plus grand agrément de cette ville* (Rouen, 1806), p. 9.

46. Berthollet, *Eléments*, p. 218; Chaptal, *Chimie*, p. 292.

47. Dubuc, *Traité sur les parements et encollages dont l'emploi permet aux tisserands de travailler ailleurs que dans les caves et autres bas-fonds non éclairés et généralement mal-sains* (Rouen, 1829), p. ix.

48. Koechlin-Schouch, "Essai sur l'emploi du son dans le débouillissage des toiles peintes," *Bulletin de la Société Industrielle de Mulhouse*, 2 (1829), p. 292.

49. The Swiss process described in the *Mémoires de la Société d'Agriculture de Berne*, 1766, was used. The Constituent (law of 27 September 1791), then the National Assembly (law of 23 May 1792), nationalized the finding of saltpeter and the making of gunpowder according to traditional processes. Saltpeter was manufactured synthetically after 1830: 53.45% nitric acid + 46.35% potash.

50. Laborie et al., *Observations*, p. 107; and Janin, *Antiméphitique*, p. xxiv.

51. Dupuy, *Urbanisme*, Part 2.

52. Guillerme, *Corps à corps sur la route: les routes, les chemins et l'organisation des services, 1836–1920* (Paris, Presses de l'Ecole Nationale des Ponts et Chaussées, 1984).

53. The first Conseil de Salubrité (health board) was set up in 1802 under the auspices of the prefecture of Paris, composed first of four members, then seven in 1807, to which were added two doctors for epidemics. This board was to keep watch over unhealthy factories and workshops; gather observations on epidemics; have the markets, rivers, slaughterhouses, pavements, cemeteries, and public baths inspected; establish medical statistics and mortality records; look for ways to keep public halls, hospitals, and other places clean, and suggest cost estimates. The second board was created in Nantes in 1817 for the Loire Inférieure. Rouen set one up on the models of Nantes and Paris, with twelve members: three doctors, three chemists, one botanist, two veterinarians, one architect, one engineer from the Ponts et Chaussées, and one manufacturer. The balance was thus not favorable to crafts. Health boards were set up in all the Départements in 1851.

Conclusion

1. See *Science and Society 1600–1900*, especially Mathias, "Who Unbound Prometheus? Science and Technical Change, 1600–1800," p. 63.

2. "Préface à l'histoire de l'Académie des Sciences," *MARS*, 1699, p. vii. For Rohaut, physics is "the science that teaches us the reasons and causes of all the effects that nature produces" (*Traité*, I, p. 1; this work went through twenty editions between 1671 and 1720). At the end of the eighteenth century, physics still included all the human sciences, including medicine, botany, and natural history. See also Heilbron, *Electricity*, pp. 11–14, and *Elements of Early Modern Physics* (Berkeley, Los Angeles, and London: University of California Press, 1982), pp. 1–5.

3. As early as the fourteenth century, mills began to multiply. Water courses were diverted and dynamized, unlike urban waters. In the middle of the eighteenth century, milling reached an energy saturation point and brought about flooding. The rural world of northern France used the same technology, based on fermentation, as did the city, and this remained unchanged until the beginning of the twentieth century. It is true that, here again, the prohibition of death would take much longer to come into effect.

4. I will perhaps be called to task for having passed too rapidly over the relationship between medieval urban technology and its mentality. But, to my knowledge, no analysis of the *Weltanschauung* of the High Middle Ages has been undertaken, at least such as has been developed by Philippe Ariès. But the valuable works of Marc Bloch, Georges Duby, and Jacques Le Goff prove that both feudal and urban society loved life, without hiding death. Thus I think, as I have stressed, it is more along the lines of the theme of liberty—"city air makes freedom"—close to the theme of life, that the technical forms of the eleventh to the thirteenth century will have to be sketched.

Bibliography

For local monographs (in France), the list of works to consult is given in the *Bibliographie d'histoire de villes de France*, P. Wolff and P. Dollinger, eds. (Paris: Kincksieck, 1967).

L'Histoire de la France urbaine, G. Duby, general editor (Paris: Le Seuil, 1980, 5 vols.), and *L'Histoire des techniques*, B. Gille, general editor (Paris: Gallimard, 1978), provide a vast bibliography. For my own project, I add the following works:

Printed Sources

A. General Works

Acta Sanctorum ordini S. Benedicti. Coll. J. Bollandus. Anvers, 1643 ff. (3rd ed., 1863 ff.).

Actes du Comité de Salut Public. Paris, 1900–1901.

Bernier, A. *Monuments inédits de l'Histoire de France (1400–1600)*. Paris and Senlis, 1835.

Bouchard, J. J. *Confessions suivies de son voyage de Paris à Rome en 1630*. Paris, 1881.

Buffon, G. *Histoire naturelle*. 3 vols. Paris, 1749.

Catalogue des actes de François Ier. 10 vols. Paris, 1887–1908.

Compte rendu et présenté au corps législatif . . . par l'Institut National des Sciences et de Arts. Paris, an VI.

Du Cange. *Glossarium mediae et infimae latinitatis*. 7 vols. Paris, 1840–50.

Duples-Agier, H. "Ordonnances inédites de Philippe le Bel et de Philippe le Long sur la police de la pêche fluviale." *BEC* 18 (1857): 265–70.

Durand, G. *Rational ou manuel des divins offices*. Ed. Barthélémy. 5 vols. Paris, 1854.

Encyclopédie ou dictionnaire raisonné des sciences, des arts et des métiers. 17 vols. Paris, 1751–72.

Enguerrand de Monstrelet. *Chronique 1400–1444*. Ed. Douet d'Arcq. 3 vols. Paris, 1857–62.

Bibliography

Flodoard. *Historiae remensis ecclesiae.* Ed. Lejeune. Reims, 1854.

Giry, A. *Documents sur la Relation de la Royauté avec les villes de France de 1180 à 1314.* Paris, 1885.

Gregoire de Tours. *Historia francorum.* Ed. and trans. Halphen. 2 vols. Paris, 1965.

Guibert de Nogent. *Histoire de sa vie (1053–1124).* Ed. Labande. Paris, 1982.

Guillaume de Poitiers. *Histoire de Guillaume le Conquérant.* Ed. Foreville. Paris, 1952.

Guillaume le Breton. *Philippide.* Ed. Delaborde. Paris, 1885.

Institut de France—Académie des Sciences Ordre de lectures et prix, 1778–1829. 2 vols. Paris, 1837–52.

Isambert, DeCrusy, and Armet, eds. *Recueil général des anciennes lois françaises depuis l'an 420 jusqu'à la révolution de 1789.* 28 vols. Paris, 1835–80.

La Mare, N. de. *Traité de Police.* 4 vols. Paris, 1768–72.

Luchaire, A. *Etude sur les actes de Louis VII.* Paris, 1885.

Montrenet, E. de. *Chroniques 1400–1444.* Ed. Douet d'Arques. 4 vols. Paris. 1857–62.

Monumenta Germaniae Historica—Scriptorum rerum mero-vingicarum. 7 vols. Hanover, 1885–1909.

Monumenta Germaniae Historica—Poetae Latini aevi carolini. 3 vols. Berlin, 1886–1923.

Monumenta Germaniae Historica—Concilia. 3 vols. Hanover, 1888–1912.

Mortet, V. *Recueil de textes relatifs à l'architecture et à la condition des architectes en France au Moyen-Age, XI–XIIe siècles.* Paris, 1911.

———, and Deschamps, P. *Recueil de textes relatifs à l'architecture et à la condition des architectes en France au Moyen-Age, XII–XIIIe siècles.* Paris, 1929.

Newman, W. *Catalogue des actes de Robert II, Roi de France.* Paris, 1937.

Orderic, Vital. *Historia ecclesiastica.* Ed. Le Prevost. 2 vols. Paris, 1840.

Piganiol de la Force, J. *Nouvelle description de la France dans lequel on voit le gouvernement général de ce royaume, celui de chaque province en particulier et les descriptions des villes.* 6 vols. Paris, 1718.

Poterlet, J. *Code des dessèchements ou recueil des règlements rendus sur cette matière, depuis le règne de Henri IV jusqu'à nos jours.* Paris, 1807.

Prou, M., ed. *Recueil des actes de Philippe Ier,* Paris, 1908.

Ravinet, J. *Dictionnaire hydrographique de la France contenant la description des rivières et canaux flottables et navigables dépendants du domaine public . . . suivi de la collection complète des tarifs des droits de navigation.* 2 vols. Paris, 1824.

Recueil général des anciennes lois de France. Ed. Isambert. Paris, 1830–45.

Recueil des monuments inédits de l'histoire du Tiers-Etat. Ed. Thierry. Paris, 1850.

Recueil des historiens des Gaules et de la France. 27 vols. Paris, 1738–1904.

Richer. *Histoire de France.* Ed. La Touche. Paris, 1935–37.

Samaran, C. *Recueil des actes de Philippe Auguste, Roi de France.* 3 vols. Paris, 1954–66.

Savary des Bruslons, J. *Dictionnaire universel de commerce, contenant tout ce qui concerne le commerce qui se fait dans les quatre parties du monde.* 3 vols. Paris, 1723–30.

Say, J. *Des canaux de navigation dans l'état actuel de la France.* Paris, 1815.

———. *Cours complet d'économie politique.* 7 vols. Paris, 1828–29.

Soehnee, F. *Catalogue des actes de Philippe Ier, Roi de France (1031–1060).* Paris, 1907.

Sulpice, Sévère. *Vie de Saint Martin.* Ed. Fontaine. 3 vols. Paris, 1967–68.

Turgot, A. *Oevres complètes.* 2 vols. Paris, 1807–1808.

Ursins, J. des. *Histoire de Charles VI, Roi de France.* Paris, 1841.

Vie des Saints et des bienheureux selon l'ordre du calendrier. 13 vols. Paris, 1935–59.

Vitruve. *Les Dix Livres d'architecture.* Book IX. Paris, 1978.

Young, A. *Travels in France.* 2 vols. London, 1752.

B. Poliorcetics

Bardet de Villuneuve, P. *Cours de la science militaire à l'usage de l'infanterie, de la cavalerie, de l'artillerie, du génie et de la marine.* The Hague, 1740–57.

Billon, J. de. *Les Principes de l'art militaire, où il est sommairement traité de la plupart des charges et devoirs des hommes qui sont en une armée . . . divisez en trois livres—suites des principes de l'art militaire, où il est amplement traité des devoirs du sergent major.* Lyons, 1622.

Blondel, J. *Nouvelle manière de fortifier les places.* Paris, 1711.

Carnot, L. *Mémoire présenté au Conseil de la Guerre, au sujet des places fortes qui doivent être démolies ou abandonnées; ou examen de cette question; est-il avantageux au Roi de France qu'il y ait des places fortes sur les frontières de ses Etats.* Paris, 1789.

Cataneo, J. *Le Capitaine . . . contenant la manière de fortifier les places, assaillir et défendre. Avec l'ordre qu'on doit tenir pour asseoir un camp, et mespartir les logis d'iceluy.* Lyons, 1624.

Cormontaingne, L. de. *Architecture militaire, ou l'art de fortifier.* The Hague, 1741.

Dürer, A. *Instruction sur la fortification des villes, bourgs et châteaux.* Nuremberg, 1524; Paris, 1870.

Errard, J. *La Fortification démontrée et réduicte en art.* Paris, 1600.

Fabre, J. *Les Pratiques du Sieur Fabre, sur l'ordre et règle de fortifier, garder, attaquer et défendre les places, avec un facile moyen pour level toutes sortes de plans, tant des places et des bastimens, que la campagne pour les cartes.* Paris, 1629.

Feuquières, A. de. *Mémoires sur la Guerre, où l'on a rassemblé les maximes les plus nécessaires dans les opérations de l'art militaire.* Amsterdam, 1730 (2d ed., 1735; 3 vols., London, 1736).

Folard, J. de. *Nouvelles découverts sur la guerre dans une dissertation sur Polybe.* Paris, 1726.

Gautier, H. *Traité des fortifications contenant la démonstration et l'examen de tout ce qui regarde l'art de fortifier les places tant régulières qu'irrégulières.* Lyons, 1865.

Goldmann, N. *La Nouvelle Fortification*. Leiden, 1654.

La Font de Bois Guérin, G. de. *Discours sur la défense des places*. Paris, 1675.

Lanteri, G. *Delle offese et diffese delle città et fortezze*. Venice, 1601.

La Treille, F. de. *Discours des villes, chasteaux et forteresses, batues, assaillies et prises par la force de l'artillerie durant les règnes des roys Henry Second et Charles IX, estant maistre et capitaine général d'icelle le siegneur Destrées*. Paris, 1563.

Le Blond, G. *Elémens de fortifications à l'usage des jeunes officiers*. Paris, 1739 (2d ed., 1742; 3rd ed., 1752; 4th ed., 1756; 5th ed., 1764; 6th ed., 1770; 7th ed., 1775; 8th ed., 1786).

Lupicini, P. *Discorso . . . sopra i ripari delle mondazioni di Fiorenza*. Florence, 1594.

Machiavelli. *Oeuvres complètes*. Ed. Barincou. Paris, 1952.

Mandar, C. *De l'architecture des forteresses, ou l'art de fortifier les places*. Paris, 1801.

Manesson-Mallet, A. *Les Travaux de Mars ou la fortification nouvelle tant régulière qu'irrégulière*. 3 vols. Paris, 1671, 1684, 1685.

Michaud D'Arcon, A. *Considérations militaires et politiques sur les fortifications*. Paris, n.d.

Rozard, M. *Nouvelle fortification française où il est traité de la construction des places, ensemble l'explication des trois systèmes du Maréchal de Vauban*. Nuremberg, 1731.

Saint Julien, A. de. *Architecture militaire ou l'art de fortifier les villes*. The Hague, 1705.

Sturm, L. C. *Architectura militaris hypothetico-electica oder gründliche Anleitung zu der Kriegsbaukunst aus denen Hypothesibus und Erfindungen derer meisten und besten Ingenieurs dargestellet*. Nuremberg, 1719.

Vauban, S. de. *De l'attaque et de la défense des places*. The Hague, 1737.

Vignau, A. du. *Exercice complet sur le tracé, le relief et la construction, l'attaque et la défense des fortifications*. Paris, 1830.

Ville, A. de. *Les Fortifications . . . contenant la manière de fortifier toutes sortes de places*. Paris, 1629.

C. Hydraulics—Inland Navigation—Milling

Alembert, J. d'. *Essai d'une nouvelle théorie de la résistance des fluides*. Paris, 1752.

——. *Traité de l'équilibre et du mouvement des fluides pour servir de suite au traité de dynamique*. Paris, 1744.

Ampere, A. M. *Essai sur la philosophie des sciences, ou exposition analytique d'une classification naturelle de toutes les connaissances humaines*. 2 vols. Paris, 1834–43.

Aubuisson de Voisins, J. d'. *Traité d'hydraulique à l'usage des ingénieurs*. 2d ed. Paris, 1840.

——. *Traité élémentaire de géognésie*. 2 vols. Paris, 1828.

Barattieri, G. B. *Architettura d'acque*. 2 vols. Plaisance, 1656–63.

Becquey, E.-L. *Rapport au roi sur la navigation intérieure.* Paris, 1820.

Belanger, M. *Essai sur la solution de quelques problèmes relatifs au mouvement permanent des eaux courantes.* Paris, 1828.

Belidor, B. de. *Architecture hydraulique ou l'art de conduire, d'élever et de ménager les eaux, pour les différents besoins de la vie.* . . . 2 vols. Paris, 1737–39 (2d ed., 5 vols., 1739–70; 3rd ed., 4 vols., 1782–90; 4th ed., 1 vol., 1819).

―――. *Le Bombardier françois ou nouvelle méthode de jeter les bombes avec précision.* Paris. 1731.

―――. *Dictionnaire portatif de l'ingénieur* . . . , Paris, 1755.

―――. *La Science des ingénieurs dans la conduite des travaux de fortification et d'architecture civile.* Paris, 1729 (2d ed., 1773; 3rd ed., 1813).

―――. *Sommaire d'un cours d'architecture militaire, civile, hydrolique, et des autres traitez les plus utiles aux ingénieurs et architectes.* Paris, 1720.

Benedetti, F. *Spéculations mathématiques et physiques.* Turin, 1585.

Bernard, M. *Nouveaux principles d'hydraulique appliqués à tous les objects, particulièrement aux rivières.* Paris, 1787.

Bernoulli, D. *Hydrodynamica, sive de Viribus et motibus fluidorurum Commentarii, opus academicum.* . . . Agentotari, 1738.

Bernoulli, J. *Oeuvres.* 2 vols. Geneva, 1774.

Böckler, G.-A. *Architectura curiosa nova, das ist: Neue ergötzliche Sinn- und Kunstreiche, auch nützliche Bau und Wasser Kunst.* . . . Nuremberg, 1662.

Borda, C. de. "Mémoire sur les roues hydrauliques." *MARS*, 1767, pp. 144–76.

Bossut, C. *Traité théorique et expérimental d'hydrodynamique.* 2 vols. Paris, 1786–87.

―――, and Leroi, D. *Examen des projets et canaux de navigation entre la rivière d'Oise et la Seine au Bastion de l'arsenal de Paris.* Paris, 1795.

―――, and Viallet, P. *Recherches sur la construction la plus avantageuse des digues, ouvrage pour servir de suite à la deuxième partie de l'architecture hydraulique de M. Bélidor.* Paris, 1764.

Bouguer, J. *Traité complet de la navigation* . . . . Nantes, 1698.

Boussinesq, C. *Essai sur la théorie des eaux courantes.* Paris, 1877.

Bralle, C. *Précis des faits et observations relatifs à l'inondation qui a eu lieu dans Paris en Frimaire et Nivose de l'an X de la République Francaise.* Paris, 1803.

Brisson, B. *Essai sur le système général de navigation intérieure de la France, suivi d'un essai sur l'art de projeter les canaux à point de partage.* Paris, 1829.

Carnot, J. *Principes de l'équilibre et du mouvement.* Paris, 1803.

Castelli, B. *Della misura dell'acque correnti.* Rome, 1628.

―――. *Riposta alle oppozioni del S. Lodovico delle Colombe e del S. Vincenzio di Grazia contro al trattato del sig. Galileo Galilei, delle cose che stanno sù l'acqua o che in quella si muovono.* Florence, 1615.

―――. *Traité de la mesure des eaux courantes* . . . *traduit avec un Discours de la jonction des mers, adressé à Messeigneurs les Commissaires députés de sa Majesté. Ensemble un traité du mouvement des eaux d'Evangélico Torricelli.* Castres, 1644; Paris, 1645.

Caus, S. de. *Nouvelle invention de lever l'eau plus hault que sa source avec quelques machines mouvantes par le moyen de l'eau.* London, 1644.

Christian, M. *Traité de mécanique industrielle ou Exposé de la science de la mécanique déduite de l'expérience et de l'observation principalement à l'usage des manufactuiers et des artistes.* 3 vols. Paris, 1822–25.

Clairaut, A. *Théorie de la figure de la terre, tirée, des principes de l'hydrostatique.* Paris, 1743.

Coriolis, G. *Du calcul de l'effet des machines ou considération sur l'emploi des moteurs et sur leur évaluation.* Paris, 1829.

————. *Correspondance mathématique et physique de quelques célèbres géomètres du XVIIIe siècle.* Ed. Fuss. 2 vols. Saint Petersburg, 1842–43.

Coulomb, P. "Sur les machines mues par la force du vent." *MARS*, 1781, pp. 41–42, 65–81.

Dubuat, L. *Principes d'hydraulique; ouvrage dans lequel on traite du mouvement de l'eau dans les rivières, canaux, etc.* 3 vols. Paris 1779 (2d ed., 1786; 3rd ed., 1816).

Ducrest, C. *Essai sur les machines hydrauliques contenant des recherches sur la manière de les calculer et de perfectionner en général leur construction.* Paris, 1777.

Euler, L. "Principes généraux de l'état d'équilibre des fluides." *MAB*, 1755, pp. 215–73.

————. "Principes généraux du mouvement des fluides." *MAB*, 1755, pp. 274–315.

————. *Théorie complète de la construction et de la manoeuvre des Vaisseaux.* 2 vols. 1st ed. (Latin), Saint Petersburg, 1749; French ed., Paris, 1776.

Evans, O. *Young Mill-Wright and Miller's Guide.* Philadelphia, 1795. French trans. *(Le Guide du meunier et du constructeur de moulins)*, Benoist, Paris, 1830.

Eytelwein, J. *Manuel de mécanique et d'hydraulique.* Paris, 1823.

Ferrari, M. *Dizzertazioni idraulica.* 2 vols. Milan, 1797.

Fourier, J. *Oeuvres.* Ed. Darbouy. 2 vols. Paris, 1889–90.

Frisi, P. *Operum.* 3 vols. Milan, 1782–85.

Galilei, G. *Opera.* 2 vols. Bologna, 1656; Florence, 1890–1909.

Gennete, L. de. *Expérience sur le cours des fleuvres, ou lettre à un magistrat hollandais, dans laquelle on examine l'accrue des eaux et si, pour les faire baisser dans un fleuvre et éviter les inondations, il convient de faire des saignées ou des décharges en divisant les eaux.* Paris, 1760.

Germain, A. *Traité d'hydrographie: Levé et construction des cartes marines.* 2 vols. Paris, 1822.

Girard, P. *Essai sur le mouvement des eaux courantes et la figure qu'il convient de donner aux canaux qui les contiennent.* Paris, 1804.

————. *Mémoire sur les inondations souterraines auxquelles sont exposés périodiquement plusieurs quartiers de Paris.* Paris, 1818.

Guglielmini, D. *Opera omnia mathematica, hydraulica, medica et physica.* 2 vols. Geneva, 1719.

Jousse, M. *L'Art de charpenterie . . . corrigé de ce qu'il y a de plus curieux dans cet art et des machines les plus nécessaires à un charpentier.* Ed. de La Hire. Paris, 1702.

Juan, G. *Traité de mécanique appliqué à la construction et à la manoeuvre des vaisseaux.* Madrid, 1771.

Lacaux, P. "Mémoire sur la théorie des engrenages." *PATASBLAR* 20 (1818): 103–10.

Lahiteau, M. *Traité d'hydraulique expérimentale.* 2d ed. Paris, 1826.

La Hire, P. de. *L'Ecole des arpenteurs, où l'on enseigne toutes les pratiques de géométrie qui sont nécessaires à un arpenteur. On y a ajouté un abrégé du nivellement et les propriétés des eaux et les manières de les jauger ou mesurer.* . . . Paris, 1689.

La Place, P. de. *Essai philosophique sur les probabilités.* Paris, 1814.

———. *Théorie de l'action capillaire.* Paris, 1806–1807.

———. *Traité de mécanique céleste.* 5 vols. Paris, 1799–1825.

Leupold, J. *Theatri machinarum hydraulicarum oder Schau-Platz der Wasser Künste.* 2 vols. Leipzig, 1724–25.

———. *Theatrum machinarum hydrotechnicarum: Schau-Platz der Wasser-Bau-Kunst, oder deutlicher Unterricht und Anweisung desjenigen, was bey dem Wasser-Bau.* . . . Leipzig, 1724.

Linguet, S. *Canaux navigables ou développement des avantages qui résulteraient de l'exécution de plusieurs projets en ce genre pour la Picardie, l'Artois, la Bourgogne, la Champagne, la Bretagne.* . . . Paris, 1769.

MacLaurin, C. *Traité des fluxions.* 2 vols. Paris, 1749.

Mariotte, E. *Traité du mouvement des eaux et des autres corps fluides divisé en V parties et mis en lumière par les soins de M. de la Hire.* Paris, 1686.

Moradec, F. de. "Recueil de secrets, remèdes, observations physiques, machines nouvelles, etc." Manuscript, Ecomusée du Creusot, ca. 1700.

Moret, M. *Mémoire couronné en 1786 par l'Académie Royale des Sciences et Belles—Lettres d'Angers sur* . . . *"Quels seraient les moyens les plus simples et les moins dispendieux d'empêcher les débordements de l'Authion en Anjou et la stagnation de ses eaux, même de rendre cette rivière navigable dans une partie de son cours."* Angers, 1786.

Morin, A. *Aide-mémoire de mécanique pratique.* 4th ed. Paris, 1847.

Newton, I. *Principes mathématiques de la philosophie naturelle.* 2 vols. Paris, 1759.

Parent, M. *Recherches de mathématiques et de physique.* 2 vols. Paris, 1705.

Pascal, B. *Traité de l'équilibre des liqueurs.* Paris, 1663 (2d ed., 1694).

Pitot, H. "Remarques sur les rapports des surfaces des grands et petits corps." *MARS*, 1728, pp. 369–83.

Poinsot, L. *La Théorie générale de l'équilibre et du mouvement des systèmes.* Ed. Bailhache. Paris, 1806 (reprint, Paris, 1975).

Poisson, S. *Mémoire sur l'équilibre des fluides.* Paris, 1828.

Poleni, G. *De castellis per quae derivantur fluviorum acquae habentibus latera convergentia liber quo etiam continentur nova experimenta ad aquas fluentes atque ad percussionis vires pertinentia.* Padua, 1718.

———. *De motu aquae mixto libri duo, quibus, multi nova pertinentia ad aestuaria, ad portus atque ad flumine continentur.* Padua, 1771.

Poncelet, J. *Introduction à la mécanique industrielle physique et expérimentale.* 1870. 3rd ed. Paris.

————. *Mémoire sur les roues hydrauliques à Aubes courbes mues par-dessous.* Paris, 1804.

Prony, R. de. *Recherches physico-mathématiques sur la théorie des eaux courantes.* Paris, 1804.

————, Lacroix, and Dupin. *Rapport fait à l'Académie des Sciences sur l'essai général de la navigation intérieure de la France par M. Brisson.* Paris, 1828.

————. *Recueil d'auteurs italiens qui traitent de la vitesse de l'eau.* 3 vols. Paris, 1722–23 (2d ed., 9 vols., Paris, 1784–86).

Renau, M. *Théorie de la manoeuvre des vaisseaux.* Paris, 1689.

Riquier, J. *Traité d'économie pratique ou moyens de diriger par économie différentes constructions réparations ou entretiens, suivi de quelques principes concernant la meilleure construction des machines hydrauliques.* Amiens, 1780.

Rohault, J. *Traité de physique.* 2 vols. Paris, 1671.

Silberschlag, J.-T. *Théorie des fleuves avec l'art de batir dans leurs eaux et de prévenir leurs ravages.* Paris, 1769.

Smeaton, J. *Recherches expérimentales sur l'eau et le vent considérés comme forces motrices applicables aux moulins et autres machines à mouvement circulaire. . . .* Paris, 1827.

Stevin, S. *Oeuvres mathématiques.* Trans. Albert Girard. 4 vols. Leiden, 1634.

Torricelli, E. *Traité du mouvement des eaux . . . tiré du mesme autheur, du mouvement des corps pesans qui descendent naturellement et qui sont jetter.* Ed. Saporta. In Castelli, *Traité de la mesure des eaux courantes.* Castres, 1664.

Tredgold, Th. *Tracts on hydraulics.* 2d ed. London, 1836.

Varignon, P. *Nouvelle mécanique ou statique dont le projet fut donné en 1687.* 2 vols. Paris, 1725.

Ximenes, L. *Nuove sperienze idrauliche, fatte né canali e né fiumi, per verificare le principali leggi e fenomeni delle acque correnti.* Siena, 1780.

D. Mephitis—Pollution

Amatus Lusitanus, J. *Curationum medicinalium centuriae duae, tertia et quarta.* Lyon, 1556.

Baumer, J. W. *Anthropologia anatomico-physica.* Frankfurt, 1784.

Baumes, J. *Mémoires sur les effets des émanations marécageuses sur l'économie vivante.* Nîmes, 1789.

Blondel, M. *Rapport sur les épidémies cholériques de 1832 et 1849 (de 1853 et de 1854) dans les établissements dépendants de l'Administration générale de l'assistance publique de la ville de Paris.* 2 vols. Paris, 1850–55.

Boerhaave, H. *Dissertatio de utilitate inspiciendorum excrementorum ut signorum.* Nijmegen, 1644.

————. *Elemens de chimie.* 3 vols. Paris, 1754.

Boishare, D. "Mémoire sur la topographie et les institutions médicales de la ville de Quilleboeuf et des lieux circonvoisins dont elle reçoit des influences." *PATASBLAR* (13), 1811, pp. 94–132.

Boubee, N. *La Géologie dans ses rapports avec la médecine et l'hygiène publique.* Paris, 1849.

Bouffey, M. *Recherches sur l'influence de l'air dans le développement, le caractère et le traitement des maladies.* Paris, 1813.

Bullet, P. *Observations sur la nature et les effets de la mauvaise odeur des lieux d'aisances et cloaques et sur l'importance dont il est d'éviter cette mauvaise odeur pour la conservation de la santé.* Paris, 1696.

Bucquet, J. *Mémoire sur la manière dont les animaux sont affectés par différents fluides, aériformes, méphitiques et sur les moyens de remédier aux effets de ces fluides.* Paris, 1778.

Carault, E. "Quelques vues générales sur le choléra-morbus." *BSLER,* 1833, pp. 172–231.

Cazeneuve, M. *Des fosses mobiles inodores, de leur nécessité et de leur avantage pour le gouvernement, les propriétaires, les locataires.* Paris, 1818.

Chaptal, J. *Mémoire sur les causes de l'insalubrité des lieux voisins de nos étangs.* Paris, 1808.

Chevreul, E. *Mémoires sur plusieurs réactions chimiques qui intéressent l'hygiène des cités populaires.* Paris, 1854.

Condorcet, M. de. "Table indicative des âges et des durées de vie des hommes et femmes de Picardie." *Gazette de Santé,* 1775, pp. 52–55.

Deparcieux, M. "Mémoire sur un moyen de se garantir de la puanteur des puisards, quand on est contraint d'en faire dans le voisinage des maisons." *MARS,* 1767, pp. 133–37.

Dubois, Huzard, and Hericard de Thury, *Rapport sur les fosses mobiles inodores de MM. Cazeneuve et Compagnie.* Paris, 1818.

Emmery, H. "Egouts et bornes fontaines. Entrées d'eau sous galerie—Relief favorable à la circulation. Lavage des ruisseaux en eaux vives." *APC* 10 (1834), pp. 241–86.

Fonseca, R. de. *De hominis excrementis libellus.* Pisa, 1613.

Fourcroy, M. de. *Rapport concernant les marres qui sont au bas de la ville de Château-Thierry.* Paris, 1788.

Franklin, B. *Correspondances.* 3 vols. Paris, 1817.

Geraud, M. *Essai sur la suppression des fosses d'aisances et de toutes espèces de voiries.* Amsterdam, 1786.

Girard, P., and Parent-Duchatelet. *Des puits forés ou artésiens employés à l'évacuation des eaux sales et infectes et à l'assainissement de quelques fabriques.* Paris, 1833.

Guyton de Morveau, L. *Traité des moyens de désinfecter l'air, de prévenir la contagion et d'en arrêter le progrès.* Paris, 1801.

Halle, M. *Recherches sur la nature et les effets du méphitisme des fosses d'aisances.* Paris, 1785.

Hecquet, R. *Traité de la peste où . . . on fait voir le danger des baraques et des infirmeries forcées.* Paris, 1722.

Heyne, J. *De febribus epidemicus romae falso in pestium censum relatis.* Amsterdam, 1710.

Homberg, L. "Observations sur les matières fécales." *MARS,* 1771, pp. 44–56.

———. "Phosphore nouveau ou suite d'observations sur les matières fécales." *MARS,* 1711, pp. 238–49.

Huguenin, S. *Mémoire sur les étangs*. Lyons, 1779.

Janin, J. *L'Antiméphitique ou moyens de détruire les eshalaisons pernicieuses et mortelles des fosses d'aisance, l'odeur infecte des égouts, celle des hôpitaux, des prisons, des vaisseaux de guerre*. . . . Paris, 1782.

Jannet, P.; Payen; and Veinant. *Bibliotheca scatologica ou catalogue raisonné des livres traitant des vertus, faits et gestes de très noble et très ingénieux Messire Luc (à Rebours), siegneur de la chasse, et autres lieux . . . traduit du prussien . . . par trois savants en us*. Scatopolis [Paris], 5850 [1849].

Jessaint, C. de. *Description topographique du départment de la Marne*. Paris, 1802.

Kircher, A. *Scrutinum physico-medicum contagiosae luis, quae pestis dicitur—Qua origo, causae, signa pregnatica pestis*. Rome, 1668.

Laborie the Younger, Cadet, and Parmentier. *Observations sur les fosses d'aisance et moyens de prévenir des inconvénients de leur vidange*. Paris, 1778.

Lancisi, G. *De noxiis paludum effluviis eorumque remedii libri duo*. Rome, 1717.

Le Cat, M. "An account of those malignant Fevers, that raged at Rouen at the End of the year 1753, and the Beginning of 1754." *PTRA*, 1755, pp. 24–30.

Lepecq de la Cloture, M. *Collections d'observations sur les maladies et constitutions épidémiques*. Rouen, 1778.

Marcorelle, E. de. *Avis pour neutraliser à peu de frais les fosses d'aisance afin d'en faire la vidange sans inconvénient et dans danger. Hints for neutralising necessary houses at a small expense in order to empty them without danger or inconvenience*. Narbonne, 1782.

Mauduyt, P. "Corruptions des caux infectées par les insectes." *Mémoire de la Société Royale de Médecine* I (1762): 24–42.

Morgagni, J. *De sedibus et causis morborum per anatomen indagatis libri V*. 2 vols. Venice, 1761.

Orlandi, M. *De exsiccandorum paludum utilitate deque infirmitatibus quae ab acquis stagnantibus orvundis*. Rome, 1783.

Paul, P. *Dissertatio de medicamentis ex corpore humano desumptis merito negligendis*. 2 vols. Leipzig, 1821.

Paullini, S. *Heilsame Dreck-Apotheke, wie nemlich mit Koth und Urin fast alle, auch, die schwersten Krumleiten curvit werden*. Franfurt-am-Main, 1696.

Platner, J. *Panegyrin medicam*. 2 vols. Leipzig, 1789–90.

Portal, M. *Rapport sur les effets des vapeurs méphitiques dans le corps de l'homme et principalement sur les vapeurs de charbon*. Paris, 1775.

Pringle, M. "An Account of Several Persons Seized with the Gaol-Fever, Working in Newgate." *PTRA*, 1753, pp. 21–27.

Ramazzini, B. *Essai sur les maladies des artisans*. . . . Trans. de Fourcroy. Paris, 1777.

Ruland, J. D. *Pharmacopoae nova de hominis stercore*. Nuremberg, 1664.

Sage, M. *Expériences propores à faire connaître que l'alkali volatil est le remède le plus efficace contre les asphyxies*. Paris, 1776 (2d ed., 1777; 3rd ed., 1778).

Tenon, J. *Mémoire sur les hôpitaux de Paris*. Paris, 1788.

Tessier, H. A. *Rapport fait à l'Institut de France sur les excréments humains*. Paris, 1797.

―――. *Rapport concernant les marres qui sont au bas de la ville de Château-Thierry, lu dans la séance tenue au Louvre par la Société Royale de Médecine le 30 août 1782*. Paris, 1782.

Thiroux d'Arconville, M. *Essai pour servir à l'histoire de la putréfaction*. Paris, 1766.

Thouvenel, P. *Mémoire chimique et médicinal sur la nature, les usages et les effets de l'air et des eaux des aliments et des médicaments relativement à l'économie animale*. Paris, 1780.

Van Helmont, J.-B. *Oeuvres . . . traitant des principes de médecine et physique pour la guérison assurée des maladies*. Lyons, 1670.

Vitalis, M. "Rapport sur les fosses mobiles inodores." *PATASBLAR* 21 (1819):86–89.

E. Manufacturing Procedures—Chemistry

Berthollet, C. *Eléments de l'art de la teinture*. 2 vols. Paris, 1791.

―――. *Essai de statique chimique*. 2 vols. Paris, 1803.

Boyle, R. *Works*. 3 vols. London, 1772.

Bucquet, J. *Introduction à l'étude des corps naturels tirés du règne minéral*. 2 vols. Paris, 1771.

―――. *Introduction à l'étude des corps naturels tirés du règne végétal*. 2 vols. Paris, 1773.

Chaptal, J. *Chimie appliquée aux arts*. 4 vols. Paris, 1807.

―――. *Principes chimiques sur l'art du teinturier-dégraisseur*. Paris, 1808.

Chevreul, E. "Note sur les urines de chameau et de cheval." *Annales de Chimie*, 1808, pp. 294–309.

―――. *Recherches chimiques sur la peinture*. Paris, 1863.

Desmarets, N. "Premier mémoire sur les principales manipulations qui sont en usage dans les papeteries de Hollande, avec l'explication physique des résultats de ces manipulations." *MARS*, 1771, pp. 335–64.

―――. "Second mémoire sur la papeterie, dans lequel, en continuant d'exposer la méthode hollandaise, l'on traite de la nature et des qualités des pâtes hollandaises et françaises; de la manière dont elles se comportent dans les procédés de la fabrication et des apprêts; enfin des différents usages auxquels peuvent être propres les produits de ces pâtes." *MARS*, 1774, pp. 599–687.

Dubuc, G. "Mémoire sur la culture ou fabrication indigène de salpêtre (nitrate de potasse)." *PATASBLAR* 28 (1826):151–75.

―――. *Traité sur les parements et encollages, dont l'emploi permet aux tisserands de travailler ailleurs que dans les caves et autres bas-fonds non éclairés et généralement mal-sains*. Rouen, 1829.

Dufay. "Observations physiques sur le mélange de quelques couleurs dans la teinture." *MARS*, 1737, pp. 253–69.

Duhamel du Monceau, H. *L'Art du chandelier*. Paris, 1764.

―――. *L'Art de la draperie, principalement pour ce qui regarde les draps fins*. Paris, 1765.

————. *L'Art de faire différentes sortes de colles.* Paris, 1771.

————. *L'Art du savonnier.* Paris, 1774.

————. *La Physique des arbres où est traité de l'anatomie des plantes et de l'économie végétale.* 2 vols. Paris, 1758.

————. *L'Art de l'amidonnier.* Paris, 1775.

Dupont de Nemours, P. *Rapport sur le droit de marque des cuirs.* Paris, an XII.

Eller, M. "Sur la nature et les propriétés de l'eau commune considérée comme un dissolvant." *MARS,* 1750, pp. 67–92.

————. *Encyclopédie méthodique.* 5 vols. Paris, 1785–1808.

Garsault, A. de. *Art du cartonnier.* Paris, 1767.

Guyton de Morveau, L., and Chaptal. "Rapport demandé à la classe de Sciences Physiques et Mathématiques de l'Institut sur la question de savoir si les manufactures qui exhalent une odeur désagréable peuvent être nuisibles à la santé." *Annales de Chimie,* an XII, pp. 86–103.

————. *Instruction sur l'établissement des nitrières et sur la fabriction du salpêtre.* Paris, 1777.

Jaubert, A. *Dictionnaire raisonné universel des arts et métiers, contenant l'histoire, la description, la police des fabriques et manufactures de France et des pays étrangers.* 2d ed. 4 vols. Paris, 1773.

La Platiere, R. de. *L'Art du fabricant d'étoffes en laines rases et sèches, unies et croisées.* Paris, 1780.

Lavoisier, A. de. *Oeuvres.* 6 vols. 1854–68.

Macquart, L. "Sur la nature du suc gastrique des animaux ruminants." *OSP,* 1788, pp. 380–404.

Macquer, P. *Dictionnaire de chimie.* 2 vols. Paris, 1766 (2d ed., 5 vols., 1773; 3d ed. 4 vols., 1779–80).

Milly, de. "Essai sur une nouvelle manière d'analyser les substances du règne animal ou végétal; et sur les moyens de diriger le feu avec précision dans les opérations délicates de la chimie." *MARS,* 1781, pp. 34–44.

Morin, M. "De la bouse de vache considérée sous le rapport de la chimie technologique." *PATASBLAR* 32 (1830): 85–94.

Pouchet, P. *Traité sur la fabrication des étoffes.* Rouen, 1788.

Reaumur, R. *Mémoires pour servir l'histoire des insectes.* 6 vols. Paris, 1734–42.

Rozier, F. "Sur la culture et le rouissage du chanvre." *OSP,* 1788, pp. 367–79.

Scheele, C. *Supplément au traité chimique de l'air et du feu.* Paris, 1785.

Thouvenel, P. *Extrait du mémoire sur la fabrication du salpêtre.* Paris, 1782.

Vauquelin, L. "Expériences sur le suint." *Annales de Chimie,* an XI, pp. 262–84.

Vitalis, M. *Cours élémentaires de teinture sur la laine, soie, coton, lin et chanvre.* Paris, 1823.

F. Natural History of Water

Baroche, P. "Le Défrichement des bois sur le sommet et la pente des montagnes." *BSLER,* 1837, pp. 94–97.

Bibliography

Bertrand, E. *Mémoires sur la structure intérieure de la terre*. Geneva, 1752.

Brisseau-Mirbel, C. *Elémens de physiologie végétale et de botanique*. 3 vols. Paris, 1815.

Cadet de Vaux, A. *Réflexions sur la diminution progressive des eaux*. Paris, 1798.

Cuvier, G., and Brongniart, A. *Essai sur la géographie minéralogique des environs de Paris*. Paris, 1811.

Dubois de Morambert, P. "Proposition sur le boisement des terres incultes." *MSASADA* 1 (1822): 52–67.

Fabricus, J. *Théologie de l'eau ou essai sur la bonté, la sagesse et la puissance de Dieu manifestées dans la création de l'eau*. The Hague, 1741.

Fludd, R. *Philosophia moysaica, in qua sapientia et scientia creationis et creaturarum sacra vereque christiana*. Gouda, 1638.

François, J. *L'Art des fontaines, c'est-à-dire pour trouver, esprouver, assembler, mesurer, distribuer et conduire les sources dans des lieux publics et particuliers d'en rendre la conduite perpétuelle; et de donner par Art des eaux courantes aux lieux où elles manquent par la nature avec l'art de niveler*. 2d ed. Rennes, 1665.

———. *La Science des eaux qui explique leur formation, communication, mouvements et meslanges, avec les arts de conduire les eaux et mesurer la grandeur tant des eaux que des terres. L'arithmétique ou l'art de compter toute sorte de nombre*. Rennes, 1653.

Gaffarel, J. *Le Monde souterrain ou description historique et philosophique de tous les plus beaux antres*. Paris, 1654.

Garnier, F. *De l'art de fontainier-sondeur et des puits artésiens*. Paris, 1822.

———. *Traité des puits artésiens ou sur les différentes espèces de terrains dans lesquels on doit chercher les eaux souterraines*. Paris, 1826.

Guettard, J. *Observations sur les plantes*. 2 vols. Paris, 1747–48.

Hales, M. *Vegetable Statiks*. 2 vols. London, 1727.

Halley, E. "An Account of the Circulation of the Watry Vapours of the Sea, and of the Cause of Springs." *PTRA* 17 (1693): 468–73.

Hassenfratz, J. "Programme du cours des mines fait à l'école polytechnique (l'année scolaire 1806)," *Journal de l'Ecole Polytechnique* 13 (1806): 345–71.

Hautefeuille, J. de. *Réflexions sur quelques machines à élever les eaux avec des descriptions d'une nouvelle pompe sans frottement et le moyen de faire des jets d'eau sans avoir besoin de réservoirs élevés*. Paris, 1682.

Hericard de Thury, L. *Considération géologique et physique sur la cause du jaillissement des eaux de puits forés ou fontaines artificielles et recherches sur l'origine ou l'invention de la sonde*. Paris, 1829.

———. *Du dessèchement des terres cultivables sujettes à être inondées*. Paris, 1831.

———. *Rapport sur l'aménagement des eaux en agriculture et le traité pratique des irrigations, du limonage et de l'établissement des étangs et réservoirs de M. Polonceau*. Paris, 1847.

———. *Rapport sur les plantations et reboisements*. Paris, 1848.

Kircher, A. *Magnes, sive de arte magnetica opus tripartitum*. Rome, 1641.

La Framboisière, N. de. *Oeuvres*. Paris, 1613.

Lamouroux, J. *Résumé d'un cours élémentaire de géographie physique*. Paris, 1829.

Bibliography

Lydyat, T. *Praelectio astronomica de natura coeli et conditionibus elementorum tum autem de causis praecipuorum motuum coeli et stellarum, item disquisitio physiologica de origine fontium . . . frigidorum et calidorum. . . .* London, 1605.

Mariotte, E. "Observations sur la quantité d'eau de pluie tombée à Paris durant prés de trois mois et la quantité d'évaporation." *MARS* 10 (1696):27–38.

Meyer, J. *Etude sur les villes en Europe occidentale du milieu du XVIIe siecle à la veille de la Revolution française,* vol. 1. Paris, 1983.

Milliet-Dechales, C. *Les Principes généraux de la géographie.* Paris, 1677.

Palissy, B. *Discours admirables de la nature des eaux et des fontaines tant naturelles qu'artificielles des métaux des sels et salines, des pierres, des terres, du feu et des émaux.* Paris, 1580. In *Oeuvres complètes,* pp. 239–303. Paris, 1777.

Paramelle, J. *L'Art de découvrir les sources.* Paris, 1856.

Passy, A. *Description géologique du département de la Seine-Inférieure.* 2 vols. Rouen, 1832.

Payen, J. *Capital et machine à vapeur au XVIIIe siècle: Les Frères Périer et l'introduction de la machine à vapeur de Watt.* Paris, 1969.

Perrault, P. *Origine des fontaines.* Paris, 1674.

Plot, R. *De origine fontium, tentamen philosophicum Oxonii.* 1695.

Pluche, A. *Le Spectacle de la nature ou entretiens sur les particularités de l'histoire naturelle qui ont paru les plus propres à rendres les jeunes gens curieux et à leur former l'esprit.* 9 vols. Paris, 1730–37.

Pryce, W. *Mineralogia Cornubiensis, a Treatise on Minerals, Mines and Mining . . . to Which Is Added an Explanation of the Terms and idioms of Miners.* London, 1778.

Recherches sur les effectifs des armées françaises des guerres d'Italie aux guerres de Religion. Paris, 1962.

Rougier de la Bergerie, J. *Mémoire au roi et aux chambres législatives sur la destruction des bois et sur les graves conséquences qui peuvent en résulter.* Paris, 1831.

———. *Les Forêts de la France, leurs rapports avec les climats, la température et l'ordre des saisons, avec la prospérité de l'agriculture et de l'industrie.* Paris, 1817.

———. *Manuel des étangs ou traité de l'art d'en construire avec économie et solidité.* Paris, 1819.

Savery, M. *Miner's Friend.* London, 1699.

Schott, C. *Anatomia physico-hydrostatica fontium ac fluminum libris VI explicata . . . ,* 2 vols. Würzburg, 1659.

Tristan, J. M. de. *Recherches sur quelques effluves terrestres.* Paris, 1826.

Volney, C. *La Loi naturelle: Leçons d'histoire.* Ed. Gaulmier. Paris, 1980.

Woodward, J. *Géographie physique ou essai sur l'histoire naturelle de la terre.* Paris, 1735.

Other Works

Abbri, F. *La chimica del'700.* Turin, 1978.

Abrahams, J. *Jewish Life in the Middle-Ages.* London, 1896.

Bibliography

Abrard, R. *Géologie régionale du bassin de Paris*. Paris, 1950.

Actes de la conférence intergouvernementale d'experts sur les bases scientifiques de l'utilisation rationnelle et de la conservation des ressources de la biosphère, Paris, 4–13 September 1968. UNESCO, 1970.

Agus, I. *Urban Civilisation in Pre-Crusade Europe: A Study of Organized Town-Life in North-Western Europe during the Tenth and Eleventh Centuries Based on the Responsa Literature*. 2 vols. New York, 1925.

Alliaume, J. *Politique de l'habitat (1800–1850)*. Paris, 1977.

Andre, J. "Sources et évolution du vocabulaire des couleurs en latin." In *Problèmes sur la couleur, colloque du Centre de Recherche de Psychologie Comparative*, pp. 327–32. Paris, 1957.

Arbois de Jubaiville, H. d'. *Histoire des ducs et des comtes de Champagne*. 2 vols. Paris, 1861.

———. *Recherches sur l'origine des propriétés foncières et des noms de lieux habités en France*. Paris, 1890.

Adarscheff, P. *Les intendants de province sous Louis XVI*. Paris, 1909.

Aries, Ph. *Essais sur l'histoire de la mort en Occident du Moyen-Age à nos jours*. Paris, 1975.

Aronius, B. *Regesten zur Geschichte der Juden in fränkischen und deutschen Reich bis zum Jahre 1273*. Berlin, 1902.

Augoyat, M. *Aperçu historique sur les fortifications, les ingénieurs et le corps du génie*. 3 vols. Paris, 1858–64.

Aussenac, G. "Influence du couvert forestier sur les précipitations." *Revue forestière* 7 (1969): 631–35.

Babeau, A. *La Ville sous l'ancien régime*. 2 vols. Paris, 1884.

Bautier, A.-M. "Les plus anciennes mentions de moulins hydrauliques industriels et de moulins à vent." *BPHCTHS*, 1960, 2, pp. 567–626.

Bautier, R.-H. "Les Foires de Champagne—Recherches sur une évolution historique." In *Recueil de la société Jean Bodin, V—La foire*, pp. 97–147. Brussels, 1953.

Beer, J. "The Historical Relations of Science and Technology." *TC*, 1965, pp. 547–52.

Benveniste, E. *Le Vocabulaire des institutions indo-européennes*. 2 vols. Paris, 1969.

Berthelot, M. "Pour l'histoire des arts mécaniques et de l'artillerie vers la fin du Moyen-Age." *Annales de chimie et de physique*, 1891, pp. 472–98.

Bibliographie d'histoire des villes de France. Paris, 1967.

Biraben, J. *Les Hommes et la peste en France et dans les pays européens et méditerranéens*. 2 vols. Paris, The Hague, 1975–76.

Blanchet, A. *Traité des monnaies gauloises*. Bologne, 1971.

Bloch, M. *La Société féodale*. 6th ed. Paris, 1968.

———. "Avènement et conquêtes du moulin à eau." *AESC*, 1935, pp. 538–63.

Blosseville, A. de. *Dictionnaire topographique du département de l'Eure*. Paris, 1877.

Blumenkranz, B. *Juifs et chrétiens dans le monde occidental, 430–1096*. Paris, 1960.

Bonhomme, C. "La formation du département de la Somme en 1790 et l'éstabissement des subdivisions depuis cette date jusqu'à nos jours." *BSAP* 33 (1929–30):380–497.

Bonnaud-Delamare, J. "Les institutions de paix en Auitaine au XIᵉ siècle." *Recueil de la société Jean-Bodin, I—La paix.* Brussels, 1962.

Bois, G. *Crise du féodalisme.* Paris, 1976.

Bouard, M. de. *Manuel d'archéologie médiévale: De la fouille à l'histoire.* Paris, 1975.

Boudon, F. "Tissu urbain et architecture: L'Analyse parcellaire comme base de l'histoire architecturale." *AESC*, 1975, pp. 773–818.

Bourgeois, G. *Hugues l'abbé, margrave de Neustrie et archichapelain de France à la fin du IXᵉ siècle.* Caen, 1885.

Boussard, J. *Le gouvernement d'Henri II Plantagenêt.* Paris, 1956.

Boutiot, Th., and Socard, E. *Dictionnaire topographique du département de l'Aube.* Paris, 1894.

Breguet, M. "Urbi et orbi—un cliché et un thème." In *Mélanges L. Renard, Latomus*, I, pp. 140–52. 1968.

Bruhl, C.-R. *Palatium und Civitas, I—Gallian.* Cologne, Böhlau. 1975.

Buissaret, J. "The Communications of France during the Reconstruction of Henri IV." *EHR*, 1965, pp. 267–77.

Cabrol, F., and LeClerc, H. *Dictionnaire d'archéologie chrétienne et de liturgie.* 12 vols. Paris, 1953.

Cardwell, D. "Power Technologies and the Advancement of Science, 1700–1825." *TC*, 1965, pp. 192–208.

Carpentier, E. "Autour de la peste noire: Famines et épidémies dans l'histoire du XIVᵉ siècle." *AESC*, pp. 1062–92.

Carolus-Barre, L. *La Formation de la ville de Compiègne.* Compiègne, 1952.

Carus-Wilson, E. "An Industrial Revolution of the Thirteenth Century." *EHR*, 1941, pp. 38–60.

———. "Technical Innovations and the Emergences of the Grande Industrie of Northern Europe." In *Produttività e Technologie nei secoli XII–XVII*, Colloque, Prato, pp. 359–60. Florence, 1981.

Champion, M. *Les inondations en France.* 6 vols. Paris, 1858–64.

Chaumartin, H. *Le Mal des Ardents et le feu Saint-Antoine.* Lausanne, 1946.

Chaume, M. *Les origines du duché de Bourgogne.* 3 vols. Dijon, 1937.

Chazan, M. "1007–1012: Initial Crisis for Northern European Jewry." *Proceedings of the American Academy for Jewish Research* 38–39 (1970–71): 125–54.

Cheret, I. *L'eau.* Paris, 1969.

Chevallier, R. *Les Voies romaines.* 1974.

———. "Cité et territoire: Solutions romaines aux problèmes de l'organisation de l'espace." In *Mélanges Vogt*, II, pp. 745–62. Berlin, 1974.

Cipolla, C. *Before the Industrial Revolution: European Society and Economy, 1000–1700.* New York, 1976.

Claude, D. *Topographie und Verfassung der Städte Bourges und Poitiers bis in das IX. Jahrhundert.* Lübeck, Hamburg, 1960.

Claudin, J. *Histoire de l'imprimerie en France aux XVᵉ et XVIᵉ siècles.* 2 vols. Paris, 1900–1904.

Colas, R. *La pollution des eaux.* 2d ed. Paris, 1968.

Coornaert, E. *Un Centre industriel d'autrefois: La Fraperie sayetterie d'Hondschoote XIV–XVIIIᵉ siècles.* Paris, 1930.

———. *Les Corporations en France avant 1789.* 2d ed. Paris, 1968.

Corbin, A. *Le Miasme et la jonquille.* Paris, 1982.

Crombie, A.-C. *Histoire des sciences de saint Augustin à Galilée (400–1650).* 2 vols. Paris, 1959–60.

Curie-Seimbres, H. *Essais sur les villes fondées dans le sud-ouest de la France aux XIIIᵉ siècles sous le nom générique de bastides.* Toulouse, 1880.

Czarnowski, P. "L'arbre d'Esus, le taureau aux trois grues et le culte des voies fluviales en Gaule." *RA* 42 (1925): 1–57.

Daumas M. *Histoire générale des techniques.* 3 vols. Paris, 1962–68.

Dauzat, M. *Glossaire étymologique des noms de rivières et des noms de montagnes en France.* Paris, 1956.

Delisle, L. *Recueil des actes de Henri II, roi d'Angleterre et duc de Normandie.* Paris, 1909.

Delumeau, J. *L'Alun de Rome—XVᵉ–XIXᵉ siècles.* Paris, 1978.

Demangeon, A. *La Picardie et les régions voisines: Artois, Cambresis, Beauvaisis.* Paris, 1905.

Denifle, L. *La Désolation des églises, monastères et hôpitaux en France vers le milieu de XVᵉ siècle.* 2 vols. Paris, 1897–99.

De Solla-Price, D. "Is Technology Historically Independent of Science? A Study in Statistical Historiography." *TC*, 1965, pp. 553–63.

Dhondt, J. "Développement urbain et initiative comtale en Flandre au XIᵉ siècle." *RDN* 30 (1941): 133–56.

———, and Rouche, M. *Le Haut Moyen-Age (VIIIᵉ–XIᵉ siècle).* Paris, 1976.

Diepgen, L. "Die Bedeutung des Mittelalters für den Fortshrift in der Medizin." In *Mélanges K. Sudhoff,* pp. 99–120. Zurich, 1924.

Dion, R. *Histoire des levées de la Loire.* Paris, 1961.

Dodds, E.-R. *Pagan and Christian in an Age of Anxiety: Some Aspects of Religious Experience from Marcus Aurelius to Constantine.* Cambridge, 1965.

Dontenville, H. *Histoire et géographie mythique de la France.* Paris, 1973.

Donzelot, J. *La Police des familles.* Paris, 1976.

Dottin, J. *La Langue gauloise.* Paris, 1952.

Duby, J. *Hommes et structures du Moyen-Age.* Paris, The Hague, 1973.

———. *Guerriers et paysans, premier essor de l'économie européenne.* Paris, 1975.

Duchesne, L. *Fastes épiscopaux de l'ancienne Gaule.* 2d ed. 2 vols. Paris, 1900–1907.

Dugas, R. *Histoire de la mécanique.* Paris, 1954.

Dumezil, G. *L'Idéologie tripartite des Indo-européens.* Brussels, 1958.

———. *Idées romaines.* Paris, 1969.

———. *Mythes et épopées.* 3 vols. Paris, 1968–73.

————. *La religion romaine archaïque*. Paris, 1974.

————. *Mariages indo-européens suivi de quinze questions romaines*. Paris, 1979.

Dupuy, G. *Urbanisme et technique: Chronique d'un mariage de raison*. Paris, 1979.

Duval, P. *Paris antique des origines au IIIᵉ siècle*. Paris, 1963.

Duvigneaud, P. *Ecosystème et biosphère*. 2d ed. Brussels, ca. 1965.

Elhai, H. *Biogéographie*. Paris, 1968.

Eliade, M. *Traité d'histoire des religions*. 2d ed. Paris, 1964.

————. *Histoire des croyances et des idées religieuses*. 2 vols. Paris, 1976–78.

Emery, R. *The Friars in Medieval France: A Catalogue of French Medicant Convents, 1200–1550*. New York, London, 1962.

Encyclopédia judaïca. 8 vols. Jerusalem, 1971.

Enlard, C. *Manuel d'archéologie française*. 4 vols. Paris, 1930–34.

Ennen, F. *Frühgeschichte der europäischen Stadt*. Bonn, 1953.

Ernoux, A., and Meillet, A. *Dictionnaire étymologique de la langue latine: Histoire des mots*. Paris, 1967.

Etude d'écologie humaine: Aspects sociaux de la pollution des eaux douces. Colloque, Brussels, Université libre, 1968.

Espinas, G. *La draperie dans la Flandre française au Moyen-Age*. 2 vols. Paris, 1923.

————, and Pirenne, H. *Recueil des documents relatifs à l'histoire de l'industrie drapière en Flandre*. 2 vols. Brussels, 1906.

Fagniez, G. *Etudes sur l'industrie et la classe industrielle à Paris aux XIIIᵉ et XIVᵉ siècles*. Paris, 1877.

Favre, E. *Eudes, comte de Paris et roi de France (887–898)*. Paris, 1893.

Ferri, M. *Vitruvio—Recensione del testo: Traduzione e note*. 2 vols. Rome, 1960.

Flach, J. *Les Origines de l'ancienne France*. 3 vols. Paris, 1894–1904.

Fossier, R. *La Terre et les hommes en Picardie jusqu'à la fin du XIIIᵉ siècle*. 2 vols. Paris, Louvain, 1968.

Foucault, M. *Histoire de la folie à l'âge classique*. Paris, 1968.

————. *Surveiller et punir*. Paris, 1975.

Fournier, G. *Le Peuplement rural en Basse-Auvergne durant le haut Moyen-Age*. 2 vols. Paris, 1962.

————. *Le Château dans la France médiévale*. Paris, 1978.

Fourquin, G. *Histoire économique de l'occident médiéval*. Paris, 1969.

Fox, R., and Weisz, G. *The Organization of Science in Nineteenth Century France*. Paris, London, 1980.

Frezouls, G. "Etudes et recherches sur les villes en Gaule.: In *Atti de Colloquis sull tema la Gallia romana, Rome 10–11 mai 1971*, pp. 153–66. Rome, 1973.

Gaignebet, R. *Le Carnaval*. Paris, 1979.

Gandilhon, M. *La Politique économique de Louis XI*. Rennes, 1940.

Ganshof, L. *Etude sur le développement des villes entre Loire et Rhin au Moyen-Age*. Paris, Brussels, 1943.

Ganshoffer, R. *L'Evolution des institutions municipales en occident et en orient au Bas-Empire*. Paris, 1963.

Garnier, J. *Dictionnaire topographique du départment de la Somme.* 2 vols. Paris, 1867–68.

Gerlac, H. *Antoine Laurent Lavoisier: Chemist and Revolutionary.* New York, 1975.

———. "Some French Antecedents of the Chemical Revolution." *Chymia,* 1959, 5, pp. 73–112.

Gibbs, M. "History of the Manufacture of Soap." *Annals of Science* 4 (1939): 169–90.

Gille, B. *Histoire des techniques.* Paris, 1978.

Giry, A. *Documents sur la relation de la royauté avec les villes de France de 1180 à 1314.* Paris, 1885.

———. *Manuel de diplomatique.* Paris, 1894.

Gleisberg, M. "Geschichte der Technologie der alten Wassermühlen." *Sächsische Heimatblätter* 18 (1962): 44–78.

Godefroy, F. *Dictionnaire de l'ancienne langue française et de ses dialectes du IXe au XVe siècle.* 10 vols. Paris, 1938.

Goffart, W. *Caput and Colonate: Towards a History of Late Roman Taxation.* Toronto, 1974.

Goubert, P. *L'ancien Régime.* 2 vols. Paris, 1969.

Grangez, P. *Précis historique et statistique des voies navigables de la France et d'une partie de la Belgique.* Paris, 1855.

Grenier, A. *Manuel d'archéologie gallo-romaine.* 4 vols. Paris, 1931–36.

Gross, H. *Gallia judaïca: Dictionnaire géographique de la France d'après les sources rabbiniques.* Paris, 1897.

Guerin, I. *La Vie rurale en Sologne aux XIV et IVe siècles.* Paris, 1960.

Guilhermoz, P. "Ordonnance inédite de Philippe le Bel sur la police de la pêche fluviale (17 mai 1293)." *BEC* 63 (1902): 331–37.

Guillerme, A. "The Influence of Deforestation on Groundwater Tables in Temperate Zones: An Historical Perspective." *Hydrological Sciences Bulletin,* 1980, pp. 75–79.

———. "Contribution de la topométrie à la classification des villes romaines." In *Présence de l'architecture et de l'urbanisme romains, Colloque,* Académie d'Architecture, Paris, 12–13 December 1981.

Guyonvarc'h, P. "Mediolanum Biturigum, deux éléments de vocabulaire religieux et de géographie sacrée." *Ogam* 13 (1961): 137–58.

———. "Etudes sur le vocabulaire gaulois, I—Le théonyme gaulois Belisama, 'La très brillante.'" *Ogam* 14 (1962): 161–73.

Habert, J. *La Poterie antique parlante.* Paris, 1893.

Haenes, A. d'. *Les Invasions normandes: Une catastrophe?* Paris, 1970.

Hahn, R. "L'Enseignement scientifique aux écoles militaires et d'artillerie." In *Enseignement et diffusion des sciences en France au XVIIIe siècle,* pp. 513–58. Paris, 1964.

Hall, A.-R. *The Scientific Revolution, 1500–1800: The Formation of the Modern Scientific Attitude.* 2d ed. London, 1962.

Halphen, L. *Paris sous les premiers capétien (987–1123): Etude de topographie historique.* Paris, 1909.

Bibliography

————. *Charlemagne et l'empire carolingien*. Paris, 1947.

Hatt, J.-J. "La résistance gauloise sous Auguste." *Celticum* 1 (1960): 47–68.

Hautecoeur, L. *Histoire de l'architecture classique en France*. 4 vols. Paris, 1963–67.

Hazard, P. *La Pensée européenne au XVIIIe siècle*. Paris, 1963.

Heers, J. *Le Clan familial au Moyen-Age*. Paris, 1974.

Heilbron, J. *Electricity in the Seventeenth and Eighteenth Centuries: A Study of Early Modern Physics*. Berkeley, Los Angeles, London, 1979.

Heyne, M. *Körperpflege und Kleidung bei den Deutschen*. Stuttgart, 1903.

Hippeau, C. *Dictionnaire topographique du département du Calvados*. Paris, 1883.

Histoire de la France rurale. 4 vols. Paris, 1976.

Histoire de la France urbaine. 5 vols. Paris, 1980.

Holder, A. *Alt-celtische Sprachschatz*. 3 vols. Leipzig, 1893–1903.

Hubert, J. "La Renaissance carolingienne et la topographie religieuse des cités épiscopales." *Spolète* 1 (1952): 219–25.

————. "L'Abbaye de Déols et les constructions monastiques de la fin de l'époque carolingienne." *CAF* 9 (1957): 112–24.

————. "L'Evolution de la topographie des villes de Gaule du Ve au Xe siècle." In *Settimane sull alto Medioevo*, VI, pp. 529–602. Spoleto, 1958.

————. "Les Cathédrales doubles de la Gaule." *Genava* 11 (1963): 105–225.

Huizinga, J. *Le Déclin du Moyen-Age*. Paris, 1962.

Jewish Encyclopedia. 6 vols. New York, London, 1902.

Jones, A. "The Cloth Industry under the Roman Empire." *EHR* 13, no. 1 (1960): 183–206.

Jourdan, A. "La Ville étudiée dans ses quartiers: Autour des halles de Paris au Moyen-Age." *AESC*, 1965, pp. 285–301.

Jullian, C. *Histoire de la Gaule*. 8 vols. Paris, 1908–1926.

Knowles, D. *The Monastic Constitution of Lanfranc*. London, 1951.

Krahe, H. "Alteuropäische Flussnamen." *Beiträge zur Namenforschung*, 1949–52.

Laet, P. "Claude et la romanisation de la Gaule septentrionale." In *Mélanges A. Piganiol*, pp. 951–61. Paris, 1964.

Lakatos, I., and Musgrave, A. *Criticism and the Growth of Knowledge*. Cambridge, 1970.

Landsberg, H.-E. *The Climate of Towns: Man's Role in Changing the Face of the Earth*. Chicago, 1956.

Lauer, Ph. "De la signification du mot France aux époques mérovingienne et carolingienne." *MSHPIF* 42 (1915): 1–20.

Lebel, P. *Principes et méthodes d'hydronymie française*. Paris, 1976.

Lecoy de La Marche, M. "Des bains au Moyen-Age: Réponse à M. Michelet." *Revue du monde catholique* 14 (1866): 870–81.

Le Goff, J. "Au Moyen-Age: Temps de l'église et temps du marchand." *AESC*, 1960, pp. 417–33.

————. "Ordres mendiants et urbanisation dans la France médiévale." *AESC*, 1970, pp. 924–46.

———. "Guerriers et bourgeois conquérants: L'Image de la ville dans la littérature française du XIIe siècle." In *Mélanges Morazé*, pp. 113–36. Toulouse, 1979.

———. *La Civilisation de l'occident médieval.* Paris, 1966.

———. *La Naissance du Purgatoire.* Paris, 1981.

Le Grand, R. *Les Ateliers révolutionnaires de salpêtre en Picardie, 1793–an IX.* Amiens, 1949.

Lehoux, F. *Le cadre de vie des médecins parisiens aux XVIe siècle.* Paris, 1976.

Leighton, A. *Transport and Communication in Early Medieval Europe,* A.D. 500–1100. London, 1971.

Lemoine, P. *Géologie du bassin de Paris.* 1911.

Le Roux, F. "Le Dieu celtique aux lions—de l'Ogmios de Lucain à l'Ogmios de Dürer." *Ogam* 12 (1960): 112–34.

———. "Note d'histoire des religions, 8: Introduction à une étude de l'Apollon gaulois." *Ogam* 11 (1959): 216–26.

———. "Note d'histoire des religions, 1: La Blancheur royale, la main d'argent du Roi Nuada et le celtibère Argantonois." *Celticum* 9 (1964): 329–34.

———. "Le Celticum d'Ambigatus et l'omphallos gaulois: La Royauté suprême des Bituriges." *Ogam* 13 (1961): 159–84.

———. *Les Druides.* Paris, 1961.

Le Roy Ladurie, E. *Time of Feast, Time of Famine: A History of Climate since the year 1000.* New York, London, 1972.

———. *Le Territoire de l'historien.* Paris, 1973.

Lesne, E. *Histoire de la propriété ecclésiastique.* 4 vols. Lille, 1936–43.

Lestoquoy, J. "Abbayes et origines des villes." *RHEF* 33 (1947): 108–12.

———. "Le paysage urbain en Gaule du Ve au IXe siècle." *AESC,* 1953, pp. 159–72.

———. "Les origines des églises collégiales." In *Mélanges Labande,* pp. 497, 500. Paris, 1974.

Lombard, M. *Espaces et réseaux au haut Moyen-Age.* Paris, The Hague, 1970.

Lombard-Jourdan, A. "Oppidum et banlieue: Sur l'origine et les dimensions du territoire urbain." *AESC,* 1972, pp. 373–95.

Longnon, A. *Atlas historique de la France.* 2 vols. Paris, 1882–84.

———. *Documents relatifs au comté de Champagne et de Brie (1172–1361).* 3 vols. Paris, 1901–14.

———. *Les Noms de lieux de France.* 9 vols. Paris, 1920–29.

Lot, F. *Les Derniers carolingiens.* Paris, 1891.

———. "La Loire, l'Aquitaine et la Seine de 862 à 866: Robert le Fort." *BEC* 76 (1915): 112–26.

———. "Mélanges carolingiens, II: Le pont de Pîtres." *MA,* 1905, pp. 1–27.

McCann, H. *Chemistry Transformed: The Paradigm Shift from Phlogiston to Oxygen.* Norwood, Pa., 1978.

MacDonald, M. *Lanfranc: A Study of His Life, Work and Writing.* London, 1944.

Mathias, P. "Who Unbound Prometheus? Science and Technical Change, 1600–1800." In *Science and Society, 1600–1900*, pp. 54–80. Cambridge, 1972.

Male, E. *La Fin du paganisme*. Paris, 1950.

Matton, A. *Dictionnaire topographique du dèpartement de l'Aisne*. Paris, 1871.

Merlet, L. *Dictionnaire topographique du département de l'Eure et Loir*. Paris, 1861.

Mollat, M. "La draperie normande." In *Produzione, commercio e consumo dei panni di lana (nei secoli XII–XVIII)*, Colloque, Prato, pp. 403–22. Florence, 1976.

Mols, R. *Introduction à la démographie historique des villes d'Europe du XIVᵉ siècle au XVIIIᵉ siècle*. 3 vols. Louvain, 1954–56.

Momigliano, M. *The Conflict between Paganism and Christianity in the Fourth Century*. Oxford, 1963.

Morlet, M.-Th. *Les noms de personnes sur le territoire de l'ancienne Gaule, du VIᵉ au XIIᵉ siècle*. Paris, 1968.

Multhauf, R. P. "Sal Amoniacal: A Case History in Industrialization." *TC*, 1965, pp. 569–86.

Nahon, G. "Contribution à l'histoire des Juifs en France au XIIIᵉ siècle." *AESC*, 1969, pp. 1121–48.

———. "Les Communautés juives de la Champagne médiévale (XIᵉ–XIIᵉ siècle)." In *RACHI*, pp. 33–78. Paris, 1974.

Newman, P. *Catalogue des actes de Robert II, Roi de France*. Paris, 1937.

Parent, M., and Verroust, J. *Vauban*. Paris, 1971.

Partington, J.-R. *A History of Chemistry*. 2 vols. London, 1961.

Paschould, F. *Roma aeterna: Etude sur le patriotisme romain dans l'occident latin à l'époque des grandes invasions*. Rome, 1967.

Payan, R. *L'Évolution d'un monopole: L'Industrie des poudres avant la loi du 13 fructidor an V*. Paris, 1934.

Pedelabore, P. *Le Climat du bassin parisien*. Paris, 1957.

Penman, H. *Vegetation and Hydrology*. London, 1963.

Perroy, E. *Le Monde carolingien*. Paris, 1974.

———. *Le Travail dans la région du Nord du XIᵉ au début du XIVᵉ siècle*. Paris, 1962.

Petit-Dutaillis, Ch. *Les Communes françaises*. Paris, 1946.

Petrikovits, P. von. "Fortifications in the Northwestern Roman Empire from the Third to the Fifth Centuries A.D." *JRS* 61 (1971): 178–88.

Pfister, Ch. *Etude sur le règne de Robert le Pieux*. Paris, 1885.

Picard, Ch. "Le culte de Jupiter-Taranis dans le bassin de la Loire." *Caesarodunum* 10 (1975): 124–36.

Piquemal, M. "Le choléra de 1832 en France et la pensée médicale." *Thalès*, 1959, pp. 27–73.

Poerck, G. de. *La Draperie médiévale en Flandre et en Artois*. Bruges, 1951.

Polorny, J. *Indogermanisches etymologisches Wörterbuch*. 10 vols. Berne, 1959–69.

Prentout, H. *Essai sur les origines et la fondation du duché de Normandie*. Caen, 1911.

Bibliography

Preaux, L. "Les quatre vertus païennes et chrétiennes: Apothéose et Ascension." In *Mélanges L. Renard*, I, pp. 639–57. Paris, 1973.

Quantin, M. *Dictionnaire topographique du département de l'Yonne*. Paris, 1862.

Quef, P. *Histoire de la tannerie*. Paris, Namur, 1858.

Rattansi, P. M. "The Social Interpretation of Science in the Seventeenth Century." In *Science and Society, 1600–1900*, pp. 1–32. Cambridge, 1972.

Reinach, P. "Teutatès, Esus, Taranis." *RC* 18 (1897): 143–48.

——. *Bronzes figurés de la Gaule Romaine*. Paris, 1920.

Réponse des plantes aux facteurs climatiques. Actes du colloque. Paris, 1973.

Riche, P. *Education et culture dans l'occident barbare, VIe–VIIe siècle*. Paris, 1962.

——. *La Vie quotidienne dans l'empire carolingien*. Paris, 1973.

Roche, D. *Le siècle des Lumières en Province: Académies et académiciens provinciaus, 1680–1789*. 2 vols. Paris, The Hague, 1978.

Roscher, P. *Ausführliches Lexicon der griechischen und romanischen Mythologie*. 10 vols. Leipzig, 1884–90.

Ross, P. "Esus et les trois grues." *Etudes celtiques* 9 (1960–61): 13–36.

Rossiau, P. "Prostitution, jeunesse et sociéte dans les villes du Sud-Est au XVe siècle." *AESC*, 1976, pp. 289–325.

Roux, S. "L'Habitat urbain au Moyen-Age: Le quartier de l'université de paris." *AESC*, 1969, pp. 1196–1219.

Russel, J. C. *Medieval Regions and Their Cities*. London, 1972.

Sabbe, E. *Histoire de l'industrie linière en Belgique*. Brussels, 1945.

Sarton, G. *Appréciation of Ancient and Medieval Science during the Renaissance (1450–1600)*. London, 1920.

Schilling, R. "Dea dia dans la liturgie des frères Arvales." In *Mélanges L. Renard, Latomus*, II, pp. 675–79.

Schneider, J. *La Ville de Metz aux XIIIe et XIVe siècles*. Nancy, 1950.

Schwarzfuchs, S. *Les Juifs de France*. Paris, 1975.

Seston, V. "Les Murs, les portes et les tours des enceintes urbaines et le problème des 'res sanctae' en droit romain." In *Mélanges A. Piganiol*, pp. 1489–98. Paris, 1966.

See, H. *Louis XI et les villes*. Paris, 1891.

——. "Les origines de l'industrie capitaliste en France." *RH* 144 (1923): 187–200.

Singer, Ch. *A History of Technology*. 5 vols. Oxford, 1954–58.

Smeaton, W. *Fourcroy, Chemist and Revolutionary, 1755–1809*. Cambridge, 1962.

Steensberg, A. *Farms and Mills in Denmark during Two Thousand Years*. Copenhagen, 1952.

Stein, A., and Hubert, H. *Dictionnaire topographique du département de Seine et Marne*. Paris, 1954.

Sykes, G., and Skinner, F. *Microbial Aspects of Pollution*. London, New York, 1971.

Taton, R. *Histoire générale des science.* 4 vols. Paris, 1964–71.

———. "L'École royale du génie de Mézières." In *Enseignement et diffusion des sciences en France au XVIIIe siècle,* pp. 539–615. Paris, 1964.

Thompson, M. *Economic and Social History of the Middle-Ages (300–1300).* New York, 1928.

Thorndike, M. "Technology and Inventions in the Middle-Ages." *Speculum* 15 (1940): 141–59.

Thullier, G. "Pour une histoire générale de l'eau: En Nivernais au XIXe siècle." *AESC,* 1968, pp. 49–68.

Toubert, P. *Les Structures du Latium aux Xe et XIe Siècles.* 2 vols. Rome, 1974.

Toussaint-Duplessis. *Description de la Haute Normandie.* 2 vols. Rouen, 1820.

Vaesen, P., and Charavay, E. *Lettres de Louis XI.* 8 vols. Paris.

Vercauteren, F. *Etude sur les civitates de la Belgique Seconde.* Paris, 1934.

Verdon, F. "Les Femmes et la politique en France au Xe siècle." In *Mélanges Perroy,* pp. 108–22. Paris, 1973.

Vernant, J.-P. *Mythe et pensée chez les Grecs.* 2 vols. Paris, 1974.

Vie des Saints et des beinheureux selon l'ordre du Calendrier. 13 vols. Paris, 1935–59.

Vogt, M. *Orbis.* Freiburg, 1960.

Werckerlin, P. *Le Drap "escarlate" au Moyen-Age: Essai sur l'étymologie et la signification du mot écarlate et notes techniques sur la fabrication de ce drap de laine au Moyen-Age.* Lyons, 1905.

Weyl, Th. *Histoire de l'hygiène sociale.* Paris, 1910.

White, L. *Technologie mèdièvale et transformations sociales.* Paris, The Hague, 1969.

———. *Medieval Religion and Technology: Collected Essays.* Los Angeles, Berkeley, London, 1978.

Wickerscheimer, E. *Dictionnaire biographique des médecins de France au Moyen-Age.* 2 vols. Geneva, 1936. Supplement, Genéva, 1979.

———. *Les Manuscrits latins de médecine du haut Moyen-Age dans les bibliothèques françaises.* Paris, 1966.

Wild, J. P. *Textile Manufacture in the Northern Roman Provinces.* Cambridge, 1970.

Wolf, A. *A History of Science, Technology and Philosophy in the Eighteenth Century.* New York, 1939.

Zeldin, Th. *Histoire des passions françaises.* 5 vols. Paris, 1978.

Zukerman, A. *A Jewish Princedom in Feudal France, 768–900.* New York, 1974.

Index

Index

Index

The Age of Water was composed into type on a Linotron 202 digital phototypesetter in ten point Plantin with two points of spacing between the lines. Plantin was also selected for display. The book was designed by Cameron Poulter, composed by G & S Typesetters, Inc., printed offset by Thomson-Shore, Inc., and bound by John H. Dekker & Sons. The paper on which this book is printed bears acid-free characteristics for an effective life of at least three hundred years.

TEXAS A&M UNIVERSITY PRESS

COLLEGE STATION